THE GERMAN
IN WORLD WAR II

THE GERMAN ARMY
IN WORLD WAR II

NIGEL THOMAS

First published in Great Britain in 2002 by Osprey Publishing,
Elms Court, Chapel Way, Botley, Oxford OX2 9LP, UK.
Email: info@ospreypublishing.com

Previously published as Men-at-Arms 311: *The German Army 1939–45
(1) Blitzkrieg*, Men-at-Arms 316: *The German Army 1939–45 (2) North
Africa & Balkans*, Men-at-Arms 326: *The German Army 1939–45 (3)
Eastern Front 1941–43*, Men-at-Arms 330: *The German Army 1939–45 (4)
Eastern Front 1943–45*, Men-at-Arms 336: *The German Army 1939–45 (5)
Western Front 1943–45*

ISBN 1 84176 616 X

Series Editor: Martin Windrow
Editor: Sally Rawlings
Index by Alan Thatcher

Printed in China through World Print Ltd.

02 03 04 05 06   10 9 8 7 6 5 4 3 2 1

FOR A CATALOGUE OF ALL BOOKS PUBLISHED BY OSPREY
MILITARY AND AVIATION PLEASE CONTACT:

Osprey Direct UK,
P.O. Box 140, Wellingborough,
Northants, NN8 2FA, UK
E-mail: **info@ospreydirect.co.uk**

Osprey Direct USA, c/o MBI Publishing,
P.O. Box 1, 729 Prospect Ave, Osceola, WI 54020, USA
E-mail: **info@ospreydirectusa.com**

www.ospreypublishing.com

FRONT COVER: The first and second gunners of the section LMG team
in field uniform operating their LMG34 machine gun in France in May
1940. (© Brian Davis Collection)

BACK COVER: A signalman of the Signal Instruction Battalion in Halle,
Germany 1939. (© Brian Davis Collection)

CONTENTS

GERMAN ARMY 1939–45 (1) BLITZKRIEG

THE RECORD OF THE WEHRMACHT

On 30 January 1933 Adolf Hitler dismantled the Weimar Republic and established the Third Reich, with himself as *Führer* (leader) and head of state. On 15 March 1935 he abolished Weimar's armed forces, the *Reichswehr*, and replaced them with the *Wehrmacht*. Hitler announced that the Wehrmacht would not be bound by the restrictions imposed on the Reichswehr by the 1919 Treaty of Versailles, which limited it to 100,000 volunteers with no tanks, heavy artillery, submarines or aircraft.

The Wehrmacht expanded rapidly. On 1 September 1939, when Germany attacked Poland, it numbered 3,180,000 men. It eventually expanded to 9,500,000, and on 8/9 May 1945, the date of its unconditional surrender on the Western and Eastern Fronts, it still numbered 7,800,000. The Blitzkrieg period, from 1 September 1939 to 25 June 1940, was 10 months of almost total triumph for the Wehrmacht, as it defeated every country, except Great Britain, that took the field against it.

THE HIGH COMMAND OF THE ARMY AND THE WEHRMACHT

Hitler believed, incorrectly as events were to prove, that his political skills were matched by a unique ability as a strategic commander. His increasing influence on the Wehrmacht's conduct of the Second World War eventually proved to be disastrous.

As head of state, Hitler occupied the nominal position of *Oberster Befehlshaber der Wehrmacht* (Supreme Commander of the Armed Forces), and on 4 February 1938 he took over the most important professional position of *Oberbefehlshaber der Wehrmacht* (Commander of the Armed Forces), having forced his former protégé, Generalfeldmarschall Werner von Blomberg, to retire. Hitler held this post until his suicide on 30 April 1945, assisted by the subservient Generaloberst (later Generalfeldmarschall) Wilhelm von Keitel as *Chef des Oberkommandos der Wehrmacht* (Chief of Staff of the Armed Forces). Real power rested with Generalmajor (eventually Generaloberst) Alfred Jodl, technically Keitel's assistant as *Chef der Wehrmachtführungsamt* (Chief of the Operations Staff).

Germany, April 1934. An Obergefreiter, Oberschütze, Schütze and Gefreiter, all NCO candidates in service uniform, show the new Wehrmacht eagle on their M1916 helmets. They wear M1920 (eight-button) and M1928 (six-button) service tunics, M1920 rank insignia and M1928 marksmanship awards. (Brian Davis Collection)

10th Infantry Division in parade uniforms march past German officers, and Austrian officers absorbed into the German Army. The Austrian officers are wearing their M1933 *Bundesheer* uniforms with German breast eagles, and the characteristic Austrian *képi*. Vienna, March 1938. (Brian Davis Collection)

The Wehrmacht was divided into three arms – the Army (*Heer*), Navy (*Kriegsmarine*) and Air Force (*Luftwaffe*). The Army was the largest arm, averaging about 75% of total Wehrmacht strength, with 2,700,000 troops in September 1939, reaching a maximum strength of about 5,500,000, with 5,300,000 in May 1945.

Oberbefehlshaber des Heeres (Chief of the Army High Command) until 19 December 1941, when Hitler dismissed him and took over his post, was Generaloberst (later Generalfeldmarschall) Walther von Brauchitsch, assisted by General der Artillerie (later Generaloberst) Franz Halder as *Chef des Generalstabes des Heeres* (Chief of the Army General Staff). The Waffen-SS, formally established on 1 December 1939, was never technically part of the Wehrmacht, but it came under the control of the Army High Command.

The branches of the Army

On mobilisation on 26 August 1939 the Army was divided into the *Feldheer* (Field Army), advancing to attack the enemy, and the *Ersatzheer* (Replacement Army), remaining in Germany in support. The Field Army constituted three types of troops. Firstly, *Fechtende Truppen*, or combat troops, comprised Staffs (Armed Forces and Army High Commands; General Staff; Army Group, Army and Corps Staffs), Infantry (line, motorised, light and mountain), commando and penal units; Mobile Troops (cavalry, armour, mechanised infantry, reconnaissance and anti-tank units), Artillery, Engineers, Signals and Field Security Police Officials. Secondly, *Versorgungstruppen*, or Supply Troops, included Transport, Medical, Veterinary and Guard units, Military Police and Field Post Officials. Thirdly, *Sicherungstruppen* – Security Troops – were composed of Rear-Area commanders, second-line 'territorial rifle' (*Landeschützen*) battalions and prisoner-of-war camps. There were also Army Officials (including Chaplains), Bandmaster-Officers and Specialists (*Sonderführer*).

The organisation of the Field and Replacement Armies

The largest wartime Field Army units had no fixed organisation. There were five army groups: two (*Nord* and *Süd*) for the Polish campaign, and three more (A-C) for the Western campaigns. Each Army Group (*Heeresgruppe*) was composed of two or three armies with perhaps 400,000 men. There were 14 armies, each Army (*Armee*) comprising three or four corps with about 200,000 men, and, from June 1940, two reinforced Armoured Corps, called *Panzergruppe* or Armoured Groups (*von Kleist* and *Guderian*) each one controlling three motorised corps. There were 33 corps (1-13,17,21,23-30,38,40,42-4,46-9), each Corps (*Korps*) with two to five infantry divisions and perhaps 60,000 men; and seven motorised corps, each Motorised Corps (*Korps(mot.)*) with two or three armoured and motorised divisions, and one (XV) with three light divisions. One cavalry division and the four mountain divisions came directly under the control of their respective armies.

During the Blitzkrieg period 143 infantry divisions were formed, their quality depending on the 'Wave' (*Welle*), to which they belonged. In addition to the 35 well-established peacetime 1st Wave divisions (1-46 series), there were divisions of elderly veterans or untrained reservists or recruits hastily assembled from occupied Poland and Czechoslovakia, as well as the nine Replacement Divisions (*Ersatzdivisionen*) of the 10th Wave (270-280 series). Each infantry division (*Infanteriedivision*) of 16,977 men was made up of three infantry regiments plus divisional support units: one four-battalion artillery regiment; a reconnaissance battalion, with mounted, bicycle and support squadrons; an anti-tank battalion; an engineer battalion; a signals battalion; and divisional

An Unteroffizier of the 67th Infantry Regiment in Ruhleben, near Berlin, 1938 wearing the M1935 undress uniform, with the peaked cap usually worn by NCOs, with this uniform. He is instructing recruits, dressed in M1933 fatigue uniforms, in rifle drill with Karabiner 98k rifles. Note the typical soiled and crumpled appearance of the fatigue uniforms.
(Brian Davis Collection)

services – up to ten motorised and horsedrawn transport columns; a medical company, a motorised field hospital and veterinary company; a Military Police Troop and a Field Post Office.

An infantry regiment with 3,049 men (*Infanterieregiment*) had three infantry battalions, a 180-strong infantry gun company and a 170-strong anti-tank company. A battalion (*Bataillon*) of 860 men had three rifle companies and a 190-strong machine gun (actually a support) company. A 201-strong rifle company (*Schützenkompanie*) had three rifle platoons, and each 50-strong rifle platoon (*Schützenzug*) was composed of a platoon staff, a light-grenade-launcher team and four rifle sections, each section (*Schützengruppe*) having ten men.

All units of a motorised division (*Infanteriedivision(mot.)*) were armoured or motorised, and in early 1940 motorised divisions were reduced to two motorised regiments, giving a divisional total of 14,319 men. A mountain division (*Gebirgsdivision*) had 14,131 men with two 6,506-strong mountain regiments, plus support units and services, all with mountain capability.

A 14,373-strong armoured division (*Panzerdivision*) had an armoured brigade (two regiments of 1,700 men divided into two battalions) and a 4,409-strong motorised rifle brigade (rifle regiment and motorcycle battalion), the remaining support units and the services being armoured or motorised.

A 10-11,000-strong light division (*Leichte Division*) had between one and four 638-strong armoured battalions and one or two 2,295-strong motorised cavalry regiments, before reorganising as Panzer Divisions 6-9 in October 1939–January 1940. The 16,000-strong 1 Cavalry Division (*1.Kavalleriedivision*) had four 1,440-strong mounted (*Reiter*) regiments (each with two mounted battalions), a cavalry (*Kavallerie*) regiment (one mounted, one bicycle battalion) and a bicycle battalion, other support units and services being mounted or motorised.

Guderian on the day of his promotion to General der Panzertruppen and his appointment as Commander of Mobile Troops, 20 November 1938. He is wearing the M1935 officers' service uniform with a particularly good example of the M1935 peaked cap. Note the First World War bravery and Wehrmacht long-service awards. (Brian Davis Collection)

15 March 1939. Reconnaissance troops in field uniform, wearing the regulation M1934 rubberised greatcoats, ride a BMW R12 745cc motorcycle combination through the streets of the conquered city of Prague. They carry minimal field equipment appropriate for this unopposed invasion. Note the dejected appearance of the local citizens. (Brian Davis Collection)

In 1937 Germany was divided into 13 military districts, numbered I–XIII, and from 1939 these were the bases of the Replacement Army. The depots, schools and training units of a *Wehrkreis* (district), manned and equipped initially one, and later as many as five, corps, for the Field Army, keeping them supplied with a continuous stream of reinforcements. As Germany expanded its territory at its neighbours' expense to form *Großdeutschland* (Greater Germany) the existing districts were expanded and six new ones formed from August 1938–October 1942. They provided conscripts for the war-effort, many of whom were not ethnic Germans or even sympathetic to the German cause.

THE STRATEGY

German strategy combined two concepts: the traditional 'Decisive Manoeuvre', developed by Prussian General von Moltke in the 1850s, and the 'Armoured Concept', usually known as *Blitzkrieg*, proposed by Heinz Guderian in the late 1920s. Both required rapidly mobilised forces to attack on consecutive fronts, mounting a concentrated surprise attack on one front, defeating the enemy in a few days or weeks, before regrouping to attack on the second front, thus avoiding a costly defensive two-front war which Germany would inevitably lose.

'Decisive Manoeuvre', used infantry to attack the enemy's line of retreat, trapping it in pockets. Blitzkrieg, however used concentrations of tanks, mechanised infantry and Luftwaffe dive-bombers to punch a hole in the enemy line, and penetrate into rear areas to destroy the enemy command centre, forcing a total collapse in enemy morale. The Polish and Scandinavian campaigns were conducted according to the principles of 'Decisive Manoeuvre', while the Western Offensive was Blitzkrieg.

Both strategies demanded that Germany be the aggressor, a position in line with the Third Reich's xenophobic and expansionist ideology. Germany had the vital advantages of surprise and of choosing the time, place and conditions of the battles. Its opponents pinned their hopes on neutrality, diplomatic skills and static frontier defences. They were psychologically unwilling to fight, and reluctant to prepare for war.

The Flower Wars

Hitler's political manoeuvrings, and Franco-British reluctance to risk war, gave the German Army five bloodless victories before September 1939. Hitler's troops annexed neighbouring territories in operations known as the *Blumenkriege*, or Flower Wars, a reference to the flowers often thrown by local ethnic Germans to welcome German forces.

On 7 March 1936 30,000 troops from the 5th, 9th, 15th and 16th Infantry Divisions marched across the Rhine and occupied the demilitarised Saar region on the west bank. On 12 March 1938 200,000 troops of the 8th Army (VII and XIII Corps, and 2.Panzerdivision) invaded Austria, annexing it, dividing it into *Wehrkreise* XVII and XVIII in April 1938, and absorbing the Austrian Army as 44th and 45th Infantry, 4th Light and 2nd and 3rd Mountain Divisions.

The Army had originally expected to deploy 39 divisions in five armies (numbers 2,8,10,12,14) against Czechoslovakia in 'Operation

An Oberst im Generalstab relaxes in his garden. He is wearing undress uniform with Kolben collar-patches and M1935 adjutants' aiguillettes for General Staff officers, the M1935 field tunic and the M1938 field cap. Germany, 1939. (Brian Davis Collection)

Troops of the Artillery Instruction Regiment in Jütebog, responsible for training artillery officer cadets in Germany, 1939. Wearing the M1935 field uniform, they demonstrate firing a 3.7cm Pak 35/36 L/45 anti-tank gun. Note the Karabiner 98k rifles and the minimal field equipment – M1931 canvas bread-bags and M1938 gas mask canisters, but no Y-straps.
(Brian Davis Collection)

Green', but following the Munich Agreement in September 1938, it occupied the Sudetenland border areas without bloodshed from 1 to 10 October 1938 with elements of the five neighbouring German corps – IV, VII, VIII, XIII, XVII, XVIII. The Sudetenland was incorporated into *Wehrkreise* IV, VII, VIII, XIII and XVII. On 15 March 1939 these units occupied the rest of Bohemia-Moravia, designated *Wehrkreis Böhmen und Mähren* in October 1942. Finally, on 23 March 1939 elements of I Corps annexed the Memel district of Western Lithuania to *Wehrkreis I.*

The 600-man volunteer *Gruppe Imker*, consisting of the Panzergruppe *Drohne* armoured unit with two signals companies and anti-tank, supply and repair elements, saw limited combat in the Spanish Civil War from July 1936 to May 1939 as part of the Luftwaffe's Condor Legion.

The Polish campaign and the Phoney War

On 26 August 1939 the Wehrmacht began a secret partial mobilisation for 'Operation White', the invasion of Poland, leading to full mobilisation on 3 September. On 1 September the army attacked, joining up with *Bau-Lehr Bataillon zbV 800* commandos and other Army Intelligence (*Abwehr*) units who had already infiltrated the region to secure vital bridges.

The invasion force, consisting of 1,512,000 men, was organised in two army groups totalling 53 divisions (37 infantry, four motorised, three mountain, three light, six Panzer). It attacked on three fronts. Army Group *Nord*, under Generaloberst Fedor von Bock with 3rd and 4th Armies, attacked from north-east Germany and East Prussia. *Süd*, commanded by Generaloberst Gerd von Rundstedt with 8th, 10th and 14th Armies, advanced from south-east Germany and northern Slovakia, supported by 1st and 2nd Slovak divisions. The 1,100,000-strong Polish Army, organised in 40 infantry divisions, two mechanised and 11 mounted cavalry brigades, and deployed too close to the German frontier, was already being outflanked when, on 17 September, seven armies (41 divisions and equivalents) of the Soviet Red Army attacked them in the rear. Threatened on four fronts, the heavily outnumbered Polish Army officially surrendered on 27 September, and had ceased all hostilities on 6 October. Occupied Poland came under military control – Ciechanòw and Suwalki districts were incorporated in *Wehrkreis* I in September 1939, Bialystok in August 1941; Danzig and north-west Poland as XX and western Poland as XXI in September 1939; and south-east Poland as *General-Gouvernement* in September 1942.

During the eight-month 'Phoney War', Anglo-French forces massed on the western German frontier, briefly occupying the Saar District in September 1939, giving the Wehrmacht a free hand in Poland and Scandinavia, and allowing it to choose the conditions of the Western Offensive in May 1940.

Denmark and Norway

Anxious that the Anglo-French forces might attack Germany through Norway and Denmark, Hitler decided to invade these militarily weak neutral states in a pre-emptive strike called 'Operation Weserübung', commanded by General der Infanterie Nikolaus von Falkenhorst.

On 9 April 1940 *Höheres Kommando z.b.V. XXXI* (XXXI Special Corps), with the 170th and 198th Infantry Divisions, 11th Motorised Rifle Brigade and 40th Special Panzer Battalion, attacked Denmark. The inexperienced Danish Army, with 6,600 troops organised in two infantry divisions, its strategic position hopeless, was forced to surrender after four hours' limited resistance.

On the same day XXI Corps, with 3rd Mountain, 69th and 163rd Infantry Divisions, disembarked in Norway, later reinforced by 2nd

A signalman of the Signal Instruction Battalion in Halle, Germany 1939, responsible for training artillery officer cadets. He wears standard M1935 field uniform and, for the purposes of the gas exercise, a M1938 gas mask, whilst operating a M1933 field telephone. His unit letter is shown on his M1933 pointed shoulder-straps without piping. (Brian Davis Collection)

Mountain, 181st, 196th and 214th Infantry Divisions, with 40th Special Panzer Battalion providing token armour. They totalled some 100,000 men. They engaged six infantry divisions of the Norwegian Army, (with only 25,000 of its 90,000 men mobilised), backed up by the Allied Expeditionary Force with the equivalent of two infantry divisions, and forced an Allied evacuation and a Norwegian surrender on 9 June 1940.

The Low Countries

For 'Operation Yellow', the Western Offensive, the German Army assembled 2,750,000 men in 91 divisions, divided among three army groups. 'A' under Generaloberst von Rundstedt with 4th, 12th and 16th Armies, including Panzergruppe *von Kleist*, was to advance through Belgium into France. 'B' commanded by Generaloberst von Bock with 6th and 18th Armies, would attack the Netherlands and Belgium, whilst 'C' under Generaloberst Wilhelm Ritter von Leeb, with 1st and 7th Armies, would pin down French forces on the Maginot Line. These forces totalled 75 infantry divisions (including 22nd Airlanding Division), one Luftwaffe airborne division, four motorised, one mountain, one cavalry and ten Panzer divisions, with a further 42 divisions in reserve.

The offensive began on 10 May 1940, with commandos and *Abwehr* already active in the Netherlands and Belgium. Army Group B's 18th Army, with nine divisions plus airportable and parachute troops, attacked the neutral Netherlands, rapidly overwhelming the inexperienced Dutch Army. With 250,000 men organised in ten poorly trained infantry divisions, the Dutch put up an unexpectedly spirited defence, but surrendered on 15 May following the bombing of Rotterdam.

Germany, 1939. A Sanitätsunteroffizier in M1935 undress uniform with the M1935 other ranks' field cap and Medical Corps red-cross armband, instructs in first-aid infantry stretcher-bearers, who wear black on white *Hilfskrankenträger* armbands. (Brian Davis Collection)

Luxembourg fell on 10 May to 16th Army, its 82-man 'Volunteer Company' offering only token resistance. The same day Army Group A, joined by 6th Army from Army Group B, began its advance through neutral Belgium, spearheaded by an airborne attack on Fort Eben-Emael. The 600,000-strong Belgian Army, organised in 18 infantry, two mountain and two cavalry divisions, supported by British and French troops, initially resisted strongly. Its morale declined as it retreated before the relentless German advance, led by the powerful Panzergruppe *von Kleist*'s surprise outflanking attack through the supposedly impenetrable Ardennes hill country. On 28 May the Belgian Army surrendered.

The Battle of France

On 16 May Army Groups A and B began to advance into France. They were confronted by the 4,320,000-strong French Army, organised in Army Groups 1-3, with eight armies composed of 38 infantry, one fortress, nine motorised, three light mechanised, four light cavalry, and three armoured divisions, a total of 87 divisions, supported by nine British, one Czechoslovak and four Polish infantry divisions.

A force of nine Panzer divisions, comprising Panzergruppe *von Kleist*, XV Corps and General der Panzertruppen Heinz Guderian's XIX Corps (redesignated Panzergruppe *Guderian* on 1 June) with the *Großdeutschland* Motorised Regiment, burst through the French 1st Army Group at Sedan, reaching the Channel coast on 22 May. Concerned that the unit, containing almost all Germany's armoured troops, had outrun its logistical tail and supporting infantry, and was vulnerable to an Allied counterattack, Von Rundstedt ordered a halt on 23 May, allowing the Allies to evacuate 338,226 British, French and Belgian troops from Dunkirk from 27 May to 4 June.

On 5 June Army 'Operation Red' commenced. Army Group B advanced along the French Channel and Atlantic coasts, stopping before Bordeaux on 22 June, while A headed through central France and C forced the Maginot Line. The French Army signed an armistice on 25 June. Eupen and Malmédy districts in Belgium were annexed and joined *Wehrkreis* VI, Luxembourg and Lorraine *Wehrkreis* XII, and Alsace Wehrkreis V. Northern, western and eastern France was occupied, leaving central and southern France unoccupied as a nominally independent French state under Field Marshal Pétain.

The verdict on Blitzkrieg

The Blitzkrieg period had restored the reputation of the German armed forces, but weaknesses had emerged. Success had confirmed Hitler's belief in his own genius and the corresponding inferiority of his professional generals. Jealousy between the *OKW*, the Wehrmacht High Command, and the

Two NCOs in undress uniform with M1935 field greatcoats having field rations in Germany, September 1939. Note the NCOs' sword-knot attached to the bayonet of the Feldwebel (right), the absence of shoulder-strap numbers, and the regulation mess-tins. (ECPA)

Poland, September 1939. Dispatch riders in field uniform. They wear M1934 rubberised greatcoats, with shoulder-straps removed for security, and M1935 dispatch-cases. Their M1916 helmets were already obsolete but were still widely encountered in the early years of the war. (Brian Davis Collection)

OKH, the Army High Command, exacerbated by the fact that Hitler controlled both, led to a division of authority. The Danish and Norwegian campaigns were controlled by *OKW*, and the Polish and Western campaigns by *OKH*. Panzergruppe *Kleist*'s classic Blitzkrieg tactics had proved brilliantly successful, but the infantry performance in Norway had been less decisive. Finally, the swift advances of the Blitzkrieg had enabled large numbers of enemy troops to evade capture and organise themselves as guerrilla armies, a constant threat to the German occupation authorities.

The Armies of Occupation

The Army established transit prisoner-of-war camps (*Dulags*) in occupied territory which collected enemy POWs before transfer to the officer camps (*Oflags*) and other-rank camps (*Stalags*). They were organised by each *Wehrkreis* and guarded by *Landesschützen* units unfit for front-line combat.

Occupied territories were placed under military governments – Poland under the *General-Gouvernement* (until September 1942); Denmark (from August 1943); Belgium-Northern France. The rest of occupied France was organised under *Militärbefehlshaber* (Army Governors), and Netherlands and Norway under *Wehrmacht-befehlshaber* (Armed Forces Governors). Each governor controlled regimental-level district commands (*Oberfeldkommandanture*), which in turn were subdivided into battalion-level sub-districts (*Feldkommandanture*) and then into smaller metropolitan, urban or rural commands.

In addition three conquered territories had occupation armies. Norway, from December 1940, had 'Norway Army' (*Armee Norwegen*) made up of three, sometimes four Corps. The Netherlands, from June 1942, had LXXXVIII Corps. Army Groups A, B and C remained in Occupied France, to be replaced in October 1940 by Army Group D with 1st, 7th and 15th Armies.

TABLE 1 GERMAN ARMY ORDERS OF DRESS 1 SEPTEMBER 1939 – 9 MAY 1945

Order of Dress	General-officers, Infantry officers and bandmaster officers	Technical non-commissioned officers, Infantry senior and junior non-commissioned officers and men	When worn
Großer Gesellschaftsanzug Formal ceremonial uniform	Service cap; dress tunic & medals/piped field tunic & ribbons; aiguillettes; trousers & shoes; white gloves; sword; knot.	—	Presenting reports; receptions; theatre; concerts.
Kleiner Gesellschaftsanzug Informal ceremonial uniform	Service cap; dress tunic/piped field tunic; ribbons; trousers & shoes; white gloves; sword; knot.	—	Presenting reports; receptions; church-parades; funerals; theatre; concerts.
Paradeanzug Parade uniform	Helmet/peaked cap; dress tunic; medals; aiguillettes; dress greatcoat; belt; breeches & riding-boots; grey gloves; sword; knot.	Helmet; dress tunic/field tunic; medals; dress greatcoat; marksman's lanyard; belt, piped/plain trousers, marching boots; grey gloves (NCOs); sword, knot (TNCOs, SNCOs); Y-straps, ammo-pouches, rifle, bayonet, knot (JNCOs, men).	Parades; church-parades; funerals.
Ausgehanzug Walking out uniform	Service cap; dress tunic/piped field tunic; ribbons; dress greatcoat; trousers & shoes; white gloves; sword; knot.	Service cap; dress tunic/field tunic; ribbons; dress greatcoat; marksman's lanyard; belt; piped/plain trousers, shoes; grey gloves (NCOs); sword, knot (TNCOs, SNCOs); bayonet, knot (JNCOs, men).	Walking-out; church-parades; funerals.
Meldeanzug Reporting uniform	Service cap; dress tunic/piped field tunic; ribbons; belt; breeches & riding boots; grey gloves; sword; knot.	Service cap; field tunic; ribbons; marksman's lanyard; belt; plain trousers, marching-boots; grey gloves (NCOs); sword, knot (TNCOs, SNCOs); bayonet, knot (JNCOs, men).	Presenting reports.
Dienstanzug Service uniform	Service cap; field tunic; ribbons; field greatcoat; belt; breeches & riding-boots; grey gloves; pistol; holster.	Service cap (TNCOs, SNCOs); helmet/field cap (JNCOs, men); field-tunic; ribbons; field greatcoat; belt, plain trousers, marching boots; grey gloves (NCOs); pistol, holster (TNCOs, SNCOs); Y-straps, ammo-pouches; rifle, bayonet, knot (JNCOs, men).	Manoeuvres; inspections; church-parades; funerals; courts martial; parades.
Kleiner Dienstanzug Undress uniform	Service cap; dress tunic/field tunic; ribbons; field greatcoat; breeches & riding boots/ trousers & shoes; grey gloves; pistol; holster.	Service cap/field cap; field tunic; ribbons; field greatcoat; belt; plain trousers, marching-boots; grey gloves (NCOs); pistol, holster (TNCOs, SNCOs); y-straps, ammo-pouches; rifle, bayonet, knot (JNCOs, men).	Manoeuvres; inspections; rifle-ranges; instructional classes; barracks-yards; presenting reports (officers).
Wachanzug Guard uniform	Helmet/field-cap; field tunic (dress tunic for guards of honour); ribbons; field greatcoat; belt; breeches & riding-boots; grey gloves; pistol; holster.	Helmet/field cap; field tunic; ribbons; field greatcoat; marksman's lanyard; belt; plain/piped trousers, marching boots; grey gloves (NCOs); pistol, holster (TNCOs, SNCOs); Y-straps, ammo-pouches; rifle, bayonet, knot (JNCOs, men).	Standing guard.
Feldanzug Field uniform	Helmet/field cap; field tunic; ribbons; field greatcoat; belt; breeches & riding-boots; grey gloves; equipment (not general-officers); pistol; holster.	Helmet/field cap; field tunic; ribbons; field greatcoat; belt, plain trousers, marching-boots; grey gloves (NCOs); pistol, holster (TNCOs, SNCOs); field-equipment; rifle, bayonet (JNCOs, men).	Manoeuvres; combat.
Arbeitsanzug Fatigue uniform	—	Field cap; fatigue tunic; belt; fatigue trousers, marching-boots.	Fatigue duties.

THE UNIFORM OF THE GERMAN ARMY

All dates connected with the introduction of new uniforms, equipment and insignia give the date of the Army Order. However, as in all armies, there was a delay (ranging from a few weeks to as much as two years) in new items reaching individual units, especially front-line units, remote garrisons, or in the Replacement Army. Furthermore, individual soldiers,

especially senior officers, often preferred to retain obsolete items if they were of sentimental value, or of better quality than the replacement. They gave the owner an air of individuality and marked him as an experienced 'old sweat'. An army order of 10 July 1942 decreed that all obsolete clothing could continue to be worn for the duration of the war.

The most visible symbol of the Wehrmacht was the breast eagle, the *Hoheitsabzeichen*, or 'Sovereignty Badge', worn by all ranks above the right breast pocket of most uniform items, and identifying the wearer as fit to bear arms. The Army version, introduced 17 February 1934, with effect from 1 May 1934, depicted an eagle with straight, outstretched wings grasping a circled swastika. Most other uniformed organisations, including the Waffen-SS, introduced various styles of eagle badges, but were obliged to wear them on the left upper arm, since the right breast was reserved for the Wehrmacht (and, curiously enough, the National Socialist Flying Corps, the NSFK).

The various uniform items of the new Army uniform began to appear following publication of the Dress Regulations of 8 April 1935. These uniforms and insignia were developments of, and continued the traditions of, the Army's four predecessors – the *Reichsheer* (National Army) of the Second Reich (18 January 1871–11 November 1918); the *Friedensheer* (Peacetime Army, 11 November 1918–5 March 1919); the *Vorläufige Reichswehr* (Temporary National Armed Forces, 6 March 1919–31 December 1920); and, most importantly, the *Reichsheer* (usually, but incorrectly, known as the *Reichswehr*) of the German Republic (1 January 1921–15 March 1935).

By the end of 1935 the main uniform styles were established. The basic uniform colour was a greenish-grey, introduced 2 July 1929 and given the traditional but inaccurate title of *feldgrau*, 'field grey' (originally designating a plain mid-grey introduced 23 February 1910).

An Unterfeldwebel (left), acting as section leader, in field uniform orders his infantry section to attack. He is wearing standard M1935 field uniform with M1935 helmet with a rubber band for securing camouflage, and minimal equipment – 6 x 30 issue binoculars and the M1931 canvas bread-bag. The deputy section leader (right), laden with 6 x 30 binoculars, M1935 mapcase, M1938 gas mask canister and M1931 camouflage shelter-quarter, observes the enemy in Poland, September 1939. (Brian Davis Collection)

Facings were in a bluish dark-green 'facing-cloth', finely woven to give an appearance of a thin felt, introduced 29 June 1935, and the same material was usually used for branch colour patches and pipings. *Reichswehr* uniform items, in M1929 *feldgrau* but with a darker greenish-grey facing-cloth, should have been withdrawn by 1937, but were still occasionally encountered in the 1939/40 period.

The Regulations of April 1935 prescribed ten orders of dress in peacetime for officers, two ceremonial uniforms and a parade uniform for formal occasions; a walking-out and reporting uniform for semi-formal occasions; service, undress and guard uniforms for training and barracks duties; the field uniform for combat; and sports dress (omitted in this study). (See Table 1 for more details.) Non-commissioned officers and other ranks had nine, omitting the ceremonial uniforms and adding a fatigue uniform for work-duties in barracks or in the field. Some uniform items were manufactured in different versions for officers and other ranks, while others were standard items worn by all ranks.

New regulations were issued on 28 December 1939 to cover the wartime period and the earlier strict observance of regulations eased. The types of uniforms were simplified. Service uniform could be worn on most formal and semi-formal occasions, but, inevitably, the field uniform became the most common uniform encountered in the front line and rear areas. Furthermore, Replacement Army units were often issued captured Austrian, Czech, Dutch, French, and even British uniform items, dyed and remodelled to conform to German patterns.

Officers' ceremonial uniform

The full ceremonial uniform consisted of the M1935 officers' peaked service cap, dress tunic (*Waffenrock*) with medals, aiguillettes and trousers, standard black lace-up shoes, officers' white suede gloves, and sabre. The informal ceremonial uniform omitted the aiguillettes, and substituted ribbons for medals.

Assault engineers in M1935 field uniform prepare to advance in Poland, September 1939. The sapper (left) carries the short model wire-cutters in a black leather case on his left back hip, also the M1938 gas mask canister, M1931 camouflage shelter-quarter, M1931 canvas bread-bag and M1931 canteen. His companion's bayonet and folded entrenching tool are prominently displayed. (Brian Davis Collection)

The saddle-shaped **officers' peaked cap**, introduced 10 September 1935 and worn with most officers' uniforms, had a high crown at the front falling steeply to the sides. Later caricatured as typically German, it was in fact a revolutionary design, replacing the traditional 'plate' style with its high cap-band and low circular crown. It was manufactured in *feldgrau* tricot or 'eskimo' material. The M1935 eagle and swastika badge, manufactured in bright aluminium, was worn above a stamped bright aluminium red (inner)-white-black (outer) national cockade in an oak-leaf wreath, on the bluish dark-green facing-cloth cap band. There was 2mm thick piping around the crown in branch-of-service colour, and above and below the cap band, a plain black-lacquered vulcanised fibre peak, and a matt aluminium wire chin-cord secured by two 12mm bright aluminium pebbled buttons. General-officers had gold-coloured metallic woven cord cap-pipings and gold wire; from 15 July 1938 this became yellow artificial 'celleon' wire, woven chin-cords with matt gold pebbled buttons. Hand-embroidered bright silver or bright aluminium bullion badges on a bluish dark-green facing-cloth backing were permitted on fine-cloth privately purchased caps.

The style, though not the colour, of the *feldgrau* tricot pocketless waisted **officers' dress-tunic**, adopted 29 June 1935, invoked the proud military traditions of the *Reichsheer* of the German Empire. It had bluish dark-green facing-cloth collars and cuffs, branch colour facing-cloth pipings, and bright aluminium pebbled buttons and wire braids. The piped front was secured by eight buttons, with three on each of the piped ornamental back 'tail-pockets'. Insignia consisted of the officers' superior dress-quality breast-eagle, collar-patches, cuff-patches and shoulder boards. The bright, hand-embroidered, flat aluminium bullion breast eagle had a bluish dark-green backing. The piped collar had M1935 branch colour facing-cloth collar-patches, with two bright aluminium wire embroidered 'Guards' braids' developed from those worn by élite Guards regiments of the Imperial *Reichsheer*. Similarly, the piped cuffs had two branch colour cuff-patches, each with a button and braid. For shoulder-boards see Table 3. Privately purchased tunics were usually shaped at the waist and had higher, stiffer collars.

General-officers had a bright gold bullion or golden-yellow hand-embroidered thread breast-eagle on a bluish dark-green facing-cloth backing. The collar and cuff-patches showed the bright gold bullion or 'celleon' hand-embroidered thread *Alt-Larisch* design introduced 22 March 1900. After 1939 they were in matt yellow yarn picked out in dark yellow or buff, on a bright-red facing-cloth patch.

On 21 March 1940 further manufacture of the *Waffenrock* was forbidden, and existing tunics were to be converted to field tunics by removing the facing-cloth cuffs and tail pockets and substituting field-quality insignia. In future only the **officers' 'piped field tunic'**, introduced 12 July 1937 as an alternative to the *Waffenrock*, would be worn in full-dress. This was a field tunic with

An infantryman in Poland in October 1939 wearing the M1935 field uniform, with reversed shoulder-straps to conceal unit insignia, searches a Polish prisoner. There is a particularly good view of his improvised assault-pack, consisting of a bayonet strapped to his entrenching-tool, with the M1931 camouflage shelter-quarter and the M1931 mess-kit tied to his belt with belt supporting-straps. (ECPA)

Poland, 18 September 1939. German officers in M1935 field uniform relax during negotiations with a Soviet Red Army officer (centre, in a greatcoat, carrying a map-case) over arrangements for partitioning defeated Poland between Germany and the Soviet Union. Note the German guard, in M1935 field uniform with field greatcoat, presenting arms. (Josef Charita)

branch colour collar facings, front and cuff pipings, and dress-quality collar-patches, shoulder-boards and breast-eagles. The M1920 service-tunic (introduced 22 December 1920) or the M1928 service-tunic (introduced 31 October 1928), with respectively eight or six buttons, diagonally flapped concealed hip-pockets and branch colour facing-cloth front piping, was often retained, especially by general-officers.

The standard stone-grey trousers had a 2mm branch colour piping down the outer seam, flanked on each side by a 4cm branch colour stripe for general-officers. The bright aluminium wire dress aiguillette (gold, later 'celleon' for general-officers) was introduced 29 June 1935.

Officers' formal and semi-formal uniforms

The parade uniform consisted of the standard M1935 steel helmet or officers' peaked cap; the officers' *Waffenrock* with aiguillettes, M1937 officers' dress belt; breeches with black leather riding-boots and spurs, grey gloves and sword. The officers' M1935 dress greatcoat could also be worn, if ordered.

The standard M1935 **steel helmet** was introduced 25 June 1935, a development of the M1916 and M1918 helmets, with their prominent side-lugs. Painted matt *feldgrau* a black-white-red diagonally striped aluminium national shield was fixed to the right side, and a silver-white Wehrmacht eagle on a black painted aluminium shield on the left side, as ordered on 17 February 1934. Officers could also wear lightweight aluminium *Vulkanfiber* helmets on parade.

The **officers' dress belt**, introduced 9 July 1937, was made of bright aluminium brocade with two 5cm bluish dark-green stripes. The circular buckle was stamped bright aluminium (gold-plated or galvanically gilded for general-officers) showing a Wehrmacht eagle with folded wings in a wreath. The stone-grey officers' riding-breeches were plain, general-officers retaining their pipings and broad stripes.

The superior-quality officers' *feldgrau* **dress greatcoat**, introduced 10 September 1935, had a bluish dark-green facing-cloth collar and two rows of six matt *feldgrau* buttons, a back half-belt secured by two buttons, dress-quality shoulder-boards and the back seam sewn up. General-

General der Artillerie Halder, Chief of General Staff (left) and Generaloberst von Brauchitsch, Chief of the Army High Command (right), photographed in Germany, 4 October 1939, discussing strategy in Poland. Both wear M1935 undress uniform. Halder wears a remodelled M1929 service tunic, with an impressive array of First World War and Wehrmacht long-service medal ribbons, while von Brauchitsch, in a M1935 field tunic, has only the Nazi Party badge and the 1939 Iron Cross First Class. (Brian Davis Collection)

officers had matt gold pebbled buttons, leaving the top two buttons open to show bright-red facing-cloth lapel-linings. From 14 May 1937 all officers wearing collar decorations were also permitted to leave these buttons open. General-officers also wore the leather greatcoat with plain lapel-linings

'Walking-out' uniform consisted of the officers' service-cap, standard dress-tunic or officers' piped field tunic with ribbons, dress greatcoat if ordered, long trousers, lace-up shoes, white gloves and sword. The 'reporting uniform' added the M1934 belt, breeches and riding-boots, and grey gloves. The dark-brown **leather officers' belt** and cross-strap, introduced 18 May 1934, had a pebbled matt aluminium open-claw rectangular buckle, which was matt gilt for generals. On 20 November 1939 the cross-strap was abolished.

Officers' training and barracks uniforms

Service uniform consisted of the officers' peaked cap, M1933 field tunic with ribbons, M1935 field greatcoat, leather-belt, breeches and riding-boots, grey suede gloves, standard pistol and holster.

The officers' **field tunic** was introduced 5 May 1933, replacing the M1920 *Reichswehr* service-tunic. It was manufactured from superior quality *feldgrau* cloth with five matt-grey painted pebbled buttons, four patch pockets, turn-back cuffs and a *feldgrau* cloth collar, replaced by *feldgrau* facing-cloth on 26 July 1934 and by bluish dark-green facing-cloth in March 1936. All insignia was field-quality: the breast-eagle was in matt aluminium thread on a bluish dark-green facing-cloth backing; the bluish dark-green facing-cloth collar-patches had two matt aluminium

'Guards' braids', each with a branch colour silk-embroidered centre cord. For shoulder-boards see Table 3. Many general-officers retained the M1920 or M1928 service tunic with field-quality insignia and no front piping.

The **officers' field greatcoat** was like the dress greatcoat, but with field-quality shoulder-boards and the back seam left open.

In the 'undress' uniform, officers omitted the belt and could wear standard piped long trousers and lace-up shoes. With the 'Guard' uniform they wore the helmet, the M1934 or M1938 field cap; the field tunic or, if leading a Guard of Honour, the dress tunic; field greatcoat; brown belt; breeches and riding-boots, grey suede gloves, and a pistol and holster.

The M1934 **officers' 'old-style' field cap**, introduced 24 March 1934, became the M1935 peaked cap with the addition of a bluish dark-green cap band on 10 September 1935, and the omission of the metal crown stiffener, chincords and buttons. The visor was made of soft black patent leather and, from 30 October 1935, the eagle, cockade and wreath were of bright aluminium thread on a bluish dark-green backing.

The visorless flapped M1938 **officers' 'new-style' field cap**, introduced 6 December 1938, was made of *feldgrau* cloth, piped along the crown and the front of the flap with 3mm aluminium thread cord. The narrow aluminium cord national cockade was enclosed by a branch colour chevron, point up, in facing-cloth, with a machine-woven or hand-embroidered bright aluminium thread eagle on a bluish dark-green backing above. From 24 October 1939 general-officers wore gold thread crown and flap piping and a gold artificial silk chevron.

Officers' field uniform

In the field all Army officers except platoon leaders wore the standard steel helmet, officers' field tunic, with the field greatcoat if ordered, brown belt, breeches and riding-boots and grey suede gloves. Personal

NCOs of the Army Patrol Service in M1935 service uniform, with other ranks' M1935 field greatcoats and M1935 field caps, parade for duty in a German garrison town in 1940. The obsolete M1920 adjutants' aiguillettes on their right shoulder constitute their badges of office. (ECPA)

Germany, April 1940. A private of a newly created War Correspondents' Company in M1935 undress uniform with an M1935 field cap, takes a trip on the Rhine. He wears the lemon-yellow Signals branch colour on his shoulder-straps and cap, as well as the newly introduced *Propagandakompanie* sleeve-title. (F. Herrmann)

field equipment was usually limited to the P08 Luger or P-38 Walther pistol in a smooth leather holster – general-officers and field officers favoured the smaller Walther 7.65mm PPK – and 6x30 black binoculars in a smooth black or tan leather or bakelite case carried on the right front hip. Behind the front line the M1934 or M1938 field caps replaced the helmet.

In the field the shape and colour of the helmet was often camouflaged by daubing it with mud, or tying chicken-wire or the straps of the M1931 bread-bag and securing foliage to them. On 21 March 1940 the conspicuous national shield was removed and the helmet surface roughened and repainted from matt *feldgrau* to matt slate-grey.

From 31 October 1939 all officers below general-officer in combat units were ordered to wear the M1935 other ranks' field tunic, trousers and marching-boots with the black leather belt and officers' field-quality shoulder-boards. Many officers, however, continued to wear their former uniforms or modified the other ranks' tunic by adding officers' roll-back cuffs, collar-patches and the sharper-pointed, higher officers' collars.

Subalterns acting as infantry platoon leaders wore the standard **riflemen's field equipment** adding the brown or black leather M1935 dispatch-case on the left front hip, binoculars, compass and signal-whistle. Riflemen's field equipment consisted of the standard smooth or grained black leather M1939 infantry support Y-straps with aluminium fittings (introduced 18 April 1939), supporting two sets of three black leather ammunition pouches for the rifle. The bayonet in a black scabbard with the black leather cavalry bayonet-frog (introduced 25 January

1939) and entrenching-tool were worn on the left back hip. On the right back hip, the M1931 *feldgrau* canvas bread-bag and M1931 brown felt-covered canteen and black painted aluminium cup. Webbing supported the M1931 mess-kit and M1931 camouflage shelter-quarter on the upper back, and on the lower back the M1930 or M1938 gas mask in the distinctive *feldgrau*-painted cylindrical corrugated metal canister. The dark greenish-brown gas cape hung on the chest from a thin brown leather strap and a field flashlight was usually carried on the left shoulder. By September 1939 most officers had the MP38 submachine gun, for which two olive-green canvas M1938 magazine pouches were issued to replace the black leather ammunition-pouches.

Other ranks' parade uniform

Parade Uniform for other ranks consisted of the standard M1935 steel helmet; the OR M1935 *Waffenrock* or M1933 field tunic with medals, and, if ordered, the OR M1935 dress greatcoat; standard M1935 piped or plain trousers and marching-boots; the M1936 marksman's lanyard, M1935 belt, bayonet and bayonet-frog. All NCOs wore grey suede gloves. Technical and senior NCOs carried a sword, while junior NCOs and men wore standard M1939 Y-straps, M1908 ammunition-pouches and carried a rifle.

The other ranks' **Waffenrock**, adopted 29 June 1935, was identical to the officers' pattern with bright aluminium pebbled buttons, but made of fine quality (rather than superior) *feldgrau* cloth, with other ranks' dress insignia. The collar had M1935 branch colour facings, collar-patches with two bright aluminium thread 'Guards braids'. The cuffs had two branch colour badge-cloth cuff-patches, each with a bright aluminium pebbled button on a bright aluminium thread braid. The matt silver-grey machine-woven breast eagle had a bluish dark-green facing-cloth backing. The bluish dark-green facing-cloth shoulder-straps had rounded ends and a branch colour piping around the outer edge. For

The crew of an army light anti-aircraft unit on the alert for Allied aircraft in France, May 1940. The crewmen are wearing the typically soiled M1933 drill fatigue-uniform to avoid soiling their field uniforms. (Josef Charita)

shoulder-strap and sleeve rank insignia see Table 3. NCOs wore 1.5cm wide bright aluminium 'double-diamond' pattern yarn braid introduced 10 September 1935 on the front and top edge of the stand-up collar and on the top and back edge of the cuff to indicate their status. Privately-purchased tunics could be made of officers' tricot cloth with higher collars and tighter waisting.

The **other ranks' field tunic** in *feldgrau* cloth with matt-grey painted pebbled buttons was introduced on 5 May 1933 with the colour of the collar changing from *feldgrau* facing-cloth to bluish dark-green facing-cloth 10 September 1935. It resembled the officers' tunic, but the skirt was longer and cuffs were without the turn-backs. Insignia was of other ranks' field-quality.

The bluish dark-green facing-cloth M1935 collar-patches, introduced 10 September 1935, had two *feldgrau* braid 'Guards braids' each with branch colour facing-cloth centre stripes. They were replaced on 26 November 1938 by the 'standard braid', bluish dark-green facing-cloth stripes so the collar-patches no longer indicated branch affiliation. From 30 October 1935, the breast-eagle was embroidered in white cotton on a *feldgrau* backing; from 19 June 1937 it was on a bluish dark-green backing. Embroidery changed to silver-grey on 5 February 1939, and on 4 June 1940 to mouse-grey on feldgrau backing. NCOs wore 9mm wide bright aluminium 'single-diamond' pattern yarn braid introduced 10 September 1935, or silver-grey artificial silk braid, on the front and lower edge of the field tunic collar.

The M1933 pointed *feldgrau* cloth shoulder-straps without branch colour piping changed to *feldgrau* facing-cloth on 10 December 1934 and to bluish dark-green facing-cloth on 10 September 1935. They were replaced on 26 November 1938 by rounded bluish dark-green facing-cloth shoulder-straps with branch colour piping around the outer edges as worn on the field greatcoat, and on 18 March 1939 further production of the old model straps was discontinued. For shoulder-strap and sleeve rank insignia see Table 3.

On 25 April 1940 NCO collar and shoulder-strap braid of mouse-grey artificial silk or cellulose-fibre wool was introduced, and in May 1940 the bluish-green facing-cloth collars and shoulder-straps were replaced by *feldgrau* uniform cloth, but these changes were not implemented until after the fall of France.

The **other ranks' dress greatcoat**, introduced 10 September 1935, was officer pattern but made of lesser quality *feldgrau* cloth. The shoulder-straps were of bluish dark-green facing-cloth with branch colour piping around the outer edges. The bluish dark-green facing-cloth collar was always plain.

The stone-grey trousers had 2mm branch colour piping when worn with the *Waffenrock*. The trousers were plain when worn with the field tunic, and in May 1940 the colour changed to *feldgrau* cloth. The traditional black leather hobnailed marching-boots, nicknamed *Knobelbecher* – 'dice-shakers' – were 35-39cm high from heel to ankle. They were shortened to 32-34cm on 9 November 1939 to save material.

The **M1936 marksman's lanyard**, introduced 29 June 1936 and awarded by the company commander, distinguished 12 levels of marksmanship. Award 1 consisted of a matt aluminium plaited cord with an aluminium Wehrmacht eagle on a shield, replaced in 1939 by an aluminium eagle above crossed swords on a shield all in a small wreath, suspended from the right shoulder-strap, hooked to the second tunic button. One to three aluminium acorns at the lower end designated Awards 2-4. For Awards 5-8 the M1939 badge with a larger wreath replaced the shield, and Awards 9-12 had this same badge in gilt. From 16 December 1936 artillery gunners wore the badge with artillery-shells instead of acorns.

The **other ranks' black leather belt** had a rectangular dress-quality bright aluminium pebbled buckle with the Wehrmacht eagle in a wreath with the *Gott mit uns* ('God is with us') motto, introduced 24 January 1936. The **84/98 service bayonet**, introduced in 1898, was carried in a blued steel sheath suspended from the belt by a black leather bayonet-frog. The standard ammunition pouches were of smooth or grained black leather with matt-grey aluminium fittings.

Formal and informal uniforms for other ranks

The Walking-Out Uniform for other ranks was the same as the Parade Uniform, except that the M1935 peaked cap replaced the helmet, standard black lace-up shoes the marching-boots, and ribbons the medals. The sword, Y-straps, ammunition-pouches and rifle were omitted.

The **other ranks' peaked cap**, in *feldgrau* tricot, introduced 10 September 1935, preserved the traditional 'plate' style, although privately purchased caps often took the officers' 'saddle' style.

An Artillery Wachtmeister acting as a battery sergeant major (*Hauptwachtmeisterdiensttuer*), wearing the M1935 service uniform with M1935 other ranks' field cap. Note his double cuff braids, indicating his appointment, and the lack of the usual report book stuffed into the front of his tunic. He wears a 1939 Iron Cross 2nd Class ribbon and the bronze SA Defence-Badge. France, May 1940. (Friedrich Herrmann)

Major Eberhardt Rodt (left) and Hauptmann Finster (right) in the Corn Market, Ghent, 20 May 1940 wearing the M1935 officers' field uniform, confer in a 4 x 2 Wanderer WII staff car. Finster is wearing the M1938 officers' field cap, a 1914 Iron Cross 2nd Class button-ribbon with 1939 bar, and the 1939 Iron Cross 1st Class. (Josef Charita)

Otherwise it was exactly the same as for the officers' cap, except for the 1.5cm wide patent leather or vulcanised fibre chin-strap with two black metal buckles, fixed to the cap with two 12mm smooth black lacquered buttons.

The Reporting Uniform consisted of the peaked cap, field tunic with ribbons and field-quality insignia, plain trousers and marching-boots, no field greatcoat, black belt with bayonet and bayonet-knot and marksman's lanyard.

Training and barracks uniforms for other ranks

The Service Uniform for technical and senior NCOs consisted of the peaked cap, field tunic with ribbons, M1935 field greatcoat, trousers and marching-boots, black belt with pistol and holster and grey suede gloves. Junior NCOs wore the helmet instead or the M1935 other ranks' field cap instead of the service-cap, and Y-straps, ammunition pouches and a bayonet instead of the pistol and holster. Junior NCOs also wore grey suede gloves.

The **other ranks' field greatcoat**, introduced 10 September 1935, was identical to the officers' version but was of lesser quality and the insignia was other ranks' field-quality.

The M1935 **other ranks' field cap**, introduced 10 September 1935, resembled the later M1938 officers' field cap, and was developed from the M1934 cap of 24 March 1934. It was made of *feldgrau* cloth with a *feldgrau* flap, and the eagle and swastika and national cockade was embroidered in white cotton on a *feldgrau* backing from 30 October 1935, and on a bluish dark-green backing from 19 June 1937. Embroidery changed to silver-grey on 5 February 1939, and on 4 June 1940 to mouse-grey on *feldgrau* backing. The cockade was enclosed by a 4mm woollen branch colour chevron, point-up.

For the Undress Uniform NCOs and men wore the peaked cap, the field tunic with ribbons, plain trousers and marching-boots, the field greatcoat if ordered, and the black belt with bayonet. NCOs wore grey suede gloves and technical and senior NCOs the pistol and holster, the only field equipment carried with this uniform.

The Guard Uniform consisted of the helmet or field cap, field tunic with ribbons and plain trousers with marching-boots (*Waffenrock* with piped trousers for Guards of Honour), field greatcoat if ordered, black belt, bayonet and marksman's lanyard. Technical and senior NCOs had a sword or a pistol and holster, junior NCOs and men Y-straps and ammunition-pouches. All NCOs had grey suede gloves.

Field and fatigue uniforms for other ranks

The field uniform consisted of the helmet or field cap, field tunic with ribbons, field greatcoat if ordered, plain trousers and marching-boots. All NCOs had grey suede gloves.

Technical and senior NCOs carried a pistol and holster, and other NCOs acting as infantry platoon leaders carried the riflemen's field equipment with the map-case and, if equipped with a submachine gun, two olive-green canvas M1938 magazine pouches. Other infantry NCOs and men carried the standard riflemen's field equipment.

A ten-man rifle-section had an Unteroffizier as section leader, a Gefreiter as deputy, a light machine gun team with three Schützen (gunners), and five riflemen. The section leader wore the platoon leader's equipment, but was not normally issued with a submachine gun until 1941. The First Gunner, the machine gunner, operating the LMG34 light machine gun introduced in 1936, carried a pistol and holster instead of ammunition-pouches on his left front hip; and on his right front hip he had a black-leather spares-pouch. The Second Gunner, also the replacement machine gunner, carried standard riflemen's equipment with a pistol and holster instead of one set of ammunition-pouches; four 50-round ammunition drums, a 300-round ammunition box, and a sheet-metal barrel protector with one or two spare barrels. The deputy section leader, ordinary riflemen and the Third Gunner wore standard riflemen's equipment. Gunner 3 also carried two ammunition-boxes.

Officers in M1935 field uniform hold an impromptu meeting in Lichtervelde, Belgium, May 1940. Note the M1934 field cap worn by three officers and the leather greatcoat worn by the Major (2nd left). The Hauptmann (2nd right) is saluting before shaking the hand of the Major (1st right). (Josef Charita)

The **white drill fatigue uniform** was usually worn by enlisted men and only rarely by NCOs. It consisted of the M1934 field cap, M1933 fatigue tunic, fatigue-trousers introduced 1 April 1933, black belt and marching-boots. The tunic, made of cream or off-white cotton herringbone twill, had two patch side-pockets and five matt-grey painted pebbled buttons. Badges were confined to the special rank insignia described below. In 1940 the off-white colour was replaced on 12 February 1940 by a more practical mid-green, called 'reed-green'.

Tank crew uniforms

The M1934 black uniform was closely associated with the Panzer branch, but initially only tank-crews were authorised to wear it. Later, units of other branches in Panzer divisions were allowed to wear this prestigious uniform: signals battalions from 2 April 1937, artillery regiments from mid-1938, armoured reconnaissance battalions in March 1940, and on 10 May 1940 armoured engineer battalions. However, unauthorised personnel, such as general-officers, staff officers and members of unit staffs such as doctors, paymasters and company sergeant-majors, unofficially adopted the uniform. The colour, the distinctive double-breasted jacket and the collar patch skulls were intended to evoke the prestige of the Imperial German Cavalry.

The black uniform, introduced 12 November 1934, could be worn on all occasions except ceremonial. It consisted of the standard M1934 padded beret, later replaced by the M1940 field cap; a dark-grey tricot pullover shirt and black tie; the M1934 field jacket; M1934 field trousers and black lace-up shoes.

The **padded beret** was made of thick felt or red rubber sponge covered in black wool. From 30 October 1935 officers wore an eagle and swastika in bright aluminium bullion on the front of the beret, other ranks the badge in matt silver-grey machine-woven cotton thread, above a white cotton thread, later matt silver-grey machine-woven cotton thread, cockade and wreath, all insignia on a black backing. The beret proved too cumbersome in armoured vehicles, and on 27 March 1940 it

A motorcycle combination of a Military Police Traffic Control Battalion leads a convoy of trucks in France. Both riders are wearing the M1934 rubberised field greatcoat but with minimal equipment. The driver has slung his Karabiner 98k rifle over his shoulder, and wears the M1938 gas mask canister across his chest. His passenger carries a signal-baton. Note the divisional signs on the sidecar and the WH (*Wehrmacht-Heer*) number plate. May 1940.
(Brian Davis Collection)

A dispatch-rider in the street of a town in German-occupied Flanders in May 1940. He is wearing the M1934 rubberised field greatcoat with an M1935 dispatch-case and has slung his M1938 gas mask canister on his chest, in order not to constrict his rear-passenger on his motorcycle. (ECPA)

began to be replaced by the M1940 officers' black field cap and the M1940 other ranks' black field cap. These caps were identical to the M1938 and M1934 *feldgrau* versions, but were in black cloth, with the eagle and cockade on a black cloth backing. Many officers and NCOs also favoured the *feldgrau* officers' M1935 peaked cap, M1934 peaked field cap or M1938 field cap, or other ranks' M1935 peaked cap or M1934 field cap.

The black wool double-breasted hip-length Panzer **field jacket** had a wide collar, with a 2mm branch colour facing-cloth piping, and wide lapels. The fly-front was closed by four large black horn or plastic buttons, with three smaller buttons left exposed above. Officers wore a matt aluminium thread breast-eagle, other ranks a white cotton, later a matt silver-grey, machine-woven cotton thread breast-eagle, all on a black cloth backing. All ranks wore standard black cloth collar-patches with branch colour piping and a bright aluminium stamped skull. All ranks wore field-quality shoulder and sleeve rank insignia, with black cloth replacing the bluish dark-green facing-cloth for NCOs and men. NCOs did not wear bright aluminium yarn braid collar braid. The M1934 plain black trousers tapered at the bottom to give a bloused effect, and buttoned and tied at the ankle.

When worn as a parade-uniform, officers' jackets had aiguillettes and the M1935 brocade belt, while other ranks wore the marksmen's lanyard and black belt. On 17 October 1938 a distinctive **new marksmen's lanyard** was introduced for armoured troops. It featured a matt aluminium eagle above a tank in a small ring for awards 1-4, in a large oak-leaf wreath for 5-8, in gold for 9-12, with, from 9 December 1938, aluminium acorns instead of shells. In the field all ranks wore a leather belt with a pistol and holster.

Special uniforms for other branches

General Staff officers wore bright aluminium collar and cuff-braids on the *Waffenrock* and matt aluminium thread collar-patches on the field tunic in the traditional *Kolben* pattern, whilst *OKW* and *OKH* officers wore the same insignia in bright gold thread on the *Waffenrock* and matt gold thread on the field tunic. These officers also wore general-officers' trouser and breeches pipings and braids in crimson facing-cloth on all uniforms.

Instead of the field cap, **Mountain Troops** wore the peaked mountain-cap used by German and Austro-Hungarian troops in the First World War – mountain troops were recruited heavily from Austria. The standard model, introduced about 1930, was in *feldgrau* cloth with a flap secured by two 12mm matt grey painted buttons, matt gold for general-officers. The eagle and cockade insignia was the same as for the M1938 officers' and M1934 other ranks' field caps, but officers did not adopt the aluminium and gold crown and flap pipings until 3 October 1942.

TABLE 2 RANKS OF THE GERMAN ARMY 1 SEPTEMBER 1939 – 9 MAY 1945

(omitting Army Officials; *Sonderführer;* Bandsmen NCOs and Men; Officer Candidates and *Osttruppen*)

Rank class	Rank (Staff & Infantry)	Command (Infantry)	Rank variants (other arms)	British Army
OFFIZIERE (officers)				
Reichsmarschall	—	—	Reichsmarschall des Großdeutschen Reiches[1]	—
Generale *(General officers)*	Generalfeldmarschall	Army Group	—	Field-Marshal
	Generaloberst[2]	Army, Army Group	—	General
	General der... Infanterie, Gebirgstruppe[12]	Corps, Army	General der... Kavallerie[13]/Panzertruppen[17]/ Artillerie[21]/Pioniere[24]/Nachrichtentruppe[28] Generaloberstabsarzt[32] Generaloberstabsveterinär[33] Generaloberstabsrichter[34] Generaloberstabsintendant[35]	Lieut. General
	Generalleutnant	Division, Corps	Generalstabsarzt[32] Generalstabsveterinär[33] Generalstabsrichter[34] Generalstabsintendant[35]	Major General
	Generalmajor	Brigade, Division	Generalmajor (W)[23]/(Ing)[27] Generalarzt[32] Generalveterinär[33] Generalrichter[34] Generalintendant[35]	Brigadier
Stabsoffiziere *(Field officers)*	Oberst	Regiment	Oberst i.G.[7]/(W)[23]/(Ing)[27] Oberstarzt[32] Oberstveterinär[33] Oberstrichter[34] Oberstintendant[35]	Colonel
	Oberstleutnant	Battalion, Regiment.	Oberstleutnant i.G.[7]/(W)[23]/(Ing)[27] Oberfeldarzt[32] Oberfeldveterinär[33] Oberfeldrichter[34] Oberfeldintendant[35]	Lieut.Colonel
	Major	Battalion	Major i.G.[7]/(W)[23]/(Ing)[27] Oberstabsarzt[32] Oberstabsveterinär[33] Oberstabsrichter[34] Oberstabsintendant[35]	Major
Hauptleute und Rittmeister *(Captains)*	Hauptmann	Company, Battalion.	Hauptmann i.G.[7]/(W)[23]/(Ing)[27] Rittmeister[14] Stabsarzt[32] Stabsveterinär[33] Stabsrichter[34] Stabszahlmeister[35]	Captain
Leutnante *(Subalterns)*	Oberleutnant	Platoon, Company.	Oberleutnant(W)[23]/(Ing)[27] Oberarzt[32] Oberveterinär[33] Oberzahlmeister[35]	Lieutenant
	Leutnant	Platoon	Leutnant(W)[23]/(Ing)[27] Assistenzarzt[32] Veterinär[33] Zahlmeister[35]	2nd Lieutenant
MUSIKMEISTER (Bandmaster Officers)[3]				
Musikinspizienten *(Music Directors)*	—	Inspector of Music	Obermusikinspizient[8]	L/Col, Dir/Mus
	—	Inspector of Music	Musikinspizient[8]	Maj, Dir/Mus
Stabsmusikmeister *(Senior Bandmaster)*	Stabsmusikmeister	Regimental band	—	Bandm Capt
Musikmeister *(Junior Bandmasters)*	Obermusikmeister	Regimental band	—	Bandm Lieut
	Musikmeister	Regimental band	—	Bandm 2/Lt
UNTEROFFIZIERE (Non-commissioned Officers)				
Festungswerk- meister & Hufbe- schlaglehrmeister *(Technical NCO s)*		Instructor	Oberhufbeschlaglehrmeister[33] Festungsoberwerkmeister[24]	WOI(SSM 1cl)
	—	Instructor	Hufbeschlagmeister[33] Festungswerkmeister[24]	WOI(SSM 1cl)
Unteroffiziere mit Portepee *(Senior NCOs)*	Stabsfeldwebel	Platoon, CQMS (12 years total service)	Stabswachtmeister[15] Sanitätsstabsfeldwebel[32]	WOII(RQMS)
	Hauptfeldwebel[4]	Company Serjeant Major	Hauptwachtmeister[15] Sanitätshauptfeldwebel[32]	WOII(CSM)
	Oberfeldwebel	Platoon, CQMS	Oberwachtmeister[15] Sanitätsoberfeldwebel[32]	CQMS
	Feldwebel	Platoon, 2ic	Wachtmeister[15] Sanitätsfeldwebel[32]	Serjeant

CEREMONIAL UNIFORMS
1: Oberstleutnant, Panzerregiment 8, full ceremonial uniform, Böblingen, Germany, July 1939
2: Hauptwachtmeister, Gebirgsartillerieregiment 79, parade uniform, Garmisch-Partenkirchen, Germany, July 1939
3: Fahnenjunker-Gefreiter, III (Jäg)/ Infanterieregiment 83, walking-out uniform, Hirschberg, Germany, July 1939

A

THE POLISH CAMPAIGN
1: Generalleutnant, 14.Infanteriedivision, field
   uniform, Lublin, Poland, September 1939
2: Hauptmann i.G., 14.Infanteriedivision, field uniform,
   Lublin, Poland, September 1939
3: Stabsgefreiter, Reiterregiment 2, field uniform, Rozan, Poland,
   September 1939

BLITZKRIEG RIFLE SECTION
1: Unteroffizier, Infanterieregiment 96, field uniform, Chelmo, Poland, September 1939
2: Obergefreiter, Infanterieregiment 96, field uniform, Chelmo, Poland, September 1939
3: Schütze, Infanterieregiment 96, field uniform, Chelmo, Poland, September 1939

C

DENMARK AND NORWAY
1: Unterfeldwebel, Divisional Staff, 198.Infanteriedivision, field uniform, Copenhagen, Denmark, April 1940
2: Sanitätsobergefreiter, Sanitätskompanie 1/234, field uniform, Kristiansand, Norway, April 1940
3: Oberleutnant, Gebirgsjägerregiment 138, field uniform, Narvik, Norway, May 1940

D

NETHERLANDS AND BELGIUM
1: Leutnant, Aufklärungsabteilung 254, field uniform, Breda, Netherlands, May 1940
2: Oberschütze, Infanterieregiment 49, field uniform, Namur, Belgium, May 1940
3: Gefreiter, Pionierbataillon 30, River Meuse, Belgium, May 1940

THE BATTLE OF FRANCE (1)
1: Major, Panzerregiment 25, field uniform, Cambrai, France, May 1940
2: Panzerschütze, Panzeraufklärungsabteilung 5, field uniform, Aisne, France, May 1940
3: Hauptmann, Infanterieregiment (mot.) *Großdeutschland,* field uniform, Stonne, France, May 1940

F

THE BATTLE OF FRANCE (2)
1: Oberschirrmeister, Panzerpionierbataillon 37, field uniform, Besançon, France, June 1940
2: Schütze, Infanterieregiment 154, field uniform, De Panne, Belgium, June 1940
3: Unteroffizier, Infanterieregiment (mot.) 66, fatigue uniform, Amiens, France, June 1940

THE ARMY OF OCCUPATION
1: Unteroffizier, Verkehrsregelungsbataillon 754, field uniform, Arras, France, July 1940
2: Generalmajor, 215.Infanteriedivision, service uniform, Chaumont, France, September 1940
3: Obergefreiter, Oberfeldkommandantur 672, guard uniform, Brussels, Belgium, September 1940

Rank class	Rank (Staff & Infantry)	Command (Infantry)	Rank variants (other arms)	British Army
Unteroffiziere ohne Portepee (Junior NCOs)	Unterfeldwebel	Section (6 years total service)	Unterwachtmeister[15] Sanitätsunterfeldwebel[32]	Lance-Serjeant
	Unteroffizier. Oberjäger[11]	Section	Sanitätsunteroffizier[32]	Corporal
MANNSCHAFTEN (Men)				
Mannschaften (Men)	Stabsgefreiter (neuer Art)[5]	Section member (5 years total service)	Sanitätsstabsgefreiter (neuer Art)[32]	Lance-Corpl
	Obergefreiter mit mehr als 6 Dienstjahren	Section member (6 years total service)	Sanitätsobergefreiter mit mehr als 6 Dienstjahren[32]	Lance-Corpl
	Obergefreiter mit weniger als 6 Dienstjahren	Section member (2 years total service)	Sanitätsobergefreiter mit weniger als 6 Dienstjahren[32]	Lance-Corpl
	Gefreiter	Section member (6 months total service)	Sanitätsgefreiter[32]	Lance-Corpl
	(Obersoldat[6]) Oberschütze Obergrenadier[9] Oberfüsilier[10]	Section member (1 year total service)	(Obersoldat[6]) Oberreiter[16] Panzeroberschütze[18] Panzerobergrenadier[19] Panzeroberfüsilier[37] Panzerzug-Oberschütze[20] Oberkanonier[21] Oberpionier[24] Panzeroberpionier[39] Bauobersoldat[25] /Bauoberpionier[26] Oberfunker[29] Oberfernsprecher[40] Oberkraftfahrer[30] Oberfahrer[31] Sanitätsobersoldat[32] Feldobergendarm[36]	Private
	(Soldat[6]) Schütze Grenadier[9] Füsilier[10] Jäger[11]	Section member	(Soldat[6]) Reiter[16] Panzerschütze[18] Panzergrenadier[19] Panzerfüsilier[37] Panzerzug-Schütze[20] Kanonier[21] Panzerkanonier[38] Pionier[24] Bausoldat[25]/Baupionier[26] Funker[29] Fernsprecher[40] Kraftfahrer[30] Fahrer[31] Sanitätssoldat[32] Feldgendarm[36]	Private

1 A Wehrmacht rank, held exclusively from 19.7.1940-9.5.1945 by Hermann Goering as nominally the most senior officer in the German Armed Forces.
2 Generaloberst im Range eines Generalfeldmarschalls (Acting Field Marshal) was created in 1935 as the then highest Army rank (with 4 pips) but was never held by any officer.
3 Bandmaster Officers ranked between officers and NCOs. Bandsmen's ranks have been omitted due to pressure of space.
4 An appointment, not a rank, usually held by an Oberfeldwebel, but also by a Stabsfeldwebel. A Feldwebel, Unterfeldwebel or Unteroffizier in this appointment was designated Hauptfeldwebeldiensttuer (Acting CSM).
5 Stabsgefreiter, introduced 6.1.1928, no further promotions after 1.10.1934, reintroduced 25.4.1942 as Stabsgefreiter (neuer Art), providing an extra pay-grade.
6 A generic term, covering all the variations in rank-titles.
7 General Staff officers.
8 Attached to OKH.

9 15.10.1942 for infantry regiments.
10 12.11.1942 for selected infantry regiments.
11 Light and mountain infantry.
12 Mountain infantry.
13 Mounted cavalry.
14 Mounted cavalry, reconnaissance, motor & horsedrawn transport.
15 Mounted cavalry, reconnaissance, artillery, smoke troops, signals, war correspondents (until 24.1.1943), motor and horsedrawn transport, veterinary corps.
16 Mounted cavalry, cyclist reconnaissance, veterinary corps.
17 Armoured troops.
18 Armoured troops and armoured reconnaissance.
19 3.6.1943 for mechanised infantry.
20 27.10.1942 for armoured trains.
21 Artillery.
22 Artillery and Smoke Troops.
23 Ordnance officers.
24 Engineers.

25 27.2.1940 for pioneers.
26 11.10.1939 for pioneers.
27 Engineer specialist officers.
28 Signals.
29 Signals and until 24.12.1943 war correspondents.
30 Motor transport.
31 Horsedrawn transport.
32 Medical corps.
33 Veterinary corps.
34 1.5.1944 for judge-advocate officers.
35 1.5.1944 for administrative officers.
36 Military Police. For ranks Oberst – Gefreiter add '...der Feldgendarmerie'.
37 For Großdeutschland and Feldherrnhalle mechanised infantry.
38 12.1941 for artillery regts of Panzer divisions.
39 15.4.1940 for engineer regts of Panzer divisions
40 For Signals radio operators.

Mountain Troops also wore M1935 stone-grey (from 1939 *feldgrau*) ski-trousers with *feldgrau* ankle puttees and fawn, brown or black leather studded climbing ankle-boots. They occasionally wore the greenish-khaki double-breasted close-woven calico wind-jacket, probably introduced in 1925, with shoulder-boards and straps the only authorised insignia, and the M1938 hooded reversible water-repellent fabric white-*feldgrau* anorak. Mountaineering equipment included the M1931 greenish-khaki canvas rucksack.

The commando units of **Army Intelligence** (*Abwehr*) wore German or foreign uniform appropriate to the occasion. It is known that some *Abwehr*

TABLE 3 Rank insignia of the German Army 1 September 1939 - 9 May 1945

Staff and Infantry ranks are normally given, but are in brackets where the insignia illustrates a rank variant. Most Bandmaster Officer and both Technical NCO ranks are omitted, and insignia on camouflage and fatigue tunics are excluded.

1.Generalfeldmarschall
(Field Marshal)
(1.9.1939 – 2.4.1941)

2. Generaloberst
(General)

3. General der
Infanterie etc.
(Lieutenant General)

4. Generalleutnant
(Major General)

5. Generalarzt
(General Major)
(Brigadier)

6. Oberst
(Colonel)

7. Oberfeldrichter
(Oberstleutnant)
(Lieutenant Colonel)
Judge Advocate
Service

8. Major
(Major)
Infantry Regiment
Hoch und
Deutschmeister'

9. Stabszahlmeister
(Hauptmann)
(Captain)
Administrative Service

10. Oberveterinär
(Oberleutnant)
(Lieutenant)
Veterinary Corps

11. Obermusikmeister
(Oberleutnant)
(Lieutenant)
Bandmaster

12. Leutnant
(2nd Lieutenant)
Army AA Artillery

13. Stabsfeldwebel
(WOII, RQMS)
21 Engineer
Battalion

14. Hauptfeldwebel
(WOII, CSM)

15. Oberwachtmeister
(Oberfeldwebel)
(Colour Serjeant)
11 Division Recce
Battalion

16. Wachtmeister
(Feldwebel)
(Serjeant)
Artillery

17. Unterfeldwebel
(Lance-Serjeant)
Infantry Regiment
'Großdeutschland'

18. Oberjäger
Unteroffizier
(Corporal)
Light Infantry

19. Stabsgefreiter
(Lance-Corporal
5 years total service)
24.4.1942 – 9.5.1945

20. Obergefreiter mit
mehr als 6
Dienstjahren
(Lance-Corporal
6 years total service)

21. Obergefreiter mit
mehr als 6
Dienstjahren
(Lance-Corporal
2 years total service)

22. Gefreiter
(Lance-Corporal
6 months total
service)

23. Obersoldat
(Private 6 months total
service)

24. Schüze/Grenadier
(Private) Infantry
Regiment
'Feldherrnhalle'

A good view of the M1935 field tunic worn by a Wachtmeister of Artillery in France, May 1940. His lack of field equipment and M1935 dispatch-case with modified fastener suggest assignment to the Regimental Staff. (Brian Davis Collection)

troops wore Polish, Belgian and Dutch uniforms during the Blitzkrieg period. From 13 November 1939 the inmates of the four Army **Penal Battalions** wore the standard Army uniform without any decorations, national, rank or branch insignia, and probably also a belt-buckle with a plain pebbled disc.

All ranks of mounted personnel of the **cavalry** or any other branch wore stone-grey (from April 1940) *feldgrau* riding-breeches with grey leather reinforcements. From 12 November 1934 motorcycle couriers and personnel in motorcycle reconnaissance battalions were issued feldgrau special clothing, consisting of a motorcyclist's protective greatcoat, a woollen turtle-neck sweater, long woollen stockings, and waterproof cotton gauntlets. The *feldgrau* heavy twill cloth M1934 greatcoat was rubberised on both sides and had a large *feldgrau* cloth collar, with *feldgrau* facings from 22 June 1935, bluish dark-green facings from November 1935 and finally back to *feldgrau* cloth in May 1940. Insignia was confined to shoulder-boards or straps.

Motorised Artillery and Motorised Infantry vehicle crews, Motor Transport drivers, and guards and sentries were issued the *feldgrau* waterproof M1934 surcoat. It was the same design as the field greatcoat, but ankle-length and cut generously at the waist to allow wear over a field greatcoat. **Smoke Troops** were issued protective clothing consisting of a dark-brown single-breasted leather tunic, trousers, gauntlets, peaked cap, face-mask and goggles.

On 26 August 1939 220 1,700-strong **pioneer battalions** were formed from members of the RAD (*Reichsarbeitsdienst*, the Nazi labour service) for construction duties along the eastern and western frontiers. Personnel wore RAD uniforms and insignia, changing to Army uniforms during the winter of 1939-40.

All **Medical Corps** personnel wore the M1937 white armband with a red cross on the upper left sleeve, introduced 6 March 1937. Orderlies also carried their first-aid kit in two smooth brown leather pouches.

The uniforms and insignia of Army Officials, including Chaplains and **Sonderführer** will be covered in Volume 3.

RANKS AND RESPONSIBILITIES

The rank structure of the German Army used a system established on 6 December 1920. Officers were divided into four groups: general-officers, field officers, captains and subalterns. By tradition the lieutenant-general rank indicated the officer's original branch of service, but in the case of officers of combat branches there was no differentiation in the insignia.

The first and second gunners of the section LMG team in field uniform operating their LMG34 machine gun in France in May 1940. Both soldiers have rubbed mud on their helmets as makeshift camouflage. Their M1935 field tunics have M1938 rounded shoulder-straps with unit numbers removed as per regulation. (Brian Davis Collection)

From 31 March 1936 Bandmaster Officers were grouped as a separate rank-class as Music Directors, Senior and Junior Bandmasters. Lacking power of command, they wore officers' uniforms and insignia, enjoyed officer status and were the equivalents of officers in the British and United States Armies. Music Directors, based at the OKH, were regarded as staff officers, while the Bandmasters supervised infantry, light infantry, cavalry, artillery regimental and engineer battalion bands.

NCOs were divided into three groups. Technical NCOs, established 23 September 1937, for senior instructors in the Fortress Engineers and later the Veterinary Corps; Senior NCOs, called 'sword-knot NCOs'; and Junior NCOs, or 'NCOs without the sword-knot'. The *Stabsfeldwebel* rank, introduced 14 September 1938 for NCOs re-enlisting after 12 years service, was initially held by First World War veterans. Hauptfeldwebel was not a rank, but an appointment, introduced 28 September 1938. He was the senior NCO in a company based at the company HQ and nicknamed *der Spieß* – 'the spear'. Usually an Oberfeldwebel, he out-ranked a Stabsfeldwebel (who could also be promoted to this appointment). Other NCOs receiving this appointment were designated *Hauptfeldwebeldiensttuer* (acting CSMs), but usually received rapid promotion to Oberfeldwebel.

The rank-class of 'Men' included all privates and lance-corporals, the latter, as experienced privates, constituting a larger proportion of this rank class than would be found in other armies.

Most ranks had alternative rank titles. Some, as in the Medical Corps, differentiated specialist officers without the power of field command. Others, such as *Rittmeister* or *Oberjäger*, preserved traditional titles.

Almost all officers held substantive ranks – the British system of acting ranks did not exist – so that German officers and NCOs often held higher commands than their British equivalent. It was therefore not uncommon for a Leutnant to be a company commander. While the first platoon of a typical rifle company was under a second leutnant, the second and third were often commanded by an Oberfeldwebel or Feldwebel. Promotions to the infantry ranks of Unteroffizier, Feldwebel and Oberfeldwebel depended on a unit's table of organisation, and were

TABLE 4 SELECTIVE LIST OF GERMAN ARMY BRANCH AND UNIT INSIGNIA
1 SEPTEMBER 1939 – 25 JUNE 1940

Units	In existence	Branch colour	Shoulder strap insignia	Other distinctions (comments)
Combat Troops - Staff (Kommandobehörde)				
General Officers (Generale)	1.9.1939 - 25.6.1940	Bright red	None	Larisch collar-patches, red trouser-stripes
Armed Forces High Command (OKW) officers	1.9.1939 - 25.6.1940	Crimson	None	Gold Kolben collar-patches, crimson stripes
Army High Command (OKH) officers	1.9.1939 - 25.6.1940	Crimson	None	Gold Kolben collar-patches, crimson stripes
General Staff (Generalstab) officers	1.9.1939 - 25.6.1940	Crimson	None	Silver Kolben coll.-patches, crimson stripes
5 Army Group (Heeresgruppe) Staffs	2.9.1939 - 25.6.1940	White	G (Nord, Süd, A, B, C)	
14 Army (Armee) Staffs	1.9.1939 - 25.6.1940	White	A / 1-10, 12, 14, 16, 18	
2 Armoured Group (Panzergruppe) Staffs	5.3.1940 - 25.6.1940	White	XIX, XXII	
33 Corps (Korps) Staffs	1.9.1939 - 25.6.1940	White	I - XXXIX series	
6 Motorised Corps (Korps(mot.)) Staffs	1.9.1939 - 25.6.1940	White	XIV, XV, XIX, XXII, XXXIX, XXXXI	
XVI Motorised Corps (Korps(mot.)) Staff	1.9.1939 - 25.6.1940	Pink	XVI	
Combat Troops - Infantry (Infanterie)				
143 Infantry (Infanterie) Division Staffs	1.9.1939 - 25.6.1940	White	D / 1-557 series	
431 Line Infantry (Infanterie) Regts.	1.9.1939 - 25.6.1940	White	1-664 series	
Line Infantry (Infanterie) Regt. 17	1.9.1939 - 25.6.1940	White	17	Brunswick skull cap-badge
4 Motorised (Inf.(mot.)) Division Staffs	1.9.1939 - 25.6.1940	White	D / 2, 13, 20, 29	
12 Motorised (Infanterie(mot.)) Regts.	1.9.1939 - 25.6.1940	White	5, 15, 25, 33, 66, 69, 71, 76, 86, 90, 92-3	
Infantry Regiment Großdeutschland	1.9.1939 - 30.9.1939	White	GD monogram	Großdeutschland title
Motorized Regiment Großdeutschland	1.10.1939 - 25.6.1940	White	GD monogram	Großdeutschland title
Hitler Escort (Führer-Begleit) Battalion	29.9.1939 - 25.6.1940	White	GD monogram	Führer-Hauptquartier title (12.1939)
3 Anti-Aircraft (Flak) Bns.	6.10.1939 - 25.6.1940	White	Fl / 31-2,46	
6 Light Infantry (Jäger) Bns. in Infantry Regts.	1.9.1939 - 25.6.1940	Light green	2 (I), 4 (II), 10 (I), 15 (III), 17 (III), 83 (III)	
4 Mountain (Gebirgs) Division Staffs	1.9.1939 - 25.6.1940	Light green	D / 1-3, 6	Edelweiss badges. Mountain cap
11 Mountain (Gebirgs) Regts.	1.9.1939 - 25.6.1940	Light green	98-100, 136-143	Edelweiss badges. Mountain cap
1 Commando Bn. (Bau-Lehr Bataillon zbV 800)	10.1.1940 - 31.5.1940	—	—	Any appropriate uniform
1 Commando Regt. (Brandenburg zbV 800)	1.6.1940 - 25.6.1940	—	—	Any appropriate uniform
Penal Bn. (Sonderabteilung I, II, IX, XIII) inmates	8.1.1940 - 25.6.1940	White	None (no shoulder-straps)	Uniforms without insignia
Combat Troops - Mobile Troops (Schnelle Truppen)				
1 Cavalry (Kavallerie) Division Staff	25.10.1939 - 25.6.1940	Golden yellow	D / 1	
4 Mounted (Reiter) Regts.	1.9.1939 - 25.6.1940	Golden yellow	1, 2, 21, 22	Cavalry breeches & boots
4 Mobile (leichte) Divisional Staffs	1.9.1939 - 25.6.1940	Golden yellow	D / 1-4	
7 Motorized Cav. (Kavallerieschützen) Regts.	1.9.1939 - 25.6.1940	Golden yellow	S / 4, 6-11	

SELECTIVE LIST OF GERMAN ARMY BRANCH AND UNIT INSIGNIA
CONTINUED

Units	In existence	Branch colour	Shoulder strap insignia	Other distinctions (comments)
4 Armoured (Panzer) Bns.	1.9.1939 - 25.6.1940	Pink	33, 65-67	Skull collar-patches, black
10 Armoured (Panzer) Division Staffs	1.9.1939 - 25.6.1940	Pink	D / 1-10 (6.7.39)	Skull collar-patches, black uniform
17 Armoured (Panzer) Regts.	1.9.1939 - 25.6.1940	Pink	1-8, 10-11, 15, 23, 25, 31, 33, 35, 36	Skull collar-patches, black uniform
1 Armoured Instruction (Panzer Lehr) Bn.	1.9.1939 - 25.6.1940	Pink	L	*1936 Spanien 1939* cuff-title
11 Motorised Rifle (Schützen) Regts.	1.9.1939 - 25.6.1940	Pink	S / 1-3, 12-4, 33, 69, 86, 110-1	
7 Motorised Rifle (Schützen) Regts.	1.9.1939 - 25.6.1940	Pink	S / 4, 6-11	(Ex-Motorised Cavalry Regts)
5 Motorcycle Recce. (Kradschützen) Bns.	1.9.1939 - 25.6.1940	Pink	K / 1-2, 6-8	
Motorcycle Recce. (Kradschützen) Bn. 3	1.9.1939 - 25.6.1940	Pink	K / 3	Dragoon eagle cap badge
3 Armd Recce. (Panzeraufklärung) Bns.	1.3.1940 - 25.6.1940	Pink	A / 4-5, 8	
15 Mounted Recce. (Aufklärung) Bns.	1.9.1939 - 25.6.1940	Golden yellow	A / 54 - 187 series	
Mounted Recce. (Aufklärung) Bn. 179	1.9.1939 - 25.6.1940	Golden yellow	A / 179	Dragoon eagle cap-badge
32 Div. Recce. (Divisionsaufklärung) Bns.	1.9.1939 - 25.6.1940	Golden yellow	A / 1, 3-12, 14-9, 21-8, 30-2, 35, 44-6, 156	
Div. Recce. (Divisionsaufklärung) Bns 33, 35-6.	1.9.1939 - 25.6.1940	Golden yellow	A / 33-4, 36	Dragoon eagle cap-badge
10 Motorised Recce. (Aufklärung(mot)) Bns.	1.9.1939 - 25.6.1940	Golden yellow	A / 1-8, 20, 29	
148 Antitank (Panzerabwehr) Bns.	1.9.1939 - 25.6.1940	Pink	P / 1-672 (divisional series)	
144 Antitank (Panzerjäger) Bns.	16.3.1940 - 25.6.1940	Pink	P / 1-672 (divisional series)	
3 Mtn. Antitank (Gebirgspanzerabwehr) Bns.	1.9.1939 - 25.6.1940	Pink	P / 44, 47-8	*Edelweiss* badges. Mountain cap
4 Mtn. Antitank (Gebirgspanzerjäger) Bns.	21.3.1940 - 25.6.1940	Pink	P / 44, 47-8, 55	*Edelweiss* badges. Mountain cap
Combat Troops - Artillery (Artillerie)				
147 Artillery (Artillerie) Regts.	1.9.1939 - 25.6.1940	Bright red	1-557 (divisional series)	
4 Motorised Artillery (Artillerie (mot.)) Regts.	1.9.1939 - 25.6.1940	Bright red	2, 13, 56/20, 29	
4 Mtn. Artillery (Gebirgsartillerie) Regts.	1.9.1939 - 25.6.1940	Bright red	79, 111-2, 118	*Edelweiss* badges. Mountain cap
2 Mtd. Artillery (Reitende Artillerie) Bns.	1.9.1939 - 25.6.1940	Bright red	R / 1-2	Cavalry breeches & boots
1 Mtd. Artillery (Reitende Artillerie) Regt.	10.1.1940 - 25.6.1940	Bright red	R / 1	Cavalry breeches & boots
10 Armd. Artillery (Artillerie) Regts.	1.9.1939 - 25.6.1940	Bright red	73-6, 78, 80, 90, 102-3, 116	
40 Survey (Beobachtung) Bns.	1.9.1939 - 25.6.1940	Bright red	B / 1-36, 39, 40, 43, 44	
Ordnance officers (Offiziere(W))	1.9.1939 - 25.6.1940	Bright red	Gold crossed cannon	
3 Smoke (Nebel) Bns.	1.9.1939 - 30.9.1939	Bordeaux red	1, 2, 5	
9 Rocket Projector (Nebelwerfer) Bns.	22.9.1939 - 25.6.1940	Bordeaux red	1-9	
Combat Troops - Engineers (Pioniere)				
148 Engineer (Pionier) Bns.	1.9.1939 - 25.6.1940	Black	1-557 (divisional series)	
4 Motorised Engineer (Pionier) Bns.	1.9.1939 - 25.6.1940	Black	2, 13, 20, 29	
5 Mtn. Engineer (Gebirgspionier) Bns.	1.9.1939 - 25.6.1940	Black	54, 82, 83, 85, 91	*Edelweiss* badges. Mountain cap.
10 Armd. Engineer (Pionier) Bns.	1.9.1939 - 14.5.1940	Black	37-9, 49, 57-9, 79, 86, 89	Skull collar patches. Black uniform

SELECTIVE LIST OF GERMAN ARMY BRANCH AND UNIT INSIGNIA
CONTINUED

Units	In existence	Branch colour	Shoulder strap insignia	Other distinctions (comments)
10 Armd. Engineer (Panzerpionier) Bns.	10.5.1940 - 25.6.1940	Black & white	37-9, 49, 57-9, 79, 86, 89	Skull collar-patches, black uniform
220 Pioneer (Bau) Bns.	1.9.1939 - 22.12.1939	—	None (1-360 sorties)	RAD uniforms
220 Pioneer (Bau) Bns.	23.12.1939 - 25.6.1940	Light brown	1-360 series	
15 Fortress Pioneer (Festungsbau) Bns.	9.12.1939 - 25.6.1940	Black	19-314 series	
4 Fortress Engineer (Festungspionier) Bns.	7.2.1940 - 25.6.1940	Black	305-8	
Fortress Instructors (Festungswerkmeister)	1.9.1939 - 25.6.1940	Crimson	White Fp	Black & white shoulder cords
5 Railway Eng. (Eisenbahnpionier) Regts.	1.9.1939 - 25.6.1940	Black	E / 1-4, 68	
Engineer Specialist Generals (Generale(Ing.))	1.1.1940 - 25.6.1940	Bright red	Silver cogwheel	Larisch collar-patches, red trouser-stripes
Engineer Specialist officers (Ingenieure)	1.9.1939 - 25.6.1940	Orange	Gold cogwheel	
Combat Troops - Signals (Nachrichtentruppe)				
148 Signals (Nachrichten) Bns.	1.9.1939 - 25.6.1940	Lemon yellow	1-557 (divisional series)	
4 Motorised Signals (Nachrichten) Bns.	1.9.1939 - 25.6.1940	Lemon yellow	2, 13, 20, 29	
4 Mtn. Signals (Gebirgsnachrichten) Bns.	1.9.1939 - 25.6.1940	Lemon yellow	54, 67-8, 91	Edelweiss badges. Mountain cap
10 Armd Signals (Panzernachrichten) Bns.	1.9.1939 - 25.6.1940	Lemon yellow	37-9, 77, 79, 82-5, 90	Skull collar-patches, black uniform
1 Signals Instruction (Lehr) Battalion	1.9.1939 - 25.6.1940	Lemon yellow	L	1936 Spanien 1939 cuff-title
14 War Correspondent (Propaganda) Coys.	1.9.1939 - 25.6.1940	Lemon yellow	501-690 (Field Army series)	Propagandakompanie cuff-title
Supply Troops (Versorgungstruppen)				
608? Mot. Transport (Kraftwagen) Cols.	1.9.1939 - 25.6.1940	Light-blue	N / 1-557 (divisional series)	
920? Horsedrawn Transport (Fahr) Cols.	1.9.1939 - 25.6.1940	Light-blue	N / 1-557 (divisional series)	Cavalry breeches & boots
20 Mtn. Horsedrawn Transport (Fahr) Cols.	1.9.1939 - 25.6.1940	Light-blue	N / 79, 94, 111, 112	Edelweiss badges. Mountain cap
Medical Corps (Sanitäts) General-Officers	1.9.1939 - 25.6.1940	Bright red	Silver Aesculapius staff	Larisch collar-patches, red trouser-stripes
Medical Corps (Sanitäts) officers	1.9.1939 - 25.6.1940	Dark-blue	Gold Aesculapius staff	Red cross armband
166 Horsedr.Med. (Sanitäts) Coys-NCOs & men	1.9.1939 - 25.6.1940	Dark-blue	1-557 (divisional series)	Red cross armband; medical cuff-badge
? Mot.Medical (Sanitäts) Coys – NCOs & men	1.9.1939 - 25.6.1940	Dark-blue	1-557 (divisional series)	Red cross armband; medical cuff-badge
166 Field Hospitals (Feldlazarette) – NCOs & men	1.9.1939 - 25.6.1940	Dark-blue	1-557 (divisional series)	Red cross armband; medical cuff-badge
Veterinary Corps (Veterinär) General-Officers	1.9.1939 - 25.6.1940	Bright red	Silver snake	Larisch collar-patches, red trouser-stripes
Veterinary Corps (Veterinär) officers	1.9.1939 - 25.6.1940	Crimson	Gold snake	Cavalry breeches & boots
Farrier Instructors (Hufbeschlaglehrmeister)	1.9.1939 - 25.6.1940	Crimson	White horseshoe	Yellow wool shoulder-pieces
148 Veterinary (Veterinär) Coys – NCOs & men	1.9.1939 - 25.6.1940	Crimson	1-557 (divisional series)	Cavalry breeches & boots
27 Guard (Wach) Bns.	1.9.1939 - 31.3.1940	White	502-631 series	
10 M.P. (Feldgendarmerie) Bns.	1.9.1939 - early 1940	—	(None)531, 541, 551, 561, 571, 581, 591, 682-3, 685	Gendarmerie uniform; green armband
10 M.P. (Feldgendarmerie) Bns.	Early 1940 - 25.6.1940	Orange	531, 541, 551, 561, 571, 581, 591, 682-3, 685	Sleeve-badge & Feldgendarmerie title
10 M.P. (Feldgendarmerie) Traffic Control Bns.	26.10.1939 - early 1940	—	None (751-760)	Gendarmerie uniform: pink armband

Units	In existence	Branch colour	Shoulder strap insignia	Other distinctions (comments)
10 M.P. (Feldgendarmerie) Traffic Control Bns.	Early 1940 - 25.6.1940	Orange	751-760	Sleeve-badge & Feldgendarmerie title
201 M.P. (Feldgendarmerie) Troops	1.9.1939 - early 1940	—	None (1-557)	Gendarmerie uniform: green armband
201 M.P. (Feldgendarmerie) Troops	Early 1940 - 25.6.1940	Orange	1-557 (divisional series)	Green armband
Army Patrol Service (Heeresstreifendienst)	18.11.1939 - 25.6.1940	Any colour	Original unit	Adjutant's lanyard
Security Troops (Sicherungstruppen)				
24 Army Rear-Area Commanders (Korück)	1.9.1939 - 25.6.1940	White	K / 501-672 series, Norwegen	
14 District Commands (OFK)	1.9.1939 - 25.6.1940	White	K / 540-680 series	Kommandantur gorget?
49 Territorial Rifle (Landesschützen) Regts.	1.9.1939 - 31.3.1940	White	1 / I-3 (Army District series)	
21 Territorial Rifle (Landesschützen) Regts.	1.4.1940 - 25.6.1940	White	L / 22-183 series	
306 Territorial Rifle (Landesschützen) Bns.	1.9.1939 - 31.3.1940	White	I / I-XII / XVIII (Army District series)	
238 Territorial Rifle (Landesschützen) Bns.	1.4.1940 - 25.6.1940	White	L / 201-912 series	
33 POW Camps – officers (Oflag)	1.9.1939 - 25.6.1940	White	KG / I I / A-XXI / C (Army District series)	
45 POW Camps – NCO's & men (Stalag)	1.9.1939 - 25.6.1940	White	KG / I / A-XXI / E (Army District series)	
Army Officials (Heeresbeamten) – dark-green underlay (except chaplains) Special rank insignia				
Court Martial (Reichskriegsgericht) Generals	1.9.1939 - 25.6.1940	Bright red	None	Larisch collar-patches, green stripes
Court Martial (Reichskriegsgericht) Officials	1.9.1939 - 25.6.1940	Bordeaux red	None	
District Administration (Intendantur) Generals	1.9.1939 - 25.6.1940	Bright red	Silver HV	Larisch collar-patches, green stripes
District Administration (Intendantur) Officials	1.9.1939 - 25.6.1940	Bright red	Gold HV	
Paymaster (Zahlmeister) Officials	1.9.1939 - 25.6.1940	White	Gold HV	
Field Postal Service (Feldpost) Generals	1.9.1939 - 25.6.1940	Lemon yellow	Silver FP	Larisch collar-patches, green stripes
166 Field Post (Feldpost) Offices	1.9.1939 - 25.6.1940	Lemon-yellow	Gold FP (1-557 divisional series)	
37 Field Sec.Pol. (Geheime Feldpolizei) Groups	1.9.1939 - 25.6.1940	Light blue	Gold GFP (1-637 series)	
Chaplain-General (Feldbischof)	1.9.1939 - 25.6.1940	Violet	No shoulder-boards	Gold collar-patches, violet cap-band
Chaplains (Pfarrer)	1.9.1939 - 25.6.1940	Violet	No shoulder-boards	Silver collar-patches, violet cap-band
War Substantive Chaplains (Kriegspfarrer)	1.9.1939 - 25.6.1940	Violet	No shoulder-boards	Violet cap-band
Miscellaneous				
Music Directors (Musikinspizienten)	1.9.1939 - 25.6.1940	Bright red	Lyre	Gold Kolben patches: special shoulder-boards
Bandmaster officers (Musikmeister)	1.9.1939 - 25.6.1940	Branch colour	Lyre / Number of attached regt./bn.	Special shoulder-boards
Band NCOs & men (Musiker/Trompeter)	1.9.1939 - 25.6.1940	Branch colour	Number of attached regt./bn.	Shoulder 'wings'
Special Officers and NCOs (Sonderführer)	1.9.1939 - 2.3.1940	—	None (silver Aesculapius staff or snake)	Uniform of attached unit
Special Officers and NCOs (Sonderführer)	21.3.1940 - 25.6.1940	Grey-blue	None (silver Aesculapius staff or snake)	'Old Prussian' patches, grey-blue cap-band

France, June 1940. A Hauptfeldwebel in service uniform, displaying the double cuff braids and report book of his appointment. He has reversed his shoulder-straps to conceal his unit insignia. Note his Wehrmacht long-service ribbon. His relaxed attitude and lack of equipment suggest that the Battle of France is over. (Friedrich Herrmann)

the normal progression for a capable NCO. All other NCO and lower ranks were awarded on seniority. The rank of *Obersoldat* was held by a soldier lacking even the qualities for promotion to Gefreiter, while a Stabsgefreiter was an 'old sweat' unfitted for NCO rank. The ranks of officer candidates will be covered in Volume 2.

Rank insignia

Most rank insignia was manufactured in two versions – dress-quality for the *Waffenrock*, dress greatcoat and piped field tunic, and field-quality for the field tunic and field greatcoat.

For all uniforms **general-officers** wore dress-quality plaited shoulder-boards formed from two 4mm gold bullion (or, from 15 July 1938, golden-yellow 'celleon' thread) cords with one 4mm bright flat aluminium braid central cord on a bright-red branch colour facing-cloth backing. A Generalfeldmarschall had silver crossed stylised marshal's batons, other general-officers had 3-0 German silver or white aluminium pips 2.8–3.8cm wide. Branch insignia was in silver-plated aluminium. From 3 April 1941 all three cords of the Generalfeldmarschall were in bright gold or golden-yellow 'celleon' with miniature silver marshal's batons.

Dress-quality plaited shoulder-boards for **field officers** consisted of two 5mm wide bright flat aluminium braids on a branch colour facing-cloth backing and 2-0 pips 1.5cm, 2.0cm or 2.4cm wide, made of galvanically brassed aluminium, from 7 November 1935 gilt aluminium. During wartime they were made from golden galvanised or lacquered grey aluminium. Field-quality boards had matt aluminium, later *feldgrau* braid. M1935 branch insignia, introduced 10 September 1935, was, from 7 November 1935, made of brass-plated or gilt aluminium, and, during the war, of gold-coloured galvanised or lacquered grey aluminium or zinc alloy.

A tank-driver Gefreiter, exhausted by the Panzers' 'drive to the sea' through France in May 1940, enjoys a cigarette by his tank. He has not opted to wear his M1935 *feldgrau* field greatcoat over his M1934 special tank-crew uniform to protect it from the grime of battle. Note the drivers' goggles, civilian shirt and M1936 pullover. (Brian Davis Collection)

A classic view of a tank commander, wearing the 1934 special tank-crew uniform and the 1934 padded beret with tank commander's earphones. This officer is wearing the aluminium wire aiguillettes of a General Staff officer. France, May 1940. (Friedrich Herrmann)

Dress-quality shoulder-boards for **captains and subalterns** consisted of two 7-8mm wide bright flat aluminium braids placed side-by-side on a branch colour facing-cloth backing with 2-0 gilt aluminium pips and branch insignia as for field officers. Field-quality boards had matt aluminium, later *feldgrau* braid.

Music Directors wore field officers' shoulder-boards with two 4mm wide bright flat aluminium braids with a 3mm wide bright-red central silk cord, all on a bright-red facing-cloth backing (from 18 February 1943 the branch colour as for bandmasters) with a gilt aluminium lyre and 1-0 gilt aluminium pips. Senior and Junior Bandmasters wore shoulder-boards consisting of five 7mm wide bright flat aluminium braids placed side-by-side, alternating with four 5mm bright red silk braids on a branch colour facing-cloth backing (white, light-green, bright red or golden-yellow or black) with a gilt aluminium lyre and up to two gilt aluminium pips. Field-quality boards had matt aluminium, later *feldgrau* braid.

Technical NCOs had distinctive plaited shoulder-boards with devices and pips in white aluminium; these were made from grey aluminium or zinc alloy during the war. From 23 September 1937 Farrier-Instructors wore interwoven triple golden-yellow woollen cords with a double golden-yellow woollen cord edging all on a crimson branch colour underlay, a horseshoe and 1-0 pips. From 9 January 1939 Fortress Engineer Foremen wore the same shoulder-boards in black artificial silk with a white artificial silk inner edging all on a black branch colour underlay, with a cogwheel (from 9 June 1939 a Gothic Fp) and 1-0 pips. On 7 May 1942 both sets of shoulder-boards were changed to red, with bright aluminium and red interwoven cords, with a double red cord edging. Farrier-instructors had a crimson underlay and a horseshoe, fortress-engineers a black underlay and Fp, and 2-1 pips.

Dress-quality rank insignia for **senior NCOs** consisted of 3-1 bright aluminium pips (1.8cm, 2cm or 2.4cm wide) on M1935 bluish dark-green cloth shoulder-straps, with branch colour piping and edged on all sides by 9mm wide bright aluminium 'single-diamond' pattern yarn braid introduced 10 September 1935. Field-quality rank insignia consisted of the same pips and braid on the M1933, M1934 and M1935 unpiped, and M1938 and M1940 piped field shoulder-straps. 9mm silver-grey artificial silk braid was also worn, with grey aluminium and zinc alloy pips during the war, and from 25 April 1940 *feldgrau* matt artificial silk or cellulose-fibre wool braid. Branch insignia was of the same metal as the pips. A Hauptfeldwebel/Hauptfeldwebeldiensttuer wore a second 1.5cm wide bright aluminium 'double-diamond' pattern yarn braid above the cuff of the *Waffenrock*, and two 9mm braids on the cuff of other uniforms.

Junior NCOs wore the same shoulder-straps and braids as senior NCOs, the *Unterfeldwebel* wearing braid around the shoulder-strap, the *Unteroffizier* omitting braid across the base of the strap. Dress-quality branch insignia was fully embroidered in the branch colour on the shoulder-strap, while field-quality insignia was in branch colour wool or cotton yarn, and from 19 March 1937, also in artificial silk, embroidered in a chain-stitch pattern. Engineers' black and Medical Corps' dark-blue unit insignia were outlined in white chain-stitch on bluish dark-green shoulder-straps to render them more visible. During the war the embroidery was often full flat thin yarn.

Two soldiers in M1935 field uniform, the NCO (left) carrying an MP28/II Schmeisser sub-machine gun, guard British prisoners in northern France, May 1940. Note the general absence of field equipment – M1938 gas mask canister and M1931 canvas bread-bag and bayonet – but no Y-straps. (Josef Charita)

Other ranks wore the same shoulder-straps as junior NCOs, with branch colour branch insignia but without braids. The M1936 rank insignia consisted of chevrons, point-down, of 9mm NCO braid combined with embroidered silver-grey or aluminium thread pips (hand-embroidered bright aluminium bullion on privately purchased items). The insignia was sewn on to a triangular (circular for Obersoldat) backing of bluish dark-green facing-cloth, changed in May 1940 to *feldgrau* uniform cloth, and black for tank crew uniforms. This rank insignia was adopted on 25 September 1936 (with effect from 1 October 1936) and developed from the original *Reichswehr* system adopted 22 December 1920.

From 26 November 1938 rank insignia on the white and reed-green **twill fatigue-uniforms** consisted of 1cm wide *feldgrau* fabric and 'single diamond' braid with two thin black inner pipings. A Stabsfeldwebel wore a braid ring below two braid chevrons point-up, on each lower-sleeve; Hauptfeldwebel two rings; Oberfeldwebel, a ring and a chevron, Feld-webel, a ring only. Unterfeldwebel and Unteroffizier wore braid collar edging only. This NCO insignia was replaced by new sleeve rank insignia introduced 22 August 1942. Men wore chevrons of the same braid and *feldgrau* fabric, with braid pips sewn on to white or reed-green backings.

Branch and unit insignia

A German soldier's branch of service was indicated by a branch colour, worn on the collar and shoulder-board and shoulder-straps, and as cap, tunic and trouser pipings. The system of branch colours, a development of the regimental facing-colours in the *Reichsheer* of the German Empire, was established on 22 December 1920, continued, with comparatively few changes, until 9 May 1945.

An Unteroffizier, in M1935 field
uniform, threatens French
prisoners with his Karabiner 98k
in northern France, May 1940.
He wears a single set of
ammunition-pouches and carries
standard 6 x 30 binoculars,
suggesting he is a section leader,
and is sporting a civilian scarf
against regulations. (ECPA)

Branch insignia comprised a symbol, or a letter in Gothic script, worn by certain specialised troops within a branch, above the unit insignia – an Arabic or Roman numeral, or, in the case of Army Schools, Gothic letter(s). There was a wide variety of such insignia, and so only a selection of the principal combat units is covered here.

Such precise unit identification aided personal and unit morale, but jeopardised field security and so, from 1 September 1939, troops in the Field Army were ordered to remove or conceal their unit insignia. Many troops covered the unit insignia on their field shoulder-boards and shoulder-straps with a *feldgrau* (black for Panzer units) shoulder-slide or wore their shoulder-boards/straps reversed. The branch insignia, which was less specific, was usually retained. Unit insignia could still be worn by the Replacement Army or by Field Army troops on leave in Germany. In fact, unit insignia was often worn in the field in defiance of these regulations. On 24 January 1940 3cm wide *feldgrau* shoulder-slides with branch and unit insignia in branch colour chain-stitch were introduced for NCOs and other ranks, but senior NCOs often continued to wear their white aluminium insignia. Insignia on dress uniforms not worn in the field, was unaffected.

The pre-war system of numerals on the shoulder-strap buttons of other ranks in regiments – blank for regimental staff, I–III for battalion staff; 1-14 for constituent companies – was replaced in wartime by standard blank buttons.

Certain specialised or élite units, or a few units carrying the traditions of regiments of the Imperial *Reichsheer*, wore special insignia, usually extra cap badges, worn between the eagle and swastika and the cockade, or, in a growing trend borrowed from the paramilitary *Sturmabteilung*, as sleeve-titles.

Table 4 gives a list of the principal units in existence from 1 September 1939 to 25 June 1940, with their branch colours, branch insignia, unit and special insignia. Existence of these units before or after these dates is not excluded, nor did all units necessarily see combat at this time.

From 2 May 1939 all ranks of mountain divisions wore insignia incorporating the alpine flower, the edelweiss, originally worn by German and Austro-Hungarian units in the First World War. A white aluminium edelweiss with gilt stamens was worn above the cockade on the peaked cap. A white aluminium edelweiss with a stem, two leaves and gilt stamens (war-time production used grey aluminium with yellow stamens) was worn on the left side of the mountain cap, Austrian personnel often adding a bluish dark-green facing-cloth backing. A machine-woven white edelweiss with yellow stamens, light-green stem and leaves within a mouse-grey rope wreath on a dark-green facing-cloth oval (after May 1940 *feldgrau*), was worn on the right upper sleeve of tunics and greatcoats.

Six infantry battalions also wore the light-green *Jäger* branch colour to preserve the light infantry tradition, but they remained infantry battalions – it was not until 28 June 1942 that specialised *Jäger* units were raised.

Two commemorative matt aluminium badges were worn by all ranks in certain regiments between the eagle and cockade of the service cap and, unofficially, on the field cap. From 25 February 1938 the 17th Infantry Regiment wore the Brunswick skull and crossbones to com-

memorate the Imperial 92nd Infantry Regiment. From 21 June 1937 the 3rd Motorcycle Reconnaissance Battalion, and from 26 August 1939 the 179th Mounted, 33rd, 34th and 36th Divisional Reconnaissance Battalions, wore the dragoon eagle, also called the 'Schwedt eagle' to commemorate the Imperial 2nd Dragoon Regiment.

The *Großdeutschland* Infantry Regiment was formed on 12 June 1939 from the Berlin Guard Regiment (*Wachregiment Berlin*) and developed into an élite unit. Defying field security, their insignia was worn throughout the war. The *GD* shoulder-board/strap monogram (introduced 20 June 1939) and a woven aluminium thread *Großdeutschland* and edging was worn on a bluish dark-green cuff title (introduced 20 June 1939). This was superseded for a short time in summer 1940 by a silver-grey woven Gothic-script *Inf.Rgt Großdeutschland*, which was worn on the right cuff of all uniforms. *Großdeutschland* personnel assigned to Hitler's field HQ, the *Führerbegleitbataillon*, wore a golden-yellow machine-embroidered, machine-woven or hand-embroidered (also found in silver-grey thread) Gothic-script *Führer-Hauptquartier* and edging on a black wool sleeve title.

From 21 June 1939 the Armoured and Signals Instruction battalions wore a gold machine-woven *1936 Spanien 1939* and edging on a madder-red cloth cuff title on the left cuff to commemorate their service in *Gruppe Imker* during the Spanish Civil War. From 16 August 1938 personnel of the newly formed war correspondent companies wore a machine- or hand-embroidered aluminium Gothic-script *Propagandakompanie* on a plain black sleeve-title on the right cuff.

The Military Police was formed on mobilisation on 26 August 1939 from 8,000 German *Gendarmerie*. Motorised three-company battalions were assigned to field armies, allocating a 33-man *Trupp* to an infantry division, a 47-man *Trupp* to an armoured or motorised division and a 32-man *Trupp* to a sub-district. Initially MPs wore their M1936 *Gendarmerie* uniforms with Army shoulderboards/straps and a medium-green armband with orange-yellow machine-embroidered *Feld-Gendarmerie*. This

Northern France, May 1940. A section LMG team in field uniform with the section leader (2nd left) watching for the enemy. The LMG34 is mounted on a tripod for use as a heavy machine gun. Note the machine gunner's improvised assault-pack, consisting of an M1931 mess-tin tied to the back of his belt with belt supporting-straps. (Brian Davis Collection)

53

was replaced in early 1940 by Army uniform with, on the left upper-sleeve the Police sovereignty-badge – a machine-woven or embroidered orange eagle and black swastika in an orange wreath (officers wore hand-embroidered aluminium thread) on *feldgrau* backing. On the left cuff was a machine-woven aluminium *Feldgendarmerie* on a brown sleeve-title edged in aluminium yarn, later machine-embroidered in silver-grey yarn. When on duty MPs wore the matt aluminium gorget with an eagle and *Feldgendarmerie* in aluminium on a dark-grey scroll. Traffic Control personnel wore the MP uniform without these three insignia, wearing a black cotton woven *Verkehrs-Aufsicht* on a salmon-coloured armband on the left upper sleeve. The Army Patrol Service, equivalent to British Regimental Police, wore the obsolete M1920 matt aluminium wire adjutant's lanyard on the field tunic and field greatcoat.

Music Directors wore staff-pattern bright gold, or matt gold, *Kolben* collar and cuff-patches, and from 12 April 1938 all Bandmaster Officers wore special bright aluminium and bright red silk aiguillettes on formal uniforms. On dress and field tunics regimental bandsmen wore M1935 'swallow's-nest wings' made of bright aluminium NCO braid and branch colour facing-cloth, introduced 10 September 1935, drum-majors adding aluminium fringes. Other specialist badges will be covered in Volume 2.

MEDALS

On 16 March 1936 the Wehrmacht **Long Service Decoration** was instituted as a cornflower-blue ribbon with, for the Army, a silver or gold eagle and swastika. Four or 12 years' service merited a silver or gold medal, 18 or 25 years, a silver or gold cross, and, from 10 March 1939, 40 years a gold cross with gold oakleaves on the ribbon.

Five pre-war **campaign medals** were awarded. On 1 May 1938, the matt silver '13 March 1938 Commemoration Medal', usually known as the 'Anschluss Medal', with a red, white and black ribbon, was issued to troops participating in the occupation of Austria. On 18 October 1938 the bronze '1 October 1938 Commemoration Medal' with a black and red ribbon, was issued for the occupation of Sudetenland, and on 15 March 1939, of Bohemia-Moravia. The bronze '13 March 1938 Commemoration Medal' with a red, white and green ribbon, was issued on 1 May 1939 for the occupation of Memel District. On 14 April 1939 the bronze, silver or gold Spanish Cross with swords and, the highest award, with diamonds, was instituted for service in the Spanish Civil War; it was worn as a pin-back cross on the right breast-pocket. Finally, on 2 August 1939 the bronze 'German Defensive Wall Medal' with a white and yellowish-brown ribbon was instituted for service building the Westwall – the 'Siegfried Line' fortifications on Germany's western frontier.

The most common military **bravery award** for courage in the field was the Iron Cross, reconstituted 1 September 1939 as a black and silver cross with a red, white and black ribbon. The Iron Cross 2nd Class was worn as a ribbon attached to the second button-hole of the field tunic, or as a small silver eagle, swastika and *1939* to the black and white 1914 ribbon. The Iron Cross 1st Class was a medal pinned to the left breast-pocket or as a larger eagle, above the 1914 cross. The Knight's Cross, instituted 1 September 1939, was worn from a ribbon around the neck. The War

Merit Cross, a bronze cross with a red, white and black ribbon, was worn in 2nd Class as a ribbon, or as 1st Class pinned to the left breast-pocket. It was awarded for merit or bravery in places other than the front line.

Other awards

On 22 May 1939 an oval aluminium pin-back **wound-badge** for the left breast-pocket was instituted for service in the Spanish Civil War, featuring a swastika and Spanish helmet on crossed swords within a wreath, manufactured in three versions – black, for one or two wounds; silver, for three or four wounds; and gold, for five or more, although not surprisingly, the gold was never awarded. On 1 September 1939 the badge, now with a German helmet, was introduced for the Second World War.

Four pin-back **combat qualification-badges** could be worn on the left breast pocket. The Condor Legion Tank Combat Badge, a bronze or white aluminium skull, tank and wreath, was instituted 10 July 1939. The Infantry Assault Badge, a white aluminium eagle, rifle and wreath, was issued from 20 December 1939, with a bronze version for Motorised Infantry from 1 June 1940. The Tank Combat Badge, a white aluminium eagle, tank and wreath, was instituted 20 December 1939 for tank-crews and medical support personnel, followed on 1 June 1940 by a bronze version for armoured car crews and medical personnel. The Engineers' Assault Badge, later the General Assault Badge, a white aluminium eagle, crossed bayonet and grenade and wreath, was instituted 1 June 1940, initially for assault engineers.

The Narvik Shield was awarded on 19 August 1940 for personnel who fought in Norway at the Battle of *Narvik*, 9 April–9 June 1940. It was a grey aluminium eagle above Narvik and a crossed edelweiss, propeller and anchor, worn on a *feldgrau* oval on the upper left sleeve.

Army personnel could also wear First World War medals and Nazi awards, such as the SA Defence Badge.

THE PLATES

A: CEREMONIAL UNIFORMS

A1: Oberstleutnant, Panzerregiment 8, full ceremonial uniform, Böblingen, Germany, July 1939 This battalion commander of Panzerregiment 8, which later fought in Poland, Luxembourg and France with 10.Panzerdivision, wears the regulation M1935 full ceremonial uniform with 'Flower Wars' and Nazi decorations, and the Army Long Service medal. The officers' M1935 sword-knot, made of *feldgrau* leather with an aluminium ball, introduced 7 November 1935, hangs from his privately purchased officers' sword, usually preferred to the M1922 issue sword introduced 17 February 1922.

A2: Hauptwachtmeister, Gebirgsartillerieregiment 79, parade uniform, Garmisch-Partenkirchen, Germany, July 1939 As the ranking artillery battery NCO, the Hauptwachtmeister was a formidable personality, wearing the double NCO cuff-braids of his appointment and his report-book stuffed into his dress or field tunic. He wears the marksman's lanyard, with artillery shells to denote the awards, and carries the officers' sword and sword-knot. As a member of the élite 1st Mountain Division, which later fought in Poland and France, he wears the Edelweiss arm-badge.

A3: Fahnenjunker-Gefreiter, III (Jäg)/Infanterieregiment 83, walking-out uniform, Hirschberg, Germany, July 1939 This conscript, accepted for officer-training, wears the other ranks' field tunic with officers' cuffs, branch colour pipings and dress-quality insignia as an alternative to the *Waffenrock*. The junior NCO bayonet-knot tied to the bayonet-frog is the only indication of his status.

B: THE POLISH CAMPAIGN

B1: Generalleutnant, 14.Infanteriedivision, field uniform, Lublin, Poland, September 1939 The commander of 14th Infantry Division, which fought in southern Poland with the 10th Army, and later in Belgium with the 6th Army, wears the leather greatcoat popular with general-officers over his field tunic. He wears the M1938 officers' field cap, carries the Walther PPK 7.65mm pistol on his belt, and has powerful 10 x 50 Zeiss binoculars.

B2: Hauptmann i.G., 14.Infanteriedivision, field uniform, Lublin, Poland, September 1939 General Staff officers were ranked *Generaloberst – Hauptmann im Generalstab* (Captain). This officer, the third divisional staff officer, the '1c' (Intelligence Officer), wears field-quality staff *Kolben* collar-patches and breech stripes, and the M1934 'old style' field cap. He carries a P08 Luger pistol in a hard shell holster and wears the cross-belt, which was abolished after the Polish campaign.

B3: Stabsgefreiter, Reiterregiment 2, field uniform, Rozan, Poland, September 1939 This cavalryman, a *Reichswehr* veteran promoted to Stabsgefreiter before the rank was abolished on 1 October 1934, wears the cavalry field uniform with reinforced breeches and riding boots. The 'lightning' arm badge indicates that he is a signalman in the regimental signals platoon. He carries the M1934 saddlebags for mounted personnel introduced 7 May 1934, and the M1934 Karabiner 98k, the standard German rifle. His regiment fought in Poland and France with 1st Cavalry Division.

A section of the *Großdeutschland* Regiment in M1935 guard uniform, France, June 1940. Members of this élite German infantry regiment wore the regimental cuff-title and shoulder-strap monogram on all uniforms, even in the field. Note the marksman's lanyards, as worn on this uniform, and the soldierly parade ground bearing of the troops. (ECPA)

C: BLITZKRIEG RIFLE SECTION

C1: Unteroffizier, Infanterieregiment 96, field uniform, Chelmo, Poland, September 1939 As a section leader this NCO is wearing the standard field equipment with a flashlight and 6 x 30 issue binoculars. He carries the Karabiner 98k rifle – section leaders were not normally issued submachine guns until 1941 – and a M1924 stick-grenade, known as the 'potato masher'. He has reversed his shoulder-straps to conceal his unit insignia and tied a thick rubber band to his helmet to secure his camouflage foliage. His regiment fought in Poland, Belgium and France with the 32nd Infantry Division. In the foreground lies a discarded Polish M1931 helmet.

C2: Obergefreiter, Infanterieregiment 96, field uniform, Chelmo, Poland, September 1939 This *Landser* ('German soldier') is the Section First Gunner, typically an Obergefreiter, with the 7.92mm IMG34 general-purpose light machine gun. He carries a machine gunner's field equipment: a P38 pistol in a hard-shell holster for close combat and an M34 spares pouch, a gas cape pouch across his chest in the prescribed manner, and two 50-round belts of 7.92 x 57 ammunition.

C3: Schütze, Infanterieregiment 96, field uniform, Chelmo, Poland, September 1939 The bulky M1934 backpack, introduced 10 February 1934, and the M1939, introduced 18 April 1939, was normally left with the unit's transport column, allowing infantrymen to fight in light order. The bayonet and bayonet-frog was strapped to the entrenching-tool on the left back hip, the mess-kit, camouflage shelter-quarter and gas mask canister worn on the lower back, and the bread-bag and canteen on the right back hip. The private carries a Karabiner 98k and has tied bread-bag straps to his helmet to fix camouflage foliage. In defiance of regulations he is displaying his regimental number on his shoulder-straps.

D: DENMARK AND NORWAY

D1: Unterfeldwebel, Divisional Staff, 198.Infanterie-division, field uniform, Copenhagen, Denmark, April 1940 The 198th Division staff dispatch rider wears the M1934 motorcylists' rubberised coat. He carries one set of ammunition pouches for his Karabiner 98k, the M1935 dispatch case and leather gauntlets. 'Square-lens' protective goggles are on his helmet. This division, raised in Bohemia-Moravia, occupied Denmark, taking the Danish flag as its vehicle-sign, before fighting in France.

D2: Sanitätsobergefreiter, Sanitätskompanie 1/234, field uniform, Kristiansand, Norway, April 1940 This Medical Corps orderly, assigned to a company of 163rd Infantry Division in Norway, wears the M1934 field cap and M1935 field greatcoat. He carries medical pouches on his belt, the gas mask slung on his back, and the larger, one litre, medical corps canteen at the front of his left hip. He wears the red-cross armband on his left upper sleeve and the medical qualification badge on his right cuff. He is holding a field dressing.

D3: Oberleutnant, Gebirgsjägerregiment 138, field uniform, Narvik, Norway, May 1940 This officer in 3rd Mountain Division in Poland and Norway, wears platoon leader's field equipment over his M1925 wind-jacket, with first model ammunition-pouches for his MP38 submachine gun, shown here with the stock folded. Against regulations, he retains his officers' brown belt, and carries a M1931 model rucksack, later superseded by a more utilitarian wartime model. Note the helmet's national shield, worn in the Danish and Norwegian campaigns despite orders on 21 March 1940 to remove it, and the distinctive 'T' form eagle and cockade worn on the mountain cap.

E: NETHERLANDS AND BELGIUM

E1: Leutnant, Aufklärungsabteilung 254, field uniform, Breda, Netherlands, May 1940 This Bicycle Squadron officer wears regulation platoon leader's field equipment, with the prescribed other ranks' black belt, with one MP38 ammunition-pouch and a M1935 dispatch-case. He wears the cavalry golden-yellow branch colour and the Gothic A for *Aufklärung* – 'reconnaissance' on his field shoulder-boards. His battalion invaded the Netherlands in May 1940 with 254 Infantry Division.

E2: Oberschütze, Infanterieregiment 49, field uniform, Namur, Belgium, May 1940 As Second Gunner, this infantryman wears one set of ammunition pouches for his Karabiner 98k and, for close combat, a P08 Luger pistol. He carries two 300-round ammunition boxes and an M34 single-barrel case on his back – LMG34 barrels were normally changed after 250 rounds of full automatic fire. This regiment fought in Poland, Belgium and France with 28 Infantry Division.

E3: Gefreiter, Pionierbataillon 30, River Meuse, Belgium, May 1940 This assault boat engineer has camouflaged his helmet with mud and wears simplified field equipment – an M1928 leather ammunition-pouch for his MP28/II *Schmeisser* submachine gun, a gas mask canister, bayonet

France, May 1940. An infantry Oberst in M1935 field uniform. The 'saddle-shape' of his M1935 officer's peaked cap is particularly noticeable. The distinctive officers' collar-patches, unlike those of other ranks, retained the branch colour piping throughout the Second World War. This officer is wearing the Knight's Cross, and his regimental number is concealed by a *feldgrau* slip-on shoulder strap. (Brian Davis Collection)

beret, a Walther P38 pistol in a hardshell holster and general purpose goggles. This battalion fought in Poland, Luxembourg and France with 2 Panzerdivision.

F3: **Hauptmann, Infanterieregiment (mot.)** ***Großdeutschland*, field uniform, Stonne, France, May 1940** The regiment, which fought under direct *OKH* command in Poland, Luxembourg and at Dunkirk, was the first army unit with an élite unit cuff-band and shoulder-board monogram, which was retained in battle. This battalion commander, examining a discarded French M1935 tank-crew protective helmet, has removed the national shield from his helmet. He wears the Infantry Assault Badge in bronze for motorised infantry on his left breast-pocket, carries the M35 map-case with modified fastener, a P08 Luger in a hardshell holster, and 6 x 30 standard binoculars.

G: THE BATTLE OF FRANCE (2)

G1: Oberschirrmeister, Panzerpionierbataillon 37, field uniform, Besançon, France, June 1940 From 10 May 1940 engineer battalions of Panzer divisions wore black-and-white branch colour piping, instead of black, which was invisible on

An Unteroffizier of the 17th Infantry Regiment in Germany in July 1940 in walking-out uniform, wearing the Brunswick skull and crossbones commemorative cap-badge of his regiment. Note the marksman's lanyard, the Iron Cross 2nd Class button-ribbon and the typically pre-war style of shoulder-strap numerals.
(Brian Davis Collection)

A Hauptmann in M1935 full ceremonial uniform poses with his bride on his wedding day in July 1940. He wears the Iron Cross 1st and 2nd Class, Wehrmacht long-service medals and 'Flower Wars' campaign medals, as well as the General Assault Badge. (Brian Davis Collection)

and entrenching-tool. He wears the Helmsman's qualification-badge in the aluminium machine-embroidered version introduced 7 November 1935, and, against regulations in a forward area, *feldgrau* slip-on unit shoulder-slides. He carries an assault-boat paddle and M1924 stick-grenades. His battalion fought with the 30 Infantry Division in Poland, Belgium and France.

F: THE BATTLE OF FRANCE (1)

F1: Major, Panzerregiment 25, field uniform, Cambrai, France, May 1940 This battalion commander wears the M1935 tank crew uniform and M1938 officers' *feldgrau* field cap, his *feldgrau* slip-on shoulder straps concealing his regimental number but not his rank. He carries the P08 Luger pistol in a hardshell holster, and 10 x 50 'short design' binoculars. His awards are the aluminium Tank Combat Badge on his left breast, and the 1939 Iron Cross 2nd Class ribbon from his first button-hole. He carries a tank-commander's headset with rubber earcups. His regiment fought in Belgium and France with 7 Panzerdivision.

F2: Panzerschütze, Panzeraufklärungsabteilung 5, field uniform, Aisne, France, May 1940 AFV-crews often wore their *feldgrau* field greatcoats to protect their black uniforms from dirt and grease, even though black was intended to disguise such soiling. This armoured-car driver wears the unpopular padded

M1938 gas mask canister above the M1931 bread-bag on the lower back, and the M1931 canteen on the right back hip.

G3: Unteroffizier, Infanterieregiment (mot.) 66, fatigue uniform, Amiens, France, June 1940 This member of the 13th Motorised Division, newly arrived in France, undertakes labouring duties in the M1933 white twill fatigue uniform. This uniform was already being replaced by the more practical reed-green, and junior NCO collar insignia was worn until 22 August 1942.

H: THE ARMY OF OCCUPATION

H1: Unteroffizier, Verkehrsregelungsbataillon 754, field uniform, Arras, France, July 1940 Traffic Control battalions were raised to regulate the swiftly advancing German road-traffic. Personnel wore police uniforms, adopting in early 1940 Army uniforms with orange branch colour pipings and a distinctive armband, but not the arm-badge, cuff-title and duty gorget normally associated with German Military Police. Although *feldgrau* collars, shoulder-straps and trousers were prescribed in May 1940, they were not general issue until 1941-2, and so this NCO, his battalion operating under *OKH* command in occupied northern France, still wears M1935 bluish dark-green facing-cloth collar and straps and stone-grey trousers.

H2: Generalmajor, 215.Infanteriedivision, service uniform, Chaumont, France, September 1940 The deputy commander of the 215th Infantry Division, on occupation duties with the 1st Army in eastern France, wears the officers' service uniform with the M1937 officers' piped field tunic and carries a Walther PPK 7.65mm Luger pistol in a hardshell holster. He wears the Iron Cross 1st Class on his left breast pocket, the 1914 2nd Class ribbon and bar on his second button-hole, and the Narvik Shield for service in the Norwegian campaign.

H3: Obergefreiter, Oberfeldkommandantur 672, guard uniform, Brussels, Belgium, September 1940 This soldier at the HQ of 672 District Command, covering Brussels, wears the guard uniform. It is a more formal field uniform with the marksman's lanyard and equipment limited to belt, ammunition-pouches, bayonet and scabbard. As a lance-corporal, with six years seniority and little likelihood of promotion to NCO rank, he wears the uncommon chevron and pip sleeve rank insignia worn until the end of the war by soldiers not promoted to the new Stabsgefreiter rank after 25 April 1942.

Luxembourg, 18 September 1940. A cavalry Wachtmeister in parade uniform without the usual belt, but with the steel helmet, which he has removed in favour of an M1938 field cap, as he tries to make friends with a local girl. Unlike most scenes of this type, this one does not seem to be stage-managed. He wears the Iron Cross 1st Class and seems to have been awarded the Iron Cross 2nd Class quite recently. Note the highly polished riding-boots. (Josef Charita)

their black uniforms. This reverted to black in 1941 when special *feldgrau* AFV uniforms were adopted. This Oberfeldwebel (Oberschirrmeister), supervising his company's technical equipment, wears his yellow wool embroidery trade-badge on a dark bluish-green facing-colour disc, with the aluminium wire edging denoting his NCO status. His battalion, formed 15 April 1940, fought in France with 1 Panzerdivision.

G2: Schütze, Infanterieregiment 154, field uniform, De Panne, Belgium, June 1940 The A-frame battle-pack, introduced 18 April 1939, was still comparatively rare in 1940, so infantry and assault engineers improvised, using M1939 black leather belt supporting straps to carry the M1931 shelter-quarter wrapped around the M1931 mess-kit. This infantryman, with the 58th Infantry Division in action in France and Belgium, wears the standard short entrenching-tool, bayonet, scabbard and frog on his left back hip, the

GERMAN ARMY 1939–1945 (2) NORTH AFRICA & BALKANS

THE CONTEXT OF THE NORTH AFRICAN AND BALKAN CAMPAIGNS

The Franco-German armistice of 25 June 1940 made Germany master of Western Europe. Hitler first considered an invasion of Great Britain in autumn 1940, then scheduled Operation *Barbarossa*, the conquest of the European part of the Soviet Union, for May 1941. Anxious to emulate Hitler's successes, the Italian dictator Mussolini embarked upon unnecessary military adventures in North Africa and the Balkans, which forced Hitler's intervention, diverting and depleting precious German resources, and a six-week postponement of *Barbarossa*. This contributed to German defeat on the Eastern Front and Germany's collapse in May 1945.

A member of the Africa Corps, in bleached M1940 tropical field cap and M1940 tropical shirt, stencils the Corps tactical sign to a lorry door with white paint. (Josef Charita)

The Quality of Army Units

On 31 July 1940 Hitler began to prepare for *Barbarossa*. Now the combat area dictated the quality of army divisions that were used: those in North Africa were generally makeshift units, reflecting the low priority of that theatre; the forces committed to Operation *Marita* – the invasion of Yugoslavia and Greece – were front-line divisions earmarked for *Barbarossa*. They were replaced by second-line units with limited mobility and combat potential, first-line units making limited appearances in the Balkans until August 1943 and the arrival of the formidable 2 *Panzer* Army.

The Development of Army Units in North Africa and the Balkans

From 5 October 1941 the *Panzer* group was upgraded to a *Panzer* army. Mountain corps were formed after September 1940 and motorised corps were redesignated *Panzer* corps after June 1942. Reserve corps were formed after September 1942 for reserve divisions of units training in occupied countries.

First-line infantry divisions generally retained their 1939 organisation until 1942, often adding a reinforcement battalion to allocate reinforcements. To raise morale all infantry regiments were redesignated *Grenadier* regiments on 15 October 1942 and the Rhodes garrison was designated an 'assault' division on 31 May 1943. The 22 Airlanding Division was an infantry unit with airborne training, while the 'Africa' designation reflected reduced organisation or 'non-standard' personnel – German ex-French foreign legionnaires or 'disciplinary' personnel convicted of petty offences but considered redeemable; they were also used for manning fortress units for static guard duties in Greece. 'Special purpose' (z.b.V.) referred to a staff controlling heterogeneous units.

On 13 April 1941 '700-series' infantry divisions that were only 8,000 strong were formed from second-line troops for occupation duties. There were two infantry regiments, which lacked heavy equipment, an artillery battalion, reconnaissance, engineer and signals companies and minimal logistical support. On 1 April 1943 these divisions, along with light infantry divisions (formed in December 1940 for combat in hilly terrain) and selected reserve divisions, were reorganised as rifle (*Jäger*) divisions with younger personnel and M1939 infantry organisation, but with only two rifle regiments. From 1942 territorial rifle units were gradually redesignated security units.

The most important field unit controlled by Army Intelligence (*Abwehr*) was *Brandenburg* Commando Regiment 800 (*Lehr-Regiment Brandenburg z.b.V.800*). On 20 November 1942 it was redesignated Special Unit (*Sonderverband*) *Brandenburg*, with five regiments and a signals and a coastal commando battalion; on 1 April 1943 it was redesignated the *Brandenburg* Division; and on 15 September 1944 it became the *Brandenburg* Mechanised Division.

Sonderverband 287 and *288* were mixed regiments of specialist troops originally organised for commando operations in the Persian Gulf, then reassigned for conventional warfare. *Sonderverband 287*, formed on 4 August 1942, fought in the Caucasus with two mechanised battalions, a signals battalion; AT, armoured reconnaissance and engineer companies, assault artillery and rocket projector batteries and a supply unit. From 2 May 1943 it served in Yugoslavia as 92nd Motorised Regiment.

Sonderverband 288, formed on 24 July 1941 with a staff (HQ, armoured reconnaissance and Arab companies) and eight independent companies (sabotage, mountain, motorised rifle, MG, AT, AA, engineers and signals), fought in North Africa; it became Mechanised Regiment Africa on 31 October 1942.

The 1941 *Panzer* division organisation differed from that of 1939 by having one *Panzer* regiment and two motorised rifle regiments. By August 1941 all mobile divisions had converted to *Panzer* divisions, and on 5 July 1942 motorised rifle regiments in *Panzer* and light Africa divisions were redesignated mechanised (*Panzergrenadier*) regiments. On 24 March 1943 the motorcycle reconnaissance battalions became armoured reconnaissance battalions with armoured cars, motorcycles and jeeps. Divisional *Füsilier* battalions were partly bicycle-equipped infantry introduced on 2 October 1943, replacing dis-

Part of an armoured engineers' section line up for the attack. They are wearing helmets (first issued in late 1941 to front-line troops) with hessian covers held in place by bread-bag straps, M1940 tropical field tunics, tropical breeches and 1st pattern M1940 tropical high-boots. Note the equipment of the machine gunner (right), the hessian bags for grenades and assault equipment, and the spare LMG ammunition boxes. (ECPA)

banded divisional reconnaissance battalions, and 'AA' battalions continued cavalry traditions.

In March 1940 anti-tank assault-gun batteries were formed, and on 10 August 1940 they were grouped into battalions, each with 31 self-propelled guns. Army anti-aircraft artillery battalions were introduced in February 1941, with three batteries of 8.8cm anti-aircraft guns as anti-tank guns.

Supply services were co-ordinated by the divisional supply (*Nachschub*) officer, in October 1942, redesignated the divisional supply commander, controlling the motor-transport and fuel-supply columns (from 25 November 1942 grouped into a motor-transport company), horse-drawn transport columns (from 15 November 1943 grouped into a company), workshop company and supply company (later battalion).

FOREIGN VOLUNTEERS

The increasing demands on manpower forced the recruitment of foreign nationals.

3rd Bn *Sonderverband 287*, the German-Arab instruction battalion (*Deutsch-Arabische Lehrabteilung*), was formed on 12 January 1942 and fought in Tunisia. On 22 November 1942 the Vichy-French *Phalange Africaine* (African Phalanx) was formed in Tunisia, and in March 1943 its 220 personnel fought with 334th Infantry Regiment in Tunisia. On 9 January 1943 the 'German-Arab Troops Command' (*KODAT*), also called the 'Free Arabian Legion', was established in Tunisia; eventually it comprised one Moroccan, one Algerian and two Tunisian limited combat value battalions with German cadres.

In Yugoslavia three 'Croatian Legion' infantry divisions were formed to fight Tito's Partisans: the 369th 'Devil's Division' on 21 August 1942; 373rd 'Tiger Division' on 6 January 1943; and 392nd 'Blue Division' on 17 August 1943. On 12 September 1941 a force of White Russians, eventually five regiments strong and designated Russian Corps, fought in Serbia. German-Arab Infantry Battalion 845, formed on 5 June 1943 from 3rd Bn *Sonderverband 287*, served in Greece; and Armenian Infantry Battalion I/125 fought in Albania with 297th Infantry Division.

In September 1943 perhaps the most exotic formation of the Second World War, the 1st Cossack Division, arrived in Croatia with 2nd *Panzer* Army. Formed in occupied Poland on 4 August 1943 from units who had fought with the Germans on the Eastern Front, it comprised a German cadre commanding two cavalry brigades with two Don, one Siberian, one Kuban and two Terek cavalry regiments, one artillery regiment and divisional support units. Attached to LXIX Corps in eastern Croatia on anti-partisan duties, the division achieved an unenviable reputation among the civilian population.

A *Leutnant* commanding an assault engineer platoon. Note the MP38/40 canvas ammunition pouches, the M1924 stick-grenades and the MP40 submachine gun slung over the shoulder. The officer has retained M1935 continental officers' field collar-patches and has covered his helmet with a rough hessian cover. (Friedrich Herrmann)

THE STRATEGY IN NORTH AFRICA

On 13 September 1940 the Italian 10th Army advanced from Cyrenaica (north-east Libya) into Egypt, only to be forced back into Tripolitania (north-west Libya) by the First Offensive from the British imperial garrison. Hitler decided to send a small expeditionary force to bolster Italian forces by blocking the Allied advance and prevent an Italian collapse in Libya.

Encouraged by initial successes, the German commander, *Generalleutnant* Erwin Rommel, dreamed of occupying Egypt and advancing into the Middle East, linking up with a victorious German thrust through Southern Russia into Iraq and Iran, and threatening British India. However, with the steady Allied build-up his forces (four divisions in Libya) made even the official objective unrealistic. Rommel was constrained by permanent shortages of fuel, supplies and reinforcements; much of it had to be brought by sea from Naples to Tripoli, across the western Mediterranean, which was patrolled by British forces.

The Build-up in North Africa

The contingent which disembarked at Tripoli on 14 February 1941 became the *5. Leichte Division* (5th Mobile Division) on 18 February. It had *Panzerregiment 5* with 120 tanks (instead of 44 in the usual battalion), 3rd Reconnaissance Bn, 39th Anti-Tank Bn, I/75 Artillery Bn (instead of a regiment) and motorised divisional support units – 1/83 Medical Company, 4/572 Field-Hospital, 309th Military Police Troop and 735th Field Post Office, but no engineers or signals. To this were added 2nd and 8th Machine-Gun battalions in an infantry role, 606th AA Company with 8.8cm anti-aircraft guns, and 606th Anti-Tank Battalion to form a division strong in tanks and anti-tank guns but weak in infantry. In August 1941 it became *21. Panzerdivision,* with *Panzerregiment 5,* 104th Motorised Rifle (later Mechanised) Regt, 155th Artillery Regt, 15th Motorcycle Reconnaissance Regt and divisional support units (anti-tank bn, engineer bn, signals bn, supply bn, medical company, field hospital, MP troop and field post office). On 19 February 1941 it constituted the first unit of the German Africa Corps – *Deutsches Afrikakorps (DAK)* – under Rommel, officially subordinated to the Italian 'Armed Forces High Command North Africa'.

On 1 September 1941 the *DAK* – eventually comprising 15th, 21st *Panzer,* 90th Africa and 164th Light Africa Divisions, and one to three Italian corps – became *Panzer* Group Africa; on 30 January 1942 Armoured Army Africa; on 1 October 1942 German-Italian Armoured Army; and on 22 February 1943 1st Italian Army under the Italian General Giovanni Messe. On 14 November 1942 HQ Nehring (Stab Nehring), which on 19 November was redesignated LXXX Corps and on 8 December, 5th Armoured Army, was formed for operations in Tunisia with three German divisions. Combining with 1st Italian army it formed Army Group Africa on 22 February 1943.

June 1941. *Generalmajor* Alfred Gause, just appointed liaison officer to the Italian High Command in North Africa, consults with two Italian officers. He correctly wears general-officers' continental shoulder-boards and collar-patches on his M1940 tropical field tunic, but has unofficially pinned a gold metal breast-eagle to his white tunic. He wears a Knight's Cross. (Friedrich Herrmann)

Rommel's First Offensive

On 23 March 1941 Rommel launched his First Offensive with 5th Mobile Division and three Italian divisions, storming El Agheila and advancing through Cyrenaica, before halting on 27 May at Halfaya ('Hellfire') Pass, just inside Egypt.

On 30 April *15. Panzerdivision* arrived with *Panzerregiment 8,* 15th Motorised Rifle Brigade (104th and 115th regiments), 33rd Field Reinforcement Bn, 33rd Artillery Regt, 33rd Motorised Reconnaissance Bn and divisional support units, plus 15th Motorcycle Reconnaissance Bn and 2nd Machine-Gun Bn, all motorised. By April 1942 15th Motorcycle Recce Bn and 104th Motorised Rifle Regt had left, and 115th Motorised Rifle Regt and 2nd MG Bn had formed 115th Mechanised Regt, joined by 200th Light Infantry (later Mechanised) Regt.

In August 1941 the Africa Special Purpose Division was assigned to Rommel. Formed on 26 June 1941 from 361st Reinforced Infantry Regiment with former foreign legionnaires and 155th Motorised Rifle Regt (both units redesignated Light Infantry in April 1942 and Mechanised in July 1942), the division was renamed the 90th Light Africa Division on 26 November, adding 580th Mixed Recce Company, 361st Artillery Bn, 900th Engineer Bn and 190th Signals Company. In April 1942 it was renamed 90th Light Infantry Division. On 26 July it was

An *Oberleutnant* of an anti-tank battalion – he has retained the 'P' branch symbol – in a M1940 tropical field tunic with unofficial continental M1935 collar-patches and breast-eagle and the *'AFRIKAKORPS'* cuff-title. He wears captured British anti-dust-goggles on his M1940 tropical peaked field cap with officers' aluminium pipings. He carries the powerful 10x50 binoculars with the protective lens-lid in place (ECPA)

renamed 90th Africa Division and expanded, adding 200th Mechanised Regt, 190th Artillery Regt, 190th *Panzer* Bn, 90th Armoured Recce Bn, 190th AT Bn plus motorised divisional support units.

Rommel's Second Offensive

On 18 November 1941 the British 8th Army commenced its Second British 'Crusader' Offensive into Cyrenaica, forcing Rommel back into Tripolitania. He halted at El Agheila on 31 December. There, on 21 January 1942, Rommel launched his Second Offensive, penetrating 250 miles into Egypt before stopping at El Alamein.

In July 1942 the hard-pressed Rommel received reinforcements, when the Crete Fortress Division was flown in and reformed on 15 August as a mechanised unit – 164th Light Africa Division with 125th (in 1943 Mechanised Regt Africa), 382nd and 433rd Mechanised regts, 220th Artillery Regt, 164th Armoured (1943, 220th Motorised) Reconnaissance Bn and motorised divisional support units.

The Final Retreat Through Libya

On 23 October 1942 a total of 230,000 Allied troops advanced from El Alamein, forcing back Rommel's 100,000 men (four German and 10 Italian divisions). The German-Italian Armoured Army retreated through Libya, eventually halting on the Mareth Line, 100 miles inside Tunisia, on 15 February 1943. On 19 February Rommel routed US Army forces at the Kassarine Pass before handing over to *Generaloberst* von Arnim and returning to Germany.

The End in Tunisia

On 8 November 1942 an Anglo-American expeditionary force landed in Morocco and Algeria. They had advanced to within 50 miles of Tunis when, in late November, the *10. Panzerdivision* reached Tunis as part of LXXXX Corps (later 5th Armoured Army). This unit had *Panzerregiment 7*, 10th Mechanised Brigade (69th, 86th Mechanised regts), 10th Armoured Recce Bn, 90th Armoured Artillery Regt, 302nd AA Bn and motorised divisional support units. It was joined in late December 1942 by 334th Infantry Division (formed 25 November with 754th and 755th Grenadier regts, 756th Mountain Regt, 334th Artillery Regt and divisional support units). Then, in late March 1943, 999th Africa Division arrived. Originally formed as a brigade on 6 October 1942 and expanded to a division on 2 February 1943, this unique formation, with all its sub-units carrying the 'black number' 999, was composed of disciplinary troops led by regular officers and NCOs. Organised as an infantry unit, the division comprised 961st-963rd Africa Rifle regts, 999th Artillery Regt, 999th Armoured Reconnaissance Bn and divisional support units.

5th Armoured Army also included the *21. Panzerdivision* transferred from the *DAK*, the scratch '*Manteuffel*' mixed division, two *Luftwaffe* anti-aircraft divisions and other German and Italian units. It broke out of the Tunis bridgehead in November 1942, and by February 1943 had established a 40-mile deep defensive line around Tunis. However, on 20 March the British 8th Army broke through at the Mareth Line, and on 12 May Von Arnim surrendered in Tunis.

ARMY UNIFORM IN NORTH AFRICA

Tropical Uniform Production

In July 1940 the Tropical Institute of the University of Hamburg designed a tropical uniform based on items used by German colonial troops until November 1918. By December 1940 the uniforms were in full production, with more than enough supplies to equip the 5th Mobile Division and *15. Panzerdivision*, who were deployed to Libya from February 1941.

Most items of the M1940 tropical uniform were manufactured in ribbed heavy cotton twill or cotton drill. The prescribed colour was 'light-olive', a greenish sandy brown known as 'khaki' in Great Britain and 'olive-drab' in the United States and contrasting with the plain sandy brown or 'tan' of Navy M1941 and *Luftwaffe* M1941 tropical uniforms. Consistent production of this shade was not achieved until 1941, and in 1940 it could vary from dark-greenish brown through dark brown to sandy brown. The M1940 tropical greatcoat was manufactured in deep chocolate brown wool. Unlike the continental *feldgrau* (greenish-grey)

Perhaps nostalgic for his pith helmet, this Africa Corps soldier eating from his mess-tin has against regulations pinned the pith helmet's *Wehrmacht* eagle badge to his M1940 tropical field cap, which still shows the branch colour facing-cloth chevron ordered removed on 8 September 1942. Such customising was comparatively rare in North Africa. (ECPA)

A mixed police patrol through the bazaar of Derna, Cyrenaica: two German *Feldgendarmerie* NCOs (front and back left) patrol with a Libyan *Zaptiè* (front right) and Italian *carabiniere* (back right). The Germans wear M1940 pith-helmets, tropical shirts and shorts and 1st pattern M1940 tropical ankle-boots and the MP duty gorget. (Brian Davis Collection)

clothing, almost all tropical uniform items were standard issue for officers and men.

The M1940 tropical uniform proved very popular, and in 1943 its wear was extended to the southern European theatre. Army personnel were forbidden to wear *feldgrau* continental, or navy, *Luftwaffe* or Italian tropical uniform items, but shortages of supply, especially in North Africa, and individual preference, particularly among senior officers, subverted this regulation.

Halfaya Pass, July 1941. Men of the 1st Battalion, 104th Motorised Rifle Regiment, 15th *Panzer* Division, parade to receive decorations. Note the M1940 tropical peaked field caps (several already bleached white), tropical shirts and shorts, and the grim-faced informality of the parade, suggesting men who had just fought a hard battle. (Friedrich Herrmann)

ORDERS OF DRESS

Regulations issued on 28 December 1939 which simplified the orders of dress during wartime also applied to North Africa. The Formal Ceremonial, Informal Ceremonial, Parade, Reporting, Undress and Guard uniforms were abolished, leaving all ranks with four orders of dress: for formal and semi-formal occasions, the Service Uniform or Walking-Out Uniform; for training or barracks duties, the Service Uniform; for combat, the Field Uniform. The Fatigue Uniform for work details was not worn in North Africa.

Officers' Tropical Service Uniform

This uniform consisted of the tropical pith helmet or peaked field cap, field tunic, shirt, tie, pullover, greatcoat, belt, pistol and holster, and breeches or shorts with high-boots, or long trousers with ankle-boots.

The M1940 standard tropical pith helmet was manufactured in pressed cork covered in light-olive, later tan, canvas with a brown leather chin-strap. A black-white-red diagonally striped national shield was fixed on the right side and a silver-white *Wehrmacht* eagle on the left, in stamped brass (later in stamped aluminium, as ordered in 1934 for the steel helmet). The M1942 tropical pith helmet, in seamless pressed mid-olive felt, introduced in late 1942, did not see service in North Africa. Captured British helmets and French or Dutch helmets commandeered after the 1940 *Blitzkrieg* campaign, were also worn, and the pith helmet was less popular with the troops; they preferred the tropical peaked field cap, but often retained the pith helmet for more formal occasions.

The M1940 standard tropical peaked field cap, introduced in mid 1941, was made of light-olive ribbed heavy cotton twill and styled on the M1930 *feldgrau* mountain cap, but with a longer peak, a false flap and no buttons. Insignia comprised a machine-woven bluish-grey thread eagle and swastika on a rust-brown shaped backing. Below this was a machine-woven black (outer)-white-red thread national cockade on a rust-brown diamond backing, enclosed by a branch colour facing-cloth chevron, point up (abolished on 8 September 1942). General-officers wore a gold artificial silk chevron. Officers wore a 3mm aluminium (gold for general-officers) cord piping around the crown and on the front scallop of (or right around) the false flap. Some officers unofficially retained the M1935 continental eagle and cockade in bright aluminium or aluminium bullion on bluish dark-green facing-cloth. This cap became the most distinctive and prized uniform item worn by the *DAK*. Prolonged exposure to the harsh tropical sun bleached it to an off-white colour, and it was worn with pride as the badge of the Africa Corps 'old sweat'.

The M1940 standard tropical field tunic in light-olive ribbed heavy cotton twill was based on the M1933 field tunic for NCOs and men, with plain cuffs, five (sometimes four) light-olive sprayed pebbled front buttons and four patch pockets with scalloped flaps and pleats, but adding an open collar and fashioned lapels. The M1942 tropical field tunic, seen after October 1942, omitted the pocket pleats, while the M1943 tunic, manufactured too late for the North African campaign, had straight pocket flaps and no pleats. Some officers wore privately purchased tunics and a few sported the stylish Italian tan *sahariana* tropical field tunic.

A machine-woven bluish-grey thread eagle and swastika on a rust-brown shaped backing (a larger version of the one on the field cap) was worn above the right breast-pocket of the tunic, with the swastika often overlapping onto the pocket-flap, although many officers unofficially retained the M1935 continental matt aluminium braid breast-eagle with

December 1941. Exhausted troops of 5th Mobile or 21st *Panzer* Division, forced back to El Agheila again, manage grim smiles for the camera. They wear bleached M1940 tropical peaked caps or helmets, M1940 tropical field tunics, breeches and 1st pattern M1940 tropical high-boots. The uncomfortable ties have been discarded and sometimes replaced by more practical civilian scarves. (ECPA)

A Specialist 2nd Lieutenant – a *Sonderführer Z* – presumably acting as an Italian interpreter, has an animated conversation with an Italian lieutenant. He wears a bleached M1940 tropical peaked field cap, M1940 tropical field tunic with continental *Sonderführer* shoulder-straps and collar-patches (introduced 21 March 1940) and wears the *'AFRIKAKORPS'* cuff-title. (Friedrich Herrmann)

a bluish dark-green facing-cloth backing. Two machine-woven bluish-grey guards' braids, each a rust-brown braid centre-stripe and dividing-stripe, were sewn directly to the collar of the field tunic. Continental field quality shoulder-boards were worn. Many, if not most, officers unofficially adopted the more distinctive M1935 continental bluish dark-green facing-cloth collar-patches with two matt aluminium guards' braids, each with a branch coloured silk embroidered centre-cord.

On the tunic general-officers wore matt gold sprayed buttons and the traditional M1927 continental collar-patches introduced on 1 August 1927. The latter comprised the matt yellow yarn two-leaf *Alt Larisch* design on a bright-red facing-colour patch. Unofficially most also wore a continental bright or matt gold thread breast-eagle on a bluish dark-green facing-cloth backing.

The M1940 standard tropical shirt was manufactured in light-olive cotton drill with four small composite fibre front buttons and two breast-pockets with pleats and scalloped flaps, each secured by a light-olive painted pebbled button. Ex-French Army M1935 khaki tropical shirts, with their distinctive button-down collars and three front buttons, were also worn until the end of 1942. When the shirt was worn as the outer garment, continental field quality shoulder-boards were fixed to the shoulders using detachable light-olive painted pebbled buttons. The M1940 standard tropical tie, also in light-olive cotton drill, was usually discarded on active service and was omitted if the officer wore collar decorations. The M1940 standard olive-brown wool pullover, with a roll-neck or turtle-neck, was worn under the field tunic.

The M1940 standard tropical greatcoat, essential for freezing desert nights, was manufactured in deep chocolate brown wool in the cut of the M1935 *feldgrau* field greatcoat, with two rows of six matt *feldgrau* buttons, a back half-belt secured by two buttons, turn-back cuffs and continental field quality shoulder-boards and a divided back seam. General-officers had matt gold pebbled buttons, leaving the top two buttons open to show bright-red facing-cloth lapel-linings. Other officers entitled to collar decorations also left these buttons open. Officers also wore the leather greatcoat.

The M1940 officers' tropical belt was in heavy olive-green canvas with a circular aluminium buckle painted olive-green featuring an eagle and swastika in an oak-wreath, but most officers chose to retain their brown leather continental belt with an aluminium two-claw open buckle. A P08 Luger, P38 or Walther PPK pistol was usually carried in a brown leather holster.

The M1940 standard tropical breeches were manufactured in light-olive ribbed heavy cotton twill with a concealed integral belt. General-officers retained their traditional 2mm piping down the outer seam, flanked on each side by a 4cm stripe, all in bright-red facing-cloth.

The breeches were worn with M1940 1st pattern standard tropical high-boots in light-olive canvas, with brown leather toe, instep and inner ankle reinforcements, and black laces. These were superseded in mid-1941 by the 2nd pattern, extending the leather instep; and a slightly shorter 3rd pattern, introduced in late 1941, extended the leather toe and the instep. Some senior officers, including Rommel, favoured black leather continental high-boots.

The M1940 standard light-olive ribbed heavy cotton twill tropical long trousers proved more practical than the breeches, and troops often added tapes to allow the trouser-bottoms to be pulled tight over the ankles. General-officers wore bright-red trouser-stripes The trousers were worn with M1940 1st pattern standard tropical ankle-boots, also in light-olive canvas, with brown leather toe and instep reinforcements and black laces. The 2nd pattern, introduced in late 1942, also extended the leather toe and instep reinforcements.

M1940 standard tropical light-olive ribbed heavy cotton twill shorts could also be worn, either with tropical high-boots or with M1940 light-olive knee-socks and tropical ankle-boots.

Other Ranks' Tropical Service Uniform

Other ranks (except senior NCOs) omitted the officers' pistol but otherwise wore much the same uniforms as officers; there were slight differences, usually regarding the quality of the insignia. They wore issue uniforms and insignia, and unlike officers enjoyed less latitude in adopting unofficial insignia and retaining continental uniform items and insignia. Rank insignia will be considered separately.

Other ranks wore the same tropical pith helmet, shirt and tie, breeches, trousers, shorts, knee-socks, high-boots and ankle-boots as officers, but they did not wear cord pipings on the M1940 tropical peaked field cap. NCOs wore 9mm wide copper-tan aluminium diamond-pattern collar-braid on the field tunic but none on the tropical greatcoat, which was the same cut as for officers. The other ranks' M1940

September 1942. *Generalfeldmarschall* Rommel's successor as commander of *Panzer* Army Africa, *General der Panzertruppen* Georg Stumme, inspects installations in Tobruk harbour. Stumme wears a privately purchased M1940 tropical field tunic and breeches with general-officers' trouser-stripes, and sun-goggles on his continental M1935 service cap. His aides on the right wear M1940 tropical peaked field caps and M1940 tropical field tunics, but the officer far left has shortened his bleached field tunic. (Friedrich Herrmann)

tropical belt was in heavy olive-green or light tan canvas with a square aluminium buckle painted olive-green featuring an eagle and swastika in a ring with the motto '*GOTT MIT UNS*' (God is with us) and oak leaves.

Officers' Tropical Walking-Out Uniform

This uniform consisted of the tropical pith helmet or peaked field cap, field tunic, shirt, tie, greatcoat, and breeches or shorts with high-boots, or long trousers with ankle-boots. It was identical to the Service Uniform, except that no belt, pistol or holster was worn.

For more formal occasions some senior officers preferred a privately tailored uniform, a superior quality field tunic with turn-back cuffs and continental collar-patches and breast-eagles, grey suede gloves, and trousers with black continental leather lace-up shoes. Against regulations, the M1935 saddle-shaped *feldgrau* officers' peaked cap was sometimes worn, and some general-officers had a tropical peaked cap made, with superior quality light-olive cloth replacing the *feldgrau* tricot.

Other Ranks' Tropical Walking-Out Uniform

Other ranks wore the same uniform as officers with other ranks' insignia, but with the M1940 other ranks' tropical belt and the continental M1936 marksman's lanyard, as modified in 1939. This consisted of a matt aluminium plaited cord with an aluminium *Wehrmacht* eagle above crossed swords on a shield, all in a small wreath, with one to three aluminium acorns (miniature artillery shells for gunners) designating Awards 2-4. Awards 5-8 had a larger wreath; Awards 9-12 had the same badge in gilt. The lanyard was suspended from the right shoulder-strap and hooked to the first tunic button.

Officers' Tropical Field Uniform

All officers wore the tropical pith helmet or peaked field cap (later the

23 October 1942, the day of the Allied offensive at El Alamein. *Major* Briel (left), commanding *Panzergrenadierregiment 200* of 90th Africa Division, in a battered helmet and M1940 tropical field tunic with unofficial M1935 officers' continental collar-patches and a German Cross medal talks to fellow officers. His right hand is bandaged. Note the M1940 tropical anklets worn by the middle officer. (Friedrich Herrmann)

steel helmet), field tunic, shirt, tie, pullover, greatcoat, belt, and breeches or shorts with high-boots, or long trousers with ankle-boots.

Helmets were not general issue in North Africa until early 1943, although mechanised infantry, anti-tank troops and engineers had acquired them by late 1941. The M1935 helmet and the M1942 helmet (introduced on 1 August 1942) had a silver-white *Wehrmacht* eagle on a black shield – usually stencilled – on the left side. Most soldiers painted their helmets roughly with pale yellow, mustard-beige or orange-tan vehicle-camouflage paint, sometimes mixed with sand; they often painted over the shield. The *DAK* vehicle sign, a white palm-tree and swastika, was sometimes painted unofficially on one side of the helmet. Sand-bag hessian provided practical helmet camouflage.

Officers other than infantry platoon-leaders carried a pistol and holster and 6x30 black binoculars in a smooth brown leather or bakelite case. Infantry platoon-leaders were gradually issued equipment in a modified tropical version for North Africa, and often painted metal fittings with sand-yellow camouflage paint. They wore the other ranks' M1940 olive-green canvas belt and M1940 olive-green canvas tropical infantry support Y-straps with *feldgrau* or olive-green painted aluminium fittings supporting two sets of three M1938/40 *feldgrau* canvas ammunition pouches for the MP38 or MP40 sub-machine gun on the front hips. Also worn on the left front hip was the brown or black leather M1935 dispatch-case, the 84/98 bayonet in a black scabbard in a M1940 olive-green or tan canvas tropical bayonet-frog. The M1940 folding entrenching tool was worn on the left back hip, and the M1941 brown or tan canvas tropical bread-bag and two M1931 brown felt-covered canteens with M1940 olive-green or tan tropical canvas straps and aluminium cup were worn on the right back hip. Webbing supported the M1931 mess-tin, which had M1940 olive green tropical canvas straps and a M1931 camouflage shelter-quarter on the upper back. A *feldgrau* canvas strap positioned the anti-gas cape, with a tan-coloured canvas cover strapped to the M1930 or M1938 gas-mask on the lower back. Binoculars, compass, signal whistle and field flashlight were also worn.

All members of armoured and motorised units were issued *Zeiss-Umbral* sun goggles, and some personnel – notably Rommel – sported captured British models.

Other Ranks' Tropical Field Uniform

Other ranks wore the same uniform as for officers, with other ranks' insignia.

In a ten-man infantry section, the section leader, usually an *Unteroffizier*, wore platoon-leader's equipment. The deputy section-leader and the five riflemen carried standard riflemen's equipment. This con-

Early 1943. A German *Oberfeldwebel* of *Sonderverband 287* on the cadre of an Arab *KODAT* battalion. He wears an M1935 helmet, M1940 tropical field tunic with copper-tan NCO collar and shoulder-strap braids, bright aluminium rank pips and the *Orientkorps* arm-badge that was also worn by *Sonderverband 288*. (Friedrich Herrmann)

Tunisia, January 1943. An Arab soldier of 3rd Battalion, *Sonderverband 287,* also called the German-Arab Instruction Battalion (DAL), on guard duty. He wears a plain M1935 steel helmet, M1940 tropical field tunic with white branch colour shoulder-straps, and the Free Arabia arm-badge also worn in Greece in 1943 by 845th German-Arab Infantry Battalion. (Brian Davis Collection)

sisted of a tropical belt and tropical Y-straps supporting two sets of three light-brown pebbled leather rifle-ammunition pouches (or, more commonly, continental black pebbled leather pouches, sometimes painted sand-yellow) on the front hips. On the left back hip was the bayonet, scabbard and tropical bayonet-frog and entrenching-tool; on the right back hip the tropical canteen and bread-bag; on the upper back the mess-tin and shelter-quarter; on the lower back the gas-mask; on the upper chest the anti-gas cape. *Zeiss-Umbral* sun-goggles were also widely worn.

The First Gunner – the machine gunner of the three-man light machine gun team – wore the tropical belt, with a P08 Luger or a P-38 pistol in a black holster on his left front hip and a continental black leather spares pouch on his right front hip. The Second Gunner – the replacement machine gunner – wore standard rifleman's equipment, with a pistol and black leather continental holster on his left front hip instead of ammunition pouches, and four 50-round ammunition drums, a 300-round ammunition box, and a sheet-metal barrel protector with one or two spare barrels. The Third Gunner wore standard riflemen's equipment and carried two ammunition boxes.

Tank crews' Tropical Uniforms

The M1934 black tank-crew uniform was impractical for North Africa, so tank crews wore the standard M1940 tropical uniform. However, all members of the three *Panzer* regiments – 5th, 7th and 8th, including attached administrative officials (and Assault Gun Battery 287) – pinned aluminium skulls detached from black collar-patches to the lapels of their tropical field tunics.

The M1940 standard tropical tank-crew field cap (effectively the M1940 tropical peaked field cap without the peak) was the same design as the M1934 2nd pattern *feldgrau* other ranks' field cap. Made of light-olive cotton twill it had the same insignia – eagle and swastika, cockade and, until 8 September 1942 a pink (for *Panzer* troops) branch colour facing-cloth chevron, with aluminium cord piping for officers. This cap substituted for the pith-helmet, which was unsuitable for the confines of an armoured vehicle, but it was superseded by the tropical peaked field cap. Some armoured personnel retained the black continental tank crews' M1940 officers' or other ranks' field cap, against regulations.

Special Uniforms and Insignia for Other Branches

Cadre officers, NCOs and men of the 999th Africa Division wore standard tropical uniforms and full insignia, but the disciplinary troops omitted all insignia and wore the M1940 other ranks' tropical belt with a plain pebbled disc on the belt buckle.

Brandenburg units, reporting to Army Intelligence (*Abwehr*), continued to wear German or foreign uniforms or civilian clothes, depending on their mission.

Sonderverband 287 and *288* wore standard tropical uniforms with the appropriate branch colour pipings. Early in 1942 an unofficial bronze version of the *Orientkorps* (Oriental Corps) vehicle-sign was pinned to the left breast-pocket, replaced in late 1942 by a cloth badge worn on the right upper sleeve – a machine-woven yellow rising sun behind a white palm tree, swastika and laurel wreath on a dark bluish-green oval, with a machine-embroidered version on dark bluish-green facing-cloth for the tropical greatcoat.

The two mountain units in North Africa – 756th Mountain Regiment and 2nd Company, *Sonderverband 288* – both in Tunisia in 1943, wore standard tropical field uniform, often with tropical breeches, continental brown or black leather studded climbing ankle-boots and puttees. Troops carried the standard continental M1931 tropical greenish-khaki canvas mountain rucksack and wore the M1939 mountain cap-badge – a white (later grey) aluminium Edelweiss with a stem, two leaves and gilt (later yellow) stamens on the left side of the tropical peaked field cap, and the M1939 mountain arm-badge – a machine-woven white Edelweiss with yellow stamens and a light-green stem and leaves within a mouse-grey rope wreath on a dark-green (later *feldgrau*) facing-cloth oval, on the right upper sleeve.

The M1940 tropical motorcyclists' greatcoat was a copy of the M1934 continental rubberised coat manufactured in dark olive tan ribbed heavy cotton twill. It was also worn by vehicle drivers and some officers, who preferred it to the heavier woollen overcoat.

Some personnel of the 33rd Divisional Reconnaissance Battalion, probably only former officers and NCOs of 6th Cavalry Regiment, wore the matt aluminium 'Schwedt Eagle' (also called the 'Dragoon Eagle') 'tradition badge' on the front of the M1940 field cap and peaked field cap.

Assault engineers were issued the M1940 tropical A-frame made of olive-green or tan canvas straps to carry the engineers' assault pack, with the mess tin and shelter-quarter strapped to the upper back, a light-olive canvas equipment bag strapped to each front hip or two light-olive canvas equipment bags hanging around the neck; they carried the bayonet, scabbard and bayonet-frog and entrenching-tool on the left back hip, and one or two water-bottles, the bread-bag and wire-cutters in a black leather case.

Military police wore the normal tropical uniform with continental insignia. This comprised the police arm-badge, a machine-woven or embroidered orange eagle and black swastika in an orange wreath (in hand-embroidered alu-

Tunisia, January 1943. New recruits to an Arab *KODAT* Battalion on parade, wearing M1935 French Army tunics and leather field equipment, with German helmets and armbands. The German cadre NCO wears regulation M1940 tropical field uniform. (Friedrich Herrmann)

miniym thread for officers) on a *feldgrau* backing, often omitted in the field. They had a machine-woven aluminium *Feldgendarmerie* on a brown sleeve-title edged in aluminium yarn (later machine-embroidered in silver-grey yarn) on the left cuff, and, on duty, the matt aluminium gorget. In shirt-sleeve order, only the gorget was worn.

The uniforms and insignia of army officials, including chaplains and *Sonderführer*, will be covered in Volume 3.

UNIFORMS AND INSIGNIA
OF FOREIGN VOLUNTEERS

The German cadre and the Arab personnel of *Sonderverband 287* (including the German-Arab Instruction Battalion) and 845th Infantry Battalion in Greece wore the normal tropical uniform (with infantry white branch colour pipings) with, on the right upper sleeve, a shield featuring a white, red, black and green Iraqi flag with 'Free Arabia' printed in Arabic and German. Arab personnel on labour duties wore a white turban.

Arabs of the *KODAT* battalions wore the French continental M1935 khaki field uniform and brown leather equipment with a German helmet and, on the right upper sleeve, a white armband with '*Im Dienst der deutschen Wehrmacht*' (attached to the German Armed Forces) introduced on 1 October 1941. The *Phalange Africaine* added a French tricolour helmet badge and an axe badge on the right breast-pocket. German tropical uniforms were issued for combat.

Tunisia, April 1943. Mechanised infantrymen from 15th *Panzer* Division, probably from the 115th Mechanised Regiment, taken prisoner at the Battle of Gabes Gap. Their expressions at the prospect of captivity vary from relief (third left), through trepidation (right) to dejection (second left). The troops wear M1940 pleated pocket or M1942 pleatless pocket tropical field tunics and M1940 tropical canvas belts and Y-straps. (Brian Davis Collection)

RIGHT **Tunisia, April 1943. An officer taken prisoner by British 1st Army at Medjez-el-Bab marches into captivity. He wears the M1940 tropical peaked field cap with the branch colour chevron removed (according to the Order of 8 September 1942). He wears M1935 continental field collar-patches, and the Iron Cross 1st Class and the silver General Assault Badge. (Brian Davis Collection)**

Rank Insignia

For a detailed description of ranks, responsibilities and rank insignia (see MAA 311 *German Army 1939-1945 (1) Blitzkrieg*).

General-officers, field officers, captains and subalterns wore the same field quality rank insignia as on their continental *feldgrau* uniforms on the tropical field tunic, shirt (when in shirt-sleeve order), greatcoat and motorcyclists' greatcoat.

All NCOs and men wore light-olive heavy cotton twill (olive-brown wool on the greatcoat) rounded shoulder-straps, with branch colour piping. NCOs added 9mm copper-tan aluminium diamond-pattern collar-braid with, where appropriate, continental 1.8cm, 2cm or 2.4cm wide bright aluminium pips. A *Hauptfeldwebel/ Hauptfeldwebeldiensttuer* wore two tropical NCO braids on the cuff of the field tunic and greatcoat.

Men's rank insignia consisted of arm chevrons made of tropical NCO braid combined, where appropriate, with an embroidered silver-grey or aluminium thread pip, on a light-olive ribbed heavy cotton twill triangle or disc.

On 22 August 1942 new rank insignia was prescribed for the left upper sleeve of the M1940 tropical shirt of officers and NCOs. It consisted of green and golden-yellow insignia on a black rectangle, but its relative unpopularity and supply problems suggest only limited use in North Africa. It will be described in detail in Volume 4.

Branch Insignia

The German soldier's main branch of service was indicated by a branch colour. Since, with the exception of general-officers, the collar-patches on the tropical uniform did not show the branch colour, branch affiliation was officially restricted to the officers' shoulder-board underlay, other ranks' shoulder-strap piping and, before 8 September 1942, the branch colour facing-cloth chevron on the M1940 peakless and peaked field caps.

M1940 tropical shoulder-straps for junior NCOs and men were manufactured without branch symbols or unit numerals. Officers and senior NCOs removed unit numerals from their shoulder-boards and shoulder-straps but often retained their gold-coloured galvanised, lacquered grey aluminium or zinc alloy branch symbols, such as the gothic 'P' for anti-tank units. Symbols and numerals could be worn when in rear areas or on rare leave-trips to Germany.

Tunisia, May 1943. These prisoners of war wear mountain puttees and ankle-boots instead of the unpopular tropical high boots. Note the continental M1935 bluish dark-green facing-cloth shoulder-straps worn by the man first left, and the expressions of grim resignation. (Brian Davis Collection)

Units in North Africa contained a high percentage of mobile units, so the white branch colour, principally worn by the infantry and therefore the most common colour in Europe, was comparatively rarely encountered.

Motorised rifle regiments, who wore a gothic 'S' symbol, unit numeral and the *Panzer* pink branch colour, were ordered, with effect from 25 September 1939, to drop the 'S' and adopt a grass-green (*wiesengrün*) branch colour. This was retained on 5 July 1942, when motorised rifle and light infantry were redesignated as mechanised regiments.

Individual divisional reconnaissance (*Divisionsfüsilier*) battalions derived from former cavalry regiments wore cavalry golden-yellow instead of white.

Africa Corps Cuff-Titles

On 18 July 1941 a cuff-title was prescribed for all army personnel with two months service in the *DAK*, extended on 4 November to all *Panzer* Group Africa personnel. Its wear was confined to North Africa and was rarely worn in the front line; it was permitted on continental uniforms when on leave in Germany. The cuff-title, worn on the right cuff of the tropical field tunic and greatcoat, had a machine-woven white or bright aluminium '*AFRIKAKORPS*' on a dark-green cloth background with a machine-woven white or bright aluminium inner border and a light-tan cloth outer border. In spring 1941 a few troops had briefly worn an unofficial version, with a white embroidered '*AFRIKAKORPS*' on a black woollen cuff-title, with a white embroidered edging for officers.

The official cuff-title was replaced on 15 January 1943 by the '*AFRIKA*' cuff-title, a brown ochre fine wool title with a silver-grey cotton thread '*AFRIKA*' flanked by two palm trees and edging worn on the left cuff of all tunics and greatcoats. It was awarded to personnel wounded in North Africa or with six months combat duty there (four with honourable service in April and May 1943 in Tunisia, or three if incapacitated by tropical disease). Only a few troops received the title before the German surrender in Tunis.

THE STRATEGY IN THE BALKANS

On 28 October 1940 Mussolini invaded Greece from Albania. However, damaging Greek counter-attacks, the British occupation on 31 October of strategically vital Crete (which threatened Rumanian oil-fields that were vital for the German war-machine), the arrival of a 53,000-strong Allied 'W' Force in Greece on 7 March 1941 and a pro-Allied military coup in Yugoslavia on 27 March forced Hitler to activate Operation *Marita* to prevent Greece and Yugoslavia aiding the Allies.

The Invasion of Yugoslavia

German forces comprised 2nd Army (*Generaloberst* von Weichs), with four corps – LI, LII, XXXXVI *Panzer*, XXXXIX Mountain – and most of 12th Army (*Generalfeldmarschall* List), with five corps – XVIII Mountain, XXXX *Panzer* with XI, XIV *Panzer* and XXXXI Motorised Corps in 1st *Panzer* Group (*Generaloberst* von Kleist). These forces totalled 24 divisions: eight infantry, seven *Panzer*, four mountain, two motorised, one light infantry and two SS motorised, assisted by Italian and Hungarian units.

The invasion commenced on 6 April. The 2nd Army reached Zagreb on 10 April, Belgrade on 12 April, Sarajevo on 16 April and Dubrovnik on 17 April. 1st Panzer Group's XI and XIV *Panzer* Corps captured Nis on 8 April and Belgrade on 12 April, meeting XXXXI Motorised Corps advancing from Rumania. XXXX *Panzer* Corps and elements of XVIII Corps occupied Yugoslav Macedonia, taking Strumica on 6 April, Skopje on 7 April and Monastir on 9 April before pivoting southwards towards Greece.

The 30 Yugoslav divisions were easily defeated by German *Blitzkrieg* tactics. In the north some Slovene and Croatian units refused to fight, but Serbian divisions in the south counterattacked briefly into Italian-held Albania. On 17 April the Yugoslav High Command surrendered, but many troops joined Nationalist Chetnik and later Communist Partisan guerrilla forces.

The Invasion of Greece

The Greek Army comprised 21 divisions in 1st (Epirus) Army, 2nd (Eastern Macedonian) Army and with the troops of 'W' Force.

On 6 April the German 12th Army's XXX Corps advanced into

Yugoslavia April 1941. Troops manhandle a 37mm anti-tank gun along a country road. They wear M1935 and M1940 field tunics and full field equipment. Note the MP38 submachine gun and the MP38/40 canvas ammunition pouches carried by the *Unteroffizier* section-leader on the left. (Private Collection)

western Thrace against Greek 2nd Army, taking Xanthi on 9 April. By 4 May they had occupied the Aegean islands. On 9 April XVIII Mountain Corps stormed the Metaxa Line in Greek Macedonia and advanced through eastern Greece, reaching Larisa on 19 April. XXXX *Panzer* Corps pushed through western Greece, taking Kozani on 14 April and Ioannina on 20 April, forcing the outflanked Greek 1st Army to surrender on 23 April, then pursuing 'W' Force, taking Lamia on 20 April, Thermopylae on 24 April and Athens on 27 April. On 30 April the Peloponnese were secured and 'W' Force had evacuated to Crete.

The German invasion of Crete – Operation *Merkur* (Mercury) – commenced on 20 May 1941, when the *Luftwaffe* 7th Air Division parachuted onto Crete, and from 22 May 5th Mountain Division and 6th Mountain Division's 141st Mountain Regt were flown in by glider. The 41,500 Allied defenders fought tenaciously, but on 1 June the Germans secured the island.

The Occupation of Yugoslavia

In mid-June 1941, after eight weeks' pacification duties, German 2nd and 12th army divisions transferred to the Eastern Front. Hitler divided Yugoslavia among his Italian, Hungarian and Bulgarian allies, establishing a Serbian government under Commander Serbia in Belgrade, and supporting a Croatian state that covered Croatia and Bosnia-Herzegovina.

Yugoslavia April 1941. A *Gefreiter* dispatch-rider poses on his motorcycle. He wears the M1935 field tunic with *feldgrau* M1940 shoulder-straps and M1936 rank-chevrons, and carries a leather dispatch-case. (Private Collection)

German occupation troops were limited to LXV Corps in Belgrade, redesignated Serbia Command on 1 May 1942, South-East Military Command on 13 August 1943 and finally Army Section Serbia on 26 September 1944, before abolition on 27 October 1944. In October 1942 Croatia Command (on 8 July 1943 redesignated LXIX Reserve Corps and on 20 January 1944 LXIX Corps) co-ordinated German security duties in Croatia and Bosnia, while Syrmia Command, formed January 1944, controlled east Croatia.

During the 39½-month occupation, from mid-June 1941 to 4 October 1944, when the Balkan theatre merged with the Eastern Front, German forces and their Italian, Bulgarian, Croatian and Serbian allies undertook 13 major operations. These were initially against Chetnik and Partisan guerrillas but following the Italian Armistice of 8 September 1943, they were also against Italian and, after the Bulgarian defection of 10 September 1944, Bulgarian forces.

As guerrilla activity intensified, the average number of German divisions increased from four in 1941 to five in 1942, 9½ in 1943 (when four corps of 2nd *Panzer* Army – XV, XXI Mountain, LXIX Reserve and III SS *Panzer* – arrived on 8 September 1943 to disarm the Italian Army and oppose an anticipated Allied landing) and 12 in 1944. By 4 October 1944, 24 German divisions had served in Yugoslavia: 13 infantry, one light infantry and two reserve (six reorganised as rifle divisions); three Croatian legion infantry; one mountain; one Cossack; two SS mountain and one SS mechanised.

Yugoslavia, April 1941. Both soldiers wear M1935 field tunics. The *Gefreiter* (left), probably a section-leader *(Gruppenführer)*, wears a silver wound-badge (3-4 wounds) and MP38/40 canvas ammunition pouches and carries an MP28/II *Schmeisser* submachine gun. The *Oberschütze* has M1940 *feldgrau* shoulder-straps and carries a set of rifle ammunition pouches and an LMG spares pouch. Both have M1924 stick-grenades in their belts. (Private Collection)

The Occupation of Greece

In mid-June 1941 German 12th Army divisions in Greece transferred to the Eastern Front, leaving most of Greece to Italian control, the Bulgarians in western Thrace and German forces in Athens, eastern Macedonia (with Salonika), the Greco-Turkish border region, western Crete and some islands. 12th Army HQ in Athens (from October 1941 Salonika), also called Commander-in-Chief South-East, under *Generalfeldmarschall* List, controlled XVIII Mountain Corps, with 164th Infantry Division and 125th Independent Infantry Regt in Salonika, 5th Mountain Division on Crete, 6th Mountain Division in Athens and 65th Corps in Serbia and Croatia.

With minimal Greek guerrilla activity in 1941, the Germans concentrated their forces on Crete, withdrawing 5th and 6th Mountain divisions and reorganising 164th and 713rd Infantry divisions as Crete Fortress Division. In August 1942, 22nd Airlanding Division arrived on Crete, allowing Crete Fortress Division to transfer to North Africa.

In 1943 the threats posed by Greek Nationalist EDES and Communist ELAS guerrilla forces, along with the Italian armistice and a possible Allied landing, forced a reorganisation. On 1 January 1943 the 12th Army became Army

Group E, under *Luftwaffe Generaloberst* Löhr (from August 1943 restricted to Greece), reporting to Army Group F in Belgrade, under *Generalfeldmarschall* von Weichs. Athens was garrisoned from January 1943 by 11th *Luftwaffe* Field Division; Rhodes from May by Rhodes Assault Division; eastern Greece and the Peloponnese from June by LXVIII Corps (117 Rifle, 1 *Panzer* divs) and western Greece from September by XXII Mountain Corps (104th Infantry, 1st Mountain divs). From January 1944, 41st Fortress Division, with 22 '999' fortress battalions of disciplinary troops, guarded the Peloponnese, and the Crete garrison was reorganised as 133rd Fortress Division. In August 1944 LXXXXI Corps was formed in Salonika, with fortress brigades to supervise Army Group E's retreat into Yugoslavia. This was completed by 2 November 1944, leaving the island garrisons to surrender in May 1945. Elements of the Rhodes Assault Division joined the new *Brandenburg* Mechanised Division in Belgrade on 17 October 1944.

The Occupation of Albania

On 9 September 1943 the 2nd *Panzer* Army's XXI Mountain Corps occupied Albania with 100th Rifle and 297th Infantry divisions, disarming the Italian garrison and attacking Albanian Communist UNÇS guerrillas. 100th Rifle Division left in March 1944, and was replaced in June by the Albanian 21st SS Mountain Division. On 29 November XXI Corps evacuated to Yugoslavia.

ARMY UNIFORM IN THE BALKANS

The April 1941-October 1944 Balkan Campaign overlaps with the campaign on the Eastern Front, to be covered in Volumes 3 and 4. Therefore, only specific Balkans developments will be considered here. Some of the uniform is covered in more detail in Volume 1.

Many troops wore combinations of new and old uniforms and insignia. This was the result of a bewildering succession of regulations and official orders to replace insignia only when worn out combined with supply difficulties – especially to isolated field units – and the soldier's individualism, sentimentality and inclination to retain better quality, more attractive items which suggested long battle experience. Furthermore, uniforms and insignia suffered a progressive deterioration in quality during the war years, and the OKH prescribed ingenious modifications to counteract this inevitable trend and to adapt to conditions unforeseen before 1939.

Orders of Dress

Following the regulations of 28 December 1939 Army personnel wore the Service Uniform

An officer wearing the M1934 old-style field cap, M1935 officers' field tunic showing the officers' collar-patches and a M1940 other ranks' greatcoat with *feldgrau* collar, worn open to display the Knight's Cross. Note the standard 6x30 binoculars. (Friedrich Herrmann)

ARRIVAL IN AFRICA, FEBRUARY–APRIL 1941
1: Generalmajor, *5. leichte Division*, Tripoli, Tripolitania, March 1941
2: Hauptmann, *Panzerregiment 8*, Agedabia, Cyrenaica, April 1941
3: Obergefreiter, *Kradschützenbataillon 15*, Tobruk, Cyrenaica, April 1941

2   1   3

A

CYRENAICA AND WESTERN EGYPT, MAY–NOVEMBER 1941
1: Oberschütze, *Maschinengewehrbataillon 2*, Tobruk, Cyrenaica, May 1941
2: Schütze, *Panzerjägerabteilung 33*, Halfaya Pass, Egypt, May 1941
3: Unteroffizier, *Pionierbataillon (mot.) 900*, Fort Capuzzo, Cyrenaica, November 1941

1   3   2

B

EGYPTIAN FRONTIER BATTLES, NOVEMBER 1941–OCTOBER 1942
1: Leutnant, *Aufklärungsabteilung (mot.) 33*, Gambut, Cyrenaica, November 1941
2: Hauptfeldwebel, *Panzerregiment 5*, Tobruk, Cyrenaica, May 1942
3: Gefreiter, *leichtes Infanterieregiment 361*, Bir Hacheim, Cyrenaica, May 1942

1   3   2

C

BATTLE OF EL ALAMEIN, OCTOBER 1942
1: Generalfeldmarschall Erwin Rommel, *Deutsch-italienische Panzerarmee*, El Alamein
2: Unteroffizier, *Panzergrenadierregiment 115*, Kidney Ridge, Tel el Aqqaqir
3: Oberkanonier, *Artillerieregiment 155*, Kidney Ridge, Tel el Aqqaqir

3   2   1

TUNISIAN CAMPAIGN, JANUARY–MAY 1943
1: Waffenoberfeldwebel, *Panzergrenadierregiment 200*, Kasserine Pass, February 1943
2: Feldwebel, *Gebirgsjägerregiment 756*, Longstop Hill, February 1943
3: Schütze, *Afrika-Schützenregiment 961*, Fondouk, March 1943

1   3   2

E

INVASION OF YUGOSLAVIA AND GREECE, APRIL–MAY 1941
1: Feldwebel, *Panzerregiment 33*, Nis, Yugoslavia, April 1941
2: Obergefreiter, *Infanterieregiment 330*, Zagreb, Yugoslavia, April 1941
3: Gefreiter, *Gebirgsjägerregiment 100*, Maleme Airfield, Crete, 21 May 1941

2   1   3

OCCUPATION OF YUGOSLAVIA, APRIL 1941–OCTOBER 1944
1: Schütze, *Landesschützenbataillon 562*, Belgrade, Serbia, January 1942
2: Oberstleutnant, *Grenadierregiment 370 (kroatisches)*, Gorazde, Eastern Bosnia, May 1943
3: Starshiy Prikasni, *Don-Kosak Reiterregiment 1*, Petrinja, Croatia, May 1944

1   2   3

OCCUPATION OF GREECE AND ALBANIA, APRIL 1941–NOVEMBER 1944
1: Unterarzt, *Sanitätskompanie 1/104*, Agrinion, Greece, October 1943
2: Gefreiter, *Grenadierregiment 65*, Kos, Greece, October 1943
3: Obergefreiter, *Grenadierregiment 522*, Tirana, Albania, March 1944

2   1   3

Yugoslavia, April 1941. An LMG section-team fire their MG34 from a tripod. Note the camouflaged helmet covers. (Brian Davis Collection)

The first gunner of a Section LMG team is carrying his MG34 light machine gun in the approved fashion. He wears the M1935 field tunic with M1938 standard collar-patches and M1940 shoulder-straps. He has draped camouflage netting over his helmet. Note the absence of field equipment or Y-straps. (Brian Davis Collection)

A member of the
Feldgendarmerie on traffic duty
brandishing a control baton. He
wears the M1934 rubberised
field greatcoat for motorcycle
crews, the M1935 steel helmet
with *feldgrau* woollen toque
pulled over his ears, the other
ranks' M1935J belt, a P38 hard-
shell holster and the MP duty
gorget. (Brian Davis Collection)

Walking-Out Uniform, Field Uniform or Fatigue Uniform. The Fatigue Uniform will be considered in Volume 3.

The difficulties of fighting in the hot climate of southern Europe prompted the OKH in 1943 to prescribe the M1940 Tropical Uniform which had proved so successful in North Africa for wear in Yugoslavia, Greece, Albania, Bulgaria and Rumania during the summer months (which were vaguely described as 'the hot season'). This meant that effectively each order of dress had a winter and a summer version, but many personnel wore a combination of continental and tropical uniforms.

Officers' Service Uniform

This uniform, which underwent comparatively few changes during the war years, consisted of a service cap, field tunic, field greatcoat, breeches and high-boots, gloves, and a belt with pistol and holster. In summer officers' tropical service dress could be worn.

The M1935 officers' peaked service cap was manufactured in *feldgrau* (greenish-grey) tricot or 'Eskimo' material, with a cap-band in bluish dark-green 'facing-cloth' that was finely woven to give an appearance of a thin felt. There were branch colour facing-cloth pipings, a plain black peak and matt aluminium wire chin-cords. A M1935 bright aluminium eagle and swastika was worn above a stamped bright aluminium national cockade in an oak-leaf wreath.

General-officers had gold-coloured metallic woven cord cap-pipings and gold or yellow artificial 'celleon' wire woven chin-cords, and from 16 November 1942 they had cap-badges in gilded aluminium. However, many generals, against regulations, preferred hand-embroidered bright gold bullion badges on a bluish dark-green facing-cloth backing.

The M1933 officers' field tunic, finally modified in 1935, was manufactured from superior quality *feldgrau* cloth with five matt-grey painted pebbled buttons, four patch pockets, turn-back cuffs and a bluish dark-green facing-cloth collar. All insignia was field quality and consisted of: a M1935 officers' breast-eagle in matt aluminium thread on a bluish dark-green facing-cloth backing; M1935 officers' bluish dark-green facing-cloth collar-patches with hand-embroidered, hand-woven or machine-embroidered matt aluminium guards braids, each with a branch colour silk-embroidered centre cord; and rank insignia on shoulder-boards. General-officers had a dress-quality bright or matt gold thread or golden-yellow 'celleon' hand-embroidered breast-eagle and bright-red facing-cloth collar-patches with the gold two-leaf *Alt-Larisch* design. On 19 July 1940 Hitler revived the *Generalfeldmarschall* rank with an unprecedented promotion of 9 Generals, and from 3 April 1941 a *Generalfeldmarschall* was ordered to wear collar-patches with a bright-gold wire embroidered three-leaf *Alt Larisch* pattern.

Some officers, especially general-officers, retained the six-buttoned M1928 or even the eight-buttoned M1920 service tunic, removing the front piping, or the M1937 officers' piped field tunic with field quality insignia. To counteract the deteriorating quality of the officers' field tunic, the number of front buttons were increased from five to six on 26 May 1941.

The M1935 *feldgrau* officers' field greatcoat had a bluish dark-green facing-cloth collar. General-officers left the top two buttons open to show bright-red facing-cloth lapel-linings. From 9 May 1940 the bluish-dark-green collar was to be manufactured in *feldgrau* uniform cloth, but this order was usually ignored.

The plain stone-grey officers' breeches, with general-officers adding bright-red (staff-officers crimson) facing-cloth pipings and broad stripes, were manufactured in *feldgrau* from 9 May 1940. The black high-boots, usually made of softer leather than riding boots, were retained, as were the grey suede gloves.

The brown leather M1934 officers' belt had a matt aluminium buckle, or matt gilt for generals. On 20 September 1939 the cross-belt was abolished for all officers below general-officer rank in the field army and from 29 November 1939 for all army officers. Many officers unofficially wore captured enemy officers' brown leather belts.

Oberfeldwebel Wriedt, RKT (Ritterkreuzträger – holder of the Knight's Cross), talks to admiring Hitler Youths. He wears the M1930 mountain field cap with M1939 Edelweiss cap-badge on a light-green branch colour facing-cloth backing favoured by Austrian mountain troops. He wears a M1935 field tunic with M1935 collar-patches with light-green centre stripes, and M1935 pointed shoulder-straps. He displays the Knight's Cross, Iron Cross 1st Class and Infantry Assault badge. (Brian Davis Collection)

Officers wearing the Tropical Service Uniform as summer service dress sometimes wore the M1935 service cap and added bluish dark-green collars and M1935 collar-patches and breast-eagles to the M1940 tropical field tunic.

Other Ranks' Service Uniform

The Service Uniform for technical and senior NCOs and many junior NCOs consisted of the service cap or field cap, field tunic, field greatcoat, trousers and marching-boots, a black belt with pistol and holster, and grey suede gloves. Other junior NCOs and men wore the field cap only, and a bayonet and scabbard instead of the pistol and holster.

The other ranks' M1935 service peaked cap, in *feldgrau* tricot, had a black patent leather or vulcanised fibre chin-strap. The M1935 other ranks' field cap was manufactured in *feldgrau* cloth with, from 5 February 1939, a silver-grey machine-embroidered eagle and swastika on a bluish dark-green backing and a national cockade on a bluish dark-green rhomboid. Both these were changed on 4 June 1940 to mouse-grey on *feldgrau* backing. The cockade was enclosed by a 4mm woollen branch colour chevron point-up, which was abolished on 7 July 1942. The M1942 other ranks' field cap will be described in Volume 3.

The M1935 other ranks' field tunic, manufactured in *feldgrau* cloth with a bluish dark-green facing-cloth collar and matt-grey painted pebbled buttons, had plain cuffs and other ranks' field quality insignia.

The M1937 silver-grey embroidered breast-eagle had a bluish dark-green backing; on 5 February 1939 the embroidery changed to silver-grey. The bluish dark-green facing-cloth M1938 'standard braid' collar-patches, introduced on 26 November 1938, had two *feldgrau* braid guards braids, each with bluish dark-green braid centre stripes and dividing-stripe. NCOs wore 9mm wide bright aluminium diamond-pattern yarn braid, introduced on 10 September 1935, or silver-grey artificial silk braid, on the front and lower edge of the field tunic collar. The M1935 rounded bluish dark-green facing-cloth shoulder-straps with branch colour facing-cloth piping around the outer edges, worn on the field greatcoat, were adopted for the field tunic on 26 November 1938, replacing the M1935 pointed bluish dark-green facing-cloth shoulder-straps without branch colour piping.

On 25 April 1940 NCO collar and shoulder-strap braid was changed to mouse-grey artificial silk or cellulose-fibre wool. On 9 May 1940 the bluish-dark green facing-cloth collars and shoulder-straps of the M1935 field tunic were replaced by *feldgrau* uniform cloth to form the M1940 field tunic. Also on 9 May 1940, a second pattern 'standard braid' collar-patch was introduced, this was made up of two *feldgrau* braid guards braids, with mouse-grey braid centre-stripes and dividing-stripe, sewn on to a *feldgrau* uniform cloth patch or, as from 1941, sewn directly on to the collar.

From 4 June 1940 the breast-eagle was manufactured in mouse-grey machine-embroidery on a *feldgrau* uniform cloth backing. These changes, implemented late in 1940, were evident in the Balkans from April 1941. On 26 May 1941 the number of front buttons increased to six to compensate for deteriorating quality. The M1942 and M1943 field tunics will be described in Volume 3.

1942. Four officers of a divisional staff demonstrate the variations possible with the officers' field tunic. The officer 1st right wears the eight-button modified M1920, the officer 2nd right the five-button M1935, the two on the left the six-button M1941. Note the variations in collar-shape, and the spurs worn by the second right officer. (ECPA)

After 9 May 1940 the bluish dark-green collar of the M1935 other ranks' field greatcoat was manufactured in *feldgrau* uniform cloth, and the plain trousers, designed to be worn with braces, were changed from stone-grey to *feldgrau* cloth. On 26 August 1943 M1943 trousers were introduced with belt-loops, and on 9 November 1939 the black leather marching-boots were shortened to 32-34cm to save material.

The other ranks' M1936 black leather belt had a dull aluminium (smooth sheet steel from about 1941) pebbled buckle with the *Wehrmacht* eagle in a wreath with the '*GOTT MIT UNS*' motto. The holster was black leather. The 84/98 service bayonet was carried in a blued steel sheath suspended from the belt by a black leather bayonet-frog.

Officers' Walking-Out Uniform

This uniform consisted of the peaked service cap, field tunic, field greatcoat, breeches and high-boots, or long trousers with ankle-boots, and gloves. It was identical to the Service Uniform except that it was worn without a belt, pistol or holster. Many officers wore the M1937 piped field tunic. The trousers were changed from stone-grey to *feldgrau* cloth after 9 May 1940, and then on 26 August 1943 the M1943 trousers were introduced. The ankle-boots were actually black lace-up shoes.

Other Ranks' Walking-Out Uniform

Other ranks wore the peaked service cap, field tunic, field greatcoat, long trousers with ankle-boots, black leather belt and the marksman's lanyard. NCOs wore grey suede gloves; junior NCOs and men wore the bayonet, scabbard and bayonet knot. In summer the other ranks' Tropical Walking-Out Uniform was worn.

Officers' Field Uniform

In the field all army officers except platoon-leaders wore the standard steel helmet or officers' field cap, field tunic (with the field greatcoat if ordered), brown belt, breeches and riding-boots, grey suede gloves, pistol, holster and 6x30 binoculars.

The M1935 and the M1942 standard steel helmets were painted matt greenish-grey with roughened surfaces following the order of 21 March 1940. They had a silver-white *Wehrmacht* eagle on a black shield on the left side, abolished on 28 August 1943.

The peakless flapped M1938 officers' new-style field cap, was made of *feldgrau* cloth with aluminium thread pipings. An aluminium wire-embroidered national cockade, enclosed by a branch colour facing-cloth chevron, was worn below a machine-woven or hand-embroidered bright aluminium thread eagle on a bluish dark-green facing-cloth backing.

Crete 1941. This colonel commanding the 100th Mountain Regiment, 5th Mountain Division, wears a theatrical aluminium wire cap-eagle on his M1930 *feldgrau* mountain cap and a similar breast-eagle on his M1940 tropical field tunic. Note the unofficial, but universal, M1935 officers' continental collar-patches and the bar to his First World War Iron Cross 1st Class on his left breast-pocket. (Friedrich Herrmann)

General-officers wore gold thread piping and a gold artificial silk chevron; from 16 November 1942 they wore the eagle and swastika and cockade in hand-embroidered gold thread. On 7 July 1942 all officers were required to remove the chevron. The M1943 standard peaked field cap will be described in Volume 4.

The M1934 old-style field cap, officially abolished on 1 April 1942, continued to be manufactured for officers and NCOs after that date. It was actually the officers' service cap without the metal crown stiffener, chin-cords and buttons. It had a soft black patent leather peak and a bright machine-woven aluminium thread eagle and swastika, cockade and wreath, all on a bluish dark-green facing-cloth backing. Some officers unofficially added the service-cap's matt aluminium wire chin-cords.

From 31 October 1939 all officers below general-officer in combat units were ordered to wear the other ranks' field tunic, trousers and marching-boots with the black leather belt, but many officers continued to wear their M1935 field tunic or modified the other ranks' tunic, adding officers' roll-back cuffs, collar-patches and the bluish dark-green officers' collars. In the summer months the officers' tropical field uniform was worn.

Platoon leaders wore the same field equipment as in North Africa, but retained continental items such as the brown or black leather belt, black leather M1939 Y-straps, black leather bayonet frog, M1931 olive-green or tan canvas bread-bag and M1931 canteen; tropical items may have been used in summer.

Crete, 1941. A German motorcycle combination in tropical summer uniform passes a group of Italian Fascist Youth. The motorcyclists wear sand-camouflaged steel helmets, M1940 tropical shirts and trousers and tropical canvas Y-straps. The vehicle is a *Zündapp* KS 750cc heavy motorcycle. (Josef Charita)

Other Ranks' Field Uniform

The field uniform consisted of the helmet or field cap, field tunic, field greatcoat, plain trousers and marching-boots. NCOs had grey suede gloves. Many NCOs wore the M1934 old-style field cap. The M1943 peaked field cap will be described in Volume 4. Other ranks carried the same equipment as in North Africa, but with continental instead of tropical variants. In summer the other ranks' field uniform was worn.

Tank Crews' uniforms

The M1934 special black tank crew uniform (which by May 1940 was also worn by artillery, signals and (until 1941) engineer units in *Panzer* divisions) consisted of the M1940 officers' or other ranks' black peakless field cap, with the branch colour chevron (removed 10 July 1942), the M1934 and M1936 black tank field jacket and trousers, grey shirt, black tie and black lace-up shoes. In summer tank crews wore the M1940 tropical field uniform, sometimes with M1934 black piped pink collar-patches and skulls.

Some general-officers in *Panzer* divisions, corps, groups and armies unofficially wore the black uniform with general-officers' insignia, and many officers continued to wear the M1935 *feldgrau* officers' service cap. The M1943 peaked black field cap will be described in Volume 3. In 1942 the jacket and collar were shortened slightly to save material, and the collar piping was abolished. In 1943 the buttons closing the M1936 jacket were reduced from four to three, and the three left-lapel button-holes to one.

Yugoslavia, 1942. Two members of a German tank-crew (top far left and front second left) pose in front of their ex-French Army *Hotchkiss H-39* light tank with *Chetnik* guerrillas with whom they have concluded a local truce and anti-Partisan pact. The crewman at the front wears the standard black uniform but his companion appears to have added a black collar and collar-patches to the M1933 Austrian Army field tunic. Note the bravado of the guerrilla (front far left) as he aims his submachine gun at the cameraman. (Dušan Babac Collection)

An *Unteroffizier* in an other ranks' M1940 field tunic indicates something to two officers also wearing the same model tunic but with M1935 officers' collar-patches. (Friedrich Herrmann)

The special *feldgrau* field uniform for armoured reconnaissance, assault artillery, armoured engineers (after 1941) and other units will be described in Volume 3.

Special Uniforms and Insignia for Other Branches

The Rifle (*Jäger*) Divisions and independent rifle battalions (but not rifle battalions in infantry regiments) – lightly equipped mobile troops organised for hilly terrain not requiring the specialist skills of mountain divisions – were (on 2 October 1942) issued mountain troops' uniforms with the light-green branch colour and M1939 *feldgrau* mountain-trousers, grey ankle-puttees and mountain-boots. Three bright aluminium or dark aluminium zinc oak leaves were worn on the left side of the mountain cap and a machine-embroidered or woven badge with three light-green oak-leaves on a bluish dark-green or *feldgrau* oval edged in green, grey or white rope on the right upper sleeve.

The *Grossdeutschland* Motorised Regiment, fighting in Belgrade in April 1941, adopted (7 October 1940) a new black cloth cuff-title with a hand- or machine-embroidered aluminium thread cursive '*Grossdeutschland*' and edging.

Uniforms and Insignia of Foreign Volunteers

Personnel of the Croatian Legion divisions wore a straight-sided red and white chequerboard shield stencilled to the left side of the steel helmet, and a machine-woven or machine-embroidered black-edged curved heraldic shield with '*HRVATSKA*' (Croatia) in red (this word was deleted by German cadre personnel) above a chequerboard, on the left or right upper sleeve of the field tunic and greatcoat. Veterans of the Croatian Legion, formed in July 1941, wore a silver-grey metal laurel linden leaf on the right breast-pocket.

The 1st Cossack Cavalry Division wore German cavalry uniforms with regimental fur caps, reinforced riding-breeches and the *Burka* cloak. On 18 March 1944 the lance-design collar-patches and modified Russian Tsarist rank insignia were replaced by German insignia. The Russian Corps in Serbia wore modified Tsarist Russian uniforms and insignia, changing on 30 November 1942 to German uniforms and insignia without any distinguishing unit badge.

The 845th German-Arab Infantry Battalion wore German uniforms and insignia with the 'Free Arabia' badge of *Sonderverband 287* on the right upper sleeve. In June 1943 287th Assault Gun Battery, formerly in *Sonderverband 287*, joined 1st Tank Bn, Rhodes Assault Division, its personnel still wearing *Panzer* lapel skulls and the *Orientkorps* arm-badge on their tropical uniforms.

Armenian Infantry Battalion I/125 personnel wore special collar and shoulder-strap insignia (introduced in August 1942 and replaced on 18 March 1944 by German insignia) and a machine-woven or machine-embroidered black-edged curved heraldic shield with '*ARMENIEN*' in golden-yellow or white above red, blue and golden-yellow bars, on the left upper sleeve.

Yugoslavia, 1942. The four-man crew of a 7.5cm new-style field cannon 16, a revamped First World War model – shell a village suspected of harbouring guerrillas. Note the *Unteroffizier* gun-commander far left. The men have M1940 field tunics and the minimal field equipment normally worn by artillery crews in combat. (Private Collection)

Rank Insignia

General-officers wore dress-quality plaited shoulder-boards with two gold bullion or golden-yellow 'celleon' thread cords and one bright flat aluminium braid central cord on a bright-red branch colour facing-cloth backing. A *Generalfeldmarschall* had silver-crossed marshal's batons; other general-officers had 3-0 German silver or white aluminium plated pips and branch insignia. From 3 April 1941 all three cords of the *Generalfeldmarschall* were in bright gold or golden-yellow 'celleon'.

Field-officers wore two 5mm wide matt aluminium braids on a branch colour facing-cloth backing and 2-0 gold-coloured galvanised or lacquered grey aluminium or zinc alloy pips and branch insignia. Captains and subalterns wore the same insignia on two 7-8mm wide matt aluminium (later *feldgrau* braid) braids placed side-by-side on a branch colour facing-cloth backing.

Senior NCOs wore 3-1 grey aluminium or zinc alloy pips and branch insignia on M1935 bluish dark-green facing-cloth or M1940 *feldgrau* uniform cloth shoulder-straps piped in branch colour facing-cloth and edged on all sides by 9mm wide mouse-grey artificial silk or cellulose-fibre wool diamond-pattern yarn braid. A *Hauptfeldwebel / Hauptfeldwebeldiensttuer* wore two NCO braids on the cuff of the field tunic and greatcoat.

Junior NCOs wore the same shoulder-straps and braids as senior NCOs, with the *Unterfeldwebel* wearing braid around the shoulder-strap and the *Unteroffizier* omitting braid across the base of the strap.

Men wore the same shoulder-straps and shoulder-slides as junior NCOs, insignia and M1936 NCO-braid rank chevrons and embroidered silver-grey or aluminium thread pips on a triangular (circular for *Obersoldat*) backing of bluish dark-green facing-cloth (changed on 9 May 1940 to *feldgrau* uniform cloth) and in black cloth for the black tank uniform.

Branch Insignia

From 1 September 1939 all units of the Field Army (but not the Replacement Army) were ordered, for security reasons, to remove or conceal branch symbols which identified more closely than the branch colour the type of unit, as well as the unit identifying numerals on their shoulder-boards and shoulder-straps. Officers and senior NCOs tended to retain their branch symbols. From 24 January 1940 shoulder-straps for junior NCOs and men were, with the exception of élite formations such as *Großeutschland,* manufactured without branch symbols or unit numerals. Removable *feldgrau* shoulder-slides, with branch colour wool or cotton yarn or flat thin yarn embroidered chain-stitch branch symbols and unit numerals, were issued for wear in rear areas or on leave. Engineers' black and medical corps' dark-blue insignia omitted the former white chain-stitch outline.

Two officers on the Aegean island of Leros, in summer uniform, with M1940 tropical peaked field caps with aluminium officers' piping and the branch colour chevrons removed, M1940 tropical field tunic with unofficial M1935 continental collar-patches and M1940 tropical trousers. (Josef Charita)

RIGHT Yugoslavia, 1942. The crew of a 20mm anti-aircraft gun pose with their weapon. The officer has the M1934 old-style field cap, M1935 field tunic and unidentified light-coloured breeches and high-boots. The 2nd left soldier wears the M1940 greatcoat with M1935 shoulder-straps and carries a field flashlight with clear, red and green lenses. The 2nd right soldier has the M1940 greatcoat with M1935 shoulder-straps. The 1st right soldier has a M1935 greatcoat with bluish dark-green collar. (Private Collection)

TABLE 1 INSIGNIA OF GERMAN ARMY OFFICER CANDIDATES
1 SEPTEMBER 1939 – 29 JANUARY 1940

Rank insignia	Function of rank	Rank titles
	Insignia as *soldat* Accepted for officer-training. Undergoing 4 months basic training as conscript in a Replacement Army Battalion	Fahnenjunker – branches except below Fahnenjunker (im San. Korps) – Medical Corps Fahnenjunker (im Vet. Korps) – Veterinary Corps Fahnenjunker (im Ing. Korps) – Engineer Specialists
	Insignia as *Gefreiter* plus junior NCO's bayonet-knot Accepted for officer-training. Undergoing 5 months advanced training as conscript in a Replacement Army battalion	Fahnenjunker-Gefreiter – branches except below Fahnenjunker-Gefreiter (im San. Korps) – Medical Corps Fahnenjunker-Gefreiter (im Vet. Korps) – Veterinary Corps Fahnenjunker-Gefreiter (im Ing. Korps) – Engineer specialists
	Insignia as *Unteroffizier* plus unofficial senior NCO's white metal unit insignia Attending 2 month course at military school (*Kriegsschule*)	Fahnenjunker-Unteroffizier– branches except below Fahnenjunker-Oberjäger – Rifles Fahnenjunker-Unteroffizier (im San. Korps) – Medical Corps Fahnenjunker-Unteroffizier (im Vet. Korps) –Veterinary Corps Fahnenjunker-Unteroffizier (im Ing. Korps) –Engineer specialists
	Insignia as *Unterfeldwebel* plus senior NCO's white metal unit insignia Passed out from military school. Attending 4 month course at Arm of Service school, Medical, Veterinary or Engineering academy	Fähnrich – branches except below Fähnrich (im San. Korps) – Medical Corps Fähnrich (im Vet. Corps) – Veterinary Korps Fähnrich (im Ing. Korps) – Engineer specialists
	Insignia as *Oberfeldwebel* plus officer's uniform Passed out from Arm of Service school or passed the Final Professional Examination at the Medical, Veterinary or Engineering academy. Serving 2 months in a field unit before promotion to officer	Oberfähnrich – branches except below (no symbol) Unterarzt – Medical Corps (silver aesculapius) Unterveterinär – Veterinary Corps (silver snake) Oberfähnrich (im Ing. Korps) – Engineer specialists (No symbol) Oberfeuerwerker (mit bestandener Offiziersprüfung) – Ordnance (silver cogwheel)

Rank insignia	Function of rank	Rank titles
	Insignia as *Soldat* (20.10.42 double loop) Accepted for officer-training. Completing 4 months basic training in a Replacement Army unit and 1 month with a Field Army unit	Schütze etc (OB) – all branches except below Schütze etc (SOB) – Medical Corps Schütze etc (VOB) – Veterinary Corps
	Insignia as *Gefreiter* (20.10.42 double loop) Accepted for officer-training. Undergoing 2 months platoon commander training with a field army unit	Gefreiter (OB) - all branches except below Gefreiter (SOB) – Medical Corps Gefreiter (VOB) – Veterinary Corps
	Insignia as *Unteroffizier* (20.10.42 double loop) Beginning an officer-candidate course, or professional studies at the Medical or Veterinary Academy	Unteroffizier (OA)/Fhj. Unteroffizier – all branches except below Oberjäger (OA)/Fhj. Oberjäger – Rifles Offizieranwärter (W)/Fahnenjunker (W) – Ordnance Corps Fahnenjunker (im San. Korps) – Medical Corps Fahnenjunker (im Vet. Korps) – Veterinary Corps
	Insignia as *Feldwebel* (20.10.42 double loop) Completing an officer-candidate course before promotion to officer, or after 3 months study at the Medical or Veterinary Academy	Feldwebel (OA) /Fhj. Feldwebel – all branches except below Wachtmeister (OA)/Fhj. Wachtmeister – Cav, Artillery etc Fahnenjunker-Feldwebel (im San. Korps) – Medical Corps Fahnenjunker Feldwebel (im Vet. Korps) – Veterinary Corps Fahnenjunker-Feuerwerker – Ordnance Corps
	Insignia as *Oberfeldwebel* (20.10.42 double strap loop) Former Oberfeldwebel etc attending an officer-candidate course before promotion to officer	Oberfeldwebel (OA)/Fhj. Oberfeldwebel – all branches except below Oberwachtmeister (OA)/Fhj. Oberwachtmeister – Cav, Artillery etc Fahnenjunker-Oberfeuerwerker – Ordnance Corps
	Insignia as *Stabsfeldwebel* (20.10.42 double loop) Former Stabsfeldwebel etc attending an officer-candidate course before promotion to officer	Stabsfeldwebel (OA)/Fhj. Stabsfeldwebel – all branches except below Stabswachtmeister (OA)/Fhj. Stabswachtmeister – Cav, Artillery etc Fahnenjunker-Stabsfeuerwerker – Ordnance Corps
	Insignia as *Oberfeldwebel* plus officer's uniform Passed the Preliminary Professional Examination at the Medical, Veterinary or Engineering academy. Serving some months in a field unit before resuming studies	Feldunterarzt – Medical Corps (25.7.40) (silver 'A') Feldunterveterinär – Veterinary Corps (6.2.42) (silver 'A') Fahnenjunker-Ingenieur – Engineer specialists (7.11.40) (silver cogwheel)
	Insignia as Oberfeldwebel plus officer's uniform Passed an Officer-Candidate course, or the Final Professional Examination at the Medical, Veterinary or Engineering academy. Serving 2 months in a field unit before promotion to officer	Oberfähnrich – all branches except below (1.7.43) (no symbol) Unterarzt – Medical Corps (silver aesculapius staff) Unterveterinär – Veterinary Corps (silver snake) Oberfähnrich (W) – Ordnance Corps (16.7.43) (no symbol) Feldingenieur – Engineer specialists (7.11.40) (silver cogwheel)

OTHER INSIGNIA

Officer and NCO Candidates

Until 29 January 1940 a soldier applying for training as a regular (*aktiv*) officer undertook basic training at a local Replacement Army unit, before attending an all-arms military school – *Kriegsschule* – as a cadet. There he began to wear the branch colour and uniform of his destined branch. A cadet for a combat arm then joined a specialist 'arm of service' school – *Waffenschule* – while medical, veterinary or engineering cadets attended a professional academy, then spent a period with a field unit as a Probationary 2nd Lieutenant (*Oberfähnrich*) before being commissioned.

From 30 January 1940 officer training was accelerated and senior NCOs could become officer candidates. A candidate (from 1941 known as a cadet) moved directly from basic training to a *Waffenschule*, which in 1942 was called an officer candidate school (*Schule für Offizieranwärter*) and on 28 April 1943 became a cadet school (*Schule für Fahnenjunker*) or to an academy before commissioning.

In order to alleviate the shortage of specialist officers in field units, partly qualified medical, engineering and veterinary candidates would interrupt their academy studies for service with a field unit as a field probationary 2nd Lieutenant – *Feldunterarzt* etc. In July 1943 the *Oberfähnrich* rank was restored for combat arms.

The officer candidate ranks and insignia from 1939-40, only slightly different from ordinary NCOs and men, are shown in Fig. 1.

After 30 January 1940 ordinary ranks were introduced, suffixed (OB) – *Offizierbewerber* (officer applicant) for men's ranks and (OA) – *Offizieranwärter* (officer candidate), after 1941, with the cadet – *Fahnenjunker* – prefix for NCO ranks. After 1940 officer candidate insignia was indistinguishable from that of ordinary troops, and so on 20 October 1942 all candidates and cadets added a double loop of NCO braid to their shoulder-straps (see Fig. 2).

NCO candidates (*Unteroffizieranwärter*, on 10 November 1943 redesignated *Unteroffizierbewerber* or NCO applicants) were trained at army NCO schools and wore a single loop of NCO braid on their shoulder-straps.

Serbia, spring 1944. A *Hauptmann* wearing the M1934 old-style officers' field cap and M1935 field greatcoat, carrying issue 6x30 binoculars, with his battalion's senior NCOs. Note the bright aluminium collar and shoulder-strap braid worn by the *Feldwebel* on his M1940 field tunic with M1935 bluish dark-green shoulder-straps. (Private Collection)

Trade Badges

On 22 December 1920 a range of trade badges were introduced for NCOs and men who had passed specialist courses. These technical personnel, corresponding to British technical warrant officers and NCOs, were an essential part of a modern mechanised army.

The trade badge was worn on the right cuff of the field tunic and the greatcoat and consisted of a gothic letter or symbol on a circular cloth badge (from 20 December 1920 in golden-yellow wool or silk or gold wire on *feldgrau* facing-cloth, from 10 September 1935 on bluish dark-green facing-cloth and from 9 May 1940 on *feldgrau* uniform cloth, although on black cloth for the black tank crew jacket). Trade badges for tropical uniforms were in golden-yellow wool on light-olive heavy ribbed cotton twill for the field tunic, and in olive-brown wool for the greatcoat.

The trade badges worn during the Second World War are illustrated in Fig. 3. The regulations of 15 August 1939 prescribed a 3mm bright aluminium hand-embroidered cord inner edging for qualified NCOs occupying a specialist post at regimental or battalion HQ. Qualified NCOs not yet in post, and qualified men in post, wore the badge without the edging. By 1943 many badges were also produced with a 2mm aluminium cord outer edging, as worn by *Luftwaffe* specialists.

TABLE 3 GERMAN ARMY TRADE BADGES 15 AUGUST 1939 – 9 MAY 1945

Trade	Trade-badge	Ranks	Details of trade
Hufbeschlagpersonal (farrier NCOs & men) Inf, cav, recce, art, terr. rifles, sec, horse transp, med, vet.		Stabsbeschlagmeister, Oberbeschlagmeister, Beschlagmeister; Beschlagschmied... unterwachtmeister/ unteroffizier/ stabsgefreiter/ obergefreiter/ gefreiter/ oberschütze etc/ schütze etc	NCOs run regt & bn smithies assisted by men. 15.8.39: NCOs – edging on badge when in post, none if awaiting posting. Men – no edging
Feuerwerker (Regular Artificer NCOs) Soldaten im Feuerwerkerdienst (War Sub. Artificers) Corps of Artificers		(Regular) Stabsfeuerwerker, Oberfeuerwerker, Feuerwerker, Unterfeuerwerker, Feuerwerkerunteroffizier (War Sub. 20.2.40) – Stabswachtmeister/ Oberwachtmeister/ Wachtmeister ('feldwebel')/ Unteroffizier/ Stabsgefreiter/ Gefreiter... im Feuerwerksdienst 31.7.44 – 'wachtmeister' ranks only	Heavy weapons, ammunition & equipment commissioning, inspection & administration at army, corps, div. HQ. 15.8.39: Regulars – edging on badge when in post, none if awaiting posting. 20.2.40: Regulars – edging, War Sub – no edging
Schirrmeister (Regular Technical NCOs) Kriegsschirrmeister (War Sub.Tech. NCOs)		Stabsschirrmeister, Oberschirrmeister, Schirrmeister, Schirrunterfeldwebel/ Schirrunterwachtmeister, Schirrunteroffizier (Ch)-smoke/ anti-gas, (EP)-railw.eng, (F)-Horse trans, (Fz) -Ordn, (K)-Mot, (P)-Eng, (Sch)-Searchlights	Equipment maintenance at Regt, Bn, HQ. 15.8.39: Regulars – edging on badge when in post, none if awaiting posting. 7.8.41: edging for peacetime qualified, none for wartime qualified. 8.7.43: War Sub. – braid bar
Funkunteroffiziere (Signals NCOs) Unteroffiziere im Funkmeisterdienst (War Sub. Signals NCOs) All branches		(Regular) Stabsfunkmeister, Oberfunkmeister, Funkmeister, Funkunterfeldwebel ('wachtmeister'), Funkunteroffizier (War Sub.18.8.43) – Stabsfeldwebel/ Oberfeldwebel/ Feldwebel ('wachtmeister')/ Unteroffizier ... im Funkmeisterdienst	Signals maintenance at Regt, Bn, HQ 15.8.39: Edging on badge when in post, none if awaiting posting 18.8.43: Regular – edging, War Sub. – no edging
Brieftaubenmeister (Pigeon Post NCOs) All branches		Stabsbrieftaubenmeister, Oberbrieftaubenmeister, Brieftaubenmeister, Brieftaubenunterfeldwebel/ Brieftaubenunterwachtmeister, Brieftaubenunteroffizier	Pigeon post duties at Regt & Bn HQ 15.8.39. Edging on badge when in post, none if awaiting posting
Sanitütsunterpersonal (Medical NCOs & Men) Medical Corps		Sanitäts... stabsfeldwebel/ hauptfeldwebel/ oberfeldwebel/ feldwebel/ unteroffizier/ stabsgefreiter/ obergefreiter/ gefreiter/ obersoldat/ soldat	Medically qualified orderly 15.8.39: Edging on badge for NCOs, none for men 31.12.43 edging for all ranks
Waffenunteroffiziere (Regular Armourer NCOs) Waffenmeisterdienst (War Sub.Armourer NCOs) Inf, cav, Panzer, armd inf, recce, AT, art, smoke, eng, sigs, MP, terr.rfles, sec		(Regular)Waffenstabsfeldwebel, Waffenoberfeldwebel, Waffenfeldwebel, Waffenunterfeldwebel ('wachtmeister' in cav. recce, art, smoke, sigs), Waffenunteroffizier (War Sub.18.12.40) Stabsfeldwebel/ Oberfeldwebel/ Feldwebel/ Unterfeldwebel ('wachtmeister')/ Unteroffizier.im Waffenmeisterdienst	Infantry weapons maintenance at Regt & Bn HQ 15.8.39: edging on badge when in post, none if awaiting posting 18.12.40: Regular – edging, War Sub. – no edging
Wallmeister (Defensive Line NCOs) Engineers		Wallstabsfeldwebel, Walloberfeldwebel, Wallfeldwebel, Wallunterfeldwebel, Wallunteroffizier	Workshop supervisor at Regt & Bn HQ 15.8.39: edging on badge when in post, none if awaiting posting
Festungswerkfeldwebel (Fortifications Sgts) Engineers		Festungswerkstabsfeldwebel, Festungswerkoberfeldwebel, Festungswerkfeldwebel	Fortifications construction at Regt & Bn level 15.8.39: edging on badge when in post, none if awaiting posting
Gasschutzunteroffiziere (Regular anti-Gas NCOs) Uffz. im Gasschutzdienst (War.Sub.anti-Gas NCOs) All branches		(Regular) Stabsfeldwebel, Oberfeldwebel, Feldwebel, Unterfeldwebel ('wachtmeister') Unteroffizier (War Sub.26.2.44) Stabsfeldwebel/ Oberfeldwebel/ Feldwebel/ Unterfeldwebel ('wachtmeister')/ Unteroffizier... im Gasschutzdienst	11.3.41, anti-gas equipment maintenance at Regt & Bn HQ 26.8.43: Regular – edging 26.2.44: War Sub. – no edging (From 25.9.43 GU)
Geräteverwaltungsunter-offiziere (HK/ WG) (NCO Quartermasters) Inf, armd.inf, art		Gerätfeldwebel, Gerätunterfeldwebel, Gerätunteroffizier. ('... wachtmeister' in artillery) + (HK)-garrison, (WG)-weapons & anti-gas	18.11.43. Equipment maintenance at Bn HQ Regular: edging on badge for peacetime qualified, none for wartime qualified
Kraftfahrzeug- und Panzerwärte (Motor & Tank mechanics) Armd and motorised units		These titles were associated with any rank: Kraftfahrzeug/ Panzer... wart II – Mechanic 2 Kraftfahrzeug/ Panzer... wart I – Mechanic 1 Handwerker – Craftsman, Vorhandwerker – Chargehand	1.6.43, for motor and tank maintenance, repair & recovery Mech.2 – no piping; Mech.1 – pink piping; Craftsman silver piping; Chargehand – gold piping
Panzerfunkwärte (Armd signals mechanics) Armoured units		(The title Panzerfunkwart was associated with any rank)	24.1.44 for signals equipment operation & maintenance in armoured units (gold piping)
Nachrichtenmechaniker (Signals mechanics) All branches		(The title Nachrichtenmechaniker was associated with any rank)	10.5.44 for signals equipment mechanics: Edging on badge for NCOs, none for men

TABLE 4 SELECTIVE LIST OF BRANCH AND UNIT INSIGNIA OF UNITS IN NORTH AFRICA AND THE BALKANS
14 FEBRUARY 1941 – 4 OCTOBER 1944

Units	Branch colour	Shoulder-strap insignia		Other distinctions (comments)
		Libya, Egypt, Tunisia 14.2.41 – 12.5.43	Yugoslavia, Greece, Albania 6.4.41 – 4.10.44	
Combat Troops – Staff (Kommandobehörde)				
General Officers (Generale)	Bright red	None	None	*Larisch* patches, red stripes
General Staff (Generalstab) officers	Crimson	None	None	Silver *Kolben* patches, crimson stripes
3 Army Group (Heeresgruppe) Staffs	White	G (Afrika)	G (E, F)	
2 Army (Armee) Staffs	White	–	A / 2, 12	
3 Armoured Army (Panzerarmee) Staffs	Pink	A / 5, (Afrika)	A / 2	
2 Armoured Group (Panzergruppe) Staffs	White	? (Afrika)	1	
10 Corps (Korps) Staffs	White	LXXXX, (DAK)	XI, XXX, LI–LII, LXV, LXVIII, LXIX, LXXXXI	
1 Reserve (Reservekorps) Staff	White	–	LXIX	
1 Motorised Corps (Korps (mot.)) Staff	White	–	XXXXI	
5 Mountain Corps (Gebirgskorps) Staffs	Light green	–	XV, XVIII, XXI–II, XXXXIX	*Edelweiss badges*. Mountain cap
3 Armoured Corps (Panzerkorps) Staffs	Pink	–	XIV, XXXX, XXXXVI	
Combat Troops – Infantry (Infanterie)				
26 Infantry (Infanterie) Division Staffs	White	D / 334	D / 46–718	
1 Air-Landing (Luftlande) Division Staff	White	–	D / 22	
1 Assault (Sturm) Division Staff	White	–	D (Rhodos)	
59 Line Infantry (Infanterie) Regts	White	–	16–750 series	
37 Line Infantry (Grenadier) Regts	White	754–5	359–991 series, (Rhodos)	
2 Machine-gun (Maschinengewehr) Bns	Light green	2, 8	–	
22 Reinforcement (Feldersatz) Bns	White	220, 598–9	83–392 series, (Rhodos)	
2 Africa (Afrika) Division Staffs.	White	D / 90, 999	–	
3 Africa Rifle (Afrika-Schützen) Regts	White	961–3		
2 Motorised (Inf.(mot.)) Division Staffs	White	–	D / 16, 60	
3 Motorised (Grenadier (mot.)) Regt.	White	200	120, 156	
2 Motorised (Infanterie (mot.)) Regts	White	–	60, 92	
Motorised Regiment Großdeutschland	White	–	GD monogram	*Großdeutschland* title
4 Mountain (Gebirgs) Division Staffs	Light green	–	D / 1, 4–6	*Edelweiss* badges. Mountain cap
9 Mountain (Gebirgs) Regts	Light green	756	13, 85, 91, 98–9, 100, 141, 143,	*Edelweiss* badges. Mountain cap
3 Mtn. Reinforcement (Feldersatz) Bns	Light green	–	91, 94–5	*Edelweiss* badges. Mountain cap
1 Special purpose (Div.z.b.V.) Div. Staff	White	D (Afrika)	–	
1 Special purpose (Div.z.b.V.) Regt	White	200	–	
3 Fortress (Festung) Division Staffs	White	–	D / 41, 133, (Kreta)	

TABLE 4 SELECTIVE LIST OF BRANCH AND UNIT INSIGNIA OF UNITS IN NORTH AFRICA AND THE BALKANS
CONTINUED

Units	Branch colour	Shoulder-strap insignia		Other distinctions (comments)
		Libya, Egypt, Tunisia 14.2.41 – 4.10.44	Yugoslavia, Greece, Albania 6.4.41 – 4.10.44	
3 Fortress (Festungs) Bns	White	–	F / 621–3	
22 Fortress Inf. (Festungs-Infanterie) Bns	White	–	F / (I–XIII, XVI, XVIII–XXII), 999	
6 Rifle (Jäger) Division Staffs	Light green	–	D / 42, 100, 104, 114, 117–18	Oakleaves badges. Mountain cap
12 Rifle (Jäger) Regts	Light green	–	25–750 series	Oakleaves badges. Mountain cap
2 Reserve (Reserve) Division Staffs	White	–	D / 173, 187	
5 Reserve Inf. (Reserve-Grenadier) Regts	White	–	17, 45, 130, 231, 462	
2 Anti-Aircraft (Flak) Bns	White	Fl / 606	F1/22	
1 Special Unit (Sonderverband)	Various	288	–	Orientkorps arm-badge
4 'Brandenburg' Commando Bns	Various	II/1, I/4	I/1, I/2	Any appropriate uniform
Combat Troops – Mobile Troops (Schnelle Truppen)				
1 Mobile (leichte) Division Staff	Golden-yellow	LD / 5	–	
10 Armoured (Panzer) Division Staffs	Pink	D / 10, 15, 21	D / 1, 2, 5, 8–9, 11, 14	Skull collar-patches, black uniform
10 Armoured (Panzer) Regts	Pink	5, 7, 8	1, 3, 10, 15, 31, 33, 36,	Skull collar-patches, black uniform
6 Motorcycle Recce. (Kradschützen) Bns	Grass-green	K / 15	K / 2, 8, 55, 59, 64	
1 Motorcycle Recce.(Kradschützen) Bn.	Golden-yellow	–	K / 59	
1 Motorcycle Recce. (Kradschützen) Bn.	Pink	–	K / 61	
8 Armd Recce (Panzeraufklärung) Bns.	Pink	A / 3, 10, 90, 164, 220, 999	A / 1, 59	Special collar-patches & uniforms
15 Motor Rifle (Schützen) Regts.	Grass-green	104, 115, 155	2, 8, 10–1, 13–4, 28, 110–1, 103, 108, 304	
2 Light Inf (Leichte Infanterie) Div. Staffs	Light green	D / 90	D / 101	
2 Light Africa (Leichte Afrika) Div. Staffs	Light green	D / 90, 164	–	
2 Light Infantry (Leichte Infanterie) Regts.	Light green	200, 361	–	
15 Mechanised (Panzergrenadier) Regts.	Grass green	69, 86, 104, 115, 125, 155, 200, 361, 382, 433, (Afrika)	1, 113, 382, 433	
17 Div. Recce. (Divisionsaufklärung) Bns.	Golden-yellow	A / 580	A / 42–392 series	
7 Motorised Recce. (Aufklärung(mot)) Bns.	Golden-yellow	A / 3	A / 5, 8, 9, 40, 231	
1 Motorised Recce. (Aufklärung(mot)) Bn.	Golden-yellow	A / 33		Dragoon eagle cap-badge
4 Mtn. Recce (Gebirgsaufklärung) Bns.	Golden-yellow	–	A / 54, 94–5, 112	Edelweiss badges. Mountain cap
4 Divisional Recce (Div.Füsilier) Bns	White	–	277, 334, 367, (Rhodos)	

Units	Branch colour	Shoulder-strap insignia		Other distinctions (comments)
		Libya, Egypt, Tunisia 14.2.41 – 12.5.43	Yugoslavia, Greece, Albania 6.4.41 – 4.10.44	
2 Divisional Recce (Div.Füsilier (AA)) Bns	Golden-yellow	–	181, 297	
32 Antitank (Panzerjäger) Bns	Pink	P / 33, 39, 90, 190, 334, 605, 999	P / 52–392 divisional series	
9 Motorised AT (Panzerjäger(mot.)) Bns	Pink	P / 90	P / 4, 37–8, 43, 50, 53, 160, 228	
4 Mtn. Antitank (Gebirgspanzerjäger) Bns	Pink	–	P / 47, 94–5	*Edelweiss* badges. Mountain cap
Combat Troops – Artillery (Artillerie)				
36 Artillery (Artillerie) Regts	Bright red	33, 75, 155, 220, 334, 999	83–670 divisional series	
5 Artillery (Artillerie) Bns	Bright red	361	653–4, 661, 668, 670	
2 Reserve Arty. (Reserve-Artillerie) Bns	Bright red	–	10, 96	
10 Motorized Arty (Artillerie (mot.)) Regts	Bright red	33, 190	4, 74, 80, 102, 116, 119, 146, 160	
4 Mtn. Artillery (Gebirgsartillerie) Regts	Bright red	–	79, 94–5, 118	*Edelweiss* badges. Mountain cap
4 Armd. Artillery (Panzerartillerie) Regt	Bright red	33, 90, 155	73	
3 Assault-gun (Sturmgeschütz) Bns	Bright red	–	184, 190–1	Special collar-patches & uniforms
2 Army AA (Heeresflak) Bns	Bright red	Shell / 302	Shell / 299	
1 Rocket Projector (Nebelwerfer) Bn.	Bordeaux Red	9	–	
Combat Troops – Engineers (Pioniere)				
37 Engineer (Pionier) Bns	Black	5, 220, 334, 900, 999	71–704 divisional series	
2 Reserve Engineer (Reserve-Pionier) Bns	Black	–	46, 86	
6 Engineer (Pionier) Coys	Black	–	704, 713–4, 717–8, (Rhodos)	
4 Mtn. Engineer (Gebirgspionier) Bns	Black	–	54, 91, 94–5,	*Edelweiss* badges. Mountain cap
10 Armd. Engineer (Panzerpionier) Bns	Black	33, 49, 200, 220	13, 37–8, 59, 86, 89, 209	Skull collar-patches, black uniform
1 Pioneer (Bau) Bn	Light brown	85	–	
Combat Troops – Signals (Nachrichtentruppe)				
35 Signals (Nachrichten) Bns	Lemon yellow	5, 334, 999	71–392 divisional series	
6 Signals (Nachrichten) Coys	Lemon yellow	–	704, 713–4, 717–8, (Rhodos)	
1 Reserve Sigs. (Reserve-Nachrichten) Coy.	Lemon yellow	–	1087	
4 Mtn Signals (Gebirgsnachrichten) Bns	Lemon yellow	–	54, 91, 94-5	*Edelweiss* badges. Mountain cap
12 Armd Signals (Panzernachrichten) Bns	Lemon yellow	78, 90, 190, 200, 220	4, 37–8, 77, 84–5, 341	Skull collar-patches, black uniform
3 War Correspondent (Propaganda) Coys	Yellow/*grey	(Afrika)	698, 690	*PK* cuff-title. *25.1.43
1 War Correspondent (Propaganda) Bn	Yellow/*grey	–	(Südost)	*PK* cuff-title.*25.1.43

TABLE 4 SELECTIVE LIST OF BRANCH AND UNIT INSIGNIA OF UNITS IN NORTH AFRICA AND THE BALKANS
CONTINUED

Units	Branch colour	Shoulder-strap insignia		Other distinctions (comments)
		Libya, Egypt, Tunisia 14.2.41 – 12.5.43	Yugoslavia, Greece, Albania 6.4.41 – 4.10.44	
Supply Troops *(Versorgungstruppen)*				
29 Div Supply *(Nachschubführer)* officers	Light blue	D / 5, 190, 220, 334, 999	D / 46–887 divisional series	
4 Mtn Div Supply *(Nachschubführer)* officers	Light blue	–	D / 54, 91, 94–5	
6 Mot Div Supply *(Nachschubführer (mot))*	Light blue	–	D / 4, 61, 66, 82, 85, 160	
3 Armd Div Supply *(Nachschubführer)* officers	Light blue	–	D / 59, 60, 81	
22 Div Supply *(Nachschubtruppen)* cmdrs	Light blue	D / 33, 90, 200	D / 104–717 divisional series	
2 Div Supply *(Nachschub-Kolonnen)* Bns	Light blue	D / 5, 334	–	
1 Supply *(Nachschub)* Bn	Light blue	N / 533	–	
3 Div Supply *(Versorgung)* Regts	Light blue	–	N / 297, 367, 373	
213 Mot Transport *(Kraftwagen)* Coys	Light-blue	N / 33–999 divisional series	N / 4–887 divisional series	
51? Mot Transport *(Kraftfahr)* Coys	Light-blue	KF / 33–999 divisional series	KF / 4–887 divisional series	
240? Horsedrawn Transport *(Fahr)* Coys	Light–blue	–	4–887 divisional series	Cavalry breeches & boots
35? Horsedrawn Transport *(Fahr)* Sqdns	Light-blue	–	4–887 divisional series	Cavalry breeches & boots
Medical Corps *(Sanitäts)* General-Officers	Bright red	Silver aesculapius staff	Silver aesculapius staff	*Larisch* patches, red trouser-stripes
Medical Corps *(Sanitäts)* officers	Dark blue	Gold aesculapius staff	Gold aesculapius staff	Red cross armband
35 Horse Med *(Sanitäts)* Coys-men	Dark blue	– –	46–887 divisional series	Red cross band. Medical badge
4 Mtn Med *(Gebirgssanitäts)* Coys-men	Dark blue	– –	54, 91, 94–5	*Edelweiss* & medical badges. Mtn cap
16 Mot.Medical (Sanitäts)Coys - NCO/men	Dark blue	33–999 divisional series	4–85 divisional series	Red cross band. Medical badge
37 Field Hospitals *(Feldlazarette)*-men	Dark blue	190, 334, 572	46–887 divisional series	Red cross band. Medical badge
4 Mtn Hosp *(Geb.Feldlazarette)* – NCO & men	Dark blue	–	54, 91, 94–5	*Edelweiss* & medical badges. Mtn cap
11 Mot Hosp *(Feldlazarette (mot))* – NCO/men	Dark blue	33, 200	4, 59, 60–1, 66, 81–2, 85, 160	Red cross band;medical badge
Veterinary Corps *(Veterinär)* Generals	Bright red	Silver snake	Silver snake	*Larisch* patches, red trouser-stripes
Veterinary Corps *(Veterinär)* officers	Crimson	Gold snake	Gold snake	Cavalry breeches & boots
37 Veterinary *(Veterinär)* Coys – NCO & men	Crimson	334, 999	46–887 divisional series	Cavalry breeches & boots
4 M.P. *(Feldgendarmerie)* Bns	Orange	613	501, 591, 696	Sleeve-badge & cuff-title

TABLE 4 SELECTIVE LIST OF BRANCH AND UNIT INSIGNIA OF UNITS IN NORTH AFRICA AND THE BALKANS
CONTINUED

Units	Branch colour	Shoulder-strap insignia		Other distinctions (comments)
		Libya, Egypt, Tunisia 14.2.41 – 12.5.43	Yugoslavia, Greece, Albania 6.4.41 – 4.10.44	
45 M.P. (Feldgendarmerie) Troops	Orange	33–999 divisional series	46–887 divisional series	Sleeve-badge & cuff- title
4 Mtn M.P. (Feldgendarmerie) Troops	Orange	–	54, 91, 94–5	Edelweiss & MP badges.Mtn cap
Security Troops – (Sicherungstruppen)				
1 Army Rear-Area Commander (Korück)	White	–	560	
28 Sub-district Comds (Feldkommandantur)	White	– –	538–1042 series	Kommandantur gorget
2 Territorial Rifle (Landesschützen) Regts	White	–	81, 86	
24 Territorial Rifle (Landesschützen) Bns	White	–	L / 257–977 series	
1 Security (Sicherung) Regt	White	–	S / 86	
18 Security (Sicherung) Bns	White	S / 766	S / 265–1025 series	
5 Transit POW Camps (Dulag)	White	–	KG / 160, 183, 185, 191, 202	
Foreign Troops – (excluding Croatian Legion Divisions)				
1 Cossack (Kosak) Cavalry Division Staff	Golden-yellow	–	1	Cossack/German unif. armbadge
6 Cossack (Kosak-Reiter) Cavalry Regts	Golden-yellow	–	– (1, 5 Don, 2 Sibir, 3, 4 Kuban, 6 Terek)	Cossack/German unif. armbadge
1 Cossack Artillery (Kosak-Artillerie) Regt	Bright red	–	55	Cossack/German unif. armbadge
5 White Russian (Russkiy Korpus) Regts	White	–	1–5	
1 Arab Special Unit (Sonderverband)	Various	(III) 287	–	Turban, Free Arabia armbadge
1 Arab Infantry (Infanterie) Bn	White	–	845	Free Arabia armbadge
4 Arab Infantry (KODAT) Bns	White	(Algerien, Marokko, Tunisien)	–	French uniforms. German armband
1 Armenian Field (Armen.Feld) Bn	White	–	(I)125	Armenian Legion armbadge
Army Officials (Heeresbeamten) – dark green underlay (except Chaplains and Special Officers) Special rank insignia				
45 Field Post (Feldpost) Offices	Lemon-yellow	Fp (33–999 divisional series)	Fp (4–887 divisional series)	
4 Mtn Field Post (Feldpost) Offices	Lemon-yellow	–	Fp (54, 91, 94–5)	Edelweiss badges. Mountain cap
7 Field Sec Pol (Geheime Feldpolizei) Grps	Light blue	GFP (741)	GFP (9, 171, 510, 611, 621, 640)	

Badges such as the Fb (Fortress Construction Senior NCO), Fp (Fortress Engineer Senior NCO), Rs (Regimental Saddler), Ts (Troop Saddler Candidate), V (Administrative NCO) and Zg (Ordnance Senior NCO) were obsolete in September 1939. Two new trades, Gas Precautions and Quartermaster NCOs, were established during the war.

The supply of suitable specialists could not meet wartime demand, and after 1940 it was often only specialists with the more thorough **109** peacetime qualification who wore the edging. Those who had passed a shorter wartime course, often designated as '*im... Dienst*' (in the... service), wore the badge without the edging.

Three types of badges produced after 1943 – the motor and tank mechanics, armoured signals mechanic and signals mechanic – showed a change in emphasis, as they were not restricted to NCOs and did not carry the same career pattern or prestige. They are therefore perhaps more comparable to the M1920 signals personnel, M1930 helmsman, M1936 artillery gun-aimer, M1937 smoke troop gun-aimer and M1941 mountain guide badges.

Medals and Awards

On 28 September 1941 the German Cross in Gold was instituted as an intermediate award between the Iron Cross 1st Class and the Knight's Cross. It comprised a gold wreathed black swastika in a grey aluminium star worn on the right breast-pocket.

Before October 1944 Hitler instituted three further grades of Knight's Cross to reward repeated bravery – on 3 June 1940 the Knight's Cross with oak leaves, on 21 June 1941 with oak leaves and swords and on 15 July 1941 with oak leaves and swords and diamonds. This last award had only 27 recipients, including *Generalfeldmarschall* Rommel. In early 1942 the Italian High Command awarded Africa Corps personnel the Italo-German Campaign medal, a bronze (later silver plated) circular medal with a black, white, red and green ribbon. It was removed on 29 March 1944, following the Italian Armistice.

On 16 October 1942 the Crete commemorative cuff-title was awarded to Army personnel, principally in the 5th Mountain Division and 141st Mountain Regiment in the Battle of Crete 20-27 May 1941. The white cloth title, worn on the left cuff, had '*KRETA*' flanked by flowers and an edging, all in yellow cotton embroidery.

Yugoslavia, summer 1944. An *Obergefreiter* war correspondent in summer field uniform with the M1940 tropical peaked field cap with the branch colour chevron removed and a M1940 tropical field tunic with a war correspondent's cuff-title, possibly indicating membership of the *Wehrmacht* War Correspondent Battalion. Note the tank battle badge. (ECPA)

Serbia, October 1944. Four exhausted soldiers catch a few moments' sleep in their Adler Type 3Gd *Kubelwagen* jeep. All wear M1940 greatcoats. Note the *Wehrmacht* eagle on the helmet (ordered removed 28 August 1943) and the bayonet at arm's reach. (Private Collection)

THE PLATES

A: ARRIVAL IN AFRICA, FEBRUARY–APRIL 1941

A1: *Generalmajor, 5. leichte Division*, **tropical service uniform, Tripoli, Tripolitania, March 1941** This deputy divisional commander wears a privately purchased M1940 early issue greenish-brown tropical field tunic with continental M1935 shoulder-boards and M1927 collar-patches but also a M1935 gold bullion breast-eagle instead of the standard M1940 bluish-grey thread version. He wears the M1940 pith helmet, M1940 tropical breeches with general-officers' stripes, the M1940 1st pattern tropical high-boots, a Walther PPK pistol and, unofficially, a general-officer's continental brown belt. He has the Iron Cross 1st and 2nd Class and the Knight's Cross and Pour le Mèrite, the highest First World War decoration.

A2: **Hauptmann,** *Panzerregiment* **8, tropical field uniform, Agedabia, Cyrenaica, April 1941** This 15 *Panzer* Division battalion commander wears the M1940 tropical field tunic with unofficial continental M1940 black field cap, leather belt, M1935 continental collar-patches and breast-eagle and *Panzer* lapel skulls and 10x50 Zeiss binoculars. The hard-shell P38 pistol holster, *Zeiss-Umbral* sun-goggles, M1940 tropical breeches and M1940 1st pattern tropical boots are standard. He wears the Iron Cross 1st and 2nd Class and the silver tank battle badge.

A3: *Obergefreiter, Kradschützenbataillon 15*, **tropical field uniform, Tobruk, Cyrenaica, April 1941** On 25 September 1939 motorcycle battalions officially adopted a 'K' branch symbol and grass-green branch colour, but some retained pink, golden-yellow or white. These battalions mostly ignored the 28 October 1941 change to copper-brown without the 'K' and in 1941-42 reorganised as armoured reconnaissance companies. This dispatch rider, giving the traditional German Army salute, wears the M1940 motorcyclists' greatcoat with NCO Candidates' insignia on M1940 shoulder-straps manufactured without the branch symbol, and M1936 continental chevrons, M1940 tropical field cap with sun-goggles and continental M1935 dispatch-case, and he carries M1940 tropical gauntlets and Karabiner 98k rifle.

B: CYRENAICA AND WESTERN EGYPT, MAY–NOVEMBER 1941

B1: *Oberschütze, Maschinengewehrbataillon 2*, **tropical field uniform, Tobruk, Cyrenaica, May 1941** 5th Mobile Division MG battalions wore light-green branch colour instead of white. This senior private wears the M1940 pith helmet and M1940 tropical field tunic with standard collar-patches, M1940 1st pattern tropical boots, brown leather ammunition pouches instead of black, M1940 other ranks' tropical belt and rifleman's field equipment, the tropical version of the branch colour signaller's arm-badge and the black wound-badge (1-2 wounds). He carries a Karabiner 98k with canvas breech and sight cover, and a M1924 stick-grenade.

B2: *Schütze, Panzerjägerabteilung 33*, **tropical field uniform, Halfaya Pass, Egypt, May 1941** This 15th *Panzer* Division antitank crewman wears a M1940 tan variant tropical field tunic, 1st pattern tropical boots and the M1935 helmet, which in late 1941 replaced the pith helmet with front-line units. He wears rifleman's field equipment, also worn by line and mechanised infantry, with two water-bottles and the gas-cape unofficially strapped to his gas-mask canister. In action AT crews left their equipment in the truck or half-track.

B3: *Unteroffizier, Pionierbataillon (mot.) 900*, **tropical field uniform, Fort Capuzzo, Cyrenaica, November 1941** This assault engineer section leader in 90th Light Africa Division wears the M1940 tropical field tunic with NCO tropical collar-braid, Engineers' (later redesignated General) Assault Badge, the unofficial 1st pattern Africa Corps cuff-title and M1940 2nd pattern high-boots. He has canvas bags for engineer equipment and grenades, an entrenching tool and bayonet, and an MP40 submachine gun with ammunition pouches.

C: EGYPTIAN FRONTIER BATTLES, NOVEMBER 1941–OCTOBER 1942

C1: *Leutnant, Aufklärungsabteilung (mot.) 33*, **tropical field uniform, Gambut, Cyrenaica, November 1941** This 15th *Panzer* Division Motorised Reconnaissance Battalion platoon or company commander wears standard shirt-sleeve order, with M1940 shirt, shorts, and 1st pattern tropical ankle-boots, and the unpopular officers' tropical belt with P38 pistol. The Reconnaissance branch symbol appears on his shoulder-boards and the battalion's traditional 'dragoon eagle' badge on his cap. He carries standard 6x30 binoculars painted sand camouflage.

C2: *Hauptfeldwebel, Panzerregiment 5*, **tropical field uniform, Tobruk, Cyrenaica, May 1942** This *Stabsfeldwebel* acting as company sergeant major with 21st *Panzer* Division wears the M1940 tropical field tunic with tropical cuff appointment braids, unofficial *Panzer* skull lapel badges, the silver tank battle badge and the Iron Cross 2nd Class button-ribbon. He has threaded draw-strings in his M1940 tropical trousers to create a blouse effect over the 1st pattern tropical ankle-boots. He wears an issue Dutch pith helmet and carries a M1940 peakless tropical field cap and P08 hard-shell holster.

C3: *Gefreiter, leichtes Infanterieregiment 361*, **tropical field uniform, Bir Hacheim, Cyrenaica, May 1942** Light infantry regiments wore the light-green branch colour of rifles and mountain infantry. This first gunner with 90th Light Africa Division, fighting Free French forces at Bir Hacheim, wears the M1940 tropical greatcoat with M1940 other ranks' tropical belt, P38 hard-shell holster and spares pouch and carries an MP40 light machine gun.

D: BATTLE OF EL ALAMEIN, OCTOBER 1942

D1: Generalfeldmarschall Erwin Rommel, *Deutsch-italienische Panzerarmee*, **tropical undress uniform, El Alamein** Rommel has ignored dress regulations and wears a privately purchased M1940 tropical field tunic and M1941 *Generalfeldmarschall* shoulder-boards with superseded M1927 general-officers' collar-patches and a continental M1935 breast-eagle. He wears a M1935 continental service cap and captured British sun-goggles, continental high-boots and, around his neck, the Knight's Cross with swords and diamonds and the prized Pour le Mèrite.

D2: Unteroffizier, *Panzergrenadierregiment 115*, **tropical field uniform, Kidney Ridge, Tel el Aqqaqir** This section leader with 15th *Panzer* Division wears a M1940 tropical field tunic. He has M1940 tropical trousers, 2nd pattern tropical

Germany, 1940. The elegant cadet, an *Unteroffizier* (OA) of the 83rd Infantry Regiment who, judging by his decorations – Iron Class 1st and 2nd Class, infantry assault badge and silver wound-badge – is an experienced NCO recommended for officer-training, is studying at a *Waffenschule*. He wears a M1935 field tunic with private refinements – a sharper officer-style pointed collar and stiffened shoulder-straps with his regimental number in senior NCOs' white aluminium unit numerals instead of white chain-stitch – a common affectation among officer candidates. (ECPA)

ankle-boots, a field-made hessian helmet cover, a map-case, a civilian scarf against sandstorms, and – as he awaits issue of a section leader's submachine gun – standard rifleman's equipment and Karabiner 98k rifle.

D3: *Oberkanonier*, *Artillerieregiment 155*, tropical field uniform, Kidney Ridge, Tel el Aqqaqir As he carries a shell in a wicker basket to his 15cm SFH18 medium field gun, this crewman in 21st *Panzer* Division wears his unbuttoned M1940 tropical tunic, with the Africa Corps title (rarely seen in action), without his shirt or tie in the intense desert heat. He has a M1940 tropical peaked field cap, trousers, 1st pattern tropical ankle-boots.

E: TUNISIAN CAMPAIGN, JANUARY–MAY 1943

E1: Waffenoberfeldwebel, Panzergrenadierregiment 200, tropical field uniform, Kasserine Pass, February 1943 This armourer NCO at Regimental HQ, 200th Mechanised Regiment, 90th Africa Division, wears the tropical version of his trade badge, the Africa Corps cuff title and bronze

Infantry Assault Badge, instituted on 1 June 1940 for motorised infantry, on the M1942 tropical field tunic. He has M1940 shirt and sweater, M1940 tropical trousers, 2nd pattern tropical ankle-boots and the unpopular M1940 brown webbing anklets, which from 23 February 1941 were issued to field units. He has roughly sand-camouflaged his helmet and carries a P38 pistol.

E2: *Feldwebel*, *Gebirgsjägerregiment 756*, tropical field uniform, Longstop Hill, February 1943 This member of 334th Infantry Division wears the M1942 tropical field tunic omitting, as was not uncommon, the tropical NCO collar braid. As a mountain infantryman he has the Edelweiss cap-badge on the M1940 tropical peaked cap (with the branch colour chevron removed since 8 September 1942), the Edelweiss arm badge and mountain puttees and climbing boots. As a platoon leader he carries an MP40 submachine gun and M1938/40 olive-green or tan canvas ammunition pouches.

E3: Schütze, Afrika-Schützenregiment 961, tropical field uniform, Fondouk, March 1943 Officers, NCOs and Men on the cadre of the 999th Africa Division wore normal insignia with light-green branch colour, but a disciplinary soldier (*Bewährungsschütze*) wore no insignia. This soldier has the M1942 tropical field tunic with breast-eagle, collar-patches and shoulder-straps removed, M1940 turtle-neck sweater, tropical breeches, M1935 helmet painted olive-green, plain tropical peaked cap, other ranks' tropical belt with a plain circle buckle-badge and 3rd pattern tropical high-boots. He carries standard riflemen's equipment and a Karabiner 98k rifle.

F: INVASION OF YUGOSLAVIA AND GREECE, APRIL–MAY 1941

F1: *Feldwebel*, *Panzerregiment 33*, field uniform, Niš, Yugoslavia, April 1941 This tank crewman with 9th *Panzer* Division, XXXX *Panzer* Corps, wears regulation field uniform, consisting of the M1934 special tank crew uniform modified in 1936 with three lapel button-holes, with the Iron Cross 1st Class medal and 2nd Class ribbon and silver battle badge. He has the M1940 other ranks' black peakless field cap, goggles and a P08 pistol in a hard-shell holster.

F2: *Obergefreiter*, *Infanterieregiment 330*, field uniform, Zagreb, Yugoslavia, April 1941 This member of 183rd Infantry Division wears a M1940 *feldgrau* field tunic, retaining M1935 rounded bluish dark-green shoulder-straps with NCO candidate shoulder-loops and M1936 rank chevrons, with M1940 *feldgrau* trousers. He wears a silver infantry assault badge and a black wound badge (1-2 wounds), and his helmet has, since 21 March 1940, omitted the national shield on the right side. As a deputy section leader he wears standard rifleman's equipment and he carries a Karabiner 98k rifle and a M1924 stick-grenade.

F3: *Gefreiter*, *Gebirgsjägerregiment 100*, field uniform, Maleme Airfield, Crete, 21 May 1941 This second gunner is rushing ammunition to the first gunner during 5th Mountain Division's desperate battle for Maleme Airfield. He wears an M1935 field tunic with the Edelweiss arm-badge and M1936 rank chevrons, mountain issue M1939 *feldgrau* mountain-trousers, ankle-puttees and mountain-boots, and his helmet shows the *Wehrmacht* eagle on the left side (abolished 28 August 1943). He wears second gunner's field equipment and carries a P08 *Luger* pistol.

G: OCCUPATION OF YUGOSLAVIA, APRIL 1941–OCTOBER 1944

G1: *Schütze, Landesschützenbataillon 562*, field uniform, Belgrade, Serbia, January 1942 This second-line infantryman, too old or too unfit for front-line combat, is guarding part of the Vienna-Salonika railway. He wears the M1934 other ranks' 2nd pattern field cap with M1940 mouse-grey insignia, the M1940 greatcoat, with *feldgrau* collar and shoulder-straps, and standard rifleman's black leather field equipment. He carries the 1934 early war model of the Karabiner 98k rifle.

G2: *Oberstleutnant, Grenadierregiment 370 (kroatisches)*, field uniform, Gorazde, Eastern Bosnia, May 1943 This battalion commander, fighting in Operation *Schwarz* against Yugoslav Partisans, wears the M1935 officers' field tunic with M1935 officers' field quality breast-eagle, shoulder-boards and collar-patches. He has the Iron Cross 1st Class medal and 2nd Class button-ribbon, the white aluminium infantry assault badge and, as German cadre, has folded over the '*HRVATSKA*' title of the Croatian arm-badge. His M1942 helmet shows the Croatian shield on the left side, and he carries standard 6x30 binoculars with a protective lid and a P38 hard-shell holster.

G3: *Starshiy Prikasni, Don-Kosak Reiterregiment 1*, summer field uniform, Petrinja, Croatia, May 1944 From 18 March 1944 1st Cossack Division adopted German uniforms with dark-blue or *feldgrau* breeches and spurless riding-boots. Don Cossacks – high black fur cap, thick red trouser stripes, blue-red left (5th Regt) right (1st Regt) arm badge; Siberian – high white cap, thick yellow stripes, blue-yellow right arm badge; Kuban – low black cap, thin red stripes, black-red left (3rd Regt) right (4th Regt) arm badge; Terek – low black cap, dark-blue edged black stripes, black-blue left arm badge. This *Obergefreiter* equivalent, with the 1st Class Eastern People's medal, retains rank insignia introduced on 29 May 1943 on the M1943 tropical field tunic and wears a M1935 service cap eagle and M1940 machine-woven cockade (officers and German cadre wore M1935 service-cap insignia). He carries a Cossack whip and sword and M1942 Karabiner 98k.

H: OCCUPATION OF GREECE AND ALBANIA, APRIL 1941–NOVEMBER 1944

H1: *Unterarzt, Sanitätskompanie 1/104*, summer field uniform, Agrinion, Greece, October 1943 Probationary and field probationary 2nd lieutenants wore officers' uniform and insignia with Oberfeldwebel rank insignia. This Unterarzt in 104th Rifle Division wears the M1942 rifle cap and arm-badges, M1942 tropical tunic, officers' cap piping and bright aluminium eagle and cockade on a T-shaped backing on the privately-made tropical version of the 1943 peaked field cap. He also has (unofficially) officers' M1935 continental collar-patches, breast-eagle and brown leather belt stained black with P38 hard-shell holster. He wears *Luftwaffe* tropical trousers with 2nd pattern tropical ankle-boots, a red-cross arm-band and white aluminium aesculapius staff shoulder-strap symbol, and carries a M1941 tropical bread-bag.

An armourer sergeant *(Waffenfeldwebel)* at Battalion HQ examines a *Walther* 27mm long-barrel flare pistol. He wears the M1943 standard peaked field cap, the M1935 field tunic with Iron Cross 2nd Class button-ribbon and, as a war-trained armourer, his crossed-rifles trade-badge without an edging. (Brian Davis Collection)

H2: *Gefreiter, Grenadierregiment 65*, summer field uniform, Kos, Greece, October 1943 This section-member in 22nd Airlanding Division, which captured Sevastopol in June 1942, wears the M1943 tropical field tunic with the Crimea arm-shield with M1940 tropical trousers and anklets. He has rifleman's field equipment with the 1941 model Karabiner 98k rifle, M1924 stick-grenades and M1939 egg grenades.

H3: *Obergefreiter, Grenadierregiment 522*, field uniform, Tirana, Albania, March 1944 This First Gunner in the 297th Infantry Division wears the M1943 six-buttoned field tunic with M1940 collar-patches and rank-chevrons and the M1943 standard field cap (introduced on 11 June 1943) with a M1942 mouse-grey eagle and cockade on a T-shaped *feldgrau* patch. He has standard field equipment, with a P38 soft-shell holster (introduced late 1943), and carries a MG42 light machine gun.

GERMAN ARMY 1939–45 (3)
EASTERN FRONT 1941–3

THE CONTEXT OF THE EASTERN FRONT

The High Command of the army and Wehrmacht 1941–3

As head of state, Adolf Hitler had (since 4 February 1938) held the nominal post of Supreme Commander of the Armed Forces (Oberster Befehlshaber der Wehrmacht). He became convinced that his own intellect and experience, as a regimental messenger in the First World War, had granted him a unique insight into military strategy. He continued to ignore GFM Wilhelm Keitel, as Chief of the Armed Forces High Command (Chef des Oberkommandos der Wehrmacht, the OKW) the senior professional soldier, but now even overruled the strategic and tactical decisions of the Army High Command (Oberkommando des Heeres, or OKH) and did not disguise his contempt for the generals. This dysfunctional relationship further deteriorated in late November 1941, when the German advance, which Hitler had predicted would be unstoppable, ground to a halt before Moscow. Hitler blamed the generals and on 19 December 1941 dismissed GFM Walther von Brauchitsch, the Chief of the Army High Command (Oberbefehlshaber des Heeres), taking over his post. Within six months thirty-nine more top commanders, including Gen.Obst. Heinz Guderian, the architect of *Blitzkrieg*, had been dismissed.

Hitler moved from Berlin to the 'Wolf's Lair' in Rastenburg (now Katrzyn), East Prussia, then in July 1942 to Vinnitsa in occupied Ukraine. He directed military operations isolated from the Army High Command and surrounded by the generals of its rival, the OKW, led by General der Artillerie Alfred Jodl, the Chief of the Armed Forces Operations Staff (Chef der Wehrmachtführungsamt) and Keitel's nominal deputy. Now Hitler's military advisers were easily dominated 'yes-men' such as General der Infanterie Kurt Zeitzler, who on 24 September 1942 replaced Brauchitsch's deputy, Gen.Obst. Franz Halder, as Chief of the Army General Staff (Chef des Generalstabes des Heeres).

The strategy

On 23 August 1939 Hitler had concluded an alliance of convenience with the Soviet dictator Stalin to protect Germany's eastern borders during the 1939–40 western campaign. Nevertheless the Soviet Union remained Germany's arch-enemy, and on 18 December 1940 Hitler announced that Operation Barbarossa, the attack on the Soviet Union, would commence on 15 May 1941, a date postponed to 22 June 1941 by the invasion of Yugoslavia and Greece. It would be the biggest conflict in military history, with some three million German troops and about

The German officer's service uniform remained virtually unchanged from March 1935 to May 1945. Walther von Brauchitsch, Chief of the Army High Command from 1 September 1939 to 19 December 1941, was one of the nine generals to be promoted Generalfeldmarschall by Hitler on 19 July 1940 in a move designed to devalue the importance of the German army's highest rank. He wears the M1935 officer's service peaked cap with bluish dark green cap band, gold wire pipings and chin cords and matt aluminium eagle, cockade and wreath. His M1935 officer's field tunic has a bluish dark green collar, bright red collar patches with the two-leaf *Alt-Larisch* design for general officers, gold buttons, cloth loops for his medal ribbons, a gold hand-embroidered breast-eagle on a bluish dark green facing cloth backing, and gold-silver-gold plaited shoulder boards on a bright red backing with a silver crossed marshal's batons. He wears the Knight's Cross around his neck. (ECPA)

900,000 allies facing almost 4.7 million Soviet troops, and its outcome was to colour post-war European history for 50 years.

The German army supported by the Romanian, Finnish, Hungarian and Slovak armies would attack the Soviet Union with three army groups spearheaded by Panzer and motorised divisions organised in four reinforced army corps, designated Panzergruppen. These would trap and smash the bulk of the Soviet Red Army in Belarus and occupy the three key cities of Leningrad (the cradle of Soviet communism), Moscow (the nerve centre of Soviet power), and Kiev, capital of the agriculturally rich Ukraine and gateway to the Caucasian oilfields.

The German army would then advance to the Ural Mountains–River Volga line, some 1,300 miles from the German border, build a 3,000-mile defensive line against Soviet Siberia and Central Asia, and occupy European Russia. Soviet Karelia would be awarded to Finland and Romania would annex Bessarabia, Northern Bukovina and 'Transnistria' (Moldova and Odessa). The remaining territory would be divided into four huge 'German provinces' (Reichskommissariate); Ostland (Estonia, Latvia, Lithuania, Belarus, north-western Russia), Moskau (northern and central Russia), Ukraine (Ukraine and southern Russia), and Kaukasus (Transcaucasia, Armenia, Georgia and Azerbaijan). The local populations would be ruled by up to 100 million German, Dutch and Scandinavian settlers, who would ensure permanent Nazi domination of the Eurasian land mass.

As in the 1939–40 western campaign there was a destructive tension between two strategies; Gen.Obst. Heinz Guderian's 'armoured concept', whereby armoured troops had to advance rapidly to capture the enemy power centre, and the classic 'decisive manoeuvre' strategy of Army High Command, which needed time to destroy pockets of trapped enemy forces. In the event neither strategies achieved their objectives. The rapidly advancing tanks wasted precious days waiting for supporting infantry to catch up, allowing Red Army units to reform and consolidate their defences. 'Decisive manoeuvre' inflicted heavy losses during 1941 – Soviet sources suggest 3.1 million killed and taken prisoner, German sources 7.5 million – but Moscow, the Soviet capital, was not captured, and the bulk of the Red Army was able to retreat, re-group and counter-attack in December 1941. Hitler's caution prevented the Panzer forces advancing as fast as they wanted, and he stubbornly forbade local tactical withdrawals which might have avoided disasters such as Stalingrad, but nothing in the western campaigns had prepared the Wehrmacht for the defiance, tenacity and resourcefulness of the Red Army.

Stalingrad marked a reversal of German fortunes and the turning-point in the Second World War. Henceforth it would be the Wehrmacht that was outnumbered, outequipped and outmanoeuvred and the Allies who would take, and retain, the strategic initiative until the German surrender on 8 May 1945.

The development of army units

The German army in Operation Barbarossa was organised as for the western and Balkan campaigns, with three (from 1942, five) army groups originally deployed in the western campaign. Each army group (Heeresgruppe), initially averaging one million troops commanded by a Generalfeldmarschall, controlled Army Group HQ troops and three to four armies. An infantry army (Armee), about 200,000 strong under a General-oberst, comprised Army HQ troops and two to five infantry corps and sometimes a reinforced armoured corps (a Panzer-gruppe, by January 1942 upgraded to Panzer army, or Panzerarmee) with Panzer and motorised (in June–July 1942 also designated Panzer) corps. The independent 20th Mountain Army operated on the Arctic front under OKW control.

Infantry, motorised, mountain and Panzer corps comprised about 60,000 men under a General der Infanterie (or equivalent), with corps HQ troops and two to five divisions. In September 1942 the 61st and 62nd Reserve Corps were formed to control reserve divisions in Ostland and Ukraine respectively.

The Infantry Division (Infanterie-Division) retained its 1939 organisation, with three 3,049-man infantry regiments and five divisional support units – an artillery regiment, and reconnaissance, anti-tank, engineer and signals battalions. It had fewer divisional services – about four horse-drawn and motorised transport (soon replaced by Russian *panje* cart) columns, medical company, field hospital, veterinary company, military police troop and field post office. From January 1942 many infantry divisions were reduced to two infantry regiments, theoretically offsetting this reduction with increased firepower and on 15 October 1942 all infantry regiments were redesignated 'élite' Grenadier regiments to boost morale.

Security divisions (Sicherungs-Divisionen) were formed with an infantry regiment, territorial rifle (Landesschützen) battalions and various divisional support units to garrison the occupied territories. They were joined after September 1942 by units of the home-based Replacement Army (Ersatzheer). 16,000-strong reserve divisions (Reserve-Divisionen), with two to three reserve infantry regiments and divisional support units, had the role of training recruits and undertook garrison duties, whilst training divisions (Feldausbildungs-Divisionen), with two to four regiments comprising 16,000 recruits, underwent advanced combat training and awaited allocation to front-line units.

A section first gunner on the march in June 1941, with his MG34 machine-gun slung over his back instead of over his shoulder as prescribed. Note his mess kit and shelter-quarter strapped to his A-frame and his bayonet, M1930 gas canister, M1931 bread bag and M1931 felt covered canteen and black-painted cup. (Friedrich Herrmann)

The 14,319-man M1940 Motorised Division (Infanterie-Division (mot.)) had two motorised regiments (on 15 October 1942 redesignated Motorised Grenadier) and motorised divisional support units (including a motorcycle reconnaissance battalion) and services. The army's most prestigious unit, the Großdeutschland Motorised Regiment, actually an independent reinforced regiment with four motorised battalions, support and artillery battalions and services, fought in Belarus and Central Russia. On 12 March 1942 it became a motorised division and then deployed to Southern and Central Russia.

The 13,000-man Light Infantry Division (leichte Infanterie-Division), first formed in December 1940 as an élite non-motorised 'pursuit' unit, had two infantry regiments, and from 28 June 1942 was re-designated a Rifle (Jäger) Division. The 14,131-man Mountain Division

(Gebirgs-Division) had two mountain regiments with mountain-equipped divisional support units and services.

From August 1940 to January 1941 the number of Panzer divisions was expanded to 20 at the cost of weakening existing divisions. The M1940 Panzer Division now had 1 x 2 battalion armoured regiments (instead of two); nine divisional support units, namely two motorised rifle (5 July 1942 redesignated mechanised – Panzergrenadier) regiments, one artillery (later Panzer artillery) regiment, motorcycle reconnaissance (including an armoured-car company) and motorised reconnaissance battalions (ordered to merge in 1941), motorised anti-tank, armoured engineer, armoured signals and later anti-aircraft battalions; and motorised divisional services.

The 16,000-man 1st Cavalry Division (1. Kavallerie-Division), fought in Belarus and Central Russia with three mounted regiments, one Kavallerie regiment (mounted and bicycle companies), bicycle battalion and mounted or motorised divisional support units and services. On 28 November it was reorganised as 24th Panzer Division.

Sonderverband 287, a reinforced mixed-arms regiment originally formed 4 August 1942 for commando operations in the Persian Gulf, was deployed (minus its 3rd Battalion) under Army Group 'A' in the Caucasus, and on 2 May 1943 most sub-units became 92nd Motorised Grenadier Regiment, serving in the Balkans. Sonderverband Bergmann was formed on 14 October 1941 with a German cadre commanding Georgian, North Caucasian and Azeri companies, and fought in the 1942 Caucasian campaign.

On 9 January 1941 the 'Technical Troops' were established, partly from the paramilitary 'Technical Emergency Corps' (Technische Nothilfe) to support Germany's war production, and on 15 November 1942 the 'Motor Park Troops'(Kraftfahrparktruppen) were formed to co-ordinate the units repairing and servicing motor and armoured vehicles.

European volunteers

Apart from its Romanian, Hungarian, Finnish, Slovak and Italian allies, the German army deployed huge numbers of non-German volunteers in German uniform on the eastern front, fighting to earn a favoured place in a post-war settlement after a German victory.

On 20 July 1941 Francisco Franco, the ruler of Spain (a neutral country) allowed the 250th Infantry Division – the 'Blue Division' – to be formed from 18,693 Spanish army and Fascist Falange political militia volunteers, in gratitude for German assistance in the Spanish Civil War.

ABOVE **An infantry platoon pauses for a rest whilst advancing into the Soviet Union, July 1941. Note the mixture of M1935 field tunics with bluish dark green collars and M1940 tunics with** *feldgrau* **collars. These troops are already exhibiting the front-line fighter's disregard for uniform regulations by wearing their trousers outside their boots, and the NCO platoon leader (centre foreground) is wearing his M1931 camouflage slung over his shoulder. The second gunner on his right is carrying two spare MG34 barrels. (Brian Davis)**

A Gefreiter section leader (third from left) with an MP40 submachine-gun directs his section light machine-gun team in street fighting in a Russian village, July 1941. The first gunner is firing his MG34 machine-gun, assisted by the second gunner, with the third gunner waiting behind the section leader with a spare ammunition box. (Friedrich Herrmann)

It fought on the Leningrad and Volkhov fronts until 20 October 1943, when Franco, responding to Allied pressure, had it repatriated. The 369th Reinforced Croatian Infantry Regiment was formed from 3,000 Croatian and Bosnian volunteers in July 1941 and after a lengthy training period in Germany joined 100th Light Infantry Division in Ukraine. It fought and surrendered at Stalingrad in January 1943.

The 3,000-strong 638th Reinforced French Infantry (15 October 1942 Grenadier) Regiment was formed on 27 October 1941, and fought with 4th Panzer Army attacking Moscow before relegation to anti-partisan operations in occupied Poland and Belarus and transfer to the Waffen-SS on 1 September 1944. The Walloon Legion was organised as the 373rd Walloon Infantry Battalion on 8 August 1941 from 860 French-speaking Belgian members of Léon Degrelle's Fascist Rex Party and served in South Russia with the 100th Light Infantry Division and in the Caucasus with 97th Rifle Division before transferring to the Waffen-SS on 1 June 1943.

During this period Danish, Dutch, Finnish, Flemish and Norwegian volunteers served on the eastern front with the Waffen-SS.

The Osttruppen

German divisions fighting in the Soviet Union and sustaining steady losses were surprised and delighted to accept a continuous stream of civilians and surrendered Soviet troops offering their services, and soon these men were unofficially employed as manual labour in all units and, in emergencies, as combat reinforcements. In September 1941 Hitler officially sanctioned recruitment of Soviet citizens as 'auxiliaries' (Hilfswillige, usually abbreviated to Hiwis) unsuccessfully insisting that they remain unarmed. Hiwis were still joining German divisions up to May 1945, and in 1943 their numbers were estimated at 250,000: German divisions were permitted to recruit them at up to 15% of divisional strength.

On 29 August 1941 the Germans organised the first volunteers into armed units – ten Estonian, Russian and Ingermanland security battalions and the 'Anti-Partisan Regiment' (Freijägerregiment) in Army

LEFT Weary motorcyclists from a divisional reconnaissance battalion take a break in July 1941, still sitting on their Zündapp KS 600W motorcycles. They are wearing the M1940 motorcyclist's protective coat with feldgrau collars and shoulder straps, buttoned to the legs, and have painted their helmets to blend in with the countryside, as ordered on 21 March 1940. (Author's collection)

119

Oblt. Steiner, commander of 2nd Battery, 201 Assault Artillery Battalion, poses with his command vehicle crew near Voronezh, September 1941. They are wearing the M1940 special field-grey uniform with Panzer skull collar patches. The rings around the barrel of the self-propelled gun indicate six Soviet tank 'kills'. (Friedrich Herrmann)

Group North, and five combat battalions (Kampfbataillone) in Army Group Centre. Attached to German divisions on anti-partisan duties or as front-line reinforcements these troops consistently proved their commitment and combat value: on 6 October 1941 mass recruitment of Soviet nationals as 'Eastern Troops' (Osttruppen) was permitted.

The first Cossack unit in the German army was the Red Army's 436th Infantry Regiment, which defected on 22 August 1941, and from October 1941 11 Cossack cavalry squadrons were raised for anti-partisan duties with security divisions, or mounted reconnaissance for Panzer divisions, usually with one squadron (Sotnia) per division: in late 1942 these expanded to 11 battalions. In 1942 three mounted regiments, three infantry regiments and six infantry battalions were recruited with Cossack field officers.

From 15 November 1941 seven security companies were raised from inaccurately labelled 'Turkic' Caucasian and Soviet middle-eastern

An infantry section of 16th Army advances cautiously near Lake Ilmen in September 1941. They are wearing their greatcoats strapped around the top of their M1939 A-frames and below the M1931 mess kit and M1931 camouflage shelter-quarter. The bayonet, entrenching tool, gas mask canister and M1931 bread bag are strapped to the waist belt. (Brian Davis)

An anti-tank crew pulls a 3.7cm Panzerabwehrkanone 35/36 anti-tank gun along a road littered with disabled Soviet light tanks in September 1941. They are wearing the normal infantry field uniform and equipment with Panzer pink branch-colour 'P' and piping on their shoulder straps. (Friedrich Herrmann)

nationalities, and in 1942 they expanded into six 'Eastern legions' (Ostlegionen) in occupied Poland: Armenian, Azerbaijan, Georgian, North Caucasian (Ossetians, Ingushes and Chechens etc.), Turkestan (Kazakhs, Kirkhiz, Tajiks, Turkmens, Uzbeks etc.) and Volga-Tartar (Kazan Tartars, Bashkirs, Chuvashes, Udmurts etc.) Up to the fall of Stalingrad the legions recruited civilian volunteers into five ordnance, construction, and transport battalions and 200 supply and transport companies. Ex-Red Army troops joined 34 infantry battalions numbered in the 783–844 series, and 28 field battalions carrying the divisional number, but only 28 battalions saw action on the eastern front, mostly in the Caucasus.

From 1 October 1942 Estonian, Russian, Belarussian and Ukrainian units were designated as 'Eastern battalions', mostly with Army Group Centre. Each battalion (Ostbataillon), about 950 strong, was allocated a German commander and a cadre of 36 German officers, NCOs and men. In January 1943 the 48 Eastern battalions (except Estonian battalions 658–660) and all Russian, Belarussian and Ukrainian Hiwis were nominally united as the Russian Liberation Army (Russkaya Osvoboditel'naya Armiya, or ROA).

THE EASTERN FRONT 1941–1943

Army Group North's Baltic campaign

At 4.15 a.m. on Sunday 22 June 1941 Army Group North (Heeresgruppe Nord), formerly Army Group 'C', under GFM Wilhelm Ritter von Leeb, crossed the River Niemen and began the 525-mile advance towards Leningrad with its main strike-force, 4th Panzer Group (Gen.Obst. Erich von Hoepner), with eight divisions (three Panzer, two motorised, three infantry, one Waffen-SS motorised). On 26 June, after 185 miles (296 km), it reached the Daugava (Drina) River and on 4 July Ostrov, whilst 18th Army (ten infantry divisions) advanced along the Baltic coast, capturing Riga on 1 July. The 16th Army (nine infantry divisions) guarded the Panzer group's eastern flank, completing the occupation of

Shoulder piece 1.9.39–20.3.40 7.12.42–8.5.45	Shoulder piece 21.3.40–6.12.42	Rank titles 1.9.39–20.3.40 21.3.40–6.12.42	Rank titles 7.12.42–8.5.45
1.9.39–20.3.40		**Group R (Colonel) f** 1. Regimentsführer? a 2. – 3. – 4. – 5. –	
		Group B (Major) 1. Bataillonsführer; a Abteilungsführer b 2. – 3. – 4. – 5. –	**Group B (Major)** 1. Bataillonsführer; Abteilungsführer 2. Oberkriegsarzt 3. – 4. – 5. Sonderführer (B)

		Group K (Captain)
		1. Kompanieführer a/b
		2. Bataillonsarzt; c Abteilungsarzt; c
		   Kolonnenarzt; c Abschnittsarzt; c
		   Sanitätsarzt; d Chefarzt; e
		   Abteilungsarzt e
		3. Abteilungsveterinär;
		   Ortsveterinär; Abschnittsveterinär;
		   Stationsveterinär
		4. –
		5. –
			Group K (Captain)
			1. Kompanieführer
			2. Kriegsarzt
			3. –
			4. Dolmetscher (K)
			5. Sonderführer (K)

		Group Z (2nd Lieutenant) 1. Zugführer a/b 2. Hilfsarzt c 3. Hilfsveterinär 4. Dolmetscher (Z) 5. –	**Group Z (2nd Lieutenant)** 1. Zugführer 2. Kriegsassistenzarzt 3. – 4. Dolmetscher (Z) 5. Sonderführer (Z)
		Group O (Coy Sgt.Maj.) 1. Zugführer a/b 2. Sanitätszugführer c 3. – 4. Dolmetscher (O) 5. –	
		Group G (Corporal) 1. Gruppenführer a/b 2. Sanitätsgruppenführer c 3. – 4. – 5. –	

1. General service (**a** engineers, construction engineers, railway engineers, technical troops: **b** artillery survey, signals, war reporters). No branch insignia. **f** Abolished by March 1940.

2. Medical Corps personnel (**c** attached to non-medical units: **d** in medical units: **e** in reserve field hospitals).
Gold (21.3.40–6.12.42 white aluminium) aesculapius staff for officers; yellow trade right cuff-badge for NCOs.

3. Veterinary Corps (1.9.39–6.12.42). Gold (1.9.39–20.3.40), white aluminium (21.3.40–6.12.42) snake for officers, no branch insignia for NCOs.

4. Interpreters' Service (15.5.40–30.9.43). No branch insignia.

5. Other branches (army group, army, corps and divisional staffs, administration, POW camps). No branch insignia.

Lithuania and Latvia. On 10 July 4th Panzer Group, now at Pskov on the Velikiya River, resumed the offensive, whilst 18th Army cleared Estonia, but enemy resistance in swampy terrain slowed the Panzer Group's progress and on 14 July Hitler ordered it to halt for three vital weeks on the Luga River, only 60 miles (96km) from Leningrad, to await the infantry. The advance recommenced on 8 August and on 1 September 4th Panzer Group captured Schlüsselburg on Lake Ladoga, whilst 18th Army, with the help of Estonian guerrilla forces, completed the occupation of Estonia, taking Narva on 14 July and Tallinn on 27 July

A military official with the rank equivalent of Generalmajor in officer's service uniform, with a M1935 field tunic with general officer's *Alt-Larisch* design on a dark green patch piped on three sides in bright red, and gold/silver threaded dark green/gold shoulder boards with the matt aluminium HV monogram on a bright red underlay. His decorations include the 1914 Iron Cross 1st Class with 1939 bar above the civilian Physical Training (left) and Horseman's badges. His M1935 peaked service cap's upper cap band piping is gold wire (like the crown and lower cap band pipings) not dark green facing cloth as prescribed. (Brian Davis)

before advancing to the western outskirts of Leningrad. In the south 16th Army took Novgorod on 24 August before reaching Lake Ladoga. On 4 September the Finnish army halted on 1939 Finnish–Soviet frontier on the northern approaches to Leningrad and refused to advance further for fear of provoking the Soviet Union even more.

Army Group North in North-Western Russia

On 9 September 4th Panzer Group attacked Leningrad, now only accessible to the Soviets across Lake Ladoga, but on 17 September Hitler transferred it to Army Group Centre for the attack on Moscow. Leningrad was to be besieged by 16th and 18th armies and bombarded by heavy artillery, a fatal decision that spared the city and prevented further significant advances by Army Group North. The epic siege of Leningrad lasted almost 900 days, and was finally lifted by the Red Army on 27 January 1944.

On 8 November 1941 XXXIX Armoured Corps, transferred from 3rd Panzer Group, captured Tikhvin while trying to reach Finnish forces on the River Svir, but on 5 December the Red Army unleashed its winter offensive, forcing the whole army group back 40 miles (64km) to the Volkhov River, where in January 1942 it settled down to static trench-warfare. Meanwhile Hitler replaced Von Leeb with Gen.Obst. Georg von Küchler. By April 1942 the 16th Army had retreated to the Lovat River with contingents successfully holding out in the encircled pockets at Kholm from January to May 1942, and Demyansk from February to June 1942. Finally in January 1943 Velikiye Luki fell to the Red Army.

The Arctic front

On 19th June 1941 the German Norwegen army, under OKW command, advanced from Northern Finland into Soviet Karelia with three infantry and three mountain divisions (one Waffen-SS), but was unable to capture the key port of Murmansk. By December 1941 it settled down to static warfare and in June 1942 was redesignated 20th Mountain Army under Gen.Obst. Edouard Dietl. Further south the Finnish army group under Finnish Field Marshal Gustav Mannerheim occupied ex-Finnish Karelia as far as the River Svir.

Army Group Centre in Belarus

Army Group Centre (Heeresgruppe Mitte), formerly Army Group 'B', commanded by GFM Fedor von Bock, was the strongest force. 3rd Panzer Group (Gen.Obst. Hermann Hoth), with seven divisions (four Panzer, three motorised) would advance in the north whilst the nine divisions (five Panzer, two motorised, one Waffen-SS motorised, one cavalry) of 2nd Panzer Group (Gen.Obst. Heinz Guderian) advanced in the south, trapping the bulk of the Red Army in a series of pockets in Belarus, which would be smashed by 4th Army's 19 and 9th Army's 12 infantry divisions. Then the army group would be reinforced from Army Group North for the drive on Moscow, 600 miles (960km) from the starting-point.

The initial advance through was slow with unexpectedly strong enemy resistance, but by 27 June the Panzer groups had advanced 200 miles (320km) and closed the Minsk pocket, leaving the slower infantry armies to close the Brest–Litovsk and Bialystok pockets on 28 June. The

A specialist officer with the rank of Sonderführer (K) wearing the officer's M1935 field tunic with M1940 Sonderführer collar patches and shoulder boards. As a former NCO who was awarded the Iron Cross 2nd Class button ribbon he wears an officer's collar, cap band and breast-eagle backing in bluish dark green facing cloth instead of the prescribed (and difficult to obtain) Luftwaffe grey-blue uniform cloth. (Brian Davis)

Panzer groups then advanced into Western Russia and on 18 July trapped Soviet forces in the Smolensk pocket, 200 miles (320km) from Moscow. Von Bock wanted an immediate attack on Moscow, 200 miles (320km) away, but on 19 July Hitler, anxious to ensure the capture of Kiev, sent Guderian's 2nd Panzer Group and 2nd Army, just arrived from victory in Yugoslavia, 250 miles (400km) south to support Army Group South's 1st Panzer Group's attack on the city. Guderian defeated Soviet forces at Roslavl on 9 August, Gomel on 20 August, Kiev city on 19 September and helped close the Kiev pocket on 26 September, taking 665,000 Soviet prisoners before rejoining Army Group Centre.

Army Group Centre and the attack on Moscow

On 2 October 1941, 11 weeks after the capture of Smolensk, Army Group Centre launched Operation Typhoon. Hoth's 3rd Panzer Group advanced to the north, Guderian's 2nd in the south, whilst Hoeppner's 4th was earmarked to attack Moscow itself: 2nd, 4th and 9th Armies provided support. On 7 October Orel was taken and on 12 October the Vyazma and Bryansk pockets closed, but the sudden thaw on 6 October had bogged the army group down in a sea of mud. The big freeze of 6 November allowed the advance to continue, and on 30 November advanced units of 4th Panzer Group were only 25 miles (40km) from Moscow's Red Square; but by 4 December the Germans had run out of steam.

The Soviet winter offensive hit Army Group Centre with full force on 5 December but the Germans resisted tenaciously and after a 100-mile (160km) retreat and the loss of Kalinin formed a defensive line on the Dnepr before Smolensk, Vyazma and Rzhev. This line was held until

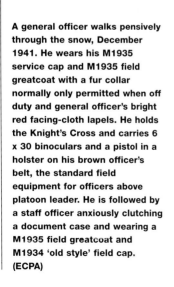

A general officer walks pensively through the snow, December 1941. He wears his M1935 service cap and M1935 field greatcoat with a fur collar normally only permitted when off duty and general officer's bright red facing-cloth lapels. He holds the Knight's Cross and carries 6 x 30 binoculars and a pistol in a holster on his brown officer's belt, the standard field equipment for officers above platoon leader. He is followed by a staff officer anxiously clutching a document case and wearing a M1935 field greatcoat and M1934 'old style' field cap. (ECPA)

A three-man section light machine-gun team from the élite **Großdeutschland** Motorised Regiment in action with their MG34 machine-gun near Tula, central Russia, in December 1941. Note the white thread GD regimental monogram on their bluish dark green white-piped shoulder straps, the bed sheets cut down to form makeshift helmet camouflage covers, and the spare ammunition boxes. (Brian Davis)

1943 with only minor losses around Smolensk. GFM Günther von Kluge replaced Von Bock on 19 December 1941.

Army Group South in Ukraine

Army Group South (Heeresgruppe Süd), formerly Army Group 'A', commanded by GFM Gerd von Rundstedt, was to occupy Ukraine. Gen.Obst. Ewald von Kleist's 1st Panzer Group with nine divisions (five Panzer, two motorised, two Waffen-SS motorised) headed straight for Kiev followed by 6th Army with 14 divisions (one Panzer, 13 infantry). 17th Army, with 13 divisions (seven infantry, two light infantry, two mountain, two Slovak) advanced through Central Ukraine, whilst 11th Army with 12 divisions (seven infantry, five Romanian) would advance along the coast with the Romanian 'Antonescu' Army Group (3rd and 4th Armies, XXI Corps).

Army Group South's advance was comparatively slow. 17th Army took the border garrison of Lvov on 30 June and on 8 August it combined with 11th Army to close the Uman pocket. On 16 October 11th Army and the Romanians took Odessa and on 27 October occupied the Crimea and besieged Sevastopol, finally capturing it on 27 June 1942. Meanwhile 1st and 4th Panzer Group took the Kiev pocket on 26 September and on 20 October 6th Army took Stalino and the Donets Basin industrial region, and on 24 October Kharkov. On 20 November 1st Panzer Group took Rostov-on-Don but GFM Walther von Reichenau, who replaced Von Rundstedt on 1 December, abandoned it on 2 December, only to die suddenly on 17 January 1942. He was succeeded by GFM von Bock.

The Soviet winter offensive made minimal gains around Kharkov, Rostov and in Eastern Crimea, and by 20 April 1942 it had ground to a halt. On 28 June Army Group South launched the fateful Operation Blue towards Stalingrad and the Caucasus and on 7 July 4th Panzer Group captured Voronezh.

Army Groups 'A' and 'B'

On 9 July 1942 Army Group South became Army Group 'B', and Army Group 'A' was formed. This army group, under GFM Wilhelm List, with 20 divisions (three Panzer, 12 infantry, two mountain, three Italian) in

An infantry section in a Russian village waits for orders, January 1942. They wear the practical snow shirt (originally only issued to mountain troops before the war) under their field equipment, and have covered their helmets with cut down bed sheets or snow shirt material. (Brian Davis)

1st Panzer Army and 17th Army, would advance into the oil-rich Caucasus region. Meanwhile Army Group 'B', commanded by GFM Maximilian Freiherr von Weichs, with 53 divisions (five Panzer, 25 infantry, two motorised, ten Romanian, five Hungarian, six Italian) in 4th Panzer Army, 2nd, 6th, 3rd and 4th Romanian, 2nd Hungarian and 8th Italian armies, would advance to the Volga and take Stalingrad.

Army Group 'B' moved forward rapidly and on 23 August 6th Army and elements of 4th Panzer Army entered Stalingrad and began to dislodge the Soviet defenders, but on 19 November the Red Army smashed through the army group's flanks, defended by Romanian and Italian units, and on 23 November had sealed the Stalingrad pocket. Hitler refused to allow the defenders to break out, believing Stalingrad could be supplied by the Luftwaffe as Demyansk had been. On 26 November he detached four armies (6th, 4th Panzer, 3rd and 4th Romanian) from Army Group 'B' to form Army Group 'Don' under GFM Erich von Manstein, in order to hold the Volga line, but on 2 February 1943 the 230 German, Romanian and Croatian troops in the Stalingrad pocket surrendered and Von Manstein retreated to Rostov-on-Don as Army Group 'B' returned to Ukraine.

Army Group 'A' had finally captured the bitterly defended Rostov-on-Don on 23 July 1942 and advanced into the Caucasus, taking Krasnodar (the capital of the Kuban Cossacks) on 9 August, and Novorossiysk on 6 September. Hitler temporally took over army group command on 10 September before appointing Gen.Obst. Ewald von Kleist on 22 November, when the offensive had halted in the Caucasian foothills before Grozny. On 23 December Army Group 'A' was ordered to evacuate the Caucasus to avoid being trapped there and by 1 February 1943 had retreated west of Rostov-on-Don.

The army of occupation

The German-occupied Soviet Union was divided vertically into four strips. The eastern strip was the combat zone with Field Army troops; the east-central strip, the division-level 'Field Army Rear Area' (Rückwärtiges Armeegebiet) with Army Rear Area commanders controlling guard and military police battalions and the west-central strip the corps-level 'Army Group Rear Area' (Rückwärtiges Heeresgebiet) with security divisions. The eastern strip comprised the Western Ostland and Ukraine provinces, nominally under German civilian administration, with district commands (Oberfeldkommandanturen).

ARMY UNIFORM

Orders of dress

Regulations issued on 28 December 1939 reduced the eleven orders of dress established on 8 April 1935 to four: the service uniform or walking-out uniform for formal and semi-formal occasions; the service uniform

Léon Degrelle, the 36-year-old leader of the right-wing Walloon Rex Movement and a volunteer in the Walloon Legion, shortly after being commissioned Leutnant and receiving the Iron Cross 1st Class in May 1942. He wears an officer's M1938 field cap with white branch-colour chevron (the Legion adopted light green later that month), an other ranks' M1935 field tunic with officer's insignia and the Legion's arm shield, and wears the Iron Cross 2nd Class button ribbon, 1st Class pin-back medal and bronze Wound badge. Hitler described Degrelle as 'the son I would most like to have had'. He is talking to an officer in an other ranks' M1940 field tunic. Behind is a Walloon Unteroffizier with full rifleman's equipment. (Josef Charita)

for training or barracks duties; the field uniform for combat, and the fatigue uniform for NCOs and men on work details.

All dates connected with the introduction of new uniform, equipment and insignia, are the date of the army order, but the actual date of introduction could be up to two years later. Logistical difficulties meant that front-line units and remote garrisons might wait up to two years to receive new items, whilst front-line combat troops often received priority issue over support units in rear areas and the Replacement Army in Germany, especially in the case of the M1942 special winter clothing. Experienced soldiers, especially senior officers, often preferred to retain obsolete items if they were of sentimental value, of superior pre-war quality, or marked them as 'old sweats', and this was often officially tolerated as an aid to morale. Finally, to reduce demand on the hard-pressed German clothing industry, which was already sub-contracting production to factories in occupied countries with a corresponding slackening of quality control, an army order of 10 July 1942 decreed that all obsolete clothing could continue to be worn for the duration of the war. Please note that only uniforms and insignia in significant use in the period June 1941–February 1943 are covered here, and readers are referred to Volume 1 (Men-at-Arms 311) for detailed descriptions of items in use before this period.

From the invasion of the Rhineland on 7 March 1936 to the attack on the Soviet Union on 22 June 1941 German units maintained a high degree of uniformity of appearance, and this continued up to the surrender of the Stalingrad pocket on 4 February 1943. Thereafter the OKH began to introduce new bravery awards, encourage élite units with non-standard uniforms and insignia, and increasingly tolerate unofficial and security-compromising unit insignia in ordinary divisions, in order to boost morale and self-confidence severely dented by the Stalingrad defeat.

Officer's service uniform

In the June 1941–February 1942 period this uniform, also worn by probationary 2nd lieutenants (Oberfähnrich and equivalent) consisted of the M1935 officer's peaked service cap, M1935 officer's field tunic with ribbons, M1935 officer's field greatcoat, M1934 officer's brown leather belt, officer's breeches and officer's black leather high-boots, grey suede gloves, standard pistol and holster.

The superior quality *feldgrau* (greenish-grey) tricot or 'eskimo' material cap had a bluish dark green, finely woven facing cloth cap-band, branch-colour facing cloth pipings, a plain black peak and bright aluminium wire chin cords. A M1935 bright aluminium eagle and swastika was worn above a stamped bright aluminium national cockade in an oak-leaf wreath. General officers had metallic woven cord cap pipings and wire chin cords in fired gold or, from 15 July 1938, in the cheaper and more durable bright yellowish-gold 'celleon' artificial material; and from 16 November 1942 their eagle, cockade and wreath were manufactured in gilded aluminium.

The superior quality *feldgrau* cloth M1933 tunic, modified 10 September 1935, was privately purchased from approved tailors, allowing for significant variations in personal taste. It had five (from 26 May 1941 six) matt grey buttons, four patch-pockets, turn-back cuffs and a bluish dark green collar. The field quality insignia consisted of the M1935 officer's hand embroidered matt aluminium thread breast-eagle on a bluish dark green facing cloth backing; M1935 officer's bluish dark green facing-cloth collar patches with hand embroidered matt aluminium guard's braids with branch-colour centre cords; and rank insignia on shoulder boards. General officers had gold buttons, a dress quality gold thread or celleon eagle and bright red collar patches with the gold two-leaf (three-leaf for Generalfeldmarschall from 3 April 1941) *Alt-Larisch* design. The eight-buttoned M1920 and six-buttoned M1928 service tunics, with distinctive diagonal lower concealed pocket flaps, were also worn.

The *feldgrau* greatcoat had two rows of six buttons and a bluish dark green collar (the 9 May 1940 order requiring a *feldgrau* collar was usually ignored) which in 1942 was widened for greater warmth, with bright red lapel linings for general officers. The plain stone grey (from 9 May 1940 *feldgrau*) breeches had bright red pipings and stripes for general officers or crimson for staff officers. The black leather high-boots were worn with spurs.

Other ranks' service uniform

The service uniform for technical NCOs (Festungswerkmeister etc.), senior NCOs (Stabsfeldwebel–Feldwebel etc.) and many junior NCOs (Unterfeldwebel–Unteroffizier etc.) consisted of the other ranks' M1935 service peaked cap or M1935 or M1942 field cap, M1935 field tunic, M1935 field greatcoat, trousers, black leather marching boots, black leather belt and holster with standard pistol and grey suede gloves. Other junior NCOs and men (Stabsgefreiter–Soldat etc.) wore the field cap only, and a bayonet and scabbard on the belt.

The other ranks' peaked cap was as for officers but in *feldgrau* tricot with a black patent leather or vulcanised fibre chin strap. The M1935 other ranks' *feldgrau* cloth field cap had a silver-grey, machine embroidered eagle and swastika on a bluish dark green backing and a cockade on a bluish dark green rhomboid, both changed on 4 June 1940 to mouse-grey on *feldgrau* backing. The cockade was enclosed in a branch-colour chevron, abolished 10 July 1942. The M1942 other ranks' *feldgrau* field cap, introduced 21 July 1942, actually the M1936 mountain cap without the peak, had double-lined flaps which could be pulled over the ears and double-buttoned under the chin in cold weather, offering better protection than the M1935 cap. The 4th Pattern M1939 mountain cap insignia – a mouse-grey woven eagle and cockade on a *feldgrau* T-shaped backing – was worn on this cap.

The *feldgrau* tunic had a bluish dark green collar, five (from 26 May 1941 six) matt grey buttons, plain cuffs and other ranks' field-quality M1937 silver-grey breast-eagle (from 4 June 1940 mouse-grey machine-embroidered) and M1938 'standard braid' collar patches, introduced 26 November 1938. NCOs wore M1935 bright aluminium collar braid or silver-grey artificial silk collar braid, replaced on 25 April 1940 by mouse-

An infantry section fords a river in Central Russia whilst tanks advance away on the opposite shore. The photograph gives a good view of a rifleman's equipment of M1931 mess kit, rolled canvas battle pack and M1931 camouflage shelter-quarter strapped to the A-frame, with the entrenching tool, M1930 gas mask canister, M1931 bread bag and M1931 canteen and cup attached to the waist belt. The section light machine-gun team first gunner (first left) is carrying his MG34 machine-gun in the regulation fashion over his shoulder. (Brian Davis)

Tank crewmen take a break, their grimy faces showing the strain of combat, July 1942. The Unteroffizier (first left) wears the M1936 black field jacket, the soldier (first right) the M1941 reed-green field jacket for tank crews (with Iron Cross 1st Class and silver Tank Combat badge) and trousers over a black tie and grey shirt, the other troops wear the grey shirt and reed-green trousers, and the soldier (second right) wears the M1941 one-piece tank overall. The other ranks' M1940 black field cap is prominent. (ECPA)

Another tank crew, June 1942. Most are wearing the M1941 one-piece tank overall over their black uniforms. Note that the trooper (second left) and the Wachtmeister at the back have removed their black ties in the summer heat, and that the M1940 black field caps still bear the Panzer pink chevron which was ordered to be removed 10 July 1942. (Friedrich Herrmann)

grey artificial silk or cellulose-fibre wool. The M1935 greatcoat round-ended bluish dark green shoulder straps piped in branch colour were worn on the tunic from 26 November 1938.

The M1940 tunic, introduced 9 May 1940, had a *feldgrau* collar and shoulder straps and M1940 'standard braid' collar patches, two *feldgrau* guard's braids with mouse-grey centre stripes and dividing stripe, sewn onto a *feldgrau* collar patch or, from 1941, directly onto the collar. The M1942 tunic, introduced in December 1941, had no pocket pleats but was not in common use until 1943.

The M1935 other ranks' *feldgrau* field greatcoat was as for officers but with other ranks' quality cloth and insignia. The belt had a dull *feldgrau* pebbled aluminium (from about 1941 smooth sheet-metal) buckle with a Wehrmacht eagle and motto. The M1940 greatcoat had *feldgrau* shoulder straps and collar, and the M1942 model had a wider collar for better protection against the cold.

Walking-out uniform

When walking-out or on leave officers wore the service uniform sometimes with the M1937 officer's piped field tunic, with stone grey or *feldgrau* trousers and no belt, holster or pistol. Technical and Senior NCOs wore the peaked cap, field tunic or greatcoat, trousers and black leather ankle-boots, belt and marksman's lanyard, junior NCOs and men adding the bayonet, scabbard and bayonet knot.

Officer's field uniform

In the field officers (except platoon leaders) wore the service uniform but with the steel helmet or field cap and increasingly (though reluctantly) from 23 February 1941, the unpopular, British-army inspired *feldgrau* or brown sailcloth anklets – 'retreat puttees' first introduced 8 August 1940 – with black lace-up ankle-boots to save shoe leather.

The M1935 steel helmet, painted matt greenish-grey with roughened surfaces after 21 March 1940, had a silver-white Wehrmacht eagle decal on a black shield on the left side. The M1942 helmet, introduced

20 April 1942, abolished the edge-crimping to simplify production but was not common in the field until 1943. The peakless M1938 officer's *feldgrau* tricot field cap had aluminium thread crown and front-flap pipings, and an aluminium wire embroidered cockade in a branch-colour chevron below an embroidered bright aluminium thread eagle on a bluish dark green backing. General officers wore gold-thread or 'celleon' piping and gold artificial silk chevron, and from 16 November 1942 gold-thread insignia. On 10 July 1942 all officers were required to remove the chevron.

The M1934 'old style' peaked field cap, officially abolished 1 April 1942, was worn by officers and NCOs until May 1945. Some officers wore the other ranks' M1942 field cap unofficially, with bright aluminium (gold for general officers) crown piping.

On 31 October 1939 all officers below general officer in combat units were ordered to wear the other ranks' field tunic, black belt, trousers and marching boots, in order not to be too conspicuous to the enemy, but many officers retained the officer's M1935 field tunic, or modified the other ranks' tunic, adding officer's roll-back cuffs, collar patches and bluish dark green, higher, more pointed collars.

Subalterns acting as infantry platoon leaders wore the other ranks' black leather belt supporting on the left back hip the 84/98 bayonet in a black-painted metal scabbard in the M1939 black leather cavalry bayonet-frog, usually secured to the black artificial leather case of the 'short shovel' or the M1938 folding shovel; and on the right back hip the M1931 *feldgrau* or M1941 greenish-brown water repellent canvas bread bag for personal effects and the M1931 brown felt-covered canteen and black (from 23 April 1941 greenish-brown) painted aluminium cup; and the black or brown leather M1935 dispatch case on the left front hip. The black leather M1920 'officer's support straps' secured two sets of three 1st pattern greenish-brown M38/40 *feldgrau* canvas ammunition

A mountain infantry company begin a route march in July 1942, singing cheerfully to impress the Propaganda-Kompanie cameraman. The men are wearing standard mountain infantry uniforms with distinctive ankle-puttees, but for coolness have unbuttoned their collars, rolled up their sleeves and slung their helmets on their belts. The officers can be recognised by their 6 x 30 issue binoculars. (Author's collection)

pouches for the MP38 or MP40 submachine-gun introduced 1940. The anti-gas cape in a greenish-brown rubberised canvas pouch (from 1942 *feldgrau* or greenish-brown linen or canvas) was usually tied with rubber bands or straps to a *feldgrau*-painted M1930 corrugated metal canister containing the M1930 or M1938 gas mask and slung from a shoulder by

TABLE 2: SELECTIVE LIST OF RANKS OF REGULAR MILITARY OFFICIALS OF THE GERMAN ARMY 1 SEPTEMBER 1939–8 MAY 1945

Branch designation (branch symbol + branch colour / secondary branch colour) (*Sample insignia illustrated)	Senior career (*Beamten des höheren Dienstes*). Gold *Kolben* collar patches (*Alt-Larisch* for Generals).			
	General der Infanterie	Generalleutnant	Generalmajor	Oberst
Court Martial (Reichskriegsgericht) (DARK GREEN / DARK RED) [1]	Ministerialdirektor im Rang eines General der Infanterie	Oberreichskriegsanwalt * Senatspräsident beim RKG *	Reichskriegsanwalt Reichskriegsgerichtsrat	Oberstkriegsgerichtsrat beim Reichskriegsgericht
District Admin. (Intendantur) (HV + DARK GREEN / BRIGHT RED) [2]	Generaloberstabsintendant (20.12.39) [3] *	Heeresintendant/Generalstabs-intendant (20.12.39)	Gruppenintendant, Korpsintendant/ Generalintendant (20.12.39)	Intendant/ Oberstintendant (20.12.39)
Paymasters (Zahlmeister) (HV + DARK GREEN / WHITE)	–	–	–	–
Mil. Admin. (Kriegsverwaltung) (EAGLE + DARK GREEN / LIGHT GREY) [4]	–	–	Kriegsverwaltungschef * Kriegsvizeverwaltungschef [6] *	Kriegsverwaltungsabteilung-schef
Field Post Office (Feldpost) (FP + DARK GREEN / LIGHT YELLOW) [8]	–	Heeresfeldpostmeister	Heeresfeldpostdirigent	Feldoberpostdirektor *
Field Security Police (GFP) (GFP + DARK GREEN / LIGHT BLUE)	–	–	Feldpolizeichef der Wehrmacht (1941–2) [11]	Heeresfeldpolizeichef [12/13]
Chaplains (Heeresgeistliche) (VIOLET) [15]	–	–	Feldbischof der Wehrmacht [16]	Wehrmachtdekan [17]
Branch designation (branch symbol + branch colour / secondary branch colour) (*Sample insignia illustrated)	Senior career (*Beamten des höheren Dienstes*). Gold *Kolben* collar patches (*Alt-Larisch* for Generals).			
	Oberstleutnant	Major	Hauptmann	Oberleutnant
Court Martial (Reichskriegsgericht) (DARK GREEN / DARK RED) [1]	Oberkriegsgerichtsrat beim RKG. Bürodirektor beim RKG.	Kriegsgerichtsrat	Kriegsgerichtsrat (unter 35 Jahren) * Kriegsrichter *	–
District Admin. (Intendantur) (HV + DARK GREEN / BRIGHT RED) [2]	Oberintendanturrat/ Oberfeldintendant (9.9.42) *	Intendanturrat/ Oberstabsintendant (9.9.42)	Intendanturrat/Stabsintendant (9.9.42) a.p. Stabsintendant	–
Paymasters (Zahlmeister) (HV + DARK GREEN / WHITE)	–	–	–	–
Mil. Admin. (Kriegsverwaltung) (EAGLE + DARK GREEN / LIGHT GREY) [4/5]	Oberkriegsverwaltungsrat/ Kriegsverwaltungsoberrat (6.4.40)	Kriegsverwaltungsrat	Kriegsverwaltungsrat (unter 35 Jahren), Kriegsverwaltungsassessor	Kriegsverwaltungsreferendar (4.11.40) *
Field Post Office (Feldpost) (FP + DARK GREEN / LIGHT YELLOW) [8]	Feldoberpostrat/ Feldpostoberrat (1942)	Feldpostrat	Feldpostrat (unter 35 Jahren)	–
Field Security Police (GFP) (GFP + DARK GREEN / LIGHT BLUE) [10]	Oberfeldpolizeidirektor (4.6.43) [13]	Feldpolizeidirektor [13] *		–
Chaplains (Heeresgeistliche) (VIOLET) [15]	Wehrmachtoberpfarrer [17]	Wehrmachtpfarrer [17]	Wehrmachtkriegspfarrer [18]	–

Branch designation (branch symbol + branch colour / secondary branch colour) (*Sample insignia illustrated)	Advanced career (*Beamten des gehobenen Dienstes*). Thick silver-wire guard's braid collar patches.			
	Oberstleutnant	**Major**	**Hauptmann**	**Oberleutnant**
Court Martial (Reichskriegsgericht) (DARK GREEN / DARK RED) [1]	–	Amtsrat beim RKG. Amtmann beim RKG	Reichskriegsgerichts-oberinspektor	Reichskriegsgerichtsinspektor Kanzleivorsteher beim RKG
District Admin. (Intendantur) (HV + DARK GREEN / BRIGHT RED) [2]	Amtsrat *	Amtmann	–	–
Paymasters (Zahlmeister) (HV + DARK GREEN / WHITE)	Oberfeldzahlmeister	Oberstabszahlmeister *	Stabszahlmeister	Oberzahlmeister *
Mil. Admin. (Kriegsverwaltung) (EAGLE + DARK GREEN / LIGHT GREY) [4/5]	–	Kriegsverwaltungsamtsrat [7] Kriegsverwaltungsamtmann	Kriegsverwaltungs-oberinspektor	Kriegsverwaltungsinspektor
Field Post Office (Feldpost) (FP + DARK GREEN / LIGHT YELLOW) [8]	–	Feldpostamtsrat Feldpostamtmann	Feldoberpostinspektor/ Feldpostoberinspektor (1942)	Feldpostinspektor
Field Security Police (GFP) (GFP + DARK GREEN / LIGHT BLUE) [10]		–	Feldpolizeikommissar [13] *	–
Chaplains (Heeresgeistliche) (VIOLET) [15]	–	–	–	–

Branch designation (branch symbol + branch colour / secondary branch colour) (*Sample insignia illustrated)	Advanced career. Thick silver-wire guard's braid collar patches.	Intermediate career (*Beamte des mittleren Dienstes*). Thick silver-wire guard's braid collar patches (thin silver braids for NCOs).		
	Leutnant	**Oberleutnant**	**Leutnant**	**Oberfeldwebel**
Court Martial (Reichskriegsgericht) (DARK GREEN / DARK RED) [1]	–	–	Reichskriegsgerichtssekretär	Oberbotenmeister beim RKG
District Admin. (Intendantur) (HV + DARK GREEN / BRIGHT RED) [2]	–	–	–	–
Paymasters (Zahlmeister) (HV + DARK GREEN / WHITE)	Zahlmeister *	–	–	–
Mil. Admin. (Kriegsverwaltung) (EAGLE + DARK GREEN / LIGHT GREY) [4/5]	–	–	Kriegssekretär/ Kriegsverwaltungssekretär (6.4.40)	Kriegsassistent/Kriegsver-waltungsassistent (6.4.40) *
Field Post Office (Feldpost) (FP + DARK GREEN / LIGHT YELLOW) [8]		Feldoberpostsekretär/ Feldpostobersekretär (1942)	Feldpostsekretär *	Feldpostassistent [9]
Field Security Police (GFP) (GFP + DARK GREEN / LIGHT BLUE) [10]	–	Feldpolizeiobersekretär (4.6.43)/ Feldpolizeiinspektor (11.2.44) [13] *	Feldpolizeisekretär [13]	Feldpolizeiassistent [14]
Chaplains (Heeresgeistliche)	–	–	–	–

a thin brown strap or strapped to the bread bag. Zeiss 6 x 30 issue binoculars were carried on the chest, a signal whistle was secured to a breast-pocket button by a plaited lanyard, and a flashlight hung from a shoulder-strap button.

Other ranks' field uniform

Other ranks wore the service uniform, sometimes with anklets and lace-up ankle-boots, adding the steel helmet and omitting the service peaked cap, except for some NCOs who wore the M1934 'old style' peaked field cap.

Branch designation (branch symbol + branch colour / secondary branch colour) (*Sample insignia illustrated)	Basic career (*Beamten des einfachen Dienstes*). Thin silver braid collar patches.	
	Feldwebel	**Unterfeldwebel**
Court Martial (Reichskriegsgericht) (DARK GREEN / DARK RED) [1]	Reichskriegsgerichts-wachtmeister *	–
District Admin. (Intendantur) (HV + DARK GREEN / BRIGHT RED) [2]	–	–
Paymasters (Zahlmeister) (HV + DARK GREEN / WHITE)	–	–
Mil. Admin. (Kriegsverwaltung) (EAGLE + DARK GREEN / LIGHT GREY) [4/5]	Kriegsbetriebsassistent / Kriegs-verwaltungsbetriebsassistent	–
Field Post Office (Feldpost) (FP + DARK GREEN / LIGHT YELLOW) [8]	Feldpostbetriebsassistent [9]	Feldpostbote [9] *
Field Security Police (GFP) (GFP + DARK GREEN / LIGHT BLUE) [10]	–	–
Chaplains (Heeresgeistliche) (VIOLET) [15]	–	–

1 1.5.44 became the TSD Legal Service.
2 1.5.44 became the TSD Administrative Service.
3 Rank held by the commander of army military officials
4 Formed 22.12.39. Renamed Militärverwaltung 15.8.41.
5 All officers had light grey collar patches piped dark green.
6 Renamed Kriegsverwaltungsvizechef 6.4.40.
7 Gold-wire thick guard's braids on collar patch.
8 Light yellow thread on officer's shoulder boards.
9 Light yellow replaced aluminium thread on shoulder boards.
10 Light blue thread on officer's shoulder boards.
11 Held by commander of army and Luftwaffe field police.
12 Held by commander of army field police.
13 The GFP branch symbol should be aluminium, but gilded aluminium was often worn.
14 This rank existed briefly in 1940. Light blue replaced aluminium thread on shoulder boards. Army NCOs and men (usually military police) seconded as auxiliary field police wore the GFP branch symbol on their original uniform.
15 No shoulder boards worn. Rank indicated by collar patches.
16 Thick gold-wire guard's braids on collar patches.
17 Thick silver-wire guard's braids on collar patches.
18 No collar patches.

Technical and senior NCOs carried a pistol in a black holster and NCOs acting as infantry platoon leaders or section leaders wore the same equipment as subaltern platoon leaders, but wore the other ranks' M1939 black leather infantry support Y-straps.

Other NCOs and men wore the standard rifleman's equipment. The black waist belt carried the bayonet, folding shovel, bread bag, canteen and cup. The M1939 infantry support Y-straps and supplementary D-ring straps supported two sets of three black leather M1911 rifle ammunition pouches on the front. On the back it held the M1939 *feldgrau* canvas A-frame, carrying the M1931 dark matt grey (from 23 April 1941 greenish-brown) painted aluminium mess kit (pot and frying pan/lid); the M1931 camouflage shelter-quarter; the greenish-brown canvas battle pack bag, carrying iron rations, eating utensils and other miscellaneous items; and the gas cape strapped to the M1930 gas canister when not worn on the canister shoulder strap.

The equipment worn by the three-man section light machine-gun team is described in Volume 1 (Men-at-Arms 311).

The summer drill uniform

The M1935 field tunic and trousers proved uncomfortably hot for the stifling temperatures encountered from June to August 1941, and so in Summer 1941 many troops adopted as a summer field uniform the M1940 reed-green drill fatigue uniform. This consisted of the off-white cotton herringbone twill tunic, with five buttons and two patch hip pockets, and trousers introduced on 1 April 1933, and from 12 February 1940 manufactured in reed-green. Officers and NCOs added shoulder-strap rank insignia and all ranks wore the breast-eagle. Its popularity led to the manufacture of the M1942 reed-green drill tunic with the same cut as the M1935 field tunic, introduced in early 1942 but not common until summer 1943.

A rather haggard three-man section light machine-gun team pause during street-fighting, August 1942. They are all wearing M1940 reed-green drill uniform as a summer field uniform with breast-eagles and shoulder straps, M1935 helmets and M1939 short-shaft marching boots. The first gunner (first right), wearing his pistol, holster and spares pouch, carries his MG34 machine-gun over his shoulder. The second gunner (first left), whose helmet still bears the tricolour national shield decal ordered removed on 21 March 1940, carries a sheet-metal barrel protector with one or two spare barrels and an ammunition box. The third gunner, with standard rifleman's equipment and more ammunition boxes, waits behind. (Friedrich Herrmann)

Winter clothing

The only issue protective clothing available for the first Soviet winter, from November 1941 to March 1942, consisted of nine uniform items. These were the *feldgrau* tube-shaped woollen balaclava; extra-thick woollen underwear; the M1936 round-neck or V-neck grey-white woollen sweater, introduced 15 March 1936 and replaced by the M1942 high turtle-neck sweater; *feldgrau* woollen mittens; the *feldgrau* sentry's water repellent, ankle-length, six button double-breasted guard coat with reinforced leather shoulders, and felt overshoes; the vehicle crew's M1934 or M1940 *feldgrau* water-repellent surcoat, cut as for the M1935 greatcoat but ankle-length and wide enough to be worn over field equipment; three-fingered fur-lined mittens in *feldgrau* surcoat cloth; and the driver's and motorcyclist's greenish-brown calico fingerless overgloves.

This clothing, whilst sufficient for Central Europe, proved totally inadequate for the eastern front. Many troops improvised with German and Soviet civilian fur coats and captured Red Army fur caps and padded field uniforms, but on 19 April 1942 new white and *feldgrau* fully reversible padded winter overclothing had been approved and was issued from Autumn 1942. This was manufactured in three weights: light – three layers (one thin white cloth and two thick *feldgrau*); medium – four layers (one thin white cloth and two thick *feldgrau*, woollen lining); and heavy – three layers (one white and one *feldgrau* heavy cotton twill with quilted wadding middle layer). The thigh-length six-buttoned hooded winter tunic had two hip pockets, the only permitted insignia being coloured sleeve field signs. There were also reversible high trousers and mittens, but the reversible hood and face-mask and white-webbing snow boots proved unpopular and were often discarded.

Other issue winter clothing consisted of ankle-length sheepskin overcoats without insignia; various styles of white, brown or black sheepskin, rabbit and artificial fur caps with service cap insignia; plain brown quilted jacket and trousers worn over the field uniform and under the greatcoat; and leather reinforced felt calf-boots. Calf-length white cotton camouflage 'snow shirts', originally prescribed for mountain troops, were issued to all branches.

Rank and branch insignia

This is covered in more detail in Volume 1 (Men-at-Arms 311). General officers wore dress quality plaited braids on their shoulder boards with two gold bullion or 'celleon' cords and one bright aluminium cord on a bright red backing. A Generalfeldmarschall had silver crossed marshal's batons (and from 3 April 1941 three gold cords), other ranks 3-0 German silver or white aluminium plated pips, branch and (exceptionally) unit insignia. Field officers had two matt aluminium (later light grey) plaited braids on a branch colour backing and 2-0 gold coloured pips, branch and unit insignia: captains and subalterns had two flat braids.

Veterinary and farrier technical NCOs had distinctive plaited shoulder boards. Senior NCOs wore 3-1 aluminium pips, branch and unit insignia on bluish dark green or *feldgrau* shoulder straps piped in branch colour and edged with M1935 bright aluminium or M1940 mouse-grey artificial silk or cellulose-fibre wool braid, whilst the Hauptfeldwebel (or equivalent) wore two braid sleeve rings. Junior NCOs wore the same shoulder strap with no pips or with a plain base, with branch and unit insignia in branch-colour chain stitch. NCOs wore special cuff and collar insignia on the reed-green fatigue uniform until 22 August 1942.

Men wore shoulder straps without braid and braid chevrons and/or aluminium pips on a bluish dark green or *feldgrau* shaped patch. On 25 April 1942 an Obergefreiter of two years seniority not suitable for junior NCO rank could be promoted to Stabsgefreiter, designated 'new style' (neuer Art) to distinguish it from the 'old style' Stabsgefreiter (effectively abolished on 1 October 1934) and many, though not all, soldiers ranking as '*Obergefreiter mit mehr als 6 Dienstjahren*' were promoted to this new pay grade.

The rectangular gold and green on black rank insignia, introduced on 22 August 1942 for officers and NCOs for wear on white winter tunics, anoraks, shirts and drill tunics, will be described in Volume 4.

A German soldier's branch of service was indicated by a branch-colour facing cloth piping worn on the collar, shoulder board/shoulder straps and on caps and tunics. Sub-branches were indicated by branch insignia, consisting of a symbol or letter worn above the unit insignia – an arabic or latin numeral. From 1 September 1939 all troops in the Field Army on campaign (but not the Replacement Army in Germany) were ordered to remove or conceal their unit insignia, but branch insignia and colours were retained. On 16 May 1941 all officers in combat divisions were ordered to remove the branch insignia from their shoulder boards, but there is evidence that all ranks wore branch and even unit insignia in the field. Some divisions wore coloured shoulder strap loops to designate regiments and battalions, a practice expressly forbidden by the Army High Command.

Special black uniform and insignia for tank crews

Most personnel in Panzer regiments and many on divisional staffs wore the black uniform introduced 12 November 1934, consisting of the helmet or field cap, field jacket and trousers, dark grey shirt, black tie and black lace-up shoes or marching boots (the latter only retained by Armoured Engineer companies after 18 January 1941).

The black M1940 officer's black field cap (with aluminium thread cord crown and front flap piping) and M1940 other ranks' field cap both had the branch-colour chevron removed 10 July 1942. Officers and NCOs also favoured the *feldgrau* officer's M1935 peaked service cap, M1934 peaked field cap or M1938 field cap, or the other ranks' M1935 peaked service cap

A rocket-launcher crew prepare the 28/32cm Nebelwerfer 41 for firing, August 1942. Most of the soldiers are wearing the issue cotton one-piece overalls, unofficially adding rank chevrons. (Friedrich Herrmann)

ARMY GROUP NORTH: JUNE–NOVEMBER 1941

1: General der Infanterie, XXVI Armeekorps, Lithuania, June 1941.

2: Leutnant, Sturmgeschützabteilung 185, Lake Peipus, Eastern Estonia, August 1941.

3: Stabszahlmeister, 21. Infanterie-Division, Novgorod, North-Western Russia, October 1941.

3

1

2

ARMY GROUP CENTRE: JUNE–NOVEMBER 1941

1: Hauptwachtmeister, Panzer-Regiment 39, Smolensk, Western Russia, July 1941.

2: Obergefreiter, Infanterie-Regiment 464, Velikiye Luki, Western Russia, August 1941.

3: Kanonier, Nebelwerfer-Regiment 51, Smolensk, Western Russia, August 1941.

B

ARMY GROUP SOUTH: JUNE–NOVEMBER 1941
1: Leutnant, Infanterie-Regiment 230, Stalin Line, Western Ukraine, July 1941.
2: Oberschütze, Infanterie-Regiment 203, Tiraspol, Bessarabia, August 1941.
3: Hilfswilliger, 13 Panzer-Division, Rostov, Southern Russia, November 1941.

C

EASTERN FRONT: DECEMBER 1941–MARCH 1942.
1: Feldwebel, Infanterie-Division 270, Leningrad, Northern Front, December 1941.
2: Schütze, Infanterie-Regiment 413, Kalinin, Central Front, December 1941.
3: Schütze, Infanterie-Regiment 117, Donets Basin, Southern Front, January 1942.

3   1   2

D

ARMY GROUP NORTH: APRIL 1942–JANUARY 1943
1: Jäger, Gebirgsjäger-Regiment 141, Murmansk, Northern Russia, April 1942.
2: Obergefreiter, Pionier-Bataillon 123, Demyansk, Northern Russia, May 1942.
3: Feldunterveterinär, Veterinär-Kompanie 181, Staraya Russa, Northern Russia, September 1942.

E

1: Wachtmeister, Panzernachrichtenabteilung 92, Orel, Western Russia, August 1942.

2: Unteroffizier, Pionier-Bataillon 267, Spass-Demensk, Western Russia, September 1942.

3: Gefreiter, Infanterie-Regiment 235, Rzhev, Western Russia, September 1942.

SOUTHERN FRONT: APRIL–AUGUST 1942
1: Unteroffizier, Panzergrenadier-Regiment 108, Kalmuck Steppes,
   North-Eastern Caucasus, August 1942.
2: Dolmetscher (Z), Georgische Infanterie-Bataillon 796, Maikop,
   North-Western Caucasus, September 1942.
3: Zugführer, Georgische Infanterie-Bataillon 796, Maikop, North-Western
   Caucasus, September 1942.

2

3

1

BATTLE OF STALINGRAD: AUGUST 1942–FEBRUARY 1943

1: Gefreiter, Grenadier-Regiment 544, December 1942.
2: Generaloberst Friedrich Paulus, 6. Armee, January 1943.
3: Panzergrenadier, Panzergrenadier-Regiment 79, January 1943.

1

2

3

H

Occasionally the 28cm, heavy, high-explosive rocket shells, each weighing more than 80kg, had to be manhandled, and muscular 'farm boys' such as this soldier were needed. He is wearing the issue cotton one-piece coveralls in *feldgrau* with a breast pocket and a thigh pocket over his field uniform but unusually has not added any insignia. August 1942. (Friedrich Herrmann)

or M1934 field cap. A black wool version of the M1942 other ranks' field cap saw limited issue.

The M1934 black wool double-breasted field jacket had a wide collar with pink branch-colour piping and four large buttons. The M1936 jacket added three small buttons and three corresponding lapel buttonholes. In late 1942 the collar was narrowed and the piping abolished. All ranks wore the black rectangular collar patch piped in pink branch colour with aluminium skull recalling the tank units of the Great War.

24th Panzer Division Staff, formed 28 November 1941 from 1st Cavalry Division, and its Panzer Regiment and Armoured Reconnaissance Battalion, retained the golden yellow cavalry branch colour. Panzer division anti-tank battalions and probably armoured train platoon crews (30 October 1941–26 June 1942) wore the pink branch colour; the Führer Escort Battalion Tank Company and Armoured-Car Platoon, white (from 1 April 1941); Armoured Reconnaissance Battalion staffs and Armoured-Car Company crews golden yellow; Armoured Engineer companies, white and black; and Armoured Signals battalions lemon yellow.

From 1941 armoured-vehicle crews and mechanics, and armoured artillery and rocket-launcher crews were issued cotton one-piece overalls in mouse-grey, *feldgrau*, off-white, light brown and reed-green (sometimes dyed black by Panzer crews). Troops usually added shoulder strap and sleeve rank insignia and a breast-eagle – the order of 22 August 1942 requiring the new sleeve rank insignia for all ranks was widely ignored. Overalls commandeered from Germany's defeated enemies between 1939 and 1941, and captured items of British and Soviet clothing were also worn.

On 5 May 1941 crews of Armoured Reconnaissance Battalion armoured-car companies were issued special clothing as a fatigue and summer field uniform in reed-green cotton herringbone twill or white or mouse-grey cotton designed to be worn over the black uniform, and this soon replaced the unpopular overalls. It consisted of a jacket, cut like the M1936 black jacket but with seven small buttons and one internal breast pocket, with black uniform collar patches and shoulder straps (in theory replaced on 22 August 1942 by sleeve rank insignia) the breast-eagle on a uniform-colour backing, and no collar piping. The trousers were cut like the M1934 black trousers. This popular uniform was officially extended to all crews wearing the black uniform in 1942.

Special field-grey uniform and insignia

On 29 May 1940 a special *feldgrau* version of the black Panzer field uniform was authorised for crews of the self-propelled guns of assault-artillery battalions, extended on 26 June 1942 to all battalion personnel. Headgear consisted of the officer's M1938 field cap, other ranks' M1934 or M1942 field cap, or steel helmet (the M1941 *feldgrau* padded beret was withdrawn 15 January 1941). The field jacket was cut like the M1936 black jacket and officially without branch-colour collar piping, the trousers like the M1934 black trousers, and the Panzer grey shirt, black tie and black lace-up boots were worn.

Normally Panzer-style *feldgrau* rectangular patches piped in bright red facing cloth with a bright aluminium stamped Panzer skull were worn, but in 1942 Panzer troops objected to assault artillery units wearing the traditional Panzer skull. Initially the assault artillery troops simply removed the skull, but on 30 January 1943 other ranks were ordered to wear M1940 mouse-grey standard guard's braids on a *feldgrau* backing sewn onto the rectangular collar patches piped in the bright red branch colour, whilst officers reverted to their M1935 matt aluminium guard's braids collar patches with bright red branch-colour centre cords on bluish dark green patches. Rank insignia and breast-eagles were as for the infantry field tunic.

A detail of three soldiers are carrying food, distributed by the company field kitchen, universally nicknamed the *Gulaschkanone* ('gulash cannon'), back to their section in battered M1931 mess kits and canteens during Army Group B's ill-fated advance to the Volga in August 1942. The men wear M1935 steel helmets and M1940 field tunic and trousers. The Schütze in the centre wears the matt aluminium braid NCO Candidate loop on his shoulder straps, a MP38/40 ammunition pouch for a submachine-gun in his belt, and an unofficial scarf against the dust. (Brian Davis)

The practical and stylish special field-grey uniform was soon extended rather haphazardly to units in Panzer divisions not entitled to, or with some personnel already wearing, the black Panzer uniform. These units wore the M1940/M1943 collar patches described above, with the appropriate branch colour. In 1941 some armoured engineer vehicle crews adopted this uniform with the black branch colour superseding the M1940 black and white. From 1942 self-propelled anti-tank units wore it with pink branch colour, whilst some units in Panzer divisions wore it with black Panzer collar patches piped pink. From 26 June 1942 Armoured Train Platoon crews wore it with pink branch colour, and from late 1942 some self-propelled armoured artillery units with bright red.

Troops entitled to the special field-grey uniform also wore the reed-green fatigue and summer field uniform with appropriate branch insignia.

Special uniforms and insignia for other branches

General staff officers wore dark bluish green collar patches with two matt aluminium *Kolben* pattern guard's braids and general officer's trouser and breeches pipings and braids in crimson branch-colour facing cloth. Officers attached to the OKW and OKH wore gold *Kolben* braids and crimson stripes until 16 November 1942, when they were ordered to wear the uniform of their original branch.

Two Terek or Kuban Cossacks from a mounted reconnaissance company (Sotnia) attached to a German Panzer division, wearing the traditional low-crowned black fur *Kubanka* caps with a red (Terek) or blue (Kuban) crown and unofficial German Panzer collar-patch skulls, carry a wounded Don Cossack, wearing a high-crowned black fur *Papacha* fur cap with a German officer's breast-eagle as a cap badge, to a German field dressing station, in July 1942. The Cossack (first right) wears a German M1940 field tunic with the shoulder straps removed, his comrade (first left) a M1929 Red Army khaki *gymnastiorka* tunic, breeches and riding boots, with a Karabiner 98k rifle slung over his right shoulder and his traditional Cossack *shashqa* sword hanging from a shoulder belt over his left. The wounded man also wears an M1929 *gymnastiorka* with a German other ranks' black belt. (Author's collection – see also Men-at-Arms 131, *Germany's Eastern Front Allies*)

A carefully posed photograph of a Feldwebel platoon leader of mechanised infantry in September 1942, wearing a M1935 helmet showing the Wehrmacht eagle decal abolished 28 August 1943, a M1940 other ranks' field tunic with M1940 *feldgrau* guard's braids collar patches and mouse-grey NCO collar and shoulder strap braid. He carries his platoon leader's map case, 6 x 30 binoculars and MP38 submachine-gun. He has the Iron Cross 2nd Class button ribbon, 1st Class pin-back medal, bronze Wound badge for one or two wounds and the bronze Tank Combat badge, awarded from 1 June 1940 to tank-associated units. (ECPA)

The élite mountain troops, largely recruited from Austria, wore a white aluminium *edelweiss* with gilt stamens above the cockade of the peaked service cap. They wore infantry field uniform with, from 2 May 1939, a bluish dark green (from May 1940 *feldgrau*) oval badge depicting a machine-woven white *edelweiss* with yellow stamens and light green stem and leaves within a mouse-grey rope on the right upper sleeve of tunics and greatcoats. Mountain troops also wore M1935 stone-grey or M1939 *feldgrau* ski trousers with *feldgrau* ankle-puttees and brown or black climbing-boots, the M1925 greenish-khaki wind-jacket, M1938 reversible anorak and M1931 canvas rucksack.

The mountain troops' M1936 peaked mountain cap, introduced 11 February 1936, had on the left side (from 2 May 1939 but not actually issued until October 1939) a white aluminium *edelweiss*, stem and leaves with gilt stamens (later grey and yellow): Austrian personnel often added a bluish dark green backing. The 1st Pattern eagle and cockade cap badge (15 March 1935) was in white aluminium; the 2nd Pattern (11 February 1936) in white embroidery on a stone-grey T; the 3rd Pattern (19 June 1937) on a bluish dark green cloth T; and the 4th Pattern (5 February 1939) mouse-grey insignia on a *feldgrau* cloth T. Officers adopted aluminium (general officers gold) crown and front flap pipings on 3 October 1942.

The Rifle (Jäger) divisions and independent rifle battalions, formed from 2 October 1942 as lightly equipped mobile units for combat in hilly terrain, wore mountain troops' uniforms with three bright or grey aluminium oak leaves on the left side of the mountain cap, and a machine-embroidered or a machine-woven bluish dark green or *feldgrau*

The days of easy German victories are now over. A rifle section in field uniform with full rifleman's equipment, stands round the grave of a dead Unteroffizier, possibly the former section leader, the cross decorated with an Iron Cross, his name, and the defiant dedication '*gefallen für Großdeutschland*' ('fallen for Greater Germany'). August 1942. (Friedrich Herrmann)

A Ukrainian ex-Red Army soldier employed as an auxiliary (*Hilfswilliger*) in a German division, September 1942. He wears a German other ranks' M1935 field cap without insignia or branch-colour chevron, the M1940 field tunic, still with the original collar patches showing M1940 *feldgrau* guard's braids, but with the shoulder straps removed. His status is indicated by the home-made white armband with non-standard black '*Im Dienst der deutschen Wehrmacht*' lettering. Against Hitler's instructions he has been issued a rifle for sentry duty. Relatively few Ukrainians joined the Osttruppen, most being directed to auxiliary Schutzmannschaften battalions under the German police. (Brian Davis)

oval sleeve badge with a green, grey or white rope edging and three light green oak leaves.

The Großdeutschland Motorised Regiment, from 12 March 1942 a motorised division, wore the GD shoulder board/strap monogram (introduced 20 June 1939) and, from 7 October 1940, the 3rd Pattern black right cuff title with a hand- or machine-embroidered aluminium thread cursive Großdeutschland cuff title and edging. 1st and 2nd Infantry regiments (renamed 1 October 1942 respectively 'Grenadier' and 'Fusilier' Regiment) wore a one or two below the shoulder strap monogram. The Divisional Anti-Aircraft Battalion wore on the right upper sleeve a bluish dark green facing cloth oval with a woven bright red winged shell. From 7 October 1940 Großdeutschland personnel forming the Führer Escort Battalion wore a golden yellow (or silver-grey thread) machine-embroidered, machine-woven or hand-embroidered gothic script '*Führer-Hauptquartier*' and edging on a black wool title on the left cuff.

271st Infantry Regiment personnel, partly formed from volunteers from the SA (Storm Troops) Guard Regiment Feldherrnhalle, wore from 9 August 1942 a woven brown title on the left cuff with an aluminium or mouse-grey cursive Feldherrnhalle and edging. Sonderverband 287 personnel probably continued to wear the Orientkorps oval arm-shield issued in 1942 in North Africa.

From 6 January 1942 until 10 January 1944 technical troops wore a bluish dark green facing colour oval with a mouse-grey woven (bright aluminium for officers) TN monogram on a cogwheel within an oak wreath on the right upper sleeve.

Uniforms and insignia of Sonderführer

On mobilisation (26 August 1939) NCOs and men with specialised technical and linguistic skills but without the necessary military training could be promoted to NCO and officer supervisory positions as 'specialist officers' (Sonderführer). They wore the uniform of their original branch with special rank insignia (see Table 1). Field officers had bright or matt aluminium plaited, captains and subalterns flat, thin thread shoulder boards with gold artificial silk 'slides', whilst NCOs had bluish dark green flat thread shoulder boards with bright aluminium thread 'slides'. 'Group O' personnel wore the Hauptfeldwebel cuff braids and medical and veterinary shoulder board and cuff speciality insignia.

In order to distinguish them more clearly from qualified officers and to encourage them to complete officer training, Sonderführer officer were required to wear on 21 March 1940 new shoulder boards with red-white-black threads with white aluminium rank pips on a grey-blue facing cloth backing. The grey-blue collar patches had a matt aluminium wire hand-embroidered pentangular *altpreußisch* braid on a grey-blue collar which was never manufactured, necessitating the use of Luftwaffe grey-blue cloth from 11 July 1941. The M1935 service cap band and breast-eagle backing was grey-blue, as were the service cap pipings and M1938 field cap inverted chevron. On 7 December 1942 Sonderführer officers reverted to the M1939 rank insignia and a new aluminium wire chin cord with grey-blue threads introduced. NCO uniforms and insignia were unchanged with the addition of aluminium NCO collar braid on 21 March 1940.

Uniforms and insignia of army officials

The German army entrusted administrative duties, which in most armies would be carried out by service personnel, to 'Officials' (Beamte), state civil servants employed by the army with limited authority over service personnel. Officials were recruited into four careers according to their educational qualifications: Senior – post-16 and university education; Advanced and Intermediate – former Senior NCOs with two years' training at service colleges; and Basic – former junior NCOs and men with minimal training.

There were about 80 branches, but Table 2 lists the seven branches whose members usually operated with the field army on campaign, and although these officials were anxious to preserve their privileged civil service status, they were increasingly militarised and Court Martial officials (lawyers), District Administration (accountants) and Paymaster officials (unit paymasters) were in May 1944 reorganised into the 'Special Troop Service' (Truppensonderdienst). Military Administration officials operated in occupied territories: the Field Post Office ran Divisional Mail offices; the Field Security Police carried out field security and counter-espionage duties in occupied territories; and Protestant and Catholic chaplains were attached to divisional staffs.

Officials wore army service, walking-out and field uniforms. The M1935 service cap and M1934 'old style' field cap pipings (crown and lower cap band pipings gold for general officer equivalents) and (since 24 October 1939) M1938 officer's and M1935 other ranks' field cap inverted chevrons (removed 10 July 1942) were in dark green facing colour. General officer equivalents wore dark green general's trouser stripes and greatcoat lapel linings. Later in the war officials unofficially wore élite unit cuff titles and black or field-grey special uniforms. The chaplains' uniform will be covered in Volume 5.

Field tunic collar patches were bluish dark green with branch-colour piping on the top, bottom and back. General officer equivalents had a bright gold bullion or yellowish-gold 'celleon' hand-embroidered thread two-leaf *Alt-Larisch* design; Senior Career officials had two matt gold wire *Kolben* pattern guard's braids; Advanced Career officials had two hand-embroidered matt aluminium guard's braids with dark green silk-embroidered centre cords; Intermediate Career officer equivalents were as for Advanced Career, then from 10 April 1940 two thin hand-embroidered matt aluminium guard's braids; and Intermediate and Basic Career Senior NCO equivalents had two thin *feldgrau* guard's braids with bluish dark green (from 9 May 1940 mouse-grey) centre stripes and dividing stripe and no NCO collar braids.

Shoulder boards usually had the HV monogram (Heeresverwaltung, or Army Administration) and rank pips in gilded aluminium (white for general officer and NCO equivalents), a branch-colour inner and dark green outer underlay. General officer equivalents had general's shoulder boards with dark green silk threads in the silver centre cord; other officer equivalents had a dark green cord dividing the bright or matt aluminium shoulder cords; Senior NCO equivalents had shoulder cords similar to technical NCOs, with two dark green wool cords separated by a bright aluminium thread cord.

Personnel with specialised skills but without the necessary educational qualifications could become War-Substantive officials

A fine study of a mechanised infantry Leutnant issuing instructions with his signal-whistle, attached to his right breast pocket button by a red plaited lanyard. He wears a M1940 other ranks' field tunic with a bluish dark green collar and M1936 officer's matt aluminium braid collar patches with grass-green branch-colour centre cords and officer's M1935 matt aluminium thread breast-eagle on a bluish dark green facing cloth backing. He wears grey leather gloves, a captured Red Army M1940 fur cap, other ranks' black belt and a P08 Luger in a black hardshell holster, and the Knight's Cross neck decoration. (Author's collection)

The positional rank titles are shown in Russian (the working language within the legions) transliterated from Russian Cyrillic, and German (the language of command). All ranks wore red (from 17.11.42 dark bluish-green piped in legion colour) collar patches with bright aluminium braid and pips. Officers had thin bright aluminium Sonderführer shoulder boards with gold braid knots (later sometimes unofficially gold-coloured aluminium German officer's pips). Other ranks had dark bluish-green facing colour (later grey-green uniform colour)

shoulder straps piped in red (from 27.11.42 in legion colour) with bright aluminium braid bars and (from 1.1.44) pips. On 29.5.43 conventional Russian rank titles were introduced. From 18.3.44 qualified personnel could wear German collar insignia and shoulder rank insignia but virtually no troops were considered suitable. The German cadre wore German uniforms and insignia with the legion arm badge.

Komandir batal'ona [1] Bataillonsführer (Hauptmann)	Komandir roty Kompanieführer (Oberleutnant)	Pomoshchnik komandir roty [2] Stellvertretender Kompanieführer (Leutnant)	Komandir vzvoda [3] Zugführer (Oberfeldwebel)	Pomoshchnik komandir vzvoda [4] Stellvertretender Zugführer (Feldwebel)
Mayor (Major)	Kapitan (Hauptmann)	Poruchik (Oberleutnant)	Podporuchik (Leutnant)	Fel'dfebel' [4/5] (Feldwebel)
Aluminium collar edging, with 1 bar and 2 pips. Aluminium shoulder board with 2 knots.	Aluminium collar edging with 2 pips. Aluminium shoulder board with 1 knot.	Aluminium collar edging with 1 pip. Aluminium shoulder board.	Aluminium collar edging. Shoulder strap with 2 bars.	Aluminium V collar edging with 2 bars. Shoulder strap with 3 bars.
Komandir otdeleniya [4] Gruppenführer (Unteroffizier)	–	Pomoshchnik komandir otdeleniya Stellvertretender Gruppenführer (Gefreiter)	–	Legioner Legionär (Soldat)
Unter-ofitser [4] (Unteroffizier)	Ober-Yefreytor [6] (Obergefreiter)	Yefreytor (Gefreiter)	Ober-Legioner [6] (Oberlegionär)	Legioner (Legionär)
Aluminium V collar edging with 1 bar. Shoulder strap with 2 bars.	Aluminium V collar edging. Shoulder strap with 1 bar and 1 pip.	Aluminium V collar edging. Shoulder strap with 1 bar.	Plain collar patch. Shoulder strap with 1 pip.	Plain collar patch and shoulder strap.

1 This rank was never held.
2 Rank first mentioned 2.6.42.
3 Originally an NCO rank this became an officer rank 29.5.43.
4 NCOs holding the appointment of Khaupt-Fel'dfebel' (Hauptfeldwebel) wore two aluminium braid sleeve rings.
5 The rank of Ober-Fel'dfebel' (Oberfeldwebel) was introduced 15.6.44: rank insignia unknown but probably identical to German Oberfeldwebel.
6 Introduced 1.1.44.

(Beamte auf Kriegsdauer), wearing insignia very similar to their army Sonderführer equivalents.

Uniforms and insignia of European volunteers

European volunteers wore German uniforms and insignia and a black machine-woven arm shield, with name of the country of origin above the national flag, also a decal depicting the flag on the right side of the steel helmet.

From 9 July 1941 Spanish troops wore a yellow 'ESPAÑA' and a red-yellow-red horizontally striped flag arm shield on the right upper sleeve and a helmet shield, whilst Falange militiamen retained their blue shirt. Croatian troops wore the greenish-grey M1941 Croatian field tunic with German collar patches and rank insignia and a red 'HRVATSKA' above a red–white chequerboard flag arm shield on the right (for many officers on the left) upper sleeve, helmet shield, German greatcoats, and the Croatian army peaked field cap and service cap and cap badges.

French volunteers wore a white 'FRANCE' and a blue-white-red horizontally striped flag shield on the right upper sleeve and a helmet shield. Walloon troops wore from 29 August 1941 a yellow 'WALLONIE' above a black-yellow-red vertically striped flag shield on the left upper sleeve, from March 1942 also a helmet shield and from May 1942 wore a mountain field cap, *edelweiss* cap and right upper sleeve badges and light green branch colour.

Uniforms and insignia of Osttruppen

Initially Hiwis wore Red Army uniforms with the insignia removed and from 1 October 1941 the '*Im Dienst der deutschen Wehrmacht*' ('Under German armed forces command') armband. German other ranks' field uniforms without cap badges, collar patches, shoulder straps or breast-eagles were officially sanctioned on 29 April 1943 but were almost certainly issued unofficially before that date.

It is unlikely that Osttruppen units, first organised in October 1941, could have functioned effectively without proper insignia, and therefore it can be assumed that the German orders issued in August 1942 and 29 May 1943 confirmed practice dating back to late 1941 and January 1943 respectively. It should also be noted that German Cadres retained their original uniforms with Osttruppen arm shields, whilst native officers and other ranks wore German other ranks' uniforms.

From April 1942 the Eastern legions wore German breast-eagles and the collar patch and shoulder board/strap rank insignia shown in Table 3. From September 1942 each legion was indicated by a Tsarist Russian-style two or three ringed coloured oval cap cockade (scalloped outer edge for officers); collar patch and shoulder strap piping, and a shield on the right upper sleeve (illustrated in Volume 5).

Infantry huddle in a trench awaiting the signal to attack, September 1942. Clearly visible are the M1931 mess tin and M1931 camouflage shelter-quarter strapped to the Y-straps, M1930 gas mask canisters and M1931 canteen and cup. The Oberfeldwebel in the foreground is carrying field equipment in a wartime version of the M1931 water-repellent greenish-brown canvas rucksack normally issued to mountain troops. (Friedrich Herrmann)

Two infantrymen wait in a slit-trench reinforced with wooden logs, on the Volkhov front, May 1942. Both soldiers wear the M1935 steel helmet with rubber camouflage band and the M1940 field tunic and *feldgrau* **trousers, and the M1939 short-shaft marching boots. The bespectacled Schütze in the foreground carries his rolled-up camouflage shelter-quarter on an improvised strap over his right shoulder and holds a folding entrenching tool in his left hand, whilst the Obergefreiter in the background, wearily awaiting a Soviet attack, is wearing the bronze Crimea Campaign shield and the M1939 Infantry Assault badge, awarded for at least three infantry assaults on separate days. (Brian Davis)**

Armenian Legion – Golden yellow (inner)/dark blue/red (outer) cockade and striped shield, golden yellow piping.

Azerbaijan Legion – green/red/blue cockade and striped shield, green piping.

Georgian Legion – black/white/red cockade and striped shield, red piping.

North Caucasian Legion – white/orange/ cockade, brown piping, blue shield/white device, 1943 red/green shield/white device.

Turkestan Legion – red/blue cockade, light blue piping, white and dark green oval shield, 1943–4 red/blue shield/white device.

Volga–Tartar Legion – blue green cockade and piping, blue/green shield white device (later modified), finally blue oval/yellow device.

In Autumn 1941 Estonian units wore M1936 Estonian army uniforms and insignia; from about April 1942 German uniforms with eastern legion collar rank insignia and rank titles; and from about May 1942 German infantry uniforms, cap badges, collar patches, breast-eagles and rank insignia. From about April 1942 other security and eastern battalions wore eastern legion collar and shoulder rank insignia, from 15 November 1942 a bluish dark green oval cap badge with a horizontal red bar and the 'Eastern' breast-eagle (mouse-grey machine-embroidered swastika on mouse-grey and *feldgrau* horizontal wings). In January 1943 ROA cap badges, collar patches, Tsarist-style shoulder rank insignia and arm shield were introduced (see Volume 4).

Cossack units, especially cavalry, often retained their traditional uniforms, often with Tsarist shoulder board rank insignia, but in about April 1942 Eastern Legion collar patch and shoulder board/red piped strap rank insignia and rank titles were introduced for those wearing German uniforms. The 15 November 1942 order introduced a bluish dark green oval cap badge with a horizontal red bar over white crossed lances, Eastern breast-eagle, white crossed lances on red collar patches edged bluish dark green (officers – bright aluminium German NCO braid) and arm shields indicated the Cossack territorial affiliation: Don, yellow/blue/red horizontally striped; Terek, black/green/red horizontally striped; and Kuban Cossacks, yellow/green diagonally quartered. NCOs (Zugführer–Gruppenführer) wore German NCO collar braid. In January 1943 ROA rank insignia was introduced.

Medals and awards

The principal medal for bravery and leadership in the front line remained the Iron Cross in two classes – 2nd Class and 1st Class – followed by five classes of 'Knight's Cross of the Iron Cross', usually given to officers: basic, with oak leaves; with oak leaves and swords (21 June 1941); with oak leaves, swords and diamonds (15 July 1941); and the Grand Cross – a courtesy award given to Reichsmarschall Hermann Goering on 19 July 1940. On 28 September 1941 the German Cross in gold was instituted to rank between the Iron Cross 1st Class and the

The Germans designated the nationalities of the Eastern Legions as Moslem 'Turkish peoples', but the Armenians and Georgians comprised ancient Christian communities. Hasmik Nasarian, a corporal (Gruppenführer) in the Armenian Legion, is wearing the M1942 field cap with the distinctive two-buttoned ear flap with (against regulations) an officer's golden-yellow/dark blue/red legion cockade with scalloped outer edge. He has an other ranks' M1935 field tunic with bluish dark green collar and bright aluminium NCO braid stitched to a red Security Battalion collar patch, altered 17 November 1942 to a dark bluish-green patch piped in the golden-yellow legion colour. The M1940 *feldgrau* shoulder straps are piped in golden-yellow. (Author's collection)

Although the Sonderverband Bergmann was primarily composed of Caucasians, all ranks wore German mountain troops' uniforms (omitting the *edelweiss* cap and arm badges) with normal German insignia. Leutnant Tataschvili, a Georgian officer, wears the M1936 mountain cap with the black and silver Caucasian *kindjal* dagger worn by all ranks, and an ill-fitting other ranks' M1935 field tunic with bluish dark green collar and M1938 other ranks' 'standard' bluish dark green collar patches with two *feldgrau* guard's braids with bluish dark green centre stripes. He wears German shoulder boards, probably with a light green mountain troops' underlay, and carries 6 x 30 platoon leader's binoculars. (Author's collection)

Knight's Cross. The War Merit Cross was instituted on 18 October 1939 with or without swords for bravery or leadership away from the front line, greater merit earning from 19 August 1940 the Knight's Cross of the War Merit Cross, with or without swords, worn on the collar.

From 18 July 1941 the army Anti-Aircraft badge, a grey aluminium Wehrmacht eagle, 88mm Flak 18 anti-aircraft gun and wreath badge worn on the left breast pocket, was awarded for service in army anti-aircraft or searchlight batteries.

Troops who had fought for 14 days in the Soviet Union between 15 November 1941 and 15 April 1942 were awarded the silver and black 'Eastern Winter Campaign 1941–2' medal, nicknamed the 'frozen meat order'. The 'Driver's Service' badge, a steering-wheel in a laurel wreath in bronze, silver or gold and worn on the left cuff, was instituted on 23 October 1942 to dispatch-riders or motor-vehicle drivers (including Hiwis) who had served in the field since 1 December 1940.

Two new grey metal campaign shields, worn on the upper left arm, were instituted during this period, although it is doubtful if any were worn in the field before February 1943. On 1 July 1942 the white metal 'Kholm Shield', depicting a Wehrmacht eagle clutching an Iron Cross, was awarded to troops who had served in the Kholm pocket in Northern Russia from 21 January to 5 May 1942. The bronze 'Crimea Shield' featuring an eagle over the Crimean peninsula and worn on a uniform-coloured cloth backing, was instituted on 25 July 1942 for troops serving there for three months between 21 September 1941 and 4 July 1942.

The 'Special badge for single-handed destruction of a tank' was instituted on 9 March 1942 and made retrospective to cover all such actions by troops other than anti-tank units using small-arms since 22 June 1941. It took the form of a black Soviet T-34 tank on a silver cord rectangle with upper and lower black edging worn on the right upper sleeve, and a gold cord badge as awarded for five tanks destroyed.

On 14 July 1942 the 'Eastern Medal' was instituted for Osttruppen and their German cadres and featured a stylised shining sun, awarded for good service, with crossed swords added for bravery. The 1st Class in gold or silver was worn on the left breast pocket, the 2nd Class hung from a ribbon: green and red for the gold award; green and white for silver; plain green for bronze. Osttruppen were also eligible for German decorations.

Units	Branch colour	Shoulder strap insignia			Other distinctions
		Northern front	Central front	Southern front	
Combat Troops – Staff (Kommandobehörde)					
General Officers (Generale)	Bright red	None	None	None	*Larisch* patches
General Staff (Generalstab) officers	Crimson	None	None	None	Silver *Kolben* patches
5 Army Group (Heeresgruppe) Staffs	White	G (Nord)	G (Mitte)	G (Süd/B, A, Don)	–
9 Army (Armee) Staffs	White	A / 11, 16, 18, (Lappland)	A / 2, 4, 9	A / 2, 6, 11, 17	–
1 Mountain Army (Gebirgsarmee) Staff	Light green	A / 20	–	–	*Edelweiss* badges
4 Armoured Group (Panzergruppe) Staffs	Pink	? (4)	? (2, 3, 4)	? (1)	–
4 Armoured Army (Panzerarmee) Staffs	Pink	–	A / 2, 3, 4	A / 1, 4	–
33 Corps (Korps) Staffs (* Corps had Latin numbers)	White	1, 2, 10, 23, 26, 28, 30, 38, 42, 50, 54	5–9, 12–3, 20, 23, 27, 30, 34–5, 43, 50, 53, 59	4, 7–8, 11, 13, 17, 29, 30, 42, 44, 51–2, 54–5	–
5 Mountain Corps (Gebirgskorps) Staff *	Light green	18–9, 36 (Norwegen)	–	49	*Edelweiss* badges
12 Motorised Corps (Korps (mot.)) Staffs *	White	39, 41, 56	24, 27, 39, 40–1, 46–8, 56–7	3, 14, 48	–
11 Armoured Corps (Panzerkorps) Staffs *	Pink	–	39, 41, 46–7, 56	3, 14, 24, 40, 48, 57	–
2 Reserve (Reserve) Corps Staffs *	White	61	–	62	–
Combat Troops – Infantry (Infanterie)					
147 Infantry (Infanterie) Division Staffs	White	1, 5, 7, 11–2, 17, 21, 23–4, 28, 30, 32, 58, 61, 67, 69, 81, 83, 93, 96, 121–3, 126, 131–2, 163, 169–170, 206, 212, 215–8, 223, 225, 227, 229, 251, 253–4, 269, 285, 290–1, 329, 385	5–8, 15, 17, 23, 26, 28, 31, 34–5, 45, 52, 56, 72, 78, 83, 86–8, 95, 98, 102, 106, 110, 112,129, 131, 134, 137, 161–3, 167, 181, 183, 197, 205–6, 208, 211, 216, 221, 246, 251–3, 255–6, 258, 260, 262–3, 267–8, 286, 292–3, 296, 299, 328, 330–1, 337, 339, 342, 385, 707	5, 9, 22, 24, 28, 44–6, 50, 56–7, 60, 62, 68, 71–3, 75–6, 79, 82, 88, 94–5, 98–9, 111, 113, 125, 132, 164, 168, 170, 196, 198, 213, 221, 239, 257, 262, 294–9, 305, 323, 335–6, 340, 370–1, 376–7, 383–5, 387, 389	–
440 Line Infantry (Infanterie) Regts	White	1–539 series	14–747 series	14–546 series	–
440 Line Infantry (Grenadier) Regts	White	1–539 series	14–747 series	14–546 series	–
7 Line Infantry (Füsilier) Regts	White	22, 26–7	34, 39	202, 230	–
8 Motorised (Inf.(mot.)) Division Staffs	White	3, 18, 20, 36	3, 10, 14, 16, 18, 20, 25, 29, 36	3, 16, 25, 29	–
20 Motorised (Infanterie (mot.)) Regts – from 15.10.42 (Grenadier (mot.))	White	8, 29, 30, 51, 69, 76, 87, 90, 118	8, 11, 15, 20, 29, 30, 35, 41, 51, 53, 60, 69, 71, 76, 86–7, 90, 118–9, 156	8, 15, 29, 35, 60, 71, 119, 156	–
1 Motorised (Inf.(mot.)) Division GD	White	–	GD	GD	Großdeutschland title
2 Motorised Regts Großdeutschland	White	–	GD/GD1, GD2	GD1, GD2	Großdeutschland title
4 Light Infantry (leichte Infanterie) Div.	Light green	8	–	97, 100–1	
8 Light Infantry (leichte Infanterie) Regts	Light green	28, 38	–	54, 204, 207, 227–9	

Units	Branch colour	Shoulder strap insignia			Other distinctions
		Northern front	Central front	Southern front	
7 Rifle (Jäger) Div. Staffs	Light green	5, 8, 28,	–	28, 97, 100–1,	Jäger badges
14 Rifle (Jäger) Regts	Light green	28, 38, 49, 56, 75, 83	–	49, 54, 83, 204, 208, 227–9	Jäger badges
7 Mountain (Gebirgs) Division Staffs	Light green	2–3, 5–7	–	1, 4	*Edelweiss* badges
15 Mountain (Gebirgs) Regts	Light green	85, 100, 136–9, 141, 143–4, 206, 218	–	13, 91, 98–9	*Edelweiss* badges
4 Reserve (Reserve) Division Staffs	White	141, 151	–	143, 153	–
11 Reserve Inf. (Reserve Grenadier) Regts	White	1, 2, 61, 206, 217	–	23, 68, 76, 208, 218, 257	–
5 Training (Feldausbildungs) Div. Staffs	White	388	390–1	381–2	–
16 Training (Feldausbildungs) Regts	White	639, 640	635–7, 718–20	381, 614–20	–
1 Special Unit (Sonderverband)	Light green	–	–	Bergmann	*Kindjal* cap badge
Combat Troops – Mobile Troops (Schnelle Truppen)					
1 Cavalry (Kavallerie) Division Staff	Gold–yellow	–	1	–	–
3 Mounted Cavalry (Reiter) Regts	Gold–yellow	–	1, 2, 22	–	Cavalry breeches/boots
1 Armoured (Panzer) Division Staff	Gold–yellow	–	–	24	Black Panzer uniform
1 Armoured (Panzer) Regt.	Gold–yellow	–	–	24	Black Panzer uniform
22 Armoured (Panzer) Division Staffs	Pink	1, 6, 8, 12	1–7, 9–12, 17–20	3, 9, 11, 13–4, 16–7, 22–3, 27	Black Panzer uniform
22 Armoured (Panzer) Regts	Pink	1, 10–1, 29	1, 3, 6–7, 11, 15, 18, 21, 25, 27, 29, 31, 33, 35, 39	2, 4, 6, 15, 33, 36, 39, 127, 201, 204	Black Panzer uniform
19 Motorcycle Recce (Kradschützen) Bns	Brown	1, 6, 8, 22	1–3, 6–7, 17–9, 20, 22, 34, 59, 61	3, 16–7, 23–4, 43, 59, 61, 64, GD	–
21 Armd Recce (Panzeraufklärung) Bns	Pink	1, 12, 57, 59	1–7, 9–12, 17–19	3, 9, 11, 13–4, 16–7, 23–4	Black Panzer uniform
44 Motor Rifle (Schützen) Regts	Grass green	1, 4, 5, 8, 25, 28, 113–4	1–7, 10–4, 25, 33, 40, 52, 59, 63, 69, 73–4, 86,1 01, 110–4, 304, 394	3, 10–1, 21, 26, 40, 63–4, 66, 79, 93, 103, 108, 110–1, 126, 128–9, 140, 394	–
41 Mechanised (Panzergrenadier) Regts	Grass green	1, 4, 5, 8, 25, 28, 113–4	1–7, 10–4, 25, 33, 40, 52, 63, 69, 73–4, 86, 101, 110–1 ,113–4, 304, 394	3, 10–1, 21, 26, 40, 63–4, 66, 79, 93, 103, 108, 110–1, 126, 128, 140, 394	–
158 Div. Recce (Divisionsaufklärung) Bns	Gold–yellow	1–385 divisional series	1–385 divisional series	1–385 divisional series	–
8 Motorised Recce (Aufklärung (mot.)) Bns	Gold–yellow	A / 18, 20, 36, 53	A / 14, 18, 20, 25, 29, 36, 53, 341	A / 18, 25, 29, 341	–
8 Mtn. Recce (Gebirgsaufklärung) Bns	Gold–yellow	A / 67, 12, 67, 95, 99, 112	–	A / 54,94	*Edelweiss* badges
182 Antitank (Panzerjäger) Bns	Pink	P / 1–385 div. series	P / 1–385 div. series, GD	P / 1–385 div. series, GD	–
8 Motorised AT (Panzerjäger (mot.)) Bns	Pink	P / 3, 18, 20, 36	P/ 3, 10, 14, 16, 18, 20, 25, 29, 36	P / 3, 16, 25, 29	–
6 Mtn. Anti-tank (Gebirgspanzerjäger) Bns	Pink	P / 47–8, 95, 99	–	P / 44, 94	*Edelweiss* badges

Units	Branch colour	Shoulder strap insignia			Other distinctions
		Northern front	Central front	Southern front	
Combat Troops – Artillery (Artillerie)					
158 Artillerie (Artillerie) Regts	Bright red	1–385 divisional series	1–385 divisional series	1–385 divisional series	–
8 Mot. Artillery (Artillerie (mot.)) Regts	Bright red	3, 18, 20, 36	3, 10, 14, 16, 18, 20, 25, 29, 36	3, 16, 25, 29, GD	–
6 Mount. Artillery (Gebirgsartillerie) Regts	Bright red	82, 95, 111–2, 118	–	79	*Edelweiss* badges
23 Armd Artillery (Panzerartillerie) Regts	Bright red	1, 6, 8, 12	1–7, 9–12, 17–20	3, 9, 11, 13–4, 16–7, 22–3, 27	Black Panzer uniform
6 Rocket Launcher (Werfer) Regts	Bord. red	–	–	51–5, 70	–
Combat Troops – Engineers (Pioniere)					
167 Engineer (Pionier) Bns	Black	1–385 series	1–385 divisional series, GD	1–385 divisional series, GD	–
6 Mount. Engineer (Gebirgspionier) Bns	Black	8–3, 91, 95, 99	–	54	*Edelweiss* badges
23 Armd Engineer (Panzerpionier) Regts	Black	1, 6, 8, 12	1–7, 9–12, 17–20	3, 9, 11, 13–4, 16–7, 22–3, 27	Black Panzer uniform
Combat Troops – Signals (Nachrichtentruppe)					
167 Signals (Nachrichten) Bns	Lemon yellow	1–385 divisional series	1–385 divisional series, GD	1–385 divisional series, GD	–
6 Mount. Signals (Gebirgsnachrichten) Bns	Lemon yellow	8–3, 91, 95, 99	–	54	*Edelweiss* badges
23 Armd Engineer (Panzerpionier) Regts	Lemon yellow	1, 6, 8, 12	1–7, 9–12, 17–20	3, 9, 11, 13–4, 16–7, 22–3, 27	Black Panzer uniform
10 War Correspondent (Propaganda) Coys	Lemon yellow	501, 621, 680	612, 698–9	637, 649, 666, 698	PK cuff title
Supply Troops (Versorgungstruppen)					
158 Div. Supply (Nachschubführer) Cdrs	Light blue	D / 1–385 div. series	D /1 385 divisional series, GD	D /1–385 div. series, GD	–
7 Mtn. Div. Supply (Nachschubführer) Cdrs	Light blue	D / 8–3, 91, 95, 99	–	D / 54, 94	*Edelweiss* badges
8 Mot. Div. Supply (Nachschubführer) Cdrs	Light blue	D / 3, 18, 20, 36	D /3, 10, 14, 16, 18, 20, 25, 29, 36	D / 3, 16, 25, 29, GD	–
Armd Div. Supply (Nachschubführer) Cdrs	Light blue	1, 6, 8, 12	1–7, 9–12, 17–20	3, 9, 11, 13–4, 16–7, 22–3, 27	Black Panzer uniform
450? Motor Transport (Nachschub) Cols	Light blue	N / 1–385 divisional series, GD	N / 385 divisional series, GD	N/1–385 divisional series, GD	–
316? Horse Transport (Nachschub) Cols	Light blue	N / 1–385 series	N / 385 divisional series, GD	N/1–385 divisional series, GD	–
Medical Corps (Sanitäts) officers	Dark blue	Gold aesculapius staff	Gold aesculapius staff	Gold aesculapius staff	Red Cross armband
158 Horse Medical (Sanitäts) Coys – men	Dark blue	1–385 series	1–385 divisional series	1–385 divisional series	Red Cross armband
7 Mtn Med. (Gebirgssanitäts) Coys – men	Dark blue	8–3, 91, 95, 99	–	54, 94	*Edelweiss* badges
32 Mot. Medical (Sanitäts) Coys – men	Dark blue	1–36 divisional series	1–36 divisional series, GD	3–29 divisional series, GD	–
Veterinary Corps (Veterinär) officers	Crimson	Gold snake	Gold snake	Gold snake	Cavalry breeches

Units	Branch colour	Shoulder strap insignia			Other distinctions
		Northern front	**Central front**	**Southern front**	
158 Veterinary (Veterinär) Coys – men	Crimson	1–385 divisional series	1–385 divisional series	1–385 divisional series	Cavalry breeches
Security Troops (Sicherungstruppen)					
13 Army Rear Area Commanders (Korück)	White	525, 583–4	532, 559, 582, 590	351, 550, 553, 580, 585, 593	–
5 Distr. Commds (Oberfeldkommandantur)	White	392, 394, 396	–	393, 579	–
198 MP (Feldgendarmerie) Troops	Orange	1–36 divisional series	1–36 divisional series, GD	3–29 divisional series, GD	Sleeve badge, cuff title
9 Security (Sicherungs) Division Staffs	White	207, 281, 285	221, 286, 403	213, 444, 454	–
17 Security (Sicherungs) Regts	White	3, 94, 107, 113	2, 45, 61, 122, 601, 608, 613	4, 57, 177, 318, 360, 375	–
Foreign Troops					
1 Spanish (Spanische) Infantry Div. Staff	White	D / 250	–	–	Spanish arm badge
3 Spanish (Spanisches) Infantry Regts	White	262–3, 269	–	–	Spanish arm badge
1 Croatian (Kroatisches) Infantry Regt.	White	–	–	369	Croatian arm badge
1 French (Französisches) Infantry Regt.	White	–	638	–	French arm badge
1 Walloon (Wallonische) Infantry Bn.	Light green	–	–	373	Belgian arm badge
48 Eastern (Ost) Bns	White	653, 658–669	82, 134, 229, 264, 406, 412, 427, 439, 441, 446–8, 601–5, 615–21, 627–30, 633–7, 642	556	–
4 Armenian Ostlegion Bns	Gold-yellow	–	I/125	II/9, 808–9	Armenian arm badge
5 Azeri Ostlegion Bns	Green	–	–	I/73, I/111, 804–6	Azeri arm badge
5 Georgian Ostlegion Bns	Red	–	I/9 (Geb)	II/4 (Geb), I/9, 795–6	Georgian arm badge
3 North Caucasian Ostlegion Bns	Brown	–	–	800–2	North Caucasian badge
11 Turkestani Ostlegion Bns	Light blue	–	–	8(Fz), 11(Fz), 156B, I/370, 450, 452, 781–2, 811, 1000–1 Geb Tr	Turkestan arm badge
10 Volga–Tartar Ostlegion Bns	Blue/Green	–	–	–	Volga–Tartar badge
3 Cossack (Kosaken) Infantry Regts	Red	–	6, 7	5	Cossack arm badge
6 Cossack (Kosaken) Infantry Bns	Red	126	622–5,631		Cossack arm badge
3 Cossack (Kosaken) Cavalry Regts	Red	–	–	Platow, Jungschultz, Pannwitz	Cossack arm badge
11 Cossack (Kosaken/Ostreiter) Cavalry Bns	Red	207	281, 443, 580, 600	403/I–IV/444, I–II/454	Cossack arm badge
Army Officials (Heeresbeamten)					
216 Field Post (Feldpost) Offices	Lemon yellow	Fp (1–385 div. series)	Fp (1–385 div. series)	Fp (1–385 div. series)	–
39 Field Security Police (GFP) Groups	Light blue	GFP (501–735 series)	GFP (570–729 series)	GFP (560–740 series)	–

THE PLATES

A. ARMY GROUP NORTH: JUNE–NOVEMBER 1941

A1. General der Infanterie, XXVI Armeekorps, Lithuania, June 1941. This 18th Army general wears the eight-buttoned M1920 service tunic with bluish dark green M1935 collar, and gold general officer's buttons, collar patches, breast-eagle and red breeches' stripes. His M1934 'old-style' peaked field cap has a soft peak, bright aluminium woven insignia and general officer's gold piping. He carries a Walther PPK 7.65mm pistol and short design 10 x 50 binoculars and wears the Knight's Cross, Iron Cross 1st Class pin-back medal and the 1914 Iron Cross 2nd Class ribbon with 1939 bar.

A2. Leutnant, Sturmgeschützabteilung 185, Lake Peipus, Eastern Estonia, August 1941. This commander of a platoon of three assault-artillery self-propelled guns wears the M1940 special *feldgrau* uniform, with the 1st pattern collar patches worn until 30 January 1943, and the M1938 officer's field cap with silver crown and front flap piping and branch-colour chevron. He carries a P08 Luger in a hard-shell holster and wind protection goggles and wears the Iron Cross 1st Class pin-back medal, Iron Cross 2nd Class button ribbon, the General Assault badge and silver Wound badge for three or four wounds.

A3. Stabszahlmeister, 21. Infanterie-Division, Novgorod, North-Western Russia, October 1941. This military official serving as regimental paymaster wears the officer's field uniform with officer's M1935 field tunic without spurs. His M1935 service cap has officials' dark green pipings, and his dark green collar patches have white branch-colour piping. As a non-combatant he has earned the War Merit Cross 2nd Class with swords button ribbon and Silver 1st Class with swords pin-back medal, but his black wound badge indicates one or two wounds, and he is armed with a P38 Walther pistol in a hardshell holster.

B. ARMY GROUP CENTRE: JUNE–NOVEMBER 1941

B1. Hauptwachtmeister, Panzer-Regiment 39, Smolensk, Western Russia, July 1941. This company sergeant-major wears his cuff rings on the M1935 special black tank crew uniform with the M1936 jacket buttoned up against the dust. He wears a privately purchased M1935 other ranks' service cap with the steel crown ring removed to give it a more battered look, an unofficial practice favoured by NCOs. He has a silver Tank Combat badge, carries a P08 Luger pistol and has 'acquired' better quality motorcycle goggles.

B2. Obergefreiter, Infanterie-Regiment 464, Velikiye Luki, Western Russia, August 1941. This section first gunner wears the still predominant M1935 other ranks' field tunic and rank chevrons with M1938 shoulder straps. He carries the M1935 helmet with M1931 *feldgrau* canvas bread bag straps, securing leaves and undergrowth for camouflage, and

All German infantry, mountain infantry, rifle and security divisions were heavily dependent on horse transport. Here a farrier corporal (Beschlagschmiedoberjäger), identifiable by his bluish dark green facing-cloth trade badge with a golden-yellow wool horseshoe trade badge, with a bright aluminium cord inner edging to indicate he is confirmed in post in a battalion smithy, repairs a cartwheel. He wears a M1940 other ranks' field tunic with M1935 shoulder straps and M1939 mountain troops *edelweiss* arm badge. September 1942. (ECPA

wears the M1934 field cap with infantry branch-colour chevron, M1940 *feldgrau* trousers and the shorter shaft marching boots introduced 9 November 1939 to save leather. He carries the 7.92mm lMG34 general purpose light machine-gun with a P38 Walther pistol for close combat and a MG34 spares pouch.

B3. Kanonier, Nebelwerfer-Regiment 51, Smolensk, Western Russia, August 1941. Occasionally rocket-launcher troops were required to manhandle the 28-cm heavy high-explosive rocket shell. This gunner wears the issue cotton one-piece coveralls in *feldgrau* over his field uniform and has unofficially added M1940 *feldgrau* shoulder straps piped in bordeaux-red branch colour and the M1940 mouse-grey machine-embroidered breast-eagle. He has removed the national shield from the left side of the helmet following the order of 23 March 1940 but retains the Wehrmacht eagle on the left side (obscured here). His M1934 field cap has a branch-colour chevron.

C. ARMY GROUP SOUTH: JUNE–NOVEMBER 1941

C1. Leutnant, Infanterie-Regiment 230, Stalin Line, Western Ukraine, July 1941. This subaltern platoon leader wears the other ranks' field uniform with M1940 tunic with Iron Cross 2nd Class button ribbon and silver Infantry Assault badge, unofficially adding the officer's collar, M1935 collar patches and breast-eagle. He has other ranks' M1940 trousers, pre-war long-shaft marching boots and a rubber bicycle inner-tube camouflage band around his M1935 helmet, also the M1920 'officer's support straps' with more practical buckles, M1935 dispatch case and 1st pattern M38/40 ammunition pouches concealing his P38 Walther hardshell holster, 6 x 30 binoculars, and MP40 submachine-gun.

C2. Oberschütze, Infanterie-Regiment 203, Tiraspol, Bessarabia, August 1941. This senior infantryman wears the M1940 field tunic and M1940 *feldgrau*-backed rank star, M1940 *feldgrau* trousers and M1939 short-shaft marching boots. He carries rifleman's equipment with standard Karabiner 98k rifle, still obediently wearing his gas-cape pouch on his chest, and has thrust a M1924 stick-grenade in his belt.

C3. Hilfswilliger, 13 Panzer-Division, Rostov, Southern Russia, November 1941. This volunteer retains the Red Army M1935 khaki infantry field uniform with a brownish-grey greatcoat, *gymnastiorka* tunic, breeches and marching boots, and M1940 fur cap. He has removed his tunic and greatcoat collar patches and red star cap badge, and wears the arm band prescribed for armed auxiliaries and an unofficial identification cap patch. Although officially non-combatant he has the German other ranks' belt and M1911 rifle ammunition pouches, M1931 bread bag and carries the obsolete Karabiner 98b rifle issued to second-line troops.

D. EASTERN FRONT: DECEMBER 1941–MARCH 1942.

D1. Feldwebel, Infanterie-Division 270, Leningrad, Northern front, December 1941. This senior NCO platoon leader wears the standard winter field uniform which proved inadequate for the eastern front – the M1935 other ranks' greatcoat, still common in 1941, a *feldgrau* tube-shaped woollen balaclava under his helmet and possibly extra underwear. He wears other ranks' M1939 infantry support Y-straps and supplementary D-ring straps, platoon leaders' issue 6 x 30 binoculars and 1st pattern MP38/40 ammunition pouches for his MP40 submachine-gun.

D2. Schütze, Infanterie-Regiment 413, Kalinin, Central front, December 1941. This sentry wears a M1934 other ranks' field cap with pulled down flaps, a woollen balaclava, and a M1941 surcoat with a wide *feldgrau* collar and shoulder straps and woollen lining, cut to go over field equipment, introduced in November 1941 for sentries but issued rapidly to combat troops. He wears three-fingered mittens, carries the Karabiner 98k rifle and has slipped his marching boots into the flimsy 1st Pattern straw overboots for static sentry duty.

D3. Schütze, Infanterie-Regiment 117, Donets Basin, Southern front, January 1942. This soldier, preparing for a trench raid, wears the M1940 other ranks' field greatcoat and woollen balaclava, but has cut down bed sheets to improvise a snow-camouflage tabard and a helmet cover. He has

limited himself to essential field equipment and carries a Karabiner 98k rifle, a M1924 stick-grenade in his belt, and has constructed a 'concentrated charge' (*geballte Ladung*) from six M1924 stick-grenade heads wired around a single stick-grenade.

E. ARMY GROUP NORTH: APRIL 1942–JANUARY 1943

E1. Jäger, Gebirgsjäger-Regiment 141, Murmansk, Northern Russia, April 1942. This mountain infantryman wears the M1936 mountain cap, with M1939 insignia and unofficial bluish dark green 'Austrian' *edelweiss* backing, the infantry field tunic, M1940 *feldgrau* ski trousers and ankle-puttees and studded climbing boots. The M1931 reversible dark/light camouflage shelter-quarter, in thickly woven, water resistant impregnated material, could be buttoned to form a one, four or eight man tent, or worn as rain protection or camouflage clothing. This soldier carries the Gewehr 33/40 short carbine issued from 16 November 1940 to mountain troops.

E2. Obergefreiter, Pionier-Bataillon 123, Demyansk, Northern Russia, May 1942. This assault engineer wears his M1940 reed-green drill fatigue uniform as a summer field uniform, retaining M1935 rank chevrons and adding a breast-eagle, and has a mosquito net over his helmet. He wears the 'engineer assault pack', introduced 27 March 1941 – a greenish-brown canvas back-pack for two 3-kg explosive charges and two side bags for gas mask, demolition charges and grenades, with small pouches for rifle ammunition clips, and P38 Walther pistol. He carries M1924 stick-grenades, a M1935 first-pattern anti-tank mine and an MP38 submachine-gun.

E3. Feldunterveterinär, Veterinär-Kompanie 181, Staraya Russa, Northern Russia, September 1942. This young veterinary student seconded to 81st Infantry Division's veterinary company wears the mounted troops' field uniform with officer's and other ranks' insignia and crimson branch

An infantry section waits in a trench before the advance on Stalingrad, September 1942. They are wearing M1935 helmets coated in mud for camouflage and M1940 other ranks' field greatcoats and rifleman's equipment strapped to the M1931 camouflage shelter-quarter. Especially prominent are the M1931 mess tin, canvas battle bag, M1931 canteen with black-painted cup, M1931 bread bag and gas mask canister. (Brian Davis)

colour. He wears the M1935 peaked officer's service cap and the M1940 other ranks' field tunic with officer's M1935 collar patches and breast-eagle and M1940 Oberfeldwebel shoulder straps with the matt aluminium Veterinary Academy 'A' monogram. He has reinforced riding breeches, riding boots with spurs, a brown officer's belt and P38 Walther pistol in a hardshell holster.

F. ARMY GROUP CENTRE: APRIL 1942–JANUARY 1943

F1. Wachtmeister, Panzernachrichtenabteilung 92, Orel, Western Russia, August 1942. This armoured signals battalion NCO wears the M1941 reed-green drill tank crew fatigue and summer uniform with M1935 black uniform shoulder straps and collar patches and breast-eagle. He also wears the M1935 black uniform grey shirt, black tie and ankle-boots and M1940 other ranks' black field cap with the lemon-yellow branch-colour chevron ordered removed on 10 July 1942. He has wind-protection goggles, a P38 Walther in a hardshell holster, and the silver Tank Combat and bronze Wound badges.

F2. Unteroffizier, Pionier-Bataillon 267, Spass-Demensk, Western Russia, September 1942. A grey leather two-piece protective suit was prescribed for flame-thrower personnel in January 1940 but was not actually worn in combat, and so this NCO wears the normal M1940 field uniform with M1939 short-shaft marching boots. He carries the standard M1941 flame-thrower, introduced spring 1942, with petrol canisters strapped to his M1939 Y-straps and D-ring straps, and for personal protection the P08 Luger in a hardshell holster.

F3. Gefreiter, Infanterie-Regiment 235, Rzhev, Western Russia, September 1942. This front-line infantryman has adapted his uniform and equipment to his personal requirements. For comfort or coolness he wears his trousers over his marching boots and for camouflage has painted out the left side eagle helmet-decal, anticipating the 29 August 1943 order. On the waist belt he carries the folding shovel in the 1st model carrier, bread bag, canteen and cup, and on the M1939 A-frame a greenish-brown painted mess kit; battle-pack bag and shelter-quarter; and gas-cape pouch strapped with rubber inner tubing to the M1930 gas mask canister. He carries the 1941 model Karabiner 98k rifle.

G. SOUTHERN FRONT: APRIL–AUGUST 1942

G1. Unteroffizier, Panzergrenadier-Regiment 108, Kalmuck Steppes, North-Eastern Caucasus, August 1942. This section leader wears standard infantry M1940 field uniform with M1940 grass-green shoulder strap piping, 'standard braid' collar patches, mouse-grey breast-eagle, Iron Cross 2nd Class button ribbon and bronze Tank Combat badge instituted on 1 June 1940 for tank-associated units. He wears M1940 *feldgrau* trousers and anklets with lace-up ankle-boots, anti-dust goggles, has cut shelter-quarter material to form a makeshift camouflage cover for his M1935 steel helmet, and carries a flashlight and two 1st pattern MP38/40 ammunition pouches for his MP40 submachine-gun.

G2. Dolmetscher (Z), Georgische Infanterie-Bataillon 796, Maikop, North-Western Caucasus, September 1942. This Russian (or less likely Georgian) interpreter attached to a Georgian Legion battalion wears other ranks' M1940 field tunic with distinctive Sonderführer M1940 collar patches and shoulder board and the non-combatant War Merit Cross 2nd Class button ribbon but has not yet received the new legion arm-shield. He also has M1940 *feldgrau* trousers and M1939 short-shaft other ranks' marching boots. His M1935 officer's service peaked cap has grey-blue pipings and a Luftwaffe grey-blue uniform-cloth cap band, and he wears an officer's belt, dispatch case and P08 Luger in a hardshell holster.

G3. Zugführer, Georgische Infanterie-Bataillon 796, Maikop, North-Western Caucasus, September 1942. This Georgian platoon leader wears the M1940 other ranks' field tunic with bluish dark green collar, red M1942 rank insignia collar patches, *feldgrau* shoulder straps with legion piping and M1942 rank insignia, German M1940 mouse-grey breast-eagle and new legion arm shield. He wears a plain M1935 steel helmet, M1940 trousers, M1939 short-shaft marching boots, other ranks' belt and Y-straps, M1931 water bottle and cup and M1931 bread bag, and, as a platoon leader, carries 6 x 30 binoculars but has only been issued the Karabiner 98k rifle and M1911 rifle ammunition pouches.

H. BATTLE OF STALINGRAD: AUGUST 1942–FEBRUARY 1943

H1. Gefreiter, Grenadier-Regiment 544, December 1942. As the second gunner of a section light machine-gun team this infantryman wears rifleman's equipment with a P38 Walther pistol replacing his left ammunition pouches and carries a 300-round machine-gun ammunition box, but no spare machine-gun barrels. He wears the M1942 field cap with flaps pulled down, the wide collared M1942 field greatcoat, woollen gloves and wool rags around his marching boots for warmth and carries a M1924 stick-grenade and, unusually, a Karabiner 98k.

H2. Generaloberst Friedrich Paulus, 6. Armee, January 1943. Paulus wears a general officer's M1935 service peaked cap with pre-16 November 1942 silver insignia in non-regulation bluish dark green backed bullion, a M1935 field tunic with Knight's Cross and general officer's collar patches, a M1935 officer's field greatcoat with general officer's bright red lapels, officer's grey suede gloves and a Walther PPK pistol. Promoted to field marshal on 31 January 1943 on the assumption that German field marshals never surrendered Paulus promptly did so, indicating his promotion in Soviet captivity with a fourth shoulder board pip.

H3. Panzergrenadier, Panzergrenadier-Regiment 79, January 1943. The mechanised infantry received the M1942 white/*feldgrau* reversible winter overclothing in late 1942. This soldier wears a red recognition field sign, woollen balaclava and leather-reinforced felt boots and a helmet painted white. He carries his gas-mask container across his shoulder, a bread bag on the back of his waist belt with a Red Army magazine pouch for his Soviet PPSh41 submachine-gun and wears woollen gloves instead of the warmer less functional three-fingered mittens. His 'short shovel' is blade-up in his belt for heart protection or easy access for close combat

GERMAN ARMY 1939-45 (4) EASTERN FRONT 1943-45

THE CONTEXT OF THE EASTERN FRONT 1943-1945

The High Command of the Army and Wehrmacht

A sentry starts guard in front of the Headquarters of Army Group North, February 1943. His M1935 helmet – still bearing the Wehrmacht eagle left-side decal – is worn over the woollen toque or tubular balaclava. He wears the M1940 surcoat over his field uniform, and M1942 sentry's overboots of felt, leather and wood. (ECPA)

Adolf Hitler, German Head of State since 30 January 1933, had, as Supreme Commander of the Armed Forces (Oberster Befehlshaber der Wehrmacht), dominated GFM Wilhelm Keitel, the Chief of the Armed Forces High Command (Chef des Oberkommandos der Wehrmacht – OKW), controlling the Army (Heer), Navy (Kriegsmarine) and Air Force (Luftwaffe). On 19 December 1941 Hitler took personal strategic command of the Wehrmacht's most important branch by appointing himself Chief of the Army High Command (Oberbefehlshaber des Heeres). Thus the highest professional military post in the German Army was held by an arrogant amateur strategist, who constantly allowed political considerations to override military imperatives – with increasingly disastrous results on the Eastern Front.

The most senior German Army officer, the Chief of the Army General Staff (Chef des Generalstabes des Heeres) had since 24 September 1942 been General der Infanterie (later Gen.Obst.) Kurt Zeitzler. Although suspected of being a protégé of Hitler and the OKW against the Army High Command (OKH), Zeitzler instead asserted the OKH's authority and successfully excluded OKW influence from the Eastern (though not from the Arctic and Balkan) Fronts. On 1 July 1944, exasperated at his lack of real authority, Zeitzler reported sick; he was ignominiously dismissed on 21 July during Hitler's purge following the unsuccessful 'Bomb Plot' of 20 July.

The Bomb Plot marked the end of the Army's remaining influence over Hitler. Henceforth the Nazi Party reigned supreme; Army personnel were forced to use the Nazi salute instead of the traditional salute, the Waffen-SS received preference, and Reichsführer-SS Heinrich Himmler was appointed Commander of the Replacement Army – the Ersatzheer – controlling all Wehrmacht troops in Germany. On 21 July 1944 Gen.Obst.Heinz Guderian, the legendary Panzer general, was appointed Acting Chief of the Army General Staff; but he was unable to prevent Hitler's 'shackling order' of 21 January 1945, which required all military decisions down to divisional level to be referred directly to him.

On 28 March 1945 Hitler, infuriated by Guderian's undisguised contempt for his strategic decisions, dismissed him. His replacement as Acting Chief was the staff officer General der Infanterie Hans Krebs; but on 25 April Hitler ordered the OKW Operations Staff (Wehrmachtführungsamt), under Gen.Obst.Alfred Jodl, to take over the military conduct of the war, with operations in the north under Admiral of the Fleet Karl Dönitz, and in the south under Luftwaffe GFM Albert

Kesselring, effectively excluding the OKH from control over Army units.

On 30 April 1945, at 15.30 hours, Hitler committed suicide by poisoning and shooting himself. On 1 May Josef Goebbels succeeded him as Prime Minister (Reichskanzler); appointed Dönitz to the revived post of German President; and immediately committed suicide himself, as did Krebs. Dönitz immediately opened negotiations with the Allies; and on 7 May, at Rheims in eastern France, Keitel signed the unconditional surrender of all German forces to the Western Allies, repeating the surrender on 9 May in Berlin for the benefit of the Soviet Red Army. Fighting was supposed to end at 23.01 hours on 8 May, but German and Croatian troops in Slovenia and Austria in fact fought on until 15 May.

Resources

On 2 February 1943 the Stalingrad garrison surrendered. From June 1941 to December 1941, and then from June to November 1942 in the Caucasus, the German Army Groups had advanced into the Soviet Union, employing the Panzer divisions and Luftwaffe bombers to penetrate Soviet lines and attack enemy command centres with *Blitzkrieg* tactics, and Panzer and infantry divisions to destroy the resultant pockets of by-passed Soviet troops in the 'Decisive Manoeuvre' tactic. This twin-track strategy required well-equipped, well-armed and well-supplied mobile forces enjoying tactical independence and room for manoeuvre; but by February 1943 all these advantages had been lost. Thereafter German divisions were defending fixed positions from which they were gradually dislodged by overwhelming Soviet superiority in weapons and manpower.

German advances in 1941-42 had been paid for by huge casualties, and by February 1943 the 3 million-strong army had already been reduced to 2,300,000. Hitler insisted on re-raising destroyed units, developing new types of divisions, and raising Waffen-SS and Luftwaffe formations which competed for resources. The result was that the number of field divisions actually increased, but potential front-line troops were diverted into support units to complete divisional tables of organization, leaving existing divisions seriously understrength but still expected to accomplish their original missions. Regiments, nominally 3,000 strong, often fought at less than 30% strength; and huge losses of junior officers meant that the company, a Hauptmann's command, was routinely led by an inexperienced Oberleutnant or Leutnant, and sometimes by an Oberfeldwebel or Feldwebel – who often lasted only a few days before being wounded or killed.

Losses in tanks had been huge, and tank and self-propelled artillery production was easily outstripped by the now-vast Soviet production capability. German armour was now often deployed in infantry support, mimicking the earlier disastrous tactics of Polish, French and British forces, and allowing the Red Army the

BELOW **Panzergrenadiers manning a Sd.Kfz.251 armoured personnel carrier, April 1943. They are still wearing M1935 field tunics with dark bluish green collars and shoulder straps with grass-green piping. Foliage attachment bands are worn on the helmets. (Author's collection)**

Infantrymen carry out a house-to-house search for partisans in a Russian village, April 1943. The soldier at left wears a M1942 field tunic, and M1940 reed-green fatigue trousers loose over his muddy marching boots. Note the full infantry equipment on his back – the mess tin and shelter-quarter strapped to his leather M1939 support Y-straps, the gas mask canister suspended from a sling, and the bayonet, bread bag and canteen fixed to his belt. Their dark green collars seem to identify the other two tunics as M1935. (Brian Davis)

initiative to adopt *Blitzkrieg* tactics. Increased issue of automatic weapons gave individual units greater firepower, but this was not enough to compensate for the shortage of manpower and heavy weapons.

A German division had traditionally recruited from a specific Military District (Wehrkreis), fostering a close regional identity which gave it great cohesion and high morale. By 1943 this system had broken down under the mounting losses, and soldiers were drafted into units in most need, destroying critical unit cohesion. Increasingly strident Nazi propaganda on the paramount need to 'defend German civilisation from the Bolshevik hordes', and a growing fear of eventual revenge by the Red Army for widely tolerated German atrocities against the Russian civilian population, went some way to stiffening fighting spirit. However, this desperation could not replace the high morale of the 1939-41 period, and incidents of desertion and indiscipline increased.

As the Eastern front line retreated inexorably towards the German heartland the understrength divisions fought ferociously and with great individual heroism; but by spring 1945, with the war clearly lost, increasing numbers of troops attempted to retreat to the Western front line in order to surrender to the Western Allies, from whom they could expect reasonable treatment in captivity.

The development of Army units

The army on the Eastern Front in 1943-45 was organized into four, later five army groups, with a sixth covering the Balkans; these comprised nine infantry and four Panzer armies, and an independent mountain army on the Arctic Front. Each Army controlled two to five infantry, Panzer, mountain, cavalry, reserve corps or army sections, each with a varying number of German and allied divisions. In autumn 1944 three armoured corps – 24th, Großdeutschland and Feldherrnhalle – were organized as powerful integrated attack formations on the Waffen-SS model, each with two divisions and supporting arms, fighting in eastern Germany in 1945.

The infantry division remained the backbone of the German army, accounting for about 82% of the divisions. From 2 October 1943 the M1939 Infantry Division (11,246-17,734 strong) was reorganized as a 12,772-strong M1944 Division, with 11,317 German personnel and 1,455 Hilfswillige auxiliaries from the Soviet Union, representing a 28% reduction in manpower but a slight increase in firepower. The M1944 division had three M1944 infantry regiments, each 1,987 strong with an anti-tank company, an infantry gun company and two infantry battalions. The six divisional support units were an artillery regiment (2,013 men), a bicycle reconaissance battalion with four Füsilier companies (708 men); a field replacement (Feldersatz) battalion, an anti-tank battalion (484 men), an engineer (620 men) and a signals (379 men) battalion. The 2,380-strong divisional services consisting of horsedrawn and motorized transport columns, a medical company, field hospital, veterinary company, military police troop and field post office.

From 30 May 1944 existing independent reinforced infantry regiments were redesignated Grenadier Brigades, on 13 July 1944 expanded into Grenadier Divisions; and on 9 October renamed People's Grenadier Divisions, joining other such units first ordered on 26 August 1944. The 10,072 strong People's Grenadier Division (Volksgrenadierdivision) was created in the aftermath of the 20 July Bomb Plot, theoretically to provide politically reliable infantry under Himmler's direct command. Usually organized from combat-weary units, it was a M1944 division with a Füsilier company instead of a battalion, but with 18% less manpower and 16% less firepower; fighting quality varied from good to wholly inadequate.

On 10 December 1944 all infantry divisions were ordered formed as M1945 Divisions, each with 11,211 German troops and 698 Hilfswillige, with divisional services reorganized as a supply regiment (Versorgungsregiment) with a motor transport company, two horsedrawn transport companies, an ordnance company, a mechanical repair platoon, an administration company, medical company, veterinary company and field post office. In March 1945 manpower was further reduced to 10,728 Germans and 642 Hilfswillige.

The M1939 Mountain Division with 13,056 men was organized as a M1939 Infantry Division but with two mountain infantry regiments and mountain-equipped support units and services. The 13,000 strong M1942 Rifle (Jäger) Division had lightly armed mobile infantry. The 1st Ski (Skijäger) Brigade was raised in September 1943 from six independent rifle battalions (2, 4, 5, 7, 9 and 11) in two ski regiments; and on 2 June 1944 it became a division, fighting in the Pripyat marshes of Belarus and later in Slovakia. Security Divisions, organized for anti-partisan duties in Army Group rear areas, usually comprised two security or infantry regiments, Eastern (locally recruited) battalions, diverse support units and minimal services. By November 1944, with no Soviet and minimal Polish occupied territory remaining, security divisions were reorganized as infantry divisions.

The motorized divisions were effectively the élite of the German infantry. In 1942-43 the 14,319-strong M1940 Motorized Divisions, with two motorized infantry regiments and motorized divisional support units and services, each received a Panzer and an anti-aircraft or assault gun battalion. On 23 June 1943 they were redesignated M1944 Armoured Infantry Divisions (singular: Panzergrenadierdivision), 14,738 strong with two motorized armoured infantry regiments (each 3,107 men) and one Panzer battalion (602 men and 52 tanks); seven divisional support units – one motorized artillery regiment (1,580 men), and field replacement (973 men), armoured reconnaissance (1,005

LEFT **May 1943: an NCO from a Panzer regiment takes a break, May 1943. His cotton one-piece coveralls may be** *feldgrau*, **mouse-grey, reed-green, or even light brown. He has fixed to them (unofficially) the M1934 black, pink-piped skull collar patches, shoulder straps with aluminium NCO braid, and M1935 aluminium breast eagle on black backing from his M1934 special black vehicle uniform. He wears standard goggles on his M1940 other ranks' field-cap. (ECPA)**

LEFT, BELOW Under their M1940 reed green fatigue trousers these troops are wearing the white collarless shirt, introduced 1 April 1933 and reissued in summer 1943 to Eastern Front units sweltering in Ukraine. The foreground soldier is removing the bolt from his Mauser Karabiner 98k for cleaning. (ECPA)

BELOW June 1943: Generaloberst Walter Model, 9th Army commander, in a leather greatcoat with *feldgrau* **cloth collar, talks to infantrymen near Kursk. The soldier in centre foreground wears an A-frame battle pack with a blanket, mess kit, bread bag and gas mask canister attached. The section light machine gun team first gunner, right, carries a IMG34 light machine gun and a M1934 carrier for two spare barrels. (Brian Davis)**

men), anti-tank (475 men), motorized anti-aircraft (635 men), motorized engineer (835 men) and motorized signals (427 men) battalions; plus 1,729-strong divisional services.

The Panzer divisions steadily lost effectiveness as their strength and weaponry declined. On 24 September 1943 all 15,600-strong M1941 Panzer Divisions were reorganized as M1944 Panzer Divisions. Each had an establishment of 14,013 German troops and 714 Hilfswillige, in a two-battalion Panzer regiment (2,006 men, 165 tanks), a 2,287-strong armoured infantry regiment (one battalion on half-tracks), and a 2,219 motorized armoured infantry regiment; divisional support units were an armoured artillery regiment (1,451 men), and armoured field replacement (973 men), anti-aircraft (635 men), armoured reconnaissance (945 men), armoured anti-tank (475 men), armoured engineer (874 men) and armoured signals (463 men) battalions; 1,979 personnel provided additional divisional services.

On 24 March 1945 all armoured divisions were ordered to be reorganized as 11,422-strong M1945 Panzer Divisions, with a mixed 1,361-strong Panzer regiment with one Panzer (767 men and 52 tanks) and one half-track-mounted armoured infantry (488 men) battalion, two motorized armoured infantry regiments (each 1,918 men), and support units and services as before.

Six élite Army divisions, which enjoyed priority in manpower and equipment but suffered disproportionately high casualties, all served on the Eastern Front. On 19 May 1943 the Großdeutschland motorized division was reorganized as a Panzergrenadier division. On 1 April 1943 the Brandenburg commando unit (Sonderverband) became a five-regiment division, and on 15 September 1944 was ordered reorganized as a Panzergrenadier division. On 28 September 1944 these two divisions formed the Panzerkorps Großdeutschland. Hitler's Escort Battalion (Führer-Begleit-Bataillon), formed on 1 October 1939, became an armoured infantry regiment in November 1944, and on 26 January 1945 the Führer-Begleit-Division. Hitler's Infantry Battalion (Führer-Grenadier-Bataillon), formed 16 September 1943, became a brigade in July 1944 and on 26 January 1945 a Panzergrenadier division, but the planned formation of a Führer-Panzerkorps never took place.

On 1 June 1943 the 44th Infantry Division was redesignated the Imperial Grenadier Division (Reichsgrenadier-Division) Hoch- und Deutschmeister, commemorating the medieval Teutonic Knights and consciously stressing Imperial Austrian military traditions. On 20 June 1943 the Panzergrenadierdivision Feldherrnhalle was formed from Sturmabteilung (SA) volunteers. It was destroyed in July 1944, reformed on 1 September, converted to a Panzer division on 27

November, and formed the Panzerkorps Feldherrnhalle with 13 Panzer Division, which in March 1945 became the second Feldherrnhalle armoured division.

From 1 April 1943 Rtm.Georg Freiherr von Boeselager raised three mounted cavalry regiments from the mounted squadrons of divisional reconnaissance regiments as Army Group tactical reserves, forming in March and May 1944 the 3rd and 4th Cavalry Brigades, from March 1945 as 11,300-strong cavalry divisions of I Cavalry Corps.

On 1 October 1943 the 18th Artillery Division was formed with three artillery regiments, assault gun, anti-aircraft and motorized battalions with support units and services, but after nine months' inconclusive trials it was disbanded on 27 July 1944.

On 25 January 1945 Hitler ordered all available units to be reorganized as infantry divisions in an attempt to stem the relentless Red Army advance. Reserve, Training (Feldausbildungs) and Replacement (Ersatz) Divisions became general numbered divisions of the Replacement Army. In February 1945 'named' infantry and Panzer divisions were raised from local schools and garrisons. Twelve town garrisons, manned by Army and Volkssturm (the Nazi Party 'home guard' established on 25 July 1944) were reorganized as fortress units for last-ditch defence. Breslau became a Fortress Corps; Danzig, Frankfurt an-der-Oder, Gotenhafen, Stettin, Swinemünde and Warschau became Fortress Divisions; Kolberg, Küstrin, Posen, Scheidemühl and Görlitz 'Fortresses'. After May 1945 all these towns, except Frankfurt-an-der-Oder, became part of Poland.

From October 1942, 200,000 Luftwaffe personnel were organized into 21 Field Divisions, organized as 7,000-strong M1942 Rifle (Jäger) Divisions; most served on the Eastern Front. On 1 November 1943, 14 field divisions transferred to the Army and were reorganized as M1944 infantry divisions with 'Rifle (L)' Regiments. On 29 March 1945 three infantry divisions named Schlageter, Friedrich Ludwig Jahn and Theodor Körner were formed from State Labour Service (RAD) personnel with Army cadres, support units and services, and saw limited action.

The Army Patrol Service (Heeresstreifendienst), established on 18 November 1939, patrolled Replacement Army garrisons and checked the papers of soldiers on leave. On 1 February 1941 it was unified under a Patrol Service Commander controlling railway guard battalions, checking documents in large railway stations. On 1 March 1944 it formed part of the Wehrmacht Patrol Service supervising station guard battalions, policing trains and railway centres. In January 1942 a Leave Supervision Commander was established for Patrol Service Groups checking soldiers travelling to and from leave. HQ Guards guarded important buildings.

On 27 November 1943 distinguished veterans and Patrol Service personnel were formed into Field Police (Feldjäger) Commands I-III, reporting directly to GFM Keitel, and holding precedence over all Patrol Service and Military Police. Each command controlled a Field Police

Panzergrenadier carrying M1941 ammunition box for the section light machine gun team, October 1943. He wears a Zeltbahn 31 camouflage shelter quarter as a poncho over his field uniform, and string netting and a band on his helmet. (ECPA)

BELOW Four junior officers, perhaps company commanders, confer with the commander (a Knight's Cross holder) of a 'Großdeutschland' armoured infantry battalion, September 1943. Note the M1938 officers' field cap (left), M1934 'old style' peaked field cap (second right), and standard M1943 peaked field cap (right); M1940 other ranks' field tunics modified with officers' dark green collars; and the divisional cuff title. (Friedrich Herrmann)

Battalion (from 25 April 1944, a Regiment) with five motorized companies each with 30 officers and 90 NCOs divided into 30 patrols; based 12 miles behind the front line, these units dealt out rough justice, including summary execution, to apparently erring Wehrmacht personnel. These were supported from December 1944 by Patrol Corps (Streifkorps) sections each comprising a senior NCO and nine other ranks.

On 24 January 1944 some Army Officials were reorganized as service personnel, and on 1 May 1944 transferred to the two branches of the newly formed Special Troop Service (Truppensonderdienst) – the Wehrmacht Legal Service for senior career court martial officials, and the Administration Service for senior and advanced career district administration officials and senior career paymaster officials.

European volunteers

On 20 October 1943 the 250th Infantry Division – the Spanish 'Blue Division' – was repatriated to Spain, leaving a 1,500-strong 'Spanish Legion' (*Legion Española de Volontarios)* which was repatriated in March 1944; this left two Spanish battalions in the Replacement Army. The three Croatian Legion infantry divisions (369, 373, 392) fought in Croatia until May 1945. The 373rd Walloon Infantry Battalion transferred to the Waffen-SS on 1 June 1943, followed on 1 September 1944 by the 638th Reinforced French Grenadier Regiment.

From September 1943 Germany's European allies began to desert the Axis cause, but small numbers of soldiers from these countries fought on in Waffen-SS national units, while some Bulgarian, Hungarian, Rumanian and Slovak troops served in Army construction units or as individual combat replacements.

The Osttruppen

Baltic troops received preferential treatment in the Wehrmacht over other Soviet nationalities. On 1 January 1943 Estonian troops were reorganized into Estonian Company 657 and Estonian Battalions 658-660, transferring to the Waffen-SS on 24 April 1944. From February six Estonian Frontier Regiments (1-6) were formed to defend Estonia, disbanding in September 1944. Twenty-two Baltic construction battalions were also formed – Latvian I-IV in 1943, Latvian ex-police 314-315, 325-328 in June and July 1944; Lithuanian I-VI in 1943, Lithuanian ex-police in 1944, and Estonian 1-5 in April and May 1944.

From 1 July 1944 Osttruppen were redesignated 'Volunteers' (Freiwillige) in recognition of the vital contribution they were making to the German war effort. Most units were deployed on rear area security, transport and construction duties, since the Germans were unwilling to test their loyalty in battle against Soviet troops; but although individuals and even some whole units deserted to Soviet lines, these represented only a small proportion of the estimated 800,000 former Soviet citizens serving in the Wehrmacht, Waffen-SS and other paramilitary organizations. All

Generalleutnant Heinz Hellmich (left foreground) – Inspector of Osttruppen from 15 December 1942 to 31 December 1943 – inspects a company of the Turkestan Legion, June 1943. He wears the M1920 eight-buttoned field tunic with M1934 'old style' peaked field cap. The legionaries wear the M1940 tropical field tunic and canvas belt permitted in Ukraine and southern Russia in the summer. Note the German cadre officer behind Hellmich, also in tropical uniform; and the officer at far left in a M1920 tunic remodelled with M1935 bellows pockets.
(Author's collection)

May 1943: three senior Russian Liberation Army (ROA) officers at Pskov, north-western Russia. *Polkovnik* (later Major-General and Deputy Chief of General Staff) V.I.Boyarskiy (left) wears a Red Army M1935 khaki *gymnastiorka* field smock and khaki service peaked cap. *Polkovnik* K.Kromiadi (centre), Vlasov's Chief of Staff, wears a white Tsarist-style summer field smock and khaki cap; and *General-Leytenant* G.N.Zhilenkov (right), Head of the Main Propaganda Department, wears a German Army general officer's uniform. All have M1943 ROA cap badges, collar patches and shoulder boards; and note the ROA armshield. (Friedrich Herrmann)

auxiliaries – Hilfswillige or 'Hiwis' – were fully integrated into German divisions and increasingly treated on a par with German troops; and from 24 October 1944 recruitment of Polish Hiwis was officially sanctioned.

In January 1943 the Eastern Battalions were transferred to the Russian Liberation Army (Russkaya Osvoboditel'naya Armiya) or ROA, under the nominal command of ex-Soviet general Andrey Vlassov. He hoped to unite all Russian volunteer units into an army to free the Soviet Union from communist control; but command of the Eastern Battalions remained firmly in German hands. A total of 71 battalions served on the Eastern Front; but from October 1943, 42 battalions from destroyed German divisions were transferred to Belgium, Denmark, France and Italy.

On 14 November 1944 the ROA was officially redesignated the Armed Forces of the Committee for the Liberation of the Russian Peoples – VS-KONR – with about 50,000 Russian troops, but the term ROA was commonly used until May 1945. The 1st Infantry (600th German) Division was formed on 1 December 1944, and fought briefly on the Oder Front in April 1945 before changing sides and helping Czech insurgents to liberate Prague from the Germans in May 1945. The 2nd (650) and 3rd (599) Divisions were never fully established. An equivalent Ukrainian Liberation Army (Ukrainske Vyzvolne Viysko), announced in January 1943 for Ukrainian Eastern Battalion personnel, was never actually formed.

On 4 August 1943 the 1st Cossack Division was formed with six cavalry regiments (1 & 5 Don, 2 Siberian, 3 & 4 Kuban, 6 Terek), divisional support units and services. It served in Croatia from October 1943, and in November 1944 transferred to Waffen-SS control, divided into 1st and 2nd Divisions and forming XV Cossack Cavalry Corps. Nine independent Cossack infantry and 19 cavalry battalions fought on the Eastern Front with German divisions.

In July 1942 the staff of the disbanded 162nd Infantry Division in occupied Poland was used to train battalions of the six newly established Armenian, Azerbaijan, Georgian, North Caucasian, Volga-Tartar and Turkestan Eastern Legions. In all 98 Eastern Legion battalions were formed (82 by the 162nd Division) and 79 served on the Eastern and Balkan Fronts 1942-45; 12 of these transferred to France and Italy in 1943-44.

CAMPAIGN SUMMARY 1943-45

The Northern Front

In February 1943 Army Group North (Heeresgruppe Nord), under Gen.Obst. (later GFM) Georg von Küchler, held the northern sector of the Eastern Front with two static infantry armies. The 18th Army, with 26 divisions (20 infantry, four Luftwaffe infantry, one Waffen-SS infantry, one mountain) besieged Leningrad, and held the Volkhov Line from Lake Ladoga to Lake Ilmen. The 16th Army's 16 divisions (15 infantry, one Luftwaffe infantry) held the northern Lovat River before Velikiye Luki. This line held throughout 1943, although on 28 February 16th Army evacuated the vulnerable Demyansk salient, and on 9 October surrendered Nevel.

On 14 January 1944 the Red Army attacked Army Group North, now under GFM Walter Model, forcing it back from Leningrad and Lake Ilmen and occupying Novgorod, Luga, Staraja Rossiya and Kholm. When the offensive halted on 1 March, Army Group North (now under Gen.Obst.Georg Lindemann, from July 1944 Gen.Obst.Johannes Frießner, then Gen.Obst.Ferdinand Schörner) had retreated to the Panther Line on the Estonian and Latvian borders. The Red Army resumed the offensive on 10 July, occupying Ostrov on 21 July, Pskov on 23 July, Narva on 28 July and, against hardening German opposition, Tartu on 25 August, and Daugavpils in eastern Latvia on 27 July.

On 14 September 1944 the Red Army attacked again, occupying Estonia and northern Latvia. Army Group North evacuated Riga on 11 October, but was cut off on the Latvian coast behind the Liepaja-Tukums line, Hitler refusing to allow a break-out or a rescue. On 25 January 1945 the Army Group was redesignated 'Kurland' (named after the Latvian province of Kurzeme), successively under Gen.Obst.Heinrich Vietinghoff, Gen.Obst.Lothar Rendulic and Gen.Obst.Carl Hilpert. It held out against Red Army attacks in six 'Kurland Battles' until 8 May 1945.

The Arctic Front

The six divisions of 20th Mountain Army (2 infantry, 3 mountain, 1 Waffen-SS mountain), under Gen.Obst.Eduard Dietl (from June 1944, Gen.Obst.Rendulic), occupied a defensive line in Soviet Karelia and guarded the Petsamo nickel mines. On 7 September 1944 Finland concluded an armistice with the USSR and declared war on Germany; under Soviet-Finnish pressure the 20th Army retreated into Norway, defending it as the Wehrmacht Command Norway under Gen. der Gebirgstruppen Franz Boehme.

The Central Front

In February 1943 GFM Günther von Kluge's Army Group Centre (Heeresgruppe Mitte) defended the Rzhev-Orel-Kharkov line in Western Russia. In March it comprised five armies

Infantrymen at ease, September 1943; all wear the M1942 field tunic and M1943 field cap. Note the silver Infantry Assault Badge worn by the two Unteroffizier section leaders at left and right; the senior NCOs' collar and shoulder strap edging braid also shows well. (Brian Davis)

(2nd Panzer, 3rd Panzer, 2nd, 4th, 9th) totalling 81 divisions (12 Panzer, one Waffen-SS Panzer, 53 infantry, five motorized, one Waffen-SS cavalry, six Luftwaffe, three Hungarian).

On 24 March 1943 the 9th Army evacuated Rzhev and the Vyazma Salient. On 4 July, 17 Panzer and 26 other divisions in 9th Army and 4th Panzer Army (Army Group South) attacked the Soviet-held Kursk Salient in Operation Zitadelle, the greatest tank battle in history; but on 17 July the attack was called off with minimal territorial gains and huge losses of men and equipment. Now the Red Army counter-attacked, taking Orel on 1 August, Smolensk and Roslavl on 24 September and Gomel on 26 November; Army Group Centre, now under GFM Ernst Busch, was forced back into Belarus.

On 22 June 1944 some two and a half million Soviet troops attacked the 400,000-strong Army Group Centre, now under GFM Walter Model. The Red Army took Vitebsk on 27 June, Mogilev on 28 June, Bobruisk on 29 June, and Minsk on 4 July, inflicting 300,000 casualties and virtually annihilating the Army Group. By mid-July the Red Army had cleared Belarus and advanced into eastern Lithuania, taking Vilna on 12 July and Kaunas on the 30th. They rolled on into eastern Poland, capturing Brest-Litovsk on 28 July, Bialystok on 29 July, and eastern Warsaw on 31 July. The Soviet armies halted on the Vistula and allowed German suppression of the Warsaw Uprising by the Polish Home Army (1 August–2 October 1944). Gen.Obst.Georg-Hans Reinhardt took over command of Army Group Centre in August 1944.

On 12 January 1945 the Red Army resumed the offensive, taking Warsaw on 17 January and advancing into eastern Germany; they halted on the River Oder on 3 February, and by 23 February had occupied most of East Prussia. On 25 January 1945 Army Group Centre was redesignated Army Group North, under Gen.Obst.Rendulic (from March 1945, Gen.Obst.Walter Weiß), with 25 divisions (two Panzer, one Luftwaffe Panzer, one Luftwaffe Panzergrenadier, 21 infantry), defending the Königsberg Pocket and Samland Peninsula. On 17 March 1945 the Red Army attacked, taking Königsberg on 9 April and Samland on 21 April.

On 24 January 1945 Army Group 'Weichsel' was formed under Reichsführer-SS Heinrich Himmler (from March, Gen.Obst.Gotthard Heinrici; from April, Luftwaffe Gen.Obst.Kurt Student), with 47 divisions (three Panzer, 35 infantry, seven Waffen-SS, one naval infantry, one parachute) in 3rd Panzer, 2nd and 9th Armies, defending the Oder Front and Pomeranian coast. On 24 February the Red Army attacked, taking Kolberg on 18 March and Danzig on 30 March. On 16

October 1943: the crew of a IMG 34 mounted on a tripod for sustained fire. The second gunner has foliage stuck through a rubber band round his helmet; the M1931 shelter-quarter is carried rolled up on the back of his belt. (Brian Davis)

GFM Ernst Busch, commander of Army Group Centre, November 1943, wearing the M1943 peaked field cap; a privately tailored sheepskin jacket with the gold-on-black M1942 arm badge of his rank; and the M1935 breeches with general officers' bright red piping and stripes. He carries a field-marshal's undress black baton, with a silver knob and a tassel in the German national colours. (Brian Davis)

LEFT A Panzergrenadier in an ice-covered slit trench, December 1943. He wears the M1942 reversible padded winter smock with a coloured field sign round the sleeve, and matching padded trousers; and a *feldgrau* toque under his whitewashed M1935 helmet. There were eight field sign variations – black or red armband on left arm, on right, or on both arms; black on left, red on right; red on left, black on right. (Brian Davis)

April Soviet roops opened the attack on Berlin, defended by 9th Army. On 1 May the Berlin garrison surrendered; and on 3 May the Red Army linked up with British and United States troops on the Elbe River.

The Southern Front

In February 1943 Ukraine was defended on the Donets River by Army Group South, formed on 12 February from Army Group Don under GFM Erich von Manstein, with 1st and 4th Panzer Armies, Armeeabteilung Kempf (later 8th Army), and Armeeabteilung Hollidt (later 6th Army), totalling 32 divisions (seven Panzer, 17 infantry, two motorized, four Waffen-SS Panzergrenadier, two Luftwaffe). The Crimea and the Taman Peninsula were held by Army Group 'A' under GFM Ewald von Kleist, with 20 divisions (one Panzer, seven infantry, two rifle, two mountain, 1 Luftwaffe, six Rumanian, one Slovak) in 17th Army, joined in October 1943 by 6th Army.

In February 1943 the Red Army advanced from Stalingrad, capturing Kursk on 8 February, Belgorod on 9 February, Rostov-on-Don on 14 February and Kharkov on 16 February. Manstein counter-attacked on 19 February with 1st Panzer Army, reoccupying Kharkov on 15 March. On 17 July the Red Army thrust once again, taking Belgorod on 5 August and Kharkov on 23 August; and on 30 September Army Group South retreated to the Dnepr River, abandoning Kiev on 6 November. Army Group 'A' evacuated the Taman Peninsula on 9 October, and by 31 October 17th Army was stranded in the Crimea.

On 24 December 1943 the Red Army resumed the offensive from its Donets bridgeheads against Army Group South, taking Zhitomir on 31 December, Nikopol on 7 February 1944, the Cherkassy (Korsun) Pocket on 15 February and Krivoi Rog on 22 February, reaching the northern Carpathian Mountains on the Rumanian border on 27 March and Brody and Tarnopol in southern Poland on 15 April. The 6th Army retreated through southern Ukraine, giving up Odessa on 10 April 1944; meanwhile 17th Army lost Sevastopol on 9 May, evacuating by sea from the Crimea to Rumania.

On 30 March 1944 Army Group South in southern Poland was redesignated Army Group North Ukraine under GFM Walter Model (from June, Gen.Obst.Josef Harpe), with three armies (1st and 4th Panzer, 1st Hungarian). On 12 July the Red Army attacked, taking Brody on 22 July, Lublin on 23 July and Lvov on 27 July. On 23 September the Army Group was redesignated Army Group 'A', adding 17th Army. On 12 January 1945 the renewed Soviet offensive hit the Army Group, which on 25 January was redesignated Army Group Centre under Gen.Obst.(in April, GFM) Ferdinand Schörner, with three armies (1st and 4th Panzer, 17th). The Red Army took Cracow on 19 January, reaching the River Oder on 25 January; Soviet forces advanced through Czechoslovakia, taking Bratislava on 4 April and Prague on 9 May 1945.

On 30 March 1944 Army Group 'A' became Army Group South Ukraine, with five armies (6th, 8th, 17th, 3rd and 4th Rumanian) in Rumania under Gen.Obst.Schörner (from July, Gen.Obst. Johannes Frießner). On 20 August the Soviets attacked, taking Iasi on 22 August and Kishinev on 24 August. Rumania and Bulgaria defected to the Allies on 23 August and 8 September respectively. On 23 August the Army Group retreated to Hungarian-held northern Transylvania, and became

Army Group South with four armies (6th, 8th; 2nd & 3rd Hungarian).

In October 1944 the Soviets pushed through eastern Hungary, taking Debrecen on 20 October and besieging Budapest from 20 December 1944 to 13 February 1945. The Army Group, now under Gen.der Infanterie Otto Wöhler, held western Hungary until 16 March 1945, when the Red Army resumed the offensive, entering eastern Austria on 1 April and taking Vienna on 13 April. On 30 April the Army Group was redesignated Army Group Ostmark with three armies (6th, 8th, 6th SS-Panzer) under Gen.Obst.Rendulic, but surrendered on 9 May 1945.

In September 1944 the Southern and Balkan Fronts merged. The Red Army entered Yugoslavia on 27 September 1944, taking Belgrade on 19 October from Army Group 'F' (2nd Panzer Army, Armeeabteilung Serbien, Army Group 'E'). In November Army Group 'E' evacuated Greece and Albania; in December 2nd Panzer Army redeployed to southern Hungary, and Army Group 'F' formed a defensive line on the Bosnian-Serb border with Croatian troops. Initially the line held well against a general offensive by Soviet, Bulgarian and Yugoslav Partisan forces launched on 15 March, and Army Group 'E' retreated in good order, evacuating Sarajevo on 7 April, Rijeka on 4 May and Zagreb on 8 May. The Army Group finally surrendered in southern Austria on 15 May 1945.

March 1944: GFM Erich von Manstein, commander of Army Group South, talks to troops who had fought in the 'Cherkassy Pocket' in the central Ukraine. He wears a privately-tailored fur cap and a fur collar on his M1935 greatcoat. Manstein's adjutant, left, wears bright aluminium wire aiguillettes and a M1934 'old style' field cap. (Brian Davis)

ARMY UNIFORM

Officers' service uniform

This uniform, also worn by probationary second lieutenants (Oberfähnrich and equivalent), consisted of the M1935 officer's peaked cap, M1935 officer's field tunic with ribbons, M1935/ M1940 officer's field greatcoat, M1934 officer's brown leather belt, officer's breeches and officer's black leather high-boots, grey suede gloves, pistol and holster.

The superior-quality *feldgrau* (greenish-grey) cap had a bluish dark-green 'facing cloth' band, facing cloth pipings in branch colour, a plain black peak and bright aluminium wire chin cords. A M1935 aluminium eagle was worn above an aluminium national cockade in an oak-leaf wreath. General officers had cord cap pipings and wire chin cords in fired gold or yellowish gold 'celleon' artificial material, and, from 16 November 1942, gilded insignia.

The superior quality *feldgrau* cloth M1935 tunic, as modified from 26 May 1941, had six matt grey buttons, four patch pockets, turn-back cuffs and a bluish dark green collar. The field quality insignia consisted of the M1935 officer's aluminium thread breast-eagle on a bluish dark green backing; M1935 officer's bluish dark green collar patches with hand-embroidered 'guards braids' with branch-colour centre cords, and shoulder boards of rank backed with branch colour. General officers had gold buttons, a dress-quality gold thread or celleon eagle, and a gold two-leaf *Alt-Larisch* design on bright red collar-patches (three-leaf for Generalfeldmarschall). From about December 1943 some tunics were produced with lapels and open collars, usually only worn by general officers and staff officers.

The *feldgrau* greatcoat had two rows of six buttons and a bluish dark green or *feldgrau* collar (widened in 1942), with bright red lapel linings for general officers. The plain stone-grey or *feldgrau* breeches had bright red seam pipings and stripes for general officers or crimson for staff officers. The black leather high-boots were worn with spurs. From 27 July 1943 the brown belt was to be stained black, an order rescinded on 30 October 1943.

Other ranks' service uniform

The service uniform for technical NCOs, senior NCOs and many junior NCOs consisted of the other ranks' M1935 service peaked cap or M1935/M1942 field cap, M1935 field tunic and M1935 field greatcoat. M1940 trousers were worn with black leather marching boots, or M1943 belted trousers with M1941 *feldgrau* canvas anklets (ironically nicknamed 'retreat gaiters' or 'Timoshenko socks') and black lace-up ankle boots. A black leather belt with an aluminium buckle (introduced 24 January 1936; from 1941, painted *feldgrau*) and holster with pistol, and grey suede gloves, were also worn. Other junior NCOs and men wore the field cap at all times, and a bayonet and scabbard on the belt.

The other ranks' peaked service cap was as for officers but in *feldgrau* tricot with a black patent leather or vulcanized fibre chin strap. The M1935 other ranks' *feldgrau* cloth field cap had a mouse-grey machine-embroidered eagle on a *feldgrau* backing and a tricolour cockade on a *feldgrau* rhomboid. The M1942 other ranks' field cap, introduced 21 July 1942, had double-lined flaps which could be folded down and buttoned under the chin in cold weather. With this cap the fourth pattern M1939 mountain cap insignia was worn – a mouse-grey woven eagle and cockade on a *feldgrau* T-shaped backing.

The M1943 peaked field cap, introduced 11 June 1943, was issued promptly to Field Army and Replacement Army units. Made of inferior quality *feldgrau* uniform cloth, with two small grey pebbled-finish flap buttons, it had a deep peak which soon bent into a crescent shape with use. It was worn with M1942 field cap insignia.

The M1940 *feldgrau* tunic had five (from 26 May 1941, six) matt grey buttons, other ranks' M1940 mouse-grey breast eagle, and M1940 'standard braid' collar patches. NCOs wore M1940 mouse-grey artificial silk or cellulose-fibre wool collar edging braid. The M1942 other ranks' field tunic omitted the pocket pleats and the M1943 tunic had straight pocket flaps. The M1943 belted trousers had a reinforced seat and tapered legs for anklets.

The M1940 other ranks' *feldgrau* field greatcoat was

January 1944: this wounded infantryman, wearing an M1942 reversible padded winter tunic over his field uniform, sits on an improvised stretcher as his comrades await a truck from the divisional medical company. The soldier at left, probably an NCO or officer, is wearing the M1942 two-piece loose cotton snow suit with a red field sign round his right sleeve; his visible kit includes a M1938 folding shovel, M1931 mess kit, bread-bag, canteen and M1935 dispatch case. The soldier at centre, a medical corps orderly in a M1935 greatcoat, carries field dressings in two medical pouches on his belt. (Friedrich Herrmann)

as for officers but with other ranks' quality cloth and insignia. The M1942 model had a wider collar for better protection against the cold.

Walking-out uniform
When walking-out or on leave officers wore the service uniform, sometimes with the M1937 officers' piped field tunic, with straight *feldgrau* trousers and no belt, holster or pistol. Technical and senior NCOs wore the peaked cap, field tunic or greatcoat, trousers and black leather ankle boots, belt and marksmanship lanyard, junior NCOs and men adding the scabbarded bayonet with knot.

Officers' field uniform
In the field all officers (except platoon leaders) wore the other ranks' M1940/M1942/M1943 or M1944 field tunic, the M1935/M1942 steel helmet or M1938/M1942 or M1943 field cap, officers' breeches with high-boots or other ranks' trousers with M1941 anklets and black lace-up ankle boots.

On 31 October 1939 all officers below general rank serving in combat units were ordered to wear the other ranks' field tunic, black belt, trousers and marching boots, in order not to be too conspicuous to the enemy; but most officers shortened the tunic skirt, adding officers' roll-back cuffs, box pleats to the pockets, officers' collar patches, and bluish dark green collars of higher and more pointed shape. Wear of the other ranks' black belt by officers was forbidden after 23 July 1943, and a blackened officers' M1934 brown belt was prescribed.

On 25 September 1944 the Felduniform 44 was introduced as a new standard field uniform for all ranks, replacing existing uniforms when they wore out. The waist-length field blouse, of inferior cloth in a browner green-grey shade designated *feldgrau 44,* had six front buttons and two plain breast pockets with straight flaps. Officers wore other ranks' M1940 *feldgrau* 'guards braids' sewn directly onto the collar, or officers' M1935 collar patches. The officers' breast eagle was either the other ranks' M1944 mouse-grey woven eagle and swastika on a *feldgrau* triangle, an officers' M1944 aluminium woven eagle on a bluish dark green triangle, or the M1935 officers' aluminium thread breast eagle on a bluish dark green backing. General officers wore a dress-quality M1935 gold thread or M1938 celleon eagle. The M1944 trousers, also in *feldgrau 44,* had an integral belt and were gathered at the ankle with a drawstring.

Iasi, north-eastern Rumania, April 1944: the unmistakable figure of Generalleutnant Hasso von Manteuffel, commanding the Panzergrenadier Division Großdeutschland (centre), wearing his M1934 'old style' field cap and a leather greatcoat, with 10x50 Zeiß binoculars with black bakelite protective lid. He confers with an officer in a sheepskin coat; and (right) a Hauptmann of the Panzer-Regiment Großdeutschland, wearing the M1942 Panzer denim uniform in reed-green herringbone twill with a large left thigh pocket; note applied collar patches, and shoulder boards with gilt 'GD' monogram. In the left background are a Rumanian general officer and captain; five months later Rumania changed sides and declared war on Germany. (Brian Davis)

TABLE 1: ARM RANK INSIGNIA OF THE GERMAN ARMY
22 AUGUST 1942 - 8 MAY 1945

This insignia was worn 10cm below the left shoulder seam of the M1938 mountain troops' wind jacket, snow shirt, M1935 grey Panzer shirt, M1940 khaki tropical shirt, M1940 reed-green fatigue jacket, M1941 AFV overalls, M1941 reed-green shirt, sheepskin overcoat, M1941 and M1942 Panzer denim jacket, M1942 reversible and camouflage winter tunic, M1942 camouflage smock, M1943 hooded camouflage smock, M1942 reed-green drill field tunic, and M1943 mountain troops' anorak, all manufactured without fastenings for shoulder boards and shoulder straps. Lower ranks (Stabsgefreiter - Obergrenadier) normally omitted their arm rank insignia, except on the M1935 grey Panzer shirt and M1940 khaki tropical shirt.

Rank titles are shown first for German line infantry, secondly in brackets for Specialist Officers (Sonderführer), introduced 10 August 1944, and thirdly in italics for Military Officials (1942 Field Post titles are given as examples) introduced 15 July 1943.

1. Generalfeldmarschall	**2.** Generaloberst	**3.** General der Infanterie *(Ministerialdirektor[1])*	**4.** Generalleutnant *Heeresfeldpostmeister*
5. Generalmajor *Heeresfeldpostdirigent*	**6.** Oberst *Feldoberpostdirektor*	**7.** Oberstleutnant *Feldpostoberrat*	**8.** Major *Feldpostrat* (Bataillonsführer)
9. Hauptmann *Feldpostrat (unter 35 J.)* (Kompanieführer)	**10.** Oberleutnant *Feldpostinspektor*	**11.** Leutnant *Feldpostsekretär* (Zugführer)	**12.** Oberfähnrich[2]
13. Stabsfeldwebel	**14.** Oberfeldwebel Oberfähnrich *Feldpostassistent*	**15.** Feldwebel *Feldpostbetriebsassistent*	**16.** Unterfeldwebel *Feldpostbote*

1. Generalfeldmarschall

2. Generaloberst

3. General der Infanterie
(*Ministerialdirektor[1]*)

4. Generalleutnant
Heeresfeldpostmeister

5. Generalmajor
Heeresfeldpostdirigent

6. Oberst
Feldoberpostdirektor

7. Oberstleutnant
Feldpostoberrat

8. Major
Feldpostrat
(Bataillonsführer)

9. Hauptmann
Feldpostrat (unter 35 J.)
(Kompanieführer)

10. Oberleutnant
Feldpostinspektor

11. Leutnant
Feldpostsekretär
(Zugführer)

12. Oberfähnrich[2]

17. Unteroffizier

The rank insignia consisted of 8.5 - 9.5 cm wide insignia on 9-10cm wide cloth rectangles of varying heights. Colours and materials were:-

1-5: White thread batons and pips, gold-yellow braid and thread leaves, on a black cloth rectangle.

6-17: Green braid and thread leaves on a black cloth rectangle, or green bars and leaves printed on a black cotton rectangle.

Footnotes

1 Court Martial Oficial rank, in the absence of an equivalent Field Post rank.

2 Unofficial insignia more accurately reflecting the rank's status.

Generals enjoyed greater latitude in their interpretation of uniform regulations. After distinguished service in North Africa, Generalmajor Fritz Bayerlein was appointed to command the newly formed élite Panzer-Lehr-Division on 10 January 1944. He is shown here in Hungary in April 1944, wearing an officers' M1935 field tunic with general officers' gold *Alt-Larisch* embroidery on bright red collar patches; and a standard M1943 field cap without generals' gold wire crown and flap-front pipings, but with an unofficial gilded aluminium eagle and swastika taken from a M1937 white undress tunic. His M1940 greatcoat does not appear to have the generals' bright red facing cloth lapel linings. He wears the Knight's Cross with Oak-leaves. (Author's collection)

The M1935 steel helmet, painted matt greenish-grey with roughened surfaces, had a silver/white on black Wehrmacht eagle decal on the left side, abolished 28 August 1943. The M1942 helmet, introduced 20 April 1942, abandoned the edge-crimping to simplify production; this was not common in the field until 1943. The peakless M1938 officers' *feldgrau* tricot field cap had aluminium thread pipings, and an aluminium wire embroidered cockade below an aluminium thread eagle on a bluish dark green backing, in gold thread or celleon for general officers. The M1934 'old style' peaked field cap, officially abolished 1 April 1942, was worn by some officers and NCOs until May 1945. Some officers wore the other ranks' M1942 field cap unofficially, with aluminium piping (gold for general officers). Officers also wore the M1943 peaked field cap with aluminium (gold or celleon for general officers) cord crown piping, and occasionally the other ranks' eagle and cockade.

Subalterns acting as infantry platoon leaders wore the other ranks' black belt supporting the 84/98 bayonet and scabbard in the M1939 bayonet-frog, usually secured to the case of the short shovel or M1938 folding shovel; the M1941 canvas bread bag; the M1931 canteen and cup; and the leather M1935 dispatch case. The black leather M1920 'officers' support straps' secured two sets of three first pattern greenish-brown *feldgrau* canvas M38/40 ammunition pouches for the MP38 or MP40 sub-machine gun. The anti-gas cape in a greenish-brown or *feldgrau* rubberized canvas or linen pouch was usually tied with rubber bands or straps to a *feldgrau*-painted M1930 gas mask canister slung from a shoulder by a strap or strapped to the bread bag. Zeiß 6x30 binoculars were carried on the chest, a signal whistle was secured to a breast pocket button by a plaited lanyard, and a flashlight hung from a shoulder strap button.

Other ranks' field uniform

Other ranks wore the service uniform, increasingly with anklets and lace-up ankle boots, adding the steel helmet and omitting the service peaked cap, except for some NCOs who wore the M1934 'old style' peaked field cap. Technical and senior NCOs carried a pistol in a black holster; and NCOs acting as infantry platoon leaders or section leaders wore the same equipment as subaltern platoon leaders, but with the other ranks' M1939 infantry support Y-straps.

The other ranks' M1944 field uniform was identical to the officers', with plain *feldgrau 44* round-ended shoulder straps with branch-colour piping, M1940 *feldgrau* 'guards braids' sewn directly onto the collar, and the other ranks' M1944 mouse-grey eagle on a *feldgrau* woven triangle. NCOs did not wear collar edging braid.

Most NCOs and men wore the standard rifleman's equipment. The waist belt carried the 84/98 bayonet, M1938 folding shovel, M1931/M1944 bread bag, M1931 canteen and cup. The M1939 infantry support Y-straps and supplementary D-ring straps supported two sets of three rifle ammunition pouches at the front, and at the back the M1939 *feldgrau* canvas A-frame, carrying the M1931 greenish-brown painted aluminium mess kit (pot and frying-pan/lid); the M1931 camouflage shelter-quarter; the canvas battle pack bag, and the gas cape strapped to the gas mask canister when not worn on the canister shoulder sling. The equipment worn by the three-man section light machine-gun team is described in Volume 1 (Men-at-Arms 311).

Summer field uniform

In summer 1941 many troops adopted as a summer field uniform the M1940 fatigue uniform, first ordered 12 February 1940, consisting of the reed-green cotton herringbone twill tunic with five buttons and two patch hip pockets, and trousers. Officers and NCOs added shoulder strap rank insignia, and all ranks wore the breast-eagle.

The M1941 reed-green pullover-style cotton shirt was introduced in early 1942 for use in warm weather as an outer garment. It had five white plastic buttons and from mid-1942 two breast pockets, with or without a centre pleat, and triangular pocket flaps. Field-quality shoulder board and shoulder strap rank insignia and arm chevrons were worn until May 1945, although from 22 August 1942 the special arm rank insignia were officially prescribed.

The M1942 reed-green herringbone twill tunic, introduced in early 1942 but not common until summer 1943, had the same cut as the M1943 field tunic, with pleatless breast pockets with straight flaps. Field-quality rank insignia and breast-eagles were worn; officers wore their M1935 collar patches, NCOs and men M1940 *feldgrau* 'guards braids' sewn directly onto the collar. Matching trousers appeared in 1943. On 25 September 1944 a reed-green drill version of the M1944 field blouse and trousers was authorized but was almost certainly never produced.

Winter clothing

Winter uniform items, first issued before March 1942, consisted of the *feldgrau* tube-shaped woollen balaclava; extra-thick woollen underwear; the M1936 and M1942 sweaters; *feldgrau* woollen mittens: the *feldgrau* sentry's double-breasted guard coat and felt overshoes; the vehicle crew's M1934 or M1940 surcoat; fur-lined mittens; and the drivers' and motorcyclists' overgloves. Many troops improvised, with civilian fleece coats and captured Red Army fleece caps and padded field uniforms. Other issue winter clothing consisted of sheepskin overcoats; fur caps; plain brown quilted jacket and trousers worn over the field uniform and under the greatcoat; leather-reinforced felt calf-boots; and mountain troops' pre-war issue calf-length white cotton 'snow shirts'. The M1933 cream or off-white cotton herringbone twill fatigue tunic and trousers, worn over the field uniform, provided makeshift snow camouflage. The neck of the M1942 polo-neck sweater, introduced early 1943, could be pulled up over the mouth for warmth.

The M1942 padded reversible white/*feldgrau* winter tunic (Winteranzug) was issued from autumn 1942 in light weight (one thin white cloth layer and two thick *feldgrau*); medium (one thin white and two thick *feldgrau*, woollen lining); and heavy weight (one white and one *feldgrau* heavy cotton twill layers, with quilted wadding interlining). The tunic was thigh length, with waist and sleeve drawcords, six white/*feldgrau* pebbled buttons, two slash waist pockets with diagonal

A major commanding an Assault Artillery Brigade – a Knight's Cross holder – confers with a battery commander, April 1944. The former wears a M1943 field cap without regulation officers' aluminium wire piping; and a M1940 special field grey jacket with M1935 officers' collar patches (these were ordered changed to *feldgrau* patches piped red on 7 May 1944). The battery commander wears the 'old style' field cap and the M1934 rubberized field greatcoat for motorcyclists; a field flashlight is hung by its tab from a button. (Brian Davis)

flaps and buttons, and an integral hood with a drawcord. A small button on each upper arm secured coloured cloth field signs to distinguish German troops from their Red Army adversaries. The M1942 trousers in the same reversible materials had two slash thigh pockets with diagonal flaps and buttons, a crutch strap, and drawcords at the ankles. M1942 reversible mittens and M1942 stiff waterproof impregnated leather-reinforced white felt snow boots were worn with this uniform, as well as the unpopular reversible separate hood and face mask.

Four other types of specially designed snow camouflage uniforms were manufactured from late 1942 and in service from early 1943. The loose four-buttoned M1942 snow coverall with side slash vents was worn over the field uniform and greatcoat. The M1942 two-piece snow suit consisted of a three-buttoned loose cotton tunic with extra-long sleeves, integral hood and trousers, which could be washed easily when dirty. The M1942 mountain troops' snow uniform, consisting of a reversible white/*feldgrau* impregnated woven anorak and over-trousers, was issued to all types of combat troops. The thigh-length M1942 anorak had an integral hood with a drawcord, waist and sleeve drawcords, a short neck vent with six sets of lace holes secured by a cord and a three-buttoned flap, above a large pleatless central chest pocket with a triangular buttoned flap flanked by two smaller pleated pockets, with two similar pleated side pockets, and arm-buttons for field signs. The over-trousers had drawcords at the ankles.

Camouflage uniforms

The Italian Army had begun issuing camouflage shelter-halves in the 1920s, but on 26 June 1930 the German Army first issued the M1931 triangular shelter-quarter (Zeltbahn 31) in tightly woven cotton drill. It was finished in the reversible first pattern light/dark green-brown-khaki angular 'splinter' scheme, for use as part of a tent or as a rain cape over field equipment; from 1939 it was also seen used as a summer camouflage cape under field equipment.

The M1942 collarless reversible Zeltbahn 31 camouflage/white smock, in cotton drill in a herringbone twill weave, was inspired by the M1938 Waffen-SS smock; worn over the field uniform, it saw limited issue from about April 1942. It was closed at the chest by a cord passing through five sets of holes; two breast slits with vertical or diagonal buttoned or buttonless openings gave access to the field tunic breast pockets; it had a waist drawcord, often two side pockets with diagonal buttoned flaps, and buttoned cuffs. The M1942 arm rank insignia was prescribed but often omitted. Over-trousers in the same material, and cut as for the M1942 snow uniform, were worn. The first pattern M1942 Zeltbahn 31 camouflage/white helmet cover was followed by a second pattern with five to seven cloth foliage loops on the camouflage side. Both patterns were secured to the helmet by a drawstring under the rim.

A few M1942 padded reversible white/*feldgrau* winter tunics, trousers and mittens were produced in reversible Zeltbahn 31 camouflage/white from April 1942 and worn from winter 1942-43, as were a non-reversible winter tunic in Zeltbahn 31 and 'marsh pattern' versions. The M1944 camouflage apron was a sleeveless, pocketless smock, closed at the chest by a buttoned flap, in Zeltbahn 31 or marsh pattern herringbone twill.

Later production smocks and winter tunics were produced in 'marsh

April 1944: a Gefreiter of infantry wearing a M1942 greatcoat with wide collar, M1940 shoulder straps piped with infantry white, M1935 arm rank badge of bright aluminium braid on a dark green facing cloth triangle, and the Kuban campaign shield. (Brian Davis)

pattern' camouflage – brown and green on khaki or greyish-green background; in second pattern M1943 angular 'splinter', issued mid-1943; and in a third pattern M1944 rounded 'blotch' version from mid-1944. The M1943 non-reversible smock in marsh pattern camouflage only, with six pairs of chest button holes and an integral hood, was issued to snipers and some Panzergrenadier units.

Personnel of the Luftwaffe field divisions, transferring to the Army in September 1943, often retained their distinctive M1942 thigh-length over-jackets in heavy duty windproof herringbone twill in the paratroopers' intricate Luftwaffe 'splinter' camouflage or marsh pattern; these had five front buttons, buttoned cuffs, and two concealed thigh pockets with straight buttoned flaps; shoulder rank insignia and breast-eagles were applied.

The camouflage uniforms proved very popular and some troops, especially officers, wore privately tailored M1943 field tunics and M1940 trousers, M1944 field tunics and trousers, and M1940 special armoured crews' tunics and trousers made up in Zeltbahn 31 or marsh pattern herringbone twill.

An Obergefreiter of a self-propelled anti-tank unit, September 1944. He wears the M1940 special field grey uniform with pink-piped *feldgrau* skull collar patches; a M1940 mouse-grey braid breast-eagle; no less than four Tank Destruction Badges for single-handed successes with hand-held weapons; the Iron Cross 1st Class medal and 2nd Class ribbon, and an unidentified metal badge. On his M1935 field cap he still wears the pink branch-colour chevron, ordered removed 10 July 1942. (Brian Davis)

Rank insignia

The officers' shoulder boards, NCOs' shoulder straps and mens' arm chevrons are covered in detail in Volume 1 (Men-at-Arms 311).

On 22 August 1942 new arm rank insignia, inspired by the M1935 Luftwaffe flying suit insignia, were ordered introduced for wear on the upper left sleeve; these are shown in Table 1. The insignia were not in widespread use until 1944, and even then were relatively unpopular. Troops often omitted them from the winter tunics and anoraks, and instead attached shoulder boards and shoulder straps to the grey, khaki and reed-green shirts, fatigue jackets and drill tunics.

Branch insignia

A selective list of branch insignia is shown in Table 3. By 1944 the German High Command recognized that the open wearing of unit insignia, officially permitted since 1939 for élite units such as Großdeutschland, had the advantages of improved morale and quick identification of personnel by military police; these now outweighed the disadvantage of compromised field security, as the general military situation was deteriorating remorselessly. Therefore, on 16 February 1944, all troops of the Field and Replacement Armies were ordered to wear full branch-colour chainstitch branch and unit insignia on *feldgrau* (or Panzer black) slip-on shoulder loops. Most officers and senior NCOs simply fixed the gold or silver metal letters and numbers already permitted when not in the field; and in fact there are many instances of troops wearing unit insignia in the field before the official authorization date.

Special black uniform and insignia for tank crews

Most personnel in Panzer regiments and many on divisional staffs wore the black uniform introduced 12 November 1934, consisting of the helmet or field cap, field jacket and trousers, dark grey shirt, black tie and black lace-up boots or marching-boots (the latter ordered retained only by Armoured Engineer Companies after 18 January 1941).

The black M1940 officers' field cap, with aluminium thread cord crown and front flap piping, and the M1940 other ranks' field cap both had the branch-colour chevron removed by an order of 10 July 1942. A black wool version of the M1942 other ranks' field cap saw limited issue. The order of 11 June 1943 authorizing the standard *feldgrau* M1943 peaked field cap prescribed a black cloth version for Panzer troops. Officers and NCOs also favoured the *feldgrau* officers' M1935 peaked service cap, M1934 peaked field cap or M1938 field cap, or the other ranks' M1935 peaked service cap or M1934 field cap, despite regulations expressly forbidding their use.

The M1942 black wool double-breasted field jacket had a wide collar (though narrower than the M1934/M1936 versions) with three lapel button holes, no collar piping, four large buttons and three small buttons. All ranks wore the black rectangular collar patch piped in pink branch-colour with applied aluminium skull. The 24th Panzer Division staff, its Panzer Regiment and Armoured Reconnaissance Battalion, and other Armoured Reconnaissance Battalion staffs and Armoured Car Company crews, wore instead the golden-yellow cavalry branch colour; Panzer Division Anti-Tank Battalions wore pink Waffenfarbe; the Führer Escort Battalion Tank Company and Armoured Car Platoon wore white; Armoured Engineer Companies, white and black twist; and Armoured Signals Battalions, lemon-yellow. Some troops had their uniforms privately modified by unit or local civilian tailors, adding extra internal jacket or trouser pockets and replacing buttons with zips.

Armoured vehicle crews and mechanics, and Armoured Artillery and Rocket-Launcher crews, were issued cotton one-piece overalls in mouse-grey, *feldgrau*, off-white, light brown and reed-green, and these were sometimes dyed black by Panzer crews. Troops usually added shoulder straps and chevrons of rank and a breast-eagle in preference to the M1942 arm rank insignia.

The overalls proved unpopular, and from 5 May 1941 crews of Armoured Reconnaissance Battalion armoured car companies wore the M1941 Panzer denim uniform in reed-green herringbone twill or in white or mouse-grey cotton as a fatigue and summer field uniform. This consisted of a jacket, cut like the M1936 black jacket but with seven small buttons and one internal breast pocket. Black uniform collar patches and shoulder straps were often applied (although in theory superseded by the M1942 arm rank insignia), as was a breast-eagle on a uniform-colour backing; there was no collar piping. The trousers were cut like the M1934 black trousers.

This uniform proved so popular that the M1942 Panzer denim uniform in reed-green

An indifferent photograph, but an intensely dramatic subject. This officer, having lost his left arm in combat as a tank commander, was recalled to the colours in September 1944 as the operations officer (1a) on the staff of a newly formed Volksgrenadier-Division, with the rank of Major im Generalstab. He wears the 'old style' field cap; M1942 reversible padded winter tunic with Zeltbahn 31 camouflage cloth outermost; and reinforced cavalry breeches with General Staff crimson piping and stripes. (Author's collection)

These two infantrymen in a Volksgrenadier-Division personify the image of the German soldier of the late war period. The soldier at left – apparently, the former conductor of the Berlin Philharmonic choir – wears the M1943 field cap, M1942 greatcoat, leather M1939 Y-straps, M1931 mess kit, and carries an MP38 sub-machine gun with leather magazine pouches. His comrade – a chartered engineer – carries a M1935 dispatch case under his M1942 greatcoat. (Author's collection)

LEFT A platoon commander, left, of the 49th Jäger Regiment, 28th Jäger Division in East Prussia, September 1944, briefs his NCOs. The usual M1942 other ranks' tunic with green officers' collar facing displays lieutenants' shoulder boards, collar patches and breast eagle, and the M1942 Jäger arm badge. The sergeant, right, has been accepted as an officer candidate (Fahnenjunker-Feldwebel), identified by the double NCO braid loop round his shoulder straps; on the collar of his M1942 tunic are M1938 *feldgrau* 'guards braids' with dark green centre-stripes on a dark green patch. The Oberjäger, centre, also wears the M1942 field tunic. All three wear the M1943 field cap, the sergeant's showing the M1942 aluminium badge for Jäger units. (Brian Davis)

herringbone twill was manufactured for all armoured vehicle crews and mechanics. This comprised a loose-fitting jacket with a large left breast pocket with buttoned scalloped flap, and two parallel rows of five buttons on the right side; the trousers had a large left thigh pocket. This suit was for wear over the special black or field-grey uniform in cold weather, and was often worn instead of them in summer.

Special field-grey uniform and insignia

The special *feldgrau* M1940 version of the black Panzer field uniform issued to Assault Artillery Battalions consisted of the M1940 *feldgrau* field jacket cut like the M1936 black jacket but without branch-colour collar piping, and with field tunic breast-eagles. Officers wore standard M1935 officers' collar patches, NCOs and men M1940 mouse-grey standard 'guards braids' on a *feldgrau* backing sewn onto rectangular collar patches piped in the bright red branch-colour. The M1940 *feldgrau* trousers were cut like M1934 black trousers; Panzer grey shirt, black tie and black lace-up boots were also worn. Headgear was the officers' M1938 field cap, other ranks' M1934 or M1942 field cap, M1943 peaked field cap, or steel helmet.

Before long this stylish uniform was already being worn by other units with appropriate branch-colour collar patch pipings, shoulder boards and shoulder straps. Armoured Engineer vehicle crews wore it with black Waffenfarbe, and self-propelled Armoured Artillery units with bright red. Normal towed Anti-Tank units and self-propelled Anti-Tank units in Infantry, Rifle or Mountain divisions or Army or Corps units wore it with the skulls on *feldgrau* collar patches piped pink. Self-propelled Anti-Tank units in Panzer or Panzergrenadier divisions or in Army or Corps units equipped with the Elefant (Ferdinand) self-propelled gun wore it with standard pink-piped black Panzer skull patches.

From 5 March 1943 crews of Anti-Tank and Infantry Gun companies mounted on half-tracks in infantry and armoured infantry units adopted this uniform with white or grass-green branch colours respectively. From 12 May 1943 Armoured Train platoons changed from the black to the field-grey special uniform with pink Waffenfarbe; Army Anti-Aircraft units adopted the uniform with bright red piping, and Armoured Rocket-Launcher batteries with bordeaux red. Signals (not Armoured Signals) personnel in armoured vehicles wore the uniform with a skull on *feldgrau* patches piped lemon-yellow; and from 1 June 1943 some personnel in the mounted Cavalry Regiments wore it with a skull on *feldgrau* patches piped golden-yellow. From September 1943 the 1st Ski Brigade wore the special field-grey uniform with M1935 officers' collar patches piped grass-green and standard M1940 other ranks' patches.

Troops entitled to the special field-grey uniform also wore the reed-green fatigue and summer field uniform with appropriate branch insignia.

Special uniforms and insignia for other branches

From 25 April 1944 only general officers of combat troops were allowed to wear bright red collar patches, shoulder board underlay and greatcoat lapel linings. **General officers of the 'special careers'** were required to substitute their branch colours (but retained their bright red trouser pipings and stripes) before

30 September 1944; but on 24 October 1944 this was effectively postponed until 1945. This order applied to general officers of the Medical Corps (dark blue branch colour), Veterinary Corps (crimson), Ordnance Corps (orange), Motor Park Troops (pink), Legal Service (bordeaux red), and Administrative Service (light blue).

From 21 August 1944 the **1st Ski Brigade (later Division)** wore the Jägers' M1942 oak-leaf field cap badge with a ski superimposed (but never wore the Jägers' arm badge modified with crossed red or white skis which was prescribed, instead retaining the M1942 Jäger arm badge).

From 1941 personnel of German units, usually Panzer and motorized divisions, were seen wearing **unofficial formation badges** on field uniforms, usually aluminium reproductions of

October 1944: an Oberst commanding a Panzer-Regiment, decorated with the Knight's Cross with Oak-leaves and Swords. He wears the M1942 special black Panzer tunic, and M1940 officers' black field cap still with the pink branch-colour chevron officially discontinued in July 1942. His colleagues both wear the M1942 reversible padded winter tunic, the officer at left in M1944 'blotch marsh pattern' camouflage, the officer at right in M1943 'splinter marsh pattern'. (Brian Davis)

the divisional vehicle sign. Typically these were applied to the left side of field caps, including the M1934 'old style' peaked field cap, just above the left ear. Divisions serving on the Eastern and Balkan Fronts in 1943-45 which are known to have worn such badges include: (Arctic Front) 2nd Mountain – deer's head; (Northern Front) 290th Infantry – sword; 5 Mountain – chamois; (Central Front) 20th Panzergrenadier – anchor; 34th Infantry – white and blue shield; (Southern Front) 1st Panzer – oak-leaf; 19th Panzer – wolf's hook rune on parallelogram; 22nd Panzer – arrow; 23rd Panzer – arrow with crossbar; 4th Mountain – blue gentian flower.

The six **élite divisions** continued to develop distinctive insignia, and general officers of these formations often unofficially wore aluminium shoulder board monograms. Großdeutschland personnel wore the GD shoulder board/strap monogram, in branch-colour chainstitch for junior NCOs and men; and the third pattern black right cuff band with a hand- or machine-embroidered aluminium thread cursive *'Großdeutschland'* title and edging, introduced on 7 October 1940. From 20 December 1944 all members of Panzerkorps Großdeutschland wore these distinctions except the Brandenburg Division, which from 17 August 1944 was authorized a machine-embroidered aluminium or light-grey Gothic *'Brandenburg'* title and edging on a bluish dark green right cuff band, the 1st and 2nd Rifle Regiments wearing Rifle and Mountain insignia respectively.

Officers of the Führer-Begleit-Bataillon/Regiment/Division attached to Hitler's personal staff wore the GD monogram and on the left cuff the *'Führer-Hauptquartier'* title, other personnel of this unit substituting the *'Großdeutschland'* cuff title. From 16 September 1943 the Führer-

NORTHERN AND CENTRAL FRONT, SPRING 1943
1: Leutnant, Panzergrenadier-Regiment 2; Rzhev Salient, March 1943
2: Hauptmann, Artillerie-Regiment 240; Leningrad, February 1943
3: Grenadier, Grenadier-Regiment 474; Demyansk, February 1943

A

SOUTHERN AND CENTRAL FRONT, SUMMER 1943
1: Obergefreiter, Panzer-Regiment 15; Kursk, July 1943
2: Oberfüsilier, Füsilier-Regiment 202; Kiev, September 1943
3: Unteroffizier, Grenadier-Regiment 37; Kursk, July 1943

B

WINTER 1943-1944
1: Obergefreiter, Grenadier-Regiment 163; Orsha, October 1943
2: Leutnant, Jäger-Regiment 204; Nikopol, January 1944
3: Panzergrenadier, Panzergrenadier-Regiment 146;
   Kamenets-Podol'skiy, March 1944

C

NORTHERN AND CENTRAL FRONTS, 1944
1: Unterfeldwebel, Estnische Bataillon 659; Narva, April 1944
2: Oberst, Kavallerie-Regiment Mitte; Pinsk, April 1944
3: Füsilier, Füsilier-Regiment Feldherrnhalle; Minsk, July 1944

CENTRAL AND SOUTHERN FRONTS, 1944
1: Gefreiter, Panzergrenadier-Regiment 103;
   Rumania, August 1944
2: Generalmajor, 454.Sicherungs-Division; Brody, July 1944
3: Panzergrenadier, Panzergrenadier-Regiment 73;
   Warsaw, September 1944

WINTER 1944-1945
1: Oberleutnant, Grenadier-Regiment 236; East Prussia, December 1944
2: Fahrer, Fahrschwadron 1/227; Latvia, December 1944
3: Oberjäger, Skijäger-Regiment 1; Slovakia, February 1945

SOUTHERN FRONT, 1945
1: Oberfeldwebel, Panzer-Pionier Bataillon 124; Vienna, April 1945
2: Oberleutnant, Panzer-Regiment 1; Hungary, March 1945
3: Stabsarzt, Sanitätskompanie 178; Czechoslovakia, May 1945

G

CENTRAL FRONT, 1945
1: Leutnant, Grenadier-Regiment 1099; Stettin, April 1945
2: Grenadier, Grenadier-Regiment 1075; Berlin, April 1945
3: Feldwebel, Panzergrenadier-Regiment Müncheberg 1;
   Seelow Heights, April 1945

1   2   3

Grenadier-Bataillon/Brigade/Division wore the Großdeutschland cuff-title and a FG shoulder monogram, replaced by the GD monogram on 19 August 1944 and removed on 26 January 1945. The planned Führer-Grenadier-Division cuff title was never manufactured.

The Feldherrnhalle Division wore the Feldherrnhalle Regiment's brown cuff band and woven title on the left cuff, and on 20 June 1943 added a shoulder monogram – the SA monogram on three victory runes (Siegrunen), all on a vertical victory rune, worn from 27 November 1944 by all Panzerkorps Feldherrnhalle personnel. From 31 December 1943 Hoch- und Deutschmeister personnel wore a grey aluminium 'Stalingrad Cross' on their shoulder boards/straps, and from 26 February 1945 a bluish dark green cloth cuff title with a silver-grey machine-embroidered edging and '*Hoch- und Deutschmeister*' title in Gothic script; an alternative was a black title with Roman script.

A tank crew photographed in January 1945; most are wearing the M1942 padded reversible winter suit with M1940 or M1943 Panzer field caps, or M1935 *feldgrau* field caps. The officer has applied major's M1942 sleeve ranking to his privately acquired collarless sheepskin jacket. (Brian Davis)

On 12 December 1943 the 199th Grenadier Regiment (from 31 August 1944, 19th Grenadier Regiment) was awarded a bluish dark green cuff-title with a matt grey or silver-grey machine-embroidered edging and title '*INFANTERIE-REGIMENT LIST*' in cursive hand-written capitals, worn on the right cuff to perpetuate the traditions of Hitler's old Great War regiment. The '*Generaloberst Dietl*' cuff title – awarded 12 August 1944 to 139th Mountain Brigade to commemorate that distinguished mountain general, killed in an accident on 23 June 1944 – was probably never issued to the unit. A locally-manufactured silver/white cuff band, with black edging and *KURLAND* between the Teutonic Order shield and a silver-white elk's head on a black shield (the badge of Liepāja town), was awarded 12 March 1945 to all Army Group Kurland personnel.

Cavalry Regiment Nord (formed 1 June 1943) had unofficially worn the aluminium 'Prussian skull' cap badge of its predecessor 5th Cavalry Regiment below the service cap eagle and the field cap one-piece eagle and cockade, a practice officially sanctioned 27 August 1944. On 3 June 1944 it was renamed 5th Cavalry Regiment, and on 4 December 1944 awarded a black left cuff band with a silver-grey machine-embroidered edging and title '*FELDMARSCHALL VON MACKENSEN*', to commemorate the distinguished Great War cavalry general. From 29 December 1944 the skull was worn as a shoulder board/strap badge, but was removed in 1945 to avoid captured cavalrymen being mistaken for Waffen-SS troops. Armoured units of this regiment wore the black Panzer uniform. Cavalry Regiment Süd (also formed 1 June 1943, and on 26 May 1944 redesignated 41st Cavalry Regiment) wore the

Troops of the ROA 1st Division parade before *General-Leytenant* A.A.Vlasov at Munsingen training camp, south-west Germany, on 10 February 1945. They wear M1942 collarless reversible white/Zeltbahn 31 camouflage smocks and trousers over field uniform. The three officers in the foreground, giving the 'German salute' practised by the ROA from July 1944 to February 1945, wear officers' service caps with the eagle and swastika above the ROA cockade (worn by personnel granted German rank insignia), and carry obsolete 9mm MP34/1 Bergmann sub-machine guns. The troops carry 98k rifles and Panzerfaust 60s. (Friedrich Herrmann)

aluminium 'Brunswick skull' cap badge of the former 3rd Cavalry Regiment; and Cavalry Regiment Mitte (formed 1 April 1944), the 'dragoon eagle' of the former 6th Cavalry Regiment.

On 27 August 1944 all personnel of the 3rd Cavalry Brigade (formed in March 1944 from Mitte) adopted the dragoon eagle badge; and 4th Cavalry Bde. (5th & 41st Cav. Regts.), except for 5th Cav. Regt., the Brunswick skull. 4th Cavalry Division (5th & 41st Cav.Regts.), formed February 1945 from 4th Cav.Bde., wore on the left upper sleeve two black horses' heads on a golden-yellow shield edged black. Also in 1945, I Cavalry Corps staff and HQ troops unofficially wore on the left upper sleeve a golden-yellow rectangle edged black with four black horseshoes between two black Ks below a black pennant.

Army Patrol Service personnel wore their original uniforms with obsolete matt aluminium thread M1920 adjutants' aiguillettes at the right shoulder. From 17 October 1941 Station Guard officers wore the brown service belt and crossbelt, other personnel an aluminium duty gorget suspended around the neck by a chain, with the inscription *'Bahnhofswache'* with the Army District number and unit number in Roman and Arabic numerals respectively. Railway Guard personnel had the duty gorget with the inscription *'Zugwachabteilung'* and an Arabic battalion number. Army members of the Wehrmacht Patrol Service wore the M1935 officers' ceremonial aiguillettes, and on the left upper sleeve a white armband with an official stamp and *'Wehrmacht/Streifendienst'* in black Gothic or Roman letters. HQ guards wore an aluminium duty gorget with the inscription *'Kommandantur'* and an Arabic unit number.

Field Police wore a Military Police duty gorget with the inscription *'Feldjägerkorps'* and on the left upper or lower sleeve a red armband with an official stamp and *'Oberkommando der Wehrmacht/Feldjäger'* in black Roman letters. Military Police retained their M1939 duty gorget, but from 19 March 1944 removed their M1939 arm badge and cuff-title to avoid reprisals when captured.

Uniforms and insignia of European volunteers

European volunteers wore German uniforms and insignia, and a black machine-woven arm shield with the name of the country of origin above the national flag colours; a shield-shaped decal depicting the flag was sometimes worn on the right side of the steel helmet.

Spanish Blue Division and Legion troops wore a yellow *ESPAÑA* and a red/yellow/red horizontally striped shield on the right upper sleeve and a helmet decal. Croatian Legion troops wore a red *HRVATSKA* o

KROATIEN (often deleted by German cadre personnel) above a red/white chequered shield on the right upper sleeve (but by many officers, on the left), and a helmet decal. French troops wore a white *FRANCE* and a blue/white/red vertically striped shield on the right upper sleeve, and a helmet decal. Walloon troops wore a yellow *WALLONIE* above a black/yellow/red vertically striped shield on the left upper sleeve, and a helmet decal; they were issued the mountain field cap, *edelweiss* cap and right upper sleeve badges, and wore light green branch colour.

Similarly shaped machine-embroidered arm patches were manufactured for Rumanian troops serving in the German Army – *ROMANIA* above a shield vertically divided yellow/blue/red; for Hungarians – *UNGARN* above a vertically divided shield with (left) white/red stripes and (right) a double-branched cross on green hills on red; and for Slovaks – *SLOWAKEI* above a double-branched cross above three blue hills on a red shield. Bulgarians were prescribed a plain straight-sided shield diagonally striped white/red/green. However, issue of these four shields to Army personnel is unconfirmed.

Uniforms and insignia of Osttruppen

Estonian, Latvian and Lithuanian troops wore standard German uniforms, cap badges, breast-eagles, collar and rank insignia. Some Estonian troops unofficially wore on the right upper arm the Estonian Police armshield – diagonal blue/black/white stripes with yellow edging and three yellow lions. From about mid-1943 Baltic troops were authorized on the right upper sleeve a cloth armshield with curved sides and a scalloped top, and diagonal stripes in national colours – blue/black/white (Estonia), dark red/white/dark red (Latvia), and yellow/green/red (Lithuania). Cockades in these colours were worn on the field cap.

From 29 April 1943 'Hiwis' wore German Army uniforms; and from 1 July 1944 they could be promoted as far as Unteroffizier. National shields, field cap cockades and ROA rank and collar insignia were officially prescribed for Russians, Belorussians and Ukrainians, but standard German insignia were usually worn. Poles wore the '*Im Dienst der deutschen Wehrmacht*' armband.

From January 1943 ROA personnel in the Eastern Battalions and the later infantry divisions wore standard German uniforms with special insignia, and could be promoted to general officer rank. Cap insignia for officers comprised a Tsarist-style blue oval cockade with a red centre and silver rays; those for NCOs and men, a plain oval blue and red cockade. The modified Tsarist rank insignia and collar insignia are illustrated in Table 2. The armshield, usually worn on the left upper sleeve, was a bluish dark green rounded shield with a straight top and machine-embroidered, printed or woven insignia consisting of a yellow 'POA' (i.e. ROA in Cyrillic

A *mayor* of the Russian Liberation Army, right, photographed while questioning a Soviet prisoner. He wears an ROA cockade on his cap (apparently a Bergmütze); and a M1940 other ranks' field tunic with officers' dark green collar, ROA collar patches, and dark green ROA armshield. Note that he has been deemed worthy to wear German shoulder boards of rank. At left is a specialist officer (Sonderführer), an interpreter second lieutenant – Dolmetscher (Z) – from a mountain infantry unit. He wears specialist officers' shoulder boards and collar patches, and an *edelweiss* badge on his field cap. (Brian Davis)

Rank titles: 1st line - ROA: 2nd line (in brackets) - Cossacks: 3rd line *(Italics)* - German infantry 1943-45.

ROA colours: 1-3 - bluish dark green strap, gold button, red piping, gold zig-zag braid, silver pips; 4-9 - bluish dark green strap, *feldgrau* button, red piping and centre-stripes, gold pips; 10 - aluminium sleeve braid; 11 - *feldgrau* strap piped in German branch-colour, *feldgrau* button, aluminium braid, silver pips; 12-17 - bluish dark green strap, *feldgrau* button, red piping, aluminium bars; 18 - dark blue, red centre, silver rays; 20 - dark blue, red centre; 21-22 - red centre, bluish dark green patch, aluminium braid, *feldgrau* button, silver wire piping. **Cossack colours:** shoulder straps as ROA or: 4-9 - silver braid strap

(gold - artillery), red piping (light blue -Terek); silver buttons, red centre-stripes (dark blue - Don, blue - Terek, black - artillery); 10-11 - as ROA with golden-yellow strap piping (bright red - artillery); 12-17 - red strap (dark blue - Don, blue - Terek, black - artillery), silver buttons, red piping (light blue - Terek), silver braid bars at button end; 19-20 - badge/rays: centre - darkblue: red (Don), dark blue: yellow (Siberian), black: red (Kuban), black: blue (Terek). 23 - red patch, white lances, bluish dark green edging. 24 - red patch, white lances, aluminium braid edging. **18 March 1944 - 8 May 1945:** German collar patches widely adopted, and for approved officers and NCOs German rank insignia.

1. General [1]
(General ot Kavalerii) [1]
General der Infanterie

2. General-Leytenant
(General-Leytenant) [1]
Generalleutnant

3. General-Mayor
(General-Mayor) [2]
Generalmajor

4. Polkovnik
(Polkovnik)
Oberst

5. Podpolkovnik
(Voyskovoy Starshina)
Oberstleutnant

6. Mayor
(Mayor)
Major

7. Kapitan
(Yesaul)
Hauptmann

8. Poruchik
(Sotnik)
Oberleutnant

9. Podporuchik
(Khorunzhiy)
Leutnant

10. Khaupt-Fel'dfebel' [3]
(Khaupt-Vakhmistr) [3]
Hauptfeldwebel

11. Ober-Fel'dfebel' [4]
(Ober-Vakhmistr) [4]
Oberfeldwebel

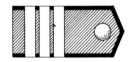

12. Fel'dfebel'
(Vakhmistr)
Feldwebel

(Cossack variant)
13. Unter-Ofitser
(Uryadnik)
Unteroffizier

14. Ober-Yefreytor [5]
(Starshiy Prikazni) [5]
Obergefreiter

(ROA/Cossack variant)
15. Yefreytor
(Prikazni)
Gefreiter

16. Ober-Soldat [5]
(Starshiy Kazak) [5]
Obergrenadier

17. Sold
(Kazak)
Grenadier

18. ROA officers' cap.
19. Cossack officers' cap.
20. All NCOs & mens' caps

ROA collar-patches
21. Officers.
22. NCOs & men

Cossack collar-patches
23. Officers.
24. NCOs & men.

Footnotes:
1 Rank authorized but never held.
2 Held from November 1944 by Ivan Nikitich Kononov, wearing German rank insignia.
3 An appointment, not a rank, usually held by a Fel'dfebel'/Vakhmistr.
4 Introduced 15.6.1944 for approved NCOs.
5 Introduced 1.1.1944

letters) above a white inner shield edged red with a blue Tsarist-style St.Andrew's Cross. From 18 March 1944 certain approved personnel, usually only officers, wore German rank insignia and collar patches, and some added an eagle and swastika to their peaked service caps above the cockade. ROA personnel usually wore the German breast eagle, but an order of 2 March 1945 specifically forbade this practice and ordered German cadres to remove their ROA armshields, to perpetuate the fiction that the ROA/KONR were independent German-allied armed forces.

The Ukrainian UVV was prescribed the same insignia with blue and yellow cockades, and an armshield showing 'УВВ' (UVV in Cyrillic) above a white Ukrainian trident on a yellow and light blue horizontally divided inner shield; but this insignia, although manufactured, was never issued.

Cossack troops retained their traditional uniforms or adopted German uniforms, and from January 1943 wore German breast eagles and the 'lance' collar patches introduced 15 November 1942. ROA rank insignia were prescribed, but most Cossacks wore them with traditional silver or gold officers' braids, pipings and centre-stripes, and other ranks' shoulder straps and pipings. From 18 March 1944 most troops adopted German collar patches and, for approved personnel, German rank insignia. The distinctive Cossack caps, and the 1st Cossack Division's armshields, are described in Volume 2 (Men-at-Arms 316). All uniforms and insignia were retained after transfer to the Waffen-SS in November 1944. German cadre personnel wore German uniforms and insignia with Cossack armshields, but many also adopted Cossack caps and cloaks, especially for parades. Some emigré Cossack officers from the Russian Revolution, who associated themselves with but were generally resented by the Cossacks, adopted eccentric mixtures of German and Cossack uniforms.

Eastern Legion battalions continued to wear German breast-eagles and collar patch and shoulder board/strap rank insignia introduced in April 1942, and the cap badges adopted in September 1942, described and illustrated in Volume 3 (Men-at-Arms 326). German officer and NCO cadres wore German uniforms and insignia with the Legion shield on the right upper arm.

Medals and awards

Since July 1941 accounts of heroic acts had been recorded in the 'Roll of Honour of the German Army', equivalent to the British Army's 'mentioned in dispatches'; and on 30 January 1944 such soldiers were awarded a gilded metal clasp in the form of a wreathed swastika, worn on the Iron Cross 2nd Class button hole ribbon.

On 25 November 1942 the Close Combat Clasp – a metal eagle and swastika above a crossed grenade and bayonet on an oak-leaf bar, worn above the left breast pocket – was instituted for 15 (bronze), 30 (silver) or 50 (gilt) days'

Infantrymen – including teenage boys and middle-aged men – wait apprehensively in a prisoner-of-war cage for further instructions. Most are wearing the Felduniform 44 with M1943 field cap, and have removed most of their equipment. Note the M1935 rank chevron still worn by the Obergefreiter, right. (ECPA)

197

This highly decorated Feldwebel is a platoon commander in the reconnaissance company of a Volksgrenadier-Division, September 1944. On the M1943 field tunic can be made out his Iron Cross 1st Class medal and 2nd Class ribbon, Close Combat Clasp and – although he is apparently an infantryman – the General Assault Badge. He carries 6x30 binoculars, and the Sturmgewehr 44 assault rifle issued as a priority to VGD personnel. (Author's collection)

hand-to-hand combat on foot unsupported by armour, counted from 1 December 1942. Hitler considered the gilt badge the highest infantry decoration, and personally awarded them from 17 August 1944.

The Anti-Partisan War Badge – a metal sword in a wreath stabbing down into writhing snakes, worn on the left breast pocket – was instituted on 30 January 1944 by Reichsführer-SS Himmler for any personnel completing 20 (bronze), 50 (silver) or 150 (gold) days' anti-partisan service.

On 20 August 1944 the Sniper's Badge – a grey cloth oval with a black eagle's head above two green oak-leaves, worn on the right cuff – was awarded in three grades: 1st Class, with a gold cord inner edging, for 60 kills; 2nd Class, silver cord, for 40 kills; and 3rd Class, without cord, for 20 kills, reckoned from 1 September 1944.

Three new campaign shields, worn on the upper left arm, were officially instituted during this period. On 25 April 1943 the white metal Demyansk Shield – depicting a Wehrmacht eagle clutching an Iron Cross above crossed swords and an aeroplane, worn without cloth backing – was awarded to 100,000 men in six infantry divisions (12, 30, 32, 123, 225, 290) of II Corps who had defended the pocket in Central Russia from 8 February to 30 June 1942. The bronze Kuban Shield – an eagle and swastika above a stylized map, worn on a *feldgrau* cloth backing – was instituted on 20 September 1943 for the 17th Army's defence of the Kuban bridgehead from 1 February to 9 October 1943. On 10 December 1944 the bronze Warsaw Shield – featuring a German eagle strangling a snake – was instituted for troops who fought against the Polish Home Army in the Warsaw Uprising from 1 August to 2 October 1944; but no shields were actually produced. (In March 1945 a grey Lappland Shield – featuring a map of the area – was instituted for 20th Mountain Army personnel, but probably never awarded.)

The 'special badge for single-handed destruction of a tank' – a black metal tank on a silver lace strip with upper and lower black edging, worn on the right upper sleeve – was awarded from 9 March 1942. On 18 December 1943 a gold tank on a gold strip was instituted for five tanks destroyed. On 12 January 1945 the same design but with an aircraft silhouette replacing the tank was instituted as the 'long-range aircraft destruction badge' for shooting down an enemy aeroplane with small arms or a light machine-gun.

Table 3: SELECTIVE LIST OF BRANCH AND UNIT INSIGNIA OF UNITS ON THE EASTERN FRONT 3 FEBRUARY 1943 - 8 MAY 1945

Units	Branch colour	Shoulder-strap insignia			Other distinctions
		Northern Front	Central Front	Southern Front *(Balkans 5.10.44-8.5.45)*	
Combat Troops - Staff *(Kommandobehörde)*					
General Officers (Generale)	Bright red	None	None	None	*Larisch* patches
General Staff *(Generalstab)* officers	Crimson	None	None	None patches	Silver *Kolben*
7 Army Group *(Heeresgruppe)* Staffs	White	G (Nord/Kurland)	G (Mitte/Nord, Weichsel) Süd /Nordukraine/ A/Mitte) *(E , F)*	G (A/Südukraine/Ostmark,	–
10 Army *(Armee)* Staffs	White	A / 16, 18	A / 2/Ostpreussen, 4, 9, 11	A / 6-9, 17	–
1 Mountain Army *(Gebirgsarmee)* Staff	Light green	A / 20	–	–	*Edelweiss* badges
4 Armoured Army *(Panzerarmee)* Staffs	Pink	–	A / 2, 3	A / 1, 4 *(2)*	–
52 Corps *(Korps)* Staffs (* Corps had Latin numbers)	White	1-7, 8, 10, 16, 26, 28, 33, 38-9, 43, 50, 54, 70-1	6-9, 12-3, 17, 20-3, 26-8,32, 35, 43, 53, 55, 59-60, 66-9, 101	5, 7-8, 11--3, 17, 24, 29, 30,32, 34, 42-4, 49, 52, 59, 72, 90 *(15, 22, 68-9)*	–
4 Mountain Corps *(Gebirgskorps)* Staff *	Light green	18-9, 36	15, 18	–	*Edelweiss* badges
11 Armoured Corps *(Panzerkorps)* Staffs *	Pink	–	39-41, 46-8, 56-7	GD, 3, 4/FH, 39, 40, 46-8, 56-7	–
1 Cavalry Corps *(Kavallerie)* Staff *	Gold-yellow	≠	1	*(1)*	-
3 Reserve *(Reserve)* Corps Staffs *	White	61	–	62 *(69)*	–
Combat Troops – Infantry *(Infanterie)*					
180 Infantry *(Infanterie)* Division Staffs	White	1-2, 11, 21, 23-4, 30, 32, 52,58, 61, 69, 74, 81, 83, 87, 93, 96, 121-3, 126, 132, 140, 163, 169-70, 199, 201, 205, 207, 210, 215, 217-8, 223, 225, 227, 230, 254, 263, 270, 274, 280-1, 285, 290, 295, 300, 328-9, 331, 389, 391, 613, 702	1, 7, 12, 14, 17, 21, 23, 30, 32, 34-6, 50, 52, 56-8, 61, 68-9, 72-3, 82-3, 85-8, 93, 95, 98, 102, 110, 112-3, 129, 131, 134 137, 169-70, 197, 201, 203, 205-6, 208, 214-6, 221, 227, 251-3, 255, 258, 260, 262-3, 267-8, 281, 286, 291-3, 296, 299, 321, 323, 327, 330-2, 339, 342, 377, 383, 391, 402, 433, 463, 604-7, 610, 707, 712	1, 9, 15, 17, 34, 38-9, 46, 48, 50, 57, 68, 72-3, 75-6, 82, 88, 94, 96-8, 106, 111-2, 123, 125, 131, 153-4, 158, 161, 168,182, 187, 193, 198, 213-4, 217, 223, 253-5, 258, 269, 275, 282, 291, 293-4, 302, 304, 306, 327-8, 332, 335-6, 339,342, 344, 356-7, 359, 367, 370-1, 376, 384, 387, 389, 404, 408, 413, 444, 454, 463-4, 546, 603, 609, 613, 616	–
14 Line Infantry *(Grenadier)* Div. Staffs	White	31	6, 541-2, 547-9, 558, 561-2	HuD, 45, 544-5	–
38 Infantry *(Volksgrenadier)* Div. Staffs	White	12, 31, 211 , 563	6, 18, 26, 31, 45, 183, 211-2, 246, 256, 277, 326, 337, 340, 349, - 541-2, 547-9, 551, 558, 561-2	6, 12, 16, 45, 62, 79, 167, 183, 211, 257, 271, 276, 320, 340, 347, 349, 361,544-5	–
1 People's Assault *(Volkssturm)* Div. Staff	White	–	78	78	–
9 Line Infantry *(Grenadier)* Brigades	White	193, 388, 503	1131-2, 1135	1133-4, 1136	–
580 Line Infantry *(Grenadier)* Regts	White	1-742 series	1-745 series	1-1090 series	–
9 Line Infantry *(Füsilier)* Regts	White	22, 26, 68	GD, 22, 26-7, 34, 39, 68, 202	GD, , 230	–
7 Rifle *(Jäger)* Div. Staffs	Light green	5, 8, 28	5, 28, 100-1	8, 28, 100-1, 117*(117-8)*	*Jäger* badges

Units	Branch colour	Shoulder-strap insignia			Other distinctions
		Northern Front	Central Front	Southern Front *(Balkans 5.10.44-8.5.45)*	
14 Rifle *(Jäger)* Regts	Light green	28, 38, 49, 56, 75, 83	49, 54, 56, 75 , 83, 227-9	28, 38, 49, 54, 83, 227-9, 737, 749	*Jäger* badges
11 Rifle Field *(Feld(L))* Div. Staffs	White	1, 9-10, 12-4, 21	4, 6	5 *(11)*	–
23 Rifle *(Feld(L))* Regts	White	1, 17-20, 23-8, 41-3	49-54	9 *(21-2)*	–
7 Mountain *(Gebirgs)* Division Staffs	Light green	2, 5-7,	3	1, 3-4 *(1)*	*Edelweiss* badges
14 Mountain *(Gebirgs)* Regts.	Light green	85, 100, 136-7, 141, 143, 206, 218	138-9	13, 91, 98-9, 138-9 *(98-9)*	*Edelweiss* badges
1 Ski *(Skijäger)* Division Staff	Light green	–	1	1	*Edelweiss* badges
2 Ski *(Skijäger)* Regts.	Light green	–	1, 2	1, 2	*Edelweiss* badges
8 Reserve *(Reserve)* Division Staffs	White		141, 151, 154 , 174	147, 153 *(173, 187)*	–
20 Reserve Inf.*(Reserve-Grenadier)*Regts.	White	–	1-266 series	23-268 series *(17-462 series)*	–
Combat Troops – Mobile Troops *Schnelle Truppen*					
1 Cavalry *(Kavallerie)* Division Staff	Gold-yellow	–	3-4	3-4 *(3-4)*	Cavalry breeches, boots
4 Mounted Cavalry *(Reiter)* Regts	Gold-yellow	–	Nord/5, Süd/41, Mitte/105	5, 31-2, 41	Cavalry breeches, boots
21 Armoured *(Panzer)* Division Staffs	Pink	4, 12, 14	2-9, 12, 18-20, 25	1-3, 6-9, 11, 13-4, 16-7, 19-20, 23, 25, 27 *(23)*	Black *Panzer* uniform
1 Armoured *(Panzer)* Division Staff	Gold-yellow	–	–	24	Black *Panzer* uniform
3 Armoured *(Panzer)* Division Staffs	Pink	–	FH1, GD	FH2, GD	Black *Panzer* uniform
5 Armoured *(Panzer)* Brigades	Pink	101	102-4	109-10	Black *Panzer* uniform
25 Armoured *(Panzer)* Regts.	Pink	29, 35-6, 118	3, 6, 8-11, 18, 21, 25 ,27, 29, 31, 33, 35, 101, 118	1-4, 6, 9-11, 15, 21, 25, 27, 33, 36, 39 *(23)*	Black *Panzer* uniform
1 Armoured *(Panzer)* Regt.	Gold-yellow	–		24	Black *Panzer* uniform
4 Armoured *(Panzer)* Regts.	Pink	–	FH/FH1, GD	BG, FH2, GD *(BG)*	Black *Panzer* uniform
26 Armd Recce.*(Panzeraufklärung)* Bns.	Pink	A / 4, 12, 14 1	A / FH, GD 2-9, 12, 18-9,	A/1-3, 6-9, 11, 13-4, 16-7, 19, 24,-5, 110, 120 *(23)*	Grey *Panzer* uniform
4 Armd.Inf.*(Panzergrenadier)* Div. Staffs	Grass green	18	10, 18, 20, 25	10, 20	Grey *Panzer* uniform
4 Armd.Inf.*(Panzergrenadier)* Div.Staffs	White	–	FB, FG, FH, GD	BG , FH1, GD *(BG)*	Grey *Panzer* uniform
1 Motorized *(Grenadier(mot.))* Brigade	White	–	–	*(92)*	–
50 Armd.Infantry *(Panzergrenadier)* Regts.	Grass green	5, 12, 25, 30, 33, 51,	2-5, 6 -7, 10-4, 20, 25, 28, 30, 33, 35, 41, 51-2, 73-4, 76, 90, 98-102, 114, 119, 146-7, 304, 394 146-7, 304, 394 *(126, 128)*	3-4, 6-7, 1 0-1, 20-1, 26, 28, 40-1, 63-4, 66, 7 3-4, 76, 79, 90, 93, 98, 103, 108, 110-1, 113-4, 140	Grey *Panzer* uniform
5 Armd.Infantry *(Panzergrenadier)* Regts.	Grass green	–	FB, FH1, GD	BG, FH3 *(BG)*	Grey *Panzer* uniform
251 Div. Recce. *(Füsilier)* Bns.	Gold-yellow	1-702 div. series	1-712 div. series	1-546 div. series	
7 Mtn. Recce.*(Gebirgsaufklärung)* Bns.	Gold-yellow	67, 91, 95, 99	95	54, 94, 112, *(54)*	*Edelweiss* badges
286 Antitank *(Panzerjäger)* Bns.	Pink	P / 1-702 div. series	P / 1-712 div. series	P / 1-546 div. series	–

Units	Branch colour	Shoulder-strap insignia			Other distinctions
		Northern Front	Central Front	Southern Front (Balkans 5.10.44-8.5.45)	
Combat Troops – Artillery (Artillerie)					
1 Artillery (Artillerie) Division Staff	Bright red	–	–	18	–
254 Artillery (Artillerie) Regts.	Bright red	1-702 series	1-712 series	1-546 series	–
7 Mount.Artill.(Gebirgsartillerie) Regts	Bright red	82, 95, 111, 118	112	79, 94, 111 (79)	Edelweiss badges
29 Armd Artillery(Panzerartillerie) Regts	Bright red	29-118 series	FB, FG, FH, GD, 2-25 series	BG, FH1, GD, 1 -27 series (23)	Black Panzer uniform
44 Assault Artillery(Sturmartillerie) Brigs	Bright red	184-5, 202, 303, 393, 600, 909, 912,	177, 1 89-90, 201-3, 209-10, 226, 228, 232, 237, 244-5, 259, 261, 270, 276, 279, 281, 286, 303, 904, 920,	177, 191203, 210, 228, 232, 239, 243-4, 249, 259, 277,300-1, 311, 322, 325, 395, 600, 905, 911	Grey Panzer uniform
4 Rocket Launcher (Werfer) Brigades	Bord. red	2	3, 6	1	–
Combat Troops – Engineers (Pioniere)					
251 Engineer (Pionier) Bns	Black	1-702 div. series	1-712 div. series	1-546 div. series	–
7 Mount. Engineer (Gebirgspionier) Bns	Black	82, 91, 95, 99	83	54, 83, 94	Edelweiss badges
29 Armd Engineer (Panzerpionier) Regts	Black	29-118 div. series	FB, FG, FH, GD, 2-25 series	BG, FH1, GD, 1 -27 series (23)	Black Panzer uniform
Combat Troops – Signals (Nachrichtentruppe)					
251 Signals (Nachrichten) Bns	Lem. yellow	29-118 div. series	FB, FG, FH , GD, 2-25 series	BG, FH1, GD, 1-27 series (23)	–
7 Mount.Sigs (Gebirgsnachrichten) Bns	Lem. yellow	67, 91, 95, 99	68	54, 68, 94	Edelweiss badges
23 Armd Sigs (Panzernachrichten) Regts	Lem. yellow	29-118 div. series	FB, FG, FH, GD, -25 series	BG, FH1, GD, (23) 1 -27 series	Black Panzer uniform
15 War Correspondent(Propaganda)Coys.	Lem.Yellow	501, 621, 680	612, 670, 689, 649, 693, 697	612, 637, 649, 666, 691, 694-5 (693)	PK cuff-title
Supply Troops (Versorgungstruppen)					
290 Div. Supply (Nachschubführer) Cdrs	Light blue	D / 1-702 div. series	D / 1-712 div. series	D / 1-546 div. series	–
290? Motor Transport (Nachschub) Cols.	Light blue	N / 1-702 div. series	N / 1-712 div. series	N / 1-546 div. series	–
380? Horse Transport (Nachschub) Cols.	Light blue	N / 1-702 div. series	N / 1-712 div. series	N / 1-546 div. series	Cavalry breeches, boots
290 Horse Medical. (Sanitäts) Coys – men	Dark blue	1-702 div. series	1-712 div. series	1-546 div. series	Red Cross armband
32 Mot.Medical (Sanitäts) Coys – men	Dark blue	1-702 div. series	1-712 div. series	1-546 div. series	–
251 Veterinary (Veterinär) Coys – men	Crimson	1-702 div. series	1-712 div. series	1-546 div. series	Cavalry breeches
Security Troops (Sicherungstruppen)					
14 Army Rear-Area Commders (Korück)	White	525, 583-4,	532, 550, 580, 590	531, 535, 550, 553, 558, 585, 593	–
11 Dist.Commds	White	394, 396	392, 399, 400, 668	242, 393, 397, 579, 679	–

Units	Branch colour	Shoulder-strap insignia			Other distinctions
		Northern Front	Central Front	Southern Front *(Balkans 5.10.44-8.5.45)*	
290 MP *(Feldgendarmerie)* Troops	Orange	1-702 div. series	1-712 div. series	1-546 div. series	Sleeve badge, cuff-title
16 Security *(Sicherungs)* Division Staffs	White	D/52, 94, 207, 281, 285, 390-1	D/52, 201, 203, 221, 286	D/213, 403, 444, 454	–
19 Security *(Sicherungs)* Regts.	White	S / 7, 88, 94, 107, 113, 601	S / 36, 57 , 61, 88, 122, 183, 601, 608, 613	S / 177, 318, 360, 375	–
Foreign Troops					
1 Spanish *(Spanische)* Infantry Div. Staff	White	D / 250	–	–	Spanish arm-badge
3 Spanish *(Spanisches)* Infantry Regts.	White	262-3, 269	–	–	Spanish arm-badge
1 Spanish *(Spanisches)* Legion	White	?	–	–	Spanish arm-badge
3 Croatian *(Kroatisches)* Infantry Div Staffs	White	–	–	*(369, 373, 392)*	Croatian arm-badge
6 Croatian *(Kroatisches)* Infantry Regts	White	–	–	*(369-70, 383-4, 846-7)*	Croatian arm-badge
1 French *(Französisches)* Infantry Regt.	White	–	638	–	French arm-badge
1 Walloon *(Wallonische)* Infantry Bn.	Light green	–	–	373	Belgian arm-badge
2 ROA Infantry *(Infanterie)* Div. Staffs	Red	–	600, 650	–	ROA right arm-badge
1 ROA Infantry Brigade	Red	–	599	–	ROA right arm-badge
6 ROA *(Grenadier)* Infantry Regts	Red	–	1601-5, 1607, 1651-3	–	ROA right arm-badge
71 ROA Eastern *(Ost)* Bns	Red	653, 658-669, 672, 674	7, 82, 134, 229, 2 63, 268, 308, 339, 406, 412, 427, 439, 441, 446-9, 559, 561, 574, 000-5, 615-21, 627-30, 633-7, 642-3, 646-9, 651, 675, 680	318, 447, 454, 550-1, 556	ROA left arm-badge
11 Armenian *Ostlegion* Bns	Gold yellow	–	I/98, I/125, 810, 814-6	II/9, III/73, 808-9 *(I/125, 422)*	Armenian arm-badge
14 Azeri *Ostlegion* Bns	Green	–	817-20, IV/101	I/4(Geb), I-II/73, I/97, I/101, I/111, 804-6	Azeri arm-badge
7 Georgian *Ostlegion* Bns	Red	–	I/1(Geb), I/9(Geb)	II/4(Geb), I/9, 795-6, *(II/125)*	Georgian arm-badge
5 North Caucasian *Ostlegion* Bns	Brown	–	–	800-2, *842-3)*	North Caucasian badge
34 Turkestani *Ostlegion* Bns	Light blue	–	I/44, I/71, I /76, I/79, I/100, I/113, I/305, I/371, I/376, I/384, I/389, 785-6, 788, 790-2	8(Fz), 11(Fz), 156, I/295, I/370, 4 50, 452, 781-4, 811, 1000-1(GebTr), *(I/297, 789)*	Turkestan arm-badge
8 Volga-Tartar *Ostlegion* Bns	Blue/Green	–	825, 828-34	–	Volga-Tartar badge
2 Cossack *(Kosaken)* Division Staffs	Gold yellow	–	–	*(1, 2)*	Cossack arm-badge
6 Cossack *(Kosaken)* Cavalry Regts	Various	–	–	1-6 *(1-6)*	Cossack arm-badge
9 Cossack *(Kosaken)* Infantry Bns	Red	126	574-5, 622, 624-5	570, 572-3 *(572-3)*	Cossack arm-badge
19 Cossack *(Kosaken/Ostreiter)* Cavalry Bns	Red	207, 285	57, 69, 780, 161, 443, 580, 622-5, 631, 638	126, 281, 403, 444, 480	Cossack arm-badge

OPPOSITE **April 1944: private in a Großdeutschland motorized regiment on look-out duty. He wears a M1943 field tunic with the two NCO braid bars of an officer candidate on his shoulder straps, and a second pattern helmet cover in M1942 Zeltbahn 31 camouflage; and is speaking into a M1933 field telephone. (ECPA)**

THE PLATES

A: NORTHERN AND CENTRAL FRONT, SPRING 1943

A1: Leutnant, Panzergrenadier-Regiment 2; Rzhev Salient, central Russia, March 1943.

Over his other ranks' M1940 field tunic with officers' M1935 collar patches this platoon commander wears the M1942 white/*feldgrau* reversible winter tunic, without the unpopular M1942 arm rank insignia – not widely worn until 1944. He also wears a *feldgrau* cloth cap lined with rabbit-fur (the most common fur cap), with unofficially added M1935 field cap insignia; M1942 reversible trousers; other ranks' belt and M1939 'short shaft' marching boots and woollen 'trigger-finger' mittens; ammunition pouches for his MP40 sub-machine gun, and a leather flare pouch. He is loading his M1928 27mm Walther short-barrel flare pistol with a red brilliant smoke cartridge.

A2: Hauptmann, Artillerie-Regiment 240; Leningrad, NW Russia, February 1943.

This artillery battalion commander wears the sentries' and horsedrawn vehicle drivers' sheepskin overcoat with *feldgrau* cloth collar, also popular with officers – generals favoured a thigh-length version with a sheepskin collar. The M1934 'old style' field cap without crown stiffening, officially abolished 1 April 1942 but worn until May 1945, has aluminium thread insignia and bright red artillery piping. He also wears a balaclava, M1942 snow boots and woollen gloves. In the absence of the M1942 arm rank insignia only the 10x50 Zeiß binoculars, M1934 officers' belt and hardshell holster for the P08 Luger suggest his commissioned rank.

A3: Grenadier, Grenadier-Regiment 474; Demyansk, central Russia, February 1943.

This sentry wears the M1942 snow coverall over his M1942 other ranks' greatcoat; note also the mittens, the balaclava rolled up under his M1935 whitewashed steel helmet, and general purpose goggles. The M1942 leather-reinforced felt overboots with wooden soles, issued for winter sentry and static defence duty, replaced the impractical straw overboots, and were sometimes worn on the move. He carries the M1931 canteen and mess kit attached to the M1941 canvas bread bag; his weapon is the Karabiner 98k, the Wehrmacht's standard rifle.

B: SOUTHERN AND CENTRAL FRONT, SUMMER 1943

B1: Obergefreiter, Panzer-Regiment 15; Kursk, central Russia, July 1943.

This tank crewman participating in the 'Death Ride of the Panzers' at Kursk wears the M1942 Panzer jacket without pink collar piping but with M1934 pink-piped skull collar patches and shoulder straps, and M1940 mouse-grey breast-eagle and (see left sleeve) rank chevrons. He has the Eastern Winter Campaign 1941/42 buttonhole ribbon, and a black Wound Badge (one and two wounds). His headgear is the short-lived M1942 black field cap; he wears M1942 reed-green herringbone twill Panzer work trousers with a large thigh pocket, ankle boots, and general purpose goggles, and carries the M1931 canteen and cup.

B2: Oberfüsilier, Füsilier-Regiment 202; Kiev, central Ukraine, September 1943.

Belonging to an infantry regiment designated 'Füsilier' on 11 June 1943 to commemorate a Great War regiment, this veteran section member wears the M1942 field tunic with M1940 insignia, M1942 field cap with buttoned flap, M1940 trousers, M1941 anklets and ankle boots, and still has the obsolete eagle decal on his M1935 steel helmet. He has M1909 leather rifle ammunition pouches, and the surplus M1940 tropical webbing infantry support Y-straps widely issued after May 1943; a gas mask canister hangs from its diagonal slinging strap, and a bayonet and entrenching shovel are worn behind his left hip. He carries a M1939 TNT 'egg' percussion grenade fixed below his right hand pouches; the unpopular Walther 7.92mm Gewehr 41(W) semi-automatic rifle; and the M1943 Panzerfaust Klein 30 recoilless anti-tank projectile launcher, trialled on the Eastern Front in July 1943 and placed in immediate production.

B3: Unteroffizier, Grenadier-Regiment 37; Kursk, central Russia, July 1943.

This sniper wears the M1942 first pattern collarless reversible white/Zeltbahn 31 'splinter' camouflage smock with matching M1935 helmet cover, M1940 *feldgrau* trousers and M1939 'short shaft' marching boots; he omits the M1942 arm rank insignia, thus concealing his NCO status. On his black other ranks' belt he wears M1909 leather ammunition pouches for his Karabiner 98k rifle, which is fitted with the extremely efficient M1939 Zeiß 4-power 'high' model turret-mounted 'scope sight issued to trained snipers. He also carries standard 6x30 binoculars with a field-made Zeltbahn 31 camouflage cover, and a bayonet.

C: WINTER 1943-1944

C1: Obergefreiter, Grenadier-Regiment 163; Orsha, eastern Belarus, October 1943.

This machine-gunner wears a M1942 greatcoat – together with the surcoat, the main winter protection for infantrymen – with M1940 left sleeve chevrons of rank. His M1935 steel helmet has a rubber tyre inner tubing band for fixing foliage camouflage, and he has scraped off the left side decal in obedience to 28 August 1943 regulations. His M1942 field cap is tucked into his belt; he wears M1940 trousers, M1941 anklets and ankle boots. He carries the MG42 light machine gun and has first gunner's belt equipment – a black leather spares pouch and a P38 Walther pistol in a hardshell holster – supported by M1939 infantry Y-straps. A gas mask canister strap is visible over his shoulder, and a bayonet and folding shovel at his hip.

C2: Leutnant, Jäger-Regiment 204; Nikopol, southern Ukraine, January 1944.

This platoon commander wears a M1942 thin two-piece snow camouflage suit with a red field sign printed on each sleeve, over his *feldgrau* field uniform and M1942 polo-neck sweater, with M1939 'short shaft' marching boots. The helmet cover is the M1942 first pattern reversible white/Zeltbahn 31 camouflage type. He carries two sets of magazine pouches for his MP40 sub-machine gun, 6x30 binoculars, and a 3kg anti-tank assault charge.

C3: Panzergrenadier, Panzergrenadier-Regiment 146; Kamenets-Podol'skiy, western Ukraine, March 1944.

This third gunner in his section's light machine gun team carries a 300-round ammunition box for the MG42. He wears the M1942 padded reversible winter tunic and trousers in first pattern white/Zeltbahn 31 camouflage, usually issued to armoured infantry units; the M1943 peaked field cap, M1941 anklets and ankle boots. He evidently prefers *feldgrau* woollen

'trigger-finger' mittens to the white/camouflage reversible mittens without a trigger-finger, a deficiency corrected in later 'marsh pattern' mittens. He has M1909 leather ammunition pouches for his Karabiner 98k mid-war production rifle, and carries M1924 stick-grenades; his M1935 helmet still bears traces of whitewash snow camouflage.

D: NORTHERN AND CENTRAL FRONTS, 1944

D1: Unterfeldwebel, Estnische Bataillon 659; Narva, Estonia, April 1944.

This volunteer wears the M1942 reed-green summer field uniform with M1940 *feldgrau* shoulder straps and M1940 NCO strap and collar braid, breast eagle and collar patches; note the M1943 Estonian armshield, Infantry Assault Badge, silver Wound Badge and Iron Cross 2nd Class buttonhole ribbon. The M1943 peaked field cap with mouse grey insignia, M1941 anklets and ankle boots complete the outfit. The M1939 Y-straps support M1909 Karabiner 98k (right) and canvas Gewehr 43 (left) ammunition pouches, folding shovel and M1931 canteen on his belt; a field flashlight is fixed at his left shoulder. He is armed with a M1924 stick grenade and a Walther 7.92mm Gewehr 43 semi-automatic rifle.

D2: Oberst, Kavallerie-Regiment Mitte; Pinsk, western Belarus, April 1944.

Following common practice this cavalry regiment commander has modified his other ranks' M1940 field tunic with a shortened skirt, bluish dark green collar, officer's collar patches and breast eagle, but not the turn-back cuffs

September 1943: an infantry company cobbler working in the field behind an array of long-shaft and M1939 short-shaft marching boots and ankle boots. His colleague, the company tailor, repairs a field tunic; unit tailors were responsible for many of the non-standard uniform items seen in 1943-45. (Brian Davis)

ABOVE, LEFT **November 1943: Unteroffizier of the Panzergrenadier-Division Großdeutschland wearing a M1935 field tunic; note white branch-colour 'GD' chainstitch monogram on his shoulder strap. The fleece-trimmed felt field cap – see also colour plate F1 – bears an aluminium machine-woven M1935 breast-eagle. Note leather M1939 support Y-straps, and 10x50 Voigtländer combat leader's binoculars. He wears the Iron Cross 1st Class, the bronze Infantry Assault Badge for motorized infantry, and the bronze DRA State Sports Badge. (ECPA)**

ABOVE **January 1944: this Oberleutnant wears a M1942 reversible padded winter tunic, with the soiled white side outwards and showing the M1942 arm rank insignia, over his field tunic showing officers' M1935 collar patches and Knight's Cross. His M1938 officers' field cap shows the aluminium wire crown and flap-front piping. (ECPA)**

sometimes seen. He has a M1935 helmet, M1940 leather-reinforced breeches, riding boots and spurs, the rare bakelite 6x30 binocular case, and a Walther P38 in a soft leather holster. The officers' M1938 field cap in his belt has aluminium thread piping, eagle and cockade, but not the aluminium Brunswick Eagle unofficially worn by this regiment since April 1943. He has the Iron Cross 1st Class medal and 2nd Class ribbon, and the General Assault Badge.

D3: Füsilier, Füsilier-Regiment Feldherrnhalle; Minsk, central Belarus, July 1944.

This former SA stormtrooper (note bronze SA Wehrabzeichen military fitness badge) wears the M1943 field tunic with M1940 collar patches and breast-eagle, embroidered 'Feldherrnhalle' cuff title and runic shoulder strap motifs. He has M1943 trousers, M1941 anklets and ankle boots; he has painted his M1942 helmet summer tan, and green and brown blotches were sometimes added. His belt, with M1909 pouches, bayonet and folding shovel, is worn without Y-straps; the slings of his 98k rifle and gas mask canister cross on his chest. His armament includes both M1924 stick and M1939 egg grenades, and a Panzerfaust 60. This unit was destroyed at Minsk.

E: CENTRAL AND SOUTHERN FRONTS, 1944

E1: Gefreiter, Panzergrenadier-Regiment 103; Iasi, Rumania, August 1944.

This machine gunner wears the M1943 field tunic and

trousers, M1941 anklets and ankle boots, M1942 helmet and camouflage net. As first gunner he carries a P38 Walther pistol in a soft shell holster on his left hip; at right front would be a spares pouch – in black leather, or black or tan pressed cardboard – for his 7.92mm MG42. The light order rifleman's equipment on his belt consists of the 84/98 bayonet, M1931 bread bag, canteen, cup and mess kit, with the M1931 shelter-quarter secured by equipment straps. He has left his gas mask and M1938 folding shovel in the Sd.Kfz.251/1 armoured personnel carrier.

E2: Generalmajor, 454.Sicherungs-Division; Brody, western Ukraine, July 1944.

This commander of a rear-area division destroyed at Brody wears the general officers' field uniform virtually unchanged

reversible white/M1943 'marsh' pattern camouflage winter suit, the tunic and trousers turned to different sides. Just visible on the left sleeve is his green-on-black M1942 rank insignia. He has leather-reinforced felt winter boots; the unofficial but common 'felt field cap', similar to the M1943 field cap, has a white fleece band and ear flap lining, and an aluminium service cap badge; the three-finger reversible mittens show the camouflage side. He carries a slightly whitewashed M1935 helmet, and short 10x50 binoculars. His blackened M1934 officer's belt supports a Walther P38 in a soft-shell holster and a dispatch case.

LEFT **September 1943: Leutnant of the Assault Artillery Battalion of Panzergrenadier-Division Großdeutschland in the cupola of his self-propelled gun. The M1940 special field grey uniform bears M1935 standard officers' collar patches with red artillery 'lights', and M1940 light grey braid shoulder boards with red badge cloth underlay and a gilded aluminium 'GD' monogram. His M1943 field cap is unpiped; note also officers' *feldgrau* suede gloves, and the bronze Infantry Assault Badge indicating previous service in the motorized infantry. (ECPA)**

BELOW **March 1944: Wachtmeister of 667th Assault Artillery Brigade. Note the brigade numerals on his shoulder straps, permitted in the field since 16 February 1944. He has removed the Panzer skulls from his red-piped *feldgrau* collar patches, but has not added the mouse-grey 'guards braids' authorized from 30 January 1943. (Brian Davis)**

from 1939. It comprises a M1935 officers' field tunic with general officers' shoulder-boards, gold buttons, breast eagle and collar patches; M1935 service cap with gold pipings and chin cords, and M1942 gilded insignia. He wears M1935 stone-grey breeches with general officers' piping and stripes, and riding boots. Partly obscured here on his left hip is a Walther PPK in a soft leather holster; his 10x50 binoculars are held down by a button tab. His decorations are an Iron Cross 1st Class medal and 2nd Class ribbon and the star of the German Cross in gold.

E3: Panzergrenadier, Panzergrenadier-Regiment 73; Warsaw, September 1944.

This section member wears the M1943 non-reversible smock with integral hood in second pattern 'marsh' camouflage over his M1943 field tunic and M1943 belted trousers. His M1942 helmet has chicken-wire netting for attaching foliage camouflage. Armoured infantry, originally with light-order equipment for mechanized combat, acquired M1939 infantry Y-straps to support heavier equipment when in the dismounted rôle. The conventional belt equipment includes rifle ammunition pouches, stick and egg grenades, bayonet and folding shovel.

F: WINTER 1944-1945

F1: Oberleutnant, Grenadier-Regiment 236; Insterburg (Chernyakhovsk), East Prussia, December 1944.

This infantry company commander wears the M1942 padded

F2: Fahrer, Fahrschwadron 1/227;
Tukums, central Latvia, December 1944.

This young driver in a horse-drawn company of a divisional supply regiment, recently transferred from Germany, gives the Nazi 'German salute' compulsory after July 1944. He wears the obsolete M1934 other ranks' field cap with mouse-grey insignia, reissued in 1944 from old stocks; the M1943 field tunic with M1940 insignia; *feldgrau* woollen balaclava rolled round his neck, woollen gloves, final pattern *feldgrau* cloth-reinforced cavalry breeches and – rare by 1944 – cavalry riding boots. He has a late-production 98k rifle, the single set of M1909 pouches issued to rear-area troops, and the 84/98 bayonet with M1942 cavalry frog. Note on his left pocket the Hitler Youth Badge of Honour.

F3: Oberjäger, Skijäger-Regiment 1;
Trstina, northern Slovakia, February 1945.

This section leader wears the mountain troops' field uniform: M1938 mountain troops' *feldgrau*/white reversible windproof anorak with three chest pockets and arm rank insignia, and reversible windproof trousers over the M1940 special field grey uniform. He also wears anklets, climbing boots, and the M1943 peaked field cap with mouse-grey insignia and the aluminium ski and oak-leaves badge. Leather M1939 Y-straps support first pattern M1943 beige canvas single-flap magazine pouches for his MP43/MP44 sub-machine gun (renamed in December 1944 the Sturmgewehr 44 assault rifle).

G: SOUTHERN FRONT, 1945

G1: Oberfeldwebel, Panzer-Pionier Bataillon 124;
Vienna, April 1945.

This NCO platoon commander in the Führer-Grenadier-Division wears the M1940 special field grey jacket with mouse-grey breast eagle, M1940 mouse-grey 'guards braids' on black-piped collar patches, and *'Großdeutschland'* right cuff title (but no GD shoulder strap monograms – these were ordered removed from 26 January 1945). His trousers are tucked into grey socks and ankle boots; he wears a second pattern Zeltbahn 31 'splinter' camouflage cover on his M1942 helmet. Decorations are the Iron Cross 2nd Class ribbon, bronze Close Combat Clasp, General Assault Badge and black Wound Badge; he displays the Demyansk armshield, indicating former service with II Corps. He has one set of beige canvas MP40 magazine pouches, a Walther P38 in a soft-shell holster, and a slung Panzerfaust 60.

G2: Oberleutnant, Panzer-Regiment 1;
Székesfehérvár, central Hungary, March 1945.

This tank company commander wears the special black Panzer uniform (the buttoned-across lapel of his jacket obscuring the M1934 aluminium breast-eagle), with M1934 pink-piped skull collar patches, and M1940 light grey braid shoulder boards with gilt rank stars and regimental numerals. The M1934 trousers are worn with ankle boots; his M1943 Panzer peaked field cap has officers' aluminium crown piping, aluminium eagle and cockade, and the unofficial 1.Panzer-Division oak-leaf badge. Note hard-shell holster for his Walther P38; grey wool gloves; motorcycle goggles; Iron

An Oberleutnant of the 290th Infantry Division wearing an M1940 other ranks' field tunic remodelled with dark green collar and officers' collar patches, breast eagle and shoulder boards. His M1934 peaked field cap, with aluminium thread eagle, cockade and wreath, also displays the unofficial divisional badge of a broadsword; even more unusually, this is repeated on his left pocket flap. This officer's decorations are the Iron Cross 1st Class medal and 2nd Class ribbon, Eastern Winter Campaign 1941/42 ribbon, Infantry Assault Badge, and – as a member of a 'Demyansk' division, – the Demyansk sleeve shield. (ECPA)

Cross 1st Class medal and 2nd Class ribbon and silver Tank Battle Badge.

G3: Stabsarzt, Sanitätskompanie 178;
Plzen, western Czechoslovakia, May 1945.

This divisional medical company commander has managed to surrender to a US 3rd Army unit. He wears officers' M1935 collar patches and breast-eagle and M1940 light grey braid shoulder boards on his other ranks' M1943 field tunic; note ribbon of the War Merit Cross with Swords in the buttonhole. M1940 *feldgrau* breeches, riding boots, and an M1943 field cap with aluminium thread insignia and crown piping complete his dress. He carries a M1942 padded reversible white/Zeltbahn 31 winter tunic. Medical personnel wore the red cross armband; nevertheless, note a P08 Luger in a hard-shell holster on his brown M1934 officers' belt. He has been permitted to retain this gun for personal protection.

H: CENTRAL FRONT, 1945

H1: Leutnant, Grenadier-Regiment 1099; Stettin, East Germany, April 1945.

This company commander in 549.Volksgrenadier-Division wears the M1944 field tunic and trousers with M1942 polo-neck sweater, and is fortunate enough to have retained M1939 short-shaft marching boots; his M1942 helmet has a rough wire cover. He displays M1935 officers' collar patches; M1940 light grey braid shoulder boards with infantry-white underlay; an other ranks' M1944 machine-woven breast-eagle on a *feldgrau 44* triangular patch; one Tank Destruction Badge and the Infantry Assault Badge. Equipment includes a M1934 brown officers' belt stained black; 6x30 binoculars; two sets of standard M1944 beige canvas magazine pouches for his Sturmgewehr 44 – issued as a priority to Volksgrenadier units; and a Panzerwurfmine 1(L) anti-tank hand grenade.

H2: Grenadier, Grenadier-Regiment 1075; Berlin, April 1945.

This 50-year-old infantryman from a battle-group of 541.Volksgrenadier-Division desperately defending Berlin, wears a M1940 surcoat with integral hood over his field uniform, with M1941 anklets and ankle boots, and the M1943 field cap with mouse-grey woven insignia. He has conventional belt and Y-strap equipment, and carries a final model Karabiner 98k rifle (without bayonet lug or cleaning rod). He also carries M1943 stick and M1939 egg grenades, and a Panzerfaust 100.

H3: Feldwebel, Panzergrenadier-Regiment Müncheberg 1; Seelow Heights, East Germany, April 1945.

This section commander defending the Oder Line wears the M1943 non-reversible winter tunic in third pattern M1944 'blotch marsh' camouflage scheme with M1942 arm rank insignia, over an M1942 sweater and M1943 field tunic; M1942 padded reversible white/*feldgrau* trousers over M1943 belted trousers; M1941 anklets and ankle boots; and a M1935 helmet smeared with mud for camouflage. He wears M1940 tropical canvas Y-straps, and beige canvas Soviet magazine pouches for his captured 7.62mm PPS.43 sub-machine gun. He also has an M1938 folding shovel, useful for hand-to-hand fighting.

GERMAN ARMY 1939-45 (5) WESTERN FRONT 1943-45

THE CONTEXT OF THE WESTERN FRONT 1943-1945

The High Command of the Army and Wehrmacht

The German Armed Forces (Wehrmacht) consisted of the Army (Heer), Navy (Kriegsmarine) and Air Force (Luftwaffe) under Chief of the Armed Forces High Command (Chef des Oberkommandos der Wehrmacht – OKW) GFM Wilhelm Keitel. The Waffen-SS, officially established in November 1939 under Reichsführer-SS Heinrich Himmler, was an independent arm, but its field units operated under Army command. There were also paramilitary units in the Police (Polizei), Border Guards (Zollgrenzschutz), Stormtroopers (SA), National Socialist Motor Corps (NSKK), State Labour Service (RAD), Todt Labour Organization (OT), and from 25 September 1944 the German Home Guard (Deutscher Volkssturm); and these all provided the Army with scratch units to defend western Germany from October 1944[1].

Adolf Hitler, as Führer and head of the German government since 30 January 1933, had appointed himself Supreme Commander of the Armed Forces (Oberster Befehlshaber der Wehrmacht) on 4 February 1938 and Chief of the Army High Command (Oberbefehlshaber des Heeres – OKH) on 19 December 1941. Hitler was essentially an armchair strategist who believed that his military experience in the ranks of the infantry during the Great War, combined with his political vision, qualified him as a gifted field commander. Accordingly he increasingly ignored the ineffective Keitel, and bypassed three successive Army Chiefs of Staff – Gen der Inf.(later GenObst) Kurt Zeitzler (24 September 1942 to 21 July 1944); GenObst Heinz Guderian (until 28 March 1945), and Gen der Inf. Hans Krebs – with predictably disastrous results. On 30 April 1945 Hitler committed suicide, and on 1 May Josef Goebbels became prime minister (Reichskanzler), appointing Admiral of the Fleet Karl Dönitz as president before himself committing suicide. On 7 May Dönitz ordered Keitel to sign the unconditional surrender of all German forces to the Western Allies at Rheims, eastern France.

Hitler encouraged rivalry and demarcation disputes in duplicated political and military institutions in order to forestall challenges to his authority. He appointed the OKW to administer France, Belgium, the Netherlands, Denmark, Norway and Italy, leaving eastern Europe and the Balkans to the OKH. This gave Army generals in the West even less power than in the East, a situation compounded by Hitler's determination to marginalise the OKH, especially after the failed Army-inspired 'Bomb Plot' of 20 July 1944.

From 25 April 1945 the OKW Operations Staff under GenObst Alfred

An overladen but determined infantryman trudges through woodland in Belgium, September 1944. He has attached foliage to his helmet, and over his field uniform and equipment he wears his Zeltbahn 31 triangular camouflaged shelter-quarter. He carries a M1943 'Panzerfaust Klein' anti-tank grenade-launcher and a box of warheads as well as his Karabiner 98k rifle and a M1924 stick grenade. (Author's collection)

---

1 See inside back cover for listing of other relevant Osprey titles on German uniformed organisations of the Third Reich period.

Jodl nominally took over the military conduct of the war, with Dönitz controlling troops in northern Germany and Luftwaffe GFM Albert Kesselring those in southern Germany, Austria and Northern Italy, thus effectively excluding the OKH from control over its own troops – though given the chaotic conditions of the last couple of weeks of hostilities, this had little practical effect .

The Army was composed of the Field Army (Feldheer) on active service outside Germany; and the Replacement Army (Ersatzheer), from July 1944 under Himmler's SS command, increasingly training replacements for field units in occupied territories. The Army decreased from a peak of 6,550,000 to 5,300,000 by May 1945, with a further 800,000 in the Waffen-SS.

Since 26 October 1940 German Army troops in occupied France – from 27 November 1942 including the former Vichy zone – Belgium and the Netherlands came under Western High Command (Oberbefehlshaber West) in Paris, also called Army Group D (Heeresgruppe D). This command was initially held by GFM Erwin von Witzleben; from 15 March 1942 by GFM Gerd von Rundstedt; from 2 July 1944 until his arrest as a conspirator in the Bomb Plot by GFM Günther von Kluge; from 15 August 1944 by GFM Walter Model; and from 5 September 1944 by Von Rundstedt again. Western High Command controlled Army Groups B and G.

Italy came under the 2nd Air Fleet (Luftflotte 2), later redesignated Southern High Command (Oberbefehlshaber Süd) and from 26 November 1943 Army South-Western High Command, under Luftwaffe GFM Albert Kesselring, controlling Army Group C and, briefly, Army Group B. As the Western and Italian Fronts merged, Western and South-Western High Command were combined on 22 April 1945 as Southern High Command, under Kesselring. The OKW administered the Netherlands, Denmark and Norway directly through the Armed Forces Commands (Wehrmachtbefehlshaber). On 11 November 1944 Netherlands Armed Forces Command became Army Group H; and on 7 April 1945 North-Western High Command, under GenObst Johannes Blaskowitz, and from 15 April 1945 GFM Ernst Busch.

The strategy

Germany's victories from September 1939 to February 1943 had been achieved by experienced generals free to apply 'Blitzkrieg tactics', with concentrations of tanks, motorised infantry and Luftwaffe ground-attack aircraft breaking through weak points in the enemy lines and destroying the enemy's command centres, while 'Decisive Manoeuvre' used infantry to trap the enemy and destroy them in isolated pockets.

Following the fall of France, the decision to postpone the invasion of Great Britain indefinitely, and his self-appointment as supreme field

RIGHT **A carefully-posed propaganda photograph intended to reassure the German public that the strong, confident German soldier would successfully resist any Allied invasion. This infantryman wears the M1942 helmet with a foliage net, and the M1935 field tunic with dark green collar bearing standard M1938 patches; he carries late-war green varnished steel 7.92mm link for his section's MG34 or MG42 light machine gun. (Author's collection)**

commander, Hitler had these tactics discontinued in favour of static defence of fortified lines – essentially the tactics he had observed as a runner at the command post of Bavarian Reserve Infantry Regiment No.16 on the Western Front during the Great War.

On 23 March 1942 Hitler ordered the OT to build the 'Atlantic Rampart' (Atlantikwall), a series of fortified seaport 'fortresses' intended to form a continuous line along the Dutch, Belgian and French Atlantic coasts as far as the Spanish border (and on the Channel Islands). These were connected by concrete coastal artillery positions and pillboxes, tank obstacles, minefields and barbed wire, to prevent the expected Anglo-American seaborne landings and allow German forces to concentrate on the Eastern and North African campaigns. The Atlantikwall was guarded by static infantry divisions with some Panzer divisions in mobile reserve; but by June 1944 the fortifications were still incomplete, and the garrisons had been stripped of manpower and tanks to provide replacements for the Eastern Front.

Hitler had reluctantly assigned the 'old warhorse' GFM Gerd von Rundstedt to defend France, Belgium and the Netherlands; but then frustrated this experienced field commander by ignoring his pleas that the Allies would land in Normandy, insisting that they would land at Calais or on the Dutch coast and consequently misdirecting vital reinforcements. Hitler also insisted until May 1945 on maintaining a large garrison in Norway, where he erroneously expected a landing.

In June 1944 the minimal infantry screen fought doggedly to defend the Normandy beaches, but valuable hours and days were lost while his generals attempted to convince a dithering Hitler, remote from the battlefield, to commit armoured reserves against the bridgehead. Thereafter GFM Walter Model, perhaps the most gifted German field commander after Rommel (but prevented by Hitler, and Allied armoured and air superiority, from deploying Blitzkrieg or Decisive Manoeuvre tactics), conducted a masterful fighting retreat under constant daytime maulings from Allied ground-attack aircraft. Hitler, wasted reinforcements by insisting on defending every inch of ground and refusing tactical withdrawals to secure defensive lines; and increasingly relied on the Waffen-SS to stiffen Army units.

Hitler's insistence, on the grounds of sustaining morale, on the reconstitution of all destroyed and depleted units actually created a deceptively large order of battle on paper, containing nominal divisions of only brigade or even regimental strength. His foolhardy gamble in counterattacking westwards in the Ardennes offensive in December 1944 squandered Rundstedt's best troops; but the depleted forces defended the western German border energetically, only collapsing in late March 1945 when defeat was clearly inevitable.

Hitler's fear of losing Italy was so great that the Italian Front commander Luftwaffe GFM Albert Kesselring was allocated good quality Army and Luftwaffe ground units. He conducted a dogged fighting withdrawal northwards across Italy's easily defensible rivers and mountains until a general collapse in April 1945. This ensured that the Italian campaign, which Winston Churchill had believed would hasten Germany's defeat, remained a comparative 'sideshow', diverting valuable Allied reinforcements from the Western Front.

THE DEVELOPMENT OF ARMY UNITS

The German army on the Western Front in 1943-45 was organised into two, later three Army Groups, with a fourth in Italy; these comprised one Panzer and eight infantry Armies, the Ligurian Italo-German Reinforced Army, and a Reinforced Corps (Armeeabteilung – actually an Army without Army HQ troops). These were supported by 1st Luftwaffe Airborne Army and 6th SS Armoured Army, with Replacement Army units briefly organised into the Upper Rhine Army Group (Heeresgruppe Oberrhein) and Blumentritt Army. Each Army controlled two to five infantry Corps; no cavalry, mountain or reserve corps served on these fronts.

Infantry Divisions

The infantry division remained the backbone of the German army and, from September 1939 to March 1945 divisions were organised according to 35 particular establishments, each designated a 'wave' (Welle). The divisional and establishment number gives a general indication of the size and quality of manpower and firepower, the higher the wave and 'house-number' the smaller the division, and the lower the quality of the troops, weapons and equipment.

Waves 1-20, in the 1934-July 1942 period (1-399, 702-719 divisional series) were organised as M1939 Divisions, with steady reductions in the number of troops (from 17,734 to 11,246). From 20 September 1942 onwards 12 'static' (bodenständig) infantry divisions, numbered 242-5, 264-6, 326 and 343-8, were formed outside the 'wave' system to guard the Atlantikwall. Each of these had two, later sometimes three fortress or infantry regiments, each with two or three battalions, usually totalling six battalions instead of the normal nine. These were older, less well-trained troops, with minimal motorisation and reduced firepower.

Losses on the Eastern Front forced M1939 Divisions in the West to be reorganised as – and for divisions in Waves 21-28 (52-237 divisional series and named divisions) from November 1943 to July 1944 to be formed as – M1944 Divisions. The M1944 Infantry Division had 12,772 men in three M1944 infantry regiments, each with an anti-tank company, infantry gun company and two infantry battalions. Six divisional support units comprised an artillery regiment, Füsilier bicycle reconnaissance, field replacement (Feldersatz), anti-tank, engineer and signals battalions. Divisional services consisted of horsedrawn and motorised transport columns, a medical company, field hospital, veterinary company, military police troop and field post office. Five of these divisions (59, 64, 226, 232, 237) were static units for the Western and Italian Fronts.

Following the Bomb Plot of 20 July 1944, Hitler from 26 August 1944 designated 54 new and reorganised divisions raised from July to August 1944 in Waves 29-32, and many reconstituted divisions (6-563 and 708 divisional series and named divisions), as People's Grenadier Divisions (Volksgrenadierdivisionen). These were intended to provide politically reliable infantry under Himmler's direct command, and would eventually represent the bulk of the infantry on the Western Front. With a nominal strength of 10,072, the People's Grenadier Division – either a reorganised combat-weary formation, or a new formation raised from

A Panzergrenadier sniper in France, carrying a Karabiner 98k fitted with a turret-mounted 'scope sight; he has pulled a helmet foliage net over his face. He wears the M1940 field tunic with *feldgrau* collar and collar patches – much less visible than the M1935 collar and M1938 patches – and *feldgrau* M1940 shoulder straps piped in the grass-green Waffenfarbe of his branch of service. (Friedrich Herrmann)

convalescent wounded and untrained recruits – was organised like a M1944 Infantry Division but with a Füsilier company instead of a battalion, with 18% less manpower and 16% less firepower. Quality varied from reasonably good to wholly inadequate.

On 10 December 1944 all existing infantry divisions, and those formed in Waves 33-35 (48-716 divisional series and named divisions), six of which were Volksgrenadierdivisionen, were reorganised as M1945 Divisions. An M1945 infantry division had 11,909 men; divisional services were reorganised as a supply regiment (Versorgungsregiment) with a motor transport company, two horsedrawn transport companies, an ordnance company and a mechanical repair platoon; administration, medical and veterinary companies, a military police troop and field post office. In March 1945 manpower was further reduced to 11,370, but it is doubtful whether any division now conformed to official establishment so late in the war. Some divisions hastily formed in spring 1945 were assigned a name rather than the usual number.

The Germans were particularly successful at forming in the field small unit remnants and individual stragglers into temporary 'battle groups'(Kampfgruppen), with no fixed organisation and named after their commanders, for particular missions. Similarly, larger assets were sometimes assembled as available into a 'divisional staff for special employment' (Division zur besonderen Verwendung – zbV) lacking a conventional divisional organisation.

From October 1939 each military district (Wehrkreis) raised several depot divisions to train Field Army depot (Ersatz) units in Germany. Each numbered depot division was organised as a M1939 infantry division; and from autumn 1944 they were increasingly deployed as field units to defend territory close to or within the German border – e.g. the deployment of 180th and 190th Depot Divisions at Arnhem in September 1944. In October 1942 many depot divisions were redesignated Reserve Divisions (141-188 series), each 16,000 strong, and deployed as static garrison units in the occupied territories. On 9 October 1944, with virtually all occupied territory recaptured by the Allies, Reserve Divisions were redesignated Infantry Divisions, as were Training Divisions (Feldausbildungs-Divisionen), each with 16,000 recruits undergoing advanced combat training and awaiting posting to front line units.

Three mountain infantry divisions (2, 6, 7) served in Norway and four (2, 5, 8, 157) on the Western and Italian Fronts. The M1939 Mountain Division with 13,056 men was organised like the M1939 Infantry Division but with two mountain regiments and mountain-equipped support units and services; whilst a 13,000-strong M1942 Rifle (Jäger) Division had lightly armed mobile infantry. No Security Divisions served on the Western or Italian Fronts.

Generalfeldmarschall Gerd von Rundstedt, commanding German forces in France, Belgium and the Netherlands in June 1944. He was the only serving officer holding a traditional appointment as Chef or 'Colonel of the Regiment', in his case of the 18th Infantry, which he commanded in 1925-26. He thus wears a unique uniform combining insignia of his rank and his honorary appointment. The eight-buttoned M1920 officer's field tunic has gold buttons and breast eagle for general's rank; the front piping prescribed for general officers in 1927 is here white for infantry. His field-marshal's shoulder boards have a white underlay, and bear both the crossed batons of rank and the regimental numerals '18'. The M1935 officer's collar patches have silver thread 'guards braids' (Litzen) on an infantry white background. He wears the Knight's Cross with Oakleaves and Swords at his throat. (ECPA)

Armoured formations and units

On 23 June 1943 the motorised infantry division was redesignated M1943 Armoured Infantry Division (Panzergrenadierdivision). This was 14,738 strong with two motorised infantry regiments and one Panzer battalion; seven divisional support units – motorised artillery regiment, field replacement, armoured reconnaissance, anti-tank, motorised anti-aircraft, motorised engineer and motorisedsignals battalions, plus divisional services. From 20 September 1944 it was reorganised as the M1944 Armoured Infantry Division, with 680 fewer support personnel and less equipment but increased firepower; the motorised infantry regiments were redesignated as Panzergrenadier regiments.

Only six army Panzer Divisions were available to fight on the Western Front and two in Italy. On 24 September 1943 all 15,600-strong M1941 Panzer Divisions were reorganised as M1944 Panzer Divisions with 14,727 men. The establishment was one two-battalion tank regiment, of which the 1st Battalion often received PzKpfw V Panthers while the 2nd retained the PzKpfw IV; two two-battalion motorised Panzergrenadier regiments, each of which had one battalion equipped with armoured half-tracks; seven divisional support units – an armoured artillery regiment, field replacement, motorised anti-aircraft, armoured reconnaissance, armoured anti-tank, armoured engineer and armoured signals battalions; and divisional services.

This organisation concealed the fact that the number of tanks had steadily declined from 328 per division in September 1939 to 165 in 1943. In practice mechanical breakdowns, shortages of spare parts, combat losses, non-arrival of replacements under skies ruled by Allied fighter-bombers, and equipment abandoned when retreating across the Seine forced GFM Model to report in September 1944 only five to ten serviceable tanks per division – which, although later greatly improved, revealed a catastrophic situation which was virtually ignored by Hitler.

On 24 March 1945 all Panzer and Panzergrenadier divisions were ordered reorganised as M1945 Panzer Divisions, with purely defensive capability and only 54 tanks; but it is unlikely that any divisions were thus organised so late in the war. Theoretically the 11,422-strong M1945 Panzer Division would have had a mixed armoured regiment with one tank battalion and one half-track Panzergrenadier battalion; two motorised Panzergrenadier regiments; and support units and services as before.

German armour was supported by assault artillery battalions allocated to Army HQs; on 25 February 1944 these were redesignated as brigades. Each had three batteries of 10-14 self-propelled guns. Panzer and Panzergrenadier divisions had army anti-aircraft battalions, each with two

Normandy, June 1944: the three-man crew of a camouflaged 7.5cm Panzerabwehrkanone 40 L/46 gun of a divisional anti-tank battalion. They wear a motley selection of field tunics, marching boots and ankle boots; the centre and right soldiers seem to have foliage straps hooked to helmets showing light blotches of camouflage paint. The man at left is armed with a MP40, the centre man with a Luger in a hard-shell holster, and the Gefreiter at right has M1911 rifle ammunition pouches and an 84/98 bayonet on his belt. Although they seem to be in light field equipment it is interesting that they retain the M1930 gas mask canister, complete with strapped-on anti-gas cape. (Friedrich Herrmann)

batteries of 88mm dual-purpose guns – devastating when used in the ground role – and two 20mm light anti-aircraft batteries. On 1 March 1944 rocket-launcher regiments were grouped into brigades; from September 1944 these came under Himmler's nominal command as 'People's Rocket Launcher Brigades', ten of which fought in the Ardennes offensive.

Elite divisions

Of the six élite army divisions formed during World War II all except the Großdeutschland divisions served, albeit often briefly, on the Western Front after June 1940. On 1 June 1943 the 44th Infantry Division was redesignated the Imperial Grenadier Division (Reichsgrenadier-Division) Hoch- und Deutschmeister, encouraging continued Austrian loyalty to the Reich by stressing Imperial Austrian military traditions; it served from August 1943 to November 1944 in Italy. On 20 June 1943 the Panzergrenadier Division Feldherrnhalle was formed from SA (Sturmabteilung) volunteers; 106th Panzer Brigade Feldherrnhalle fought on the Western Front from August 1944. Some 224 men of the Brandenburg commandos were formed into the Stielau Group and sent behind Allied lines as 56 four-man teams in US Army uniforms as saboteurs during the Ardennes offensive in December 1944; 72 soldiers were captured and shot as spies. The Führer Infantry Brigade (Führer-Grenadier-Brigade) and Führer Escort Brigade (Führer-Begleit-Brigade) participated in the final stages of the Ardennes fighting in January 1945.

Non-Army formations

On 1 November 1943, the 14 surviving Luftwaffe field divisions were transferred to the Heer and reorganised as M1944 infantry divisions with 'Rifle (L) Regiments', support units and services. On paper 14 Luftwaffe Airborne Divisions – some of these 'Green Devils' being generally considered among the best German units of the war – were formed, of which nine (2, 3, 5-8, 11, 20, Erdmann) supported the army on the Western Front and two (1, 4) on the Italian Front. The élite Hermann Goering Panzer Division served in Italy from June 1943 to July 1944. (See MAA 139, *German Airborne Troops*; and MAA 229, *Luftwaffe Field Divisions.*)

North-east France, August 1944: an Obergefreiter of Engineers prepares a charge. He wears the second pattern of camouflage cover – note its distinctive foliage loops – drawstringed to his helmet, in Zeltbahn 31 splinter-pattern. The M1935 tunic bears M1940 rank chevrons, with field-grey backing instead of the earlier dark green. (Author's collection)

A group of prisoners captured in Normandy, 12 June 1944. The Obergefreiter (left) is wearing the M1943 peaked field cap and M1940 field tunic; (far right) one soldier retains the old M1934 field cap; and (second right) note the M1943 hooded smock in marsh-pattern camouflage, as issued to snipers. (Brian Davis)

GFM Günther von Kluge (left) photographed on the Normandy front in July 1944 during his three-week tenure as Oberbefehlshaber West. The field-grey leather greatcoat was popular with high-ranking officers, but production was discontinued from 29 February 1944 in order to save strategic materials. The lapels were unlined. The Generalmajor accompanying him wears a rubberised greatcoat. (ECPA)

The Waffen-SS deployed eight divisions (1, 2, 9, 10, 12 Panzer; 17 Panzergrenadier; 34 Infantry; 6 Mountain) on the Western Front, and 16th SS-Panzergrenadier Division in Italy (see MAA 34, *The Waffen-SS).*

Military Police, Chaplains & Officials

On 1 February 1941 the Army Patrol Service (Heeresstreifendienst), supervising Replacement Army garrisons and checking the papers of soldiers on leave, was unified under a Patrol Service Commander controlling railway guard battalions and checking documents in large railway stations. From 1 December 1941 special Army Patrol Service Groups (Gruppen Heeres-Streifendienst), from 1 March 1944 redesignated Armed Forces Patrol Groups, were deployed to the occupied territories. Following the German defeat at Stalingrad in February 1943 the army's traditionally high discipline gradually eroded, requiring extra units to support these and the Military Police and Area Command (Oberfeldkommandantur) authorities.

On 27 November 1943 Field Police (Feldjäger) Commands I-III were established, reporting directly to GFM Keitel, and holding precedence over all Patrol Service and Military Police. Each command controlled a Field Police Battalion (from 25 April 1944, a Regiment) with five motorised companies; based 12 miles behind the front line, these units dealt out rough justice, including summary execution, to Wehrmacht personnel. They were supported from December 1944 by Patrol Corps (Streifkorps) sections. Each Army had a 49-strong battalion-status Secret Field Police (Geheime Feldpolizei) Group carrying out field security and anti-resistance duties, reporting to Army Intelligence (Abwehr).

A Protestant and a Catholic chaplain each served on divisional staffs, whilst Azeri, North Caucasian, Turkestani and Volga-Tartar battalions were allocated a Sunni Muslim chaplain *(Mulla).* On 24 January 1944 some branches of Army Officials, permanently assigned to the Field Army, were redesignated as service personnel, and on 1 May 1944 transferred to the two branches of the newly formed Special Troop Service (Truppensonderdienst) – the Wehrmacht Legal Service for senior career court martial officials, and the Administration Service for senior and advanced career district administration officials and senior career paymaster officials.

European volunteers

Western and northern European volunteers in the German army were not deployed on the Western Front, so as to avoid execution as traitors if captured by their compatriots. Thus the Spanish 'Blue Division', Belgian Walloon 373rd Infantry Battalion and French 638th Reinforced Grenadier Regiment served only on the Eastern Front. Belgian Flemish, Danish, Dutch, Norwegian, Swedish, Swiss and later Spanish volunteers served in the Waffen-SS on the Eastern Front, joined on 1 June 1943 by the Walloons and on 1 September 1944 by the French.

On 15 September 1943 Mussolini established the Italian Social Republic (RSI) in northern and central Italy, and the RSI armed forces continued to fight on the Italian Front as German allies in Italian uniforms. They were joined in August 1943 by the 2nd Infantry (later 2nd Technical) Division of the Slovak Army, in Slovak uniform; and on 8 May 1944 by 11 infantry battalions of the Czech Government Army *(Vládní vojsko)* in Czech uniform. Some Italian volunteers joined the Waffen-SS and others were employed by the German army in divisional service units.

The Osttruppen

The German Army on the Eastern Front had been accepting volunteers from Russia and Soviet ethnic minorities as 'Auxiliaries' (Hilfswillige, or 'Hiwis') in combat divisions since August 1941, and the success of this recruitment led to the raising of three types of independent units. Cossack cavalry squadrons and later mounted battalions, mounted regiments, infantry battalions and infantry regiments were formed from October 1941. From 8 February 1942 Armenian, Azeri, Georgian, North Caucasian, Turkestani and Volga-Tartar infantry battalions were formed into six Eastern Legions (Ostlegionen). On 1 October 1942 Estonian, Russian, Belorussian and Ukrainian units were designated Eastern Battalions (Ostbataillone); and in January 1943 Russian, Belorussian and Ukrainian units were united as the Russian Liberation Army *(Russkaya Osvoboditel'naya Armiya – ROA)* under ex-Soviet MajGen Andrey Vlasov.

On 14 November 1944 the ROA was officially redesignated the Armed Forces of the Committee for the Liberation of the Russian Peoples *(Vooruzhenni'y Sili' Komiteta Osvodobozhdeniya Narodov Rossii – VS-KONR)*, although the term ROA was commonly used until May 1945. All these units were attached to German divisions as combat or support units.

By July 1943 the German army was in inexorable retreat towards the Baltic region and into Belarus and Ukraine, and much of the home territory of the volunteers was being recaptured by Soviet forces. In order to avoid the danger of mutiny and desertion, from October 1943 67 battalions were transferred to Western Europe to expand understrength occupation divisions on the Atlantikwall, and 24 to the Italian Front. They were usually deployed as 4th Battalions of German infantry regiments. Two battalions (643rd Eastern, 823rd Georgian) even served on the Channel Islands with 319th Infantry Division. On 1 February 1944 the Volunteer Depot Division (Freiwilligen-Stamm-Division) was formed in south-eastern France with 1st-5th Regiments to train unit replacements.

There was a wide variance in morale amongst these battalions, transferred far from familiar territory and required to fight Western Allied forces instead of the Red Army, as the Germans had promised them. Allied troops were amazed to

Two well-camouflaged Panzergrenadiers in M1943 camouflage smocks and trousers lie in wait for Allied armour in a Normandy hedgerow, July 1944, armed with the lethal RPzB54 Panzerschreck. This 88mm anti-tank rocket launcher, an improved copy of the US bazooka, projected hollow charge armour-piercing rockets out to 150 yards. The projectile's rocket motor continued to burn for about 8ft after it left the muzzle – thus the need for the gunner's shield with a sighting port. His mate carries a box of RPzBGr 4322 or 4992 projectiles. (Friedrich Herrmann)

find Russian troops surrendering to their advancing forces. The Eastern Battalions proved to be the most effective, with 23 battalions serving with Army Group B in the Normandy campaign, losing ten battalions, and 11 with Army Group G in southern France. Five Cossack infantry and three cavalry battalions fought with Army Group B, losing one infantry battalion.

The Eastern Legions, recruited to liberate Transcaucasian and Central Asian homelands now well beyond the reach of the German forces, proved more problematic; 18 battalions fought in Normandy and seven in southern France. In July 1944 part of the 799th Georgian Battalion deserted to Allied lines, and the 627th Volga-Tartar Battalion mutinied; and on 5 April 1945 the 803rd North Caucasian and 822nd Georgian Battalions, stationed on Texel island off the Dutch coast, declared for the Allies and held the island against German counterattacks before surrendering to the Germans on 17 April.

The 162nd Infantry Division, formed in occupied Poland to provide units for the Eastern Legions, was mobilised with five Azeri and six Turkestani infantry and artillery battalions and German support units and services; the division was transferred to northern Italy in October 1943. One Armenian, three Georgian and two Eastern Battalions were allocated to other divisions in Italy on anti-partisan duties behind the front. No Cossack units fought in Italy, but from September 1944 to April 1945 Cossack families were billeted in Gemona, later Tolmezzo, in the north-east of that country.

CAMPAIGN SUMMARY 1943-1945

Normandy Landings 1944

France, Belgium and the Netherlands were garrisoned in June 1944 by Western High Command, controlling Army Group B (Heeresgruppe B) covering northern France, Belgium and the Netherlands,and Reinforced Army G (Armeegruppe G) in southern France.

Army Group B, commanded by GFM Erwin Rommel, the celebrated commander of German-Italian forces in North Africa, had two armies and the Netherlands garrison. *7th Army* had 12 divisions (77, 243, 265-6, 275, 343, 352-3, 709, 716 Infantry; 2 Luftwaffe Airborne, 21 Panzer) in Brittany and western Normandy, and 319 Infantry Division on the Channel Islands. Further east the *15th Army* garrisoned eastern Normandy, the Pas-de-Calais region and

An intriguing scene in eastern Normandy, August 1944: three infantrymen from an ex-Luftwaffe field division leave a knocked-out British Sherman tank carrying full jerrycans. All wear the M1942 second pattern thigh-length Luftwaffe splinter-pattern overjacket so characteristic of the Luftwaffe field units; they also retain the M1935 Luftwaffe other ranks' belt. Other photos show field division infantry wearing Luftwaffe second pattern camouflaged paratroop jump-smocks. (Friedrich Herrmann)

Belgium with 18 divisions (47-9, 84-5, 245, 326, 331, 344, 346, 348, 711-2 Infantry; 165, 182 Reserve; 17-19 Luftwaffe Rifle); while the Netherlands were defended by four divisions (347, 719 Infantry, 16 Luftwaffe Rifle, 19 Panzer). Panzer Group West, on 5 August 1944 redesignated *5th Panzer Army*, constituted Von Rundstedt's strategic reserve near Paris, with nine divisions (271-2, 276-7 Infantry; 2, 116 Panzer, Panzer-Lehr; 1, 12 SS-Panzer).

D-Day began just after midnight on Tuesday 6 June 1944, as the Allied 21 Army Group, with eight divisions (three airborne and five infantry), three armoured brigades, and total air superiority, landed in western Normandy, which was defended by three static infantry divisions (352, 709, 716) of 84 Corps, German 7th Army. Hitler's poor strategic instincts left his forces unprepared and his caution prevented a quick reaction or mobile deployment; thus only 21 Panzer Division counterattacked decisively near Caen. With daytime movement virtually excluded by Allied airpower, the deployment by late June of seven first-line mobile divisions from Panzer Group West and Army Group G (2 Panzer, Panzer-Lehr; 1, 9, 10, 12 SS Panzer; 17 SS-Panzergrenadier) was too late to destroy the Allied bridgehead. By early July this had been reinforced to total 28 American, British and Canadian divisions (three airborne, 19 infantry, six armoured) and five armoured brigades.

Northern France, Belgium and the Netherlands 1944-45

On 17 July Rommel was seriously wounded by a strafing RAF fighter, and von Kluge served as Army Group B commander until his arrest, and replacement by Model, on 17 August. The Allied bridgehead expanded slowly against determined German counterattacks, but the eventual British capture of Caen on 10 July meant that the landings were now secure. On 25 July the Allies broke out of the bridgehead, and by 7 August German 7th Army had lost Brittany. *1st Army* was briefly assigned to Army Group B but was unable to stem the Allied advance; and on 20 August the 7th Army and 5th Panzer Army, which had extricated themselves only at huge cost from encirclement in the Falaise Pocket during the westward retreat, crossed the Seine. Paris was abandoned on the 23rd.

On 25 August 1944 the Allies attacked across the Seine. Western Command and Army Group B (7th, 15th Army; 5th Panzer Army) retreated rapidly eastwards under heavy Allied air attack, evacuating northern France by 6 September – but denying valuable Channel ports to the Allies with isolated 'fortress' garrisons, some of which held out until May 1945. British progress through Belgium was even

North-east France, August 1944: the four-man crew of a six-barrelled 15cm Nebelwerfer 41 prepare to fire. All seem to wear M1942 reed-green summer field uniform and to have discarded all personal equipment while serving their devastating and much-feared weapon. (Friedrich Herrmann)

faster, with Brussels captured on 3 September, the city – but not the sea approaches – of Antwerp on 4 September, and Luxembourg on 10 September. On 15 September most of Army Group B, with minimal surviving armour and no reserves, had formed a defensive line just inside Belgium (still denying the Allies use of Antwerp's port facilities), and along the 1939 Siegfried Line (Westwall) fortifications on the Belgian-German border.

On 15 September the weary and over-extended Allies, surprised at the speed of the German collapse and short of fuel, halted, allowing the Germans valuable time to reinforce their line with dwindling reserves of Volkssturm home guards, border guards and Volksgrenadier units of mixed value. On 4 September 1944 *1st Luftwaffe Airborne Army* with seven divisions (84-5, 89, 176, 179, 353 Infantry, 6 Airborne) reinforced Army Group B in the Netherlands, just in time to help repulse – with the important assistance of 2 SS-Panzer Corps – the British airborne landings at Arnhem during 17-26 September.

However, by 21 October the Allies had occupied the southern Netherlands and Aachen, the first major town in west Germany, had fallen. On 11 November 1944 Army Group H was formed under Luftwaffe GenObst Kurt Student to defend the remainder of the Netherlands with 1st Airborne Army and 15th Army.

On 16 December 1944 the Wehrmacht attacked through the Belgian Ardennes with 24 understrength divisions (12, 18, 26, 47, 62, 246, 276-7, 326, 340, 352, 560 Volksgrenadier; 3, 15 Panzergrenadier; 2, 116 Panzer, Panzer-Lehr; 1, 2, 9, 10, 12 SS Panzer; 3, 5 Luftwaffe Airborne) from Army Group B (7th, 5th Panzer Army) and Western Command's 6th SS-Panzer Army, and depleted Luftwaffe air support. Initially the cream of the Wehrmacht remaining in the West were faced by just six Allied divisions. The Ardennes offensive, also called the Battle of the Bulge, was intended to recapture Antwerp, but after initial success the advance ground to a halt on 24 December, only four miles from the River Meuse at Dinant after a 50-mile penetration, having wasted valuable mobile forces which could have helped defend western Germany. By 20 January 1945 the German forces were back on the Siegfried Line.

Southern France 1944-45

Southern France was garrisoned by Reinforced Army G, under GenObst Johannes Blaskowitz, commanding *1st Army* in south-western France with three understrength static coastal defence divisions (708 Infantry; 158-9 Reserve), with 11 Panzer Division in strategic reserve; and *19th Army* in southern and central France with seven static divisions (242, 244, 338, 716 Infantry; 148, 157, 189 Reserve) and 198 Infantry Division, with 9 Panzer Division in reserve.

At 0800 hours on 15 August 1944 the US 7th Army with eight US and French divisions (six infantry, one armoured, one airborne) landed in

Generalleutnant Ferdinand Heim retired in August 1943 after serving as Chief of Staff of the 6th Army in Russia the previous year. He was recalled to duty, and on 1 August 1944 was given command of the Boulogne garrison. Here a dejected prisoner after surrendering to the Canadian 3rd Infantry Division on 22 September, he wears the general officer's service cap with gold-embroidered insignia. His M1935 officer's field greatcoat can be seen in the original print to have the bright red lapel linings of a general officer. It is worn open, displaying his *Alt-Larisch* collar patches and Knight's Cross. (Brian Davis)

south-eastern France in Operation Anvil. Reinforced Army G (on 12 September redesignated Army Group G), outgunned and outmanoeuvred, retreated rapidly. 19th Army abandoned Marseilles and Provence on 28 August, Lyons on 3 September and Dijon on 10 September, forcing the outflanked 1st Army to evacuate south-western France without a battle and retreat north-eastwards. When the Allies halted their offensive on 15 September 1944, Army Group G still held the Vosges mountains in Lorraine. On 21 September Gen der Pz Tr. Hermann Balck replaced Blaskowitz, who was reinstated on 24 December, by which time 1st Army had retreated into south-western Germany (15 December).Here in January 1945 it absorbed Upper Rhine Army Group (Heeresgruppe Oberrhein), formed in November 1944 from local defence and Replacement Army units. 19th Army stubbornly defended the Colmar pocket, the last German-occupied part of France, until 9 February 1945; Free French units were prominent among the Allied attackers.

Western Germany and the Netherlands 1945

Throughout January 1945 Western Command on the Dutch-Belgian and western German borders resisted local Allied attacks, but on 8 February three Allied army groups (6, 12, 21) launched a general offensive into western Germany. By 21 March 1945 the Allies had forced Army Group B (7th, 15th Army; 5th Panzer, 6th SS-Panzer Army) and most of Army Group G (1st, 19th Army) – commanded from 29 January 1945 by Waffen-SS General Paul Hausser – across the Rhine, capturing the Reichswald forest on the Dutch border after heavy fighting, Cologne on 5 March, and establishing a Rhine bridgehead at Remagen on 7 March.

The depleted Army Group H, later North-Western Command, garrisoned the Netherlands with 12 divisions in *1st Airborne Army* (84, 180, 190 Infantry; 406 zbV; 15 Panzergrenadier; 116 Panzer; 6-8 Luftwaffe Airborne; 106 Panzer Brigade), and *25th Army*, formed on 10 November 1944 (331, 346 Infantry; 2 Luftwaffe Airborne). Steady Allied pressure from 2 April forced North-West Command – joined on 9 April by German Replacement Army units organised as Armee Blumentritt – to retreat into north-west Germany on 15 April 1945, abandoning Bremen on 26 April and Hamburg on 3 May before surrendering on 4 May. On 8 May the German garrison in Denmark, with 281 and 398 District Commands, and 20 Mountain Army in Norway with 11 divisions and nine brigades, also surrendered.

Army Group B defended the central front of Western Germany with 27 divisions:
5th Panzer Army – now without significant armour – (85, 89 Infantry; 18, 26, 272, 277 Volksgrenadier; 3, 5 Luftwaffe Airborne)
15th Army (59, 176, 338, 353 Infantry; 12, 183, 363 Volksgrenadier; 476 zbV; 3 Panzergrenadier; 9, 11 Panzer, Panzer-Lehr)

Oberst Constantin Meyer, commanding the Metz garrison in Lorraine in August 1944. His field service uniform comprises the M1943 field cap – officer's silver crown piping is just visible – and M1935 field greatcoat and tunic. The coat's dark green facing cloth collar shows up better here than in the photograph of GenLt Heim; it has shoulder boards of rank on infantry white underlay, and bearing the gilt regimental numerals as ordered restored on 16 February 1944. Note the 6x30 binoculars, standard issue field flashlight and other ranks' belt. (Brian Davis)

Armeeabteilung Lüttwitz (180, Deichmann, Hamburg Infantry; 190 zbV; 116 Panzer; 2 Luftwaffe Airborne; 22 Luftwaffe Anti-Aircraft).

On 23-25 March 1945 the Allies attacked across the Rhine, and by 2 April had trapped Army Group B in the Ruhr Pocket, which surrendered on 18 April, GFM Model having committed suicide.

Army Group G, commanded from 2 April 1945 by Gen der Inf. Friedrich Schulz, defended south-west Germany with 37 divisions:
1st Army (416, 719, Rässler Infantry; 16, 19, 36, 47, 256-7, 347, 559 Volksgrenadier; 526 Reserve; 905 zbV; 2 Mountain; 17 SS-Panzergrenadier; 6 SS Mountain)
7th Army (9, 79, 167, 212, 246, 276, 326, 340, 352, 560 Volksgrenadier; 2 Panzer)
19th Army (106, 189, 198, 716 Infantry; 550 Grenadier; 16, 47, 257 Volksgrenadier; 405, 805 zbV; 1005 Infantry Brigade) – also included the 24th Army Staff formed in November 1944.

On 22 March the Allies attacked across the Rhine, taking Karlsruhe on 4 April, Stuttgart and Nuremberg on 20 April and Munich on 30 April, and reaching Salzburg in Austria on 4 May. Army Group G surrendered on 5 May.

Sicily and Southern Italy 1943

On 10 July 1943 British and US forces landed in south-eastern Sicily, defended by Italian 6th Army (four infantry, one motorised, six coastal divisions) and the German 14 Panzer Corps with three divisions (15, 29 Panzergrenadier; Hermann Göering Luftwaffe Panzer) in northern Sicily. German forces led a determined Axis defence of the island, and on 17 August retreated largely intact to Calabria in southern Italy.

The approaching loss of Sicily shocked the Italian government, which on 25 July arrested Mussolini and appointed Marshal Pietro Badoglio as prime minister. Hitler, correctly suspecting a coming Italian surrender and the prospect of Allied forces rushing to the southern Austrian border, formed the highly mobile 10th Army on 15 August 1943 around the divisions in Calabria. *10th Army*, reporting to Luftwaffe Southern Command in Rome, had ten divisions in 56 Corps (15, 29 Panzergrenadier; 16, 26 Panzer; 1 Luftwaffe Airborne) in Calabria, and three divisions (3, 90 Panzergrenadier; 2 Luftwaffe Airborne; plus 16 SS Assault Brigade Reichsführer SS) – later under 14 Panzer Corps – in reserve in central Italy.

On 3 September 1943 the Allies landed in Calabria and on 9 September at Taranto in Apulia, as 10th Army conducted a fighting retreat northwards. Italy's surrender was announced on the 8th, prompting

Highly decorated German commanders plan the destruction of the British 1st Airborne Division at Arnhem, September 1944. (Left to right) GFM Model, commanding Army Group B; General der Fallschirmtruppe Kurt Student, commanding 1st Airborne Army, wearing the Army M1934 motorcyclist's rubberised coat with field-grey cloth collar; background, a Major Kaust, who has just been decorated with the Knight's Cross, wearing the M1940 special field-grey uniform; and at far right SS-Brigadeführer und Generalmajor der Waffen-SS Heinz Harmel, commanding 10.SS-Panzer-Division 'Frundsberg', wearing the motorcyclist's coat but with dark green collar facing cloth. (Author's collection)

Hitler to send GFM Erwin Rommel's Army Group B (51, 97 Corps, 2 SS-Panzer Corps) to occupy northern Italy. Meanwhile Allied forces landed at Salerno on 9 September, but 10th Army attacked the bridgehead energetically until 18 September. Resuming its skillful retreat, 10th Army evacuated Potenza on 20 September, Foggia on 27 September and Naples on 1 October, halting on 8 October on the Capua-Termoli 'Viktor Line'.

Central and Northern Italy 1943-45

On 26 November 1943 Army Group C was formed under GFM Kesselring with 18 divisions, deployed under *10th Army* in central Italy (44, 65, 94, 305 Infantry; 15, 29, 90 Panzergrenadier; 5 Mountain; 26 Panzer; 1 Luftwaffe Airborne; Hermann Goering Panzer); and *14th Army*, formed 18 November 1943, in the north (71, 162, 278, 334, 356, 362 Infantry; 188 Reserve Mountain). 10th Army defended the narrow Italian front with great skill and resourcefulness, exacting a high price for ground lost, before halting on 27 December 1943 on the 'Gustav' or 'Hitler Line' on the Sangro and Garigliano rivers through the Monte Cassino strongpoint. On 18 January 1944 the Allies assaulted the Gustav Line, and on 22 January landed at Anzio and Nettuno; but 10th Army held the Gustav Line until 13 May 1944, and 14th Army confined the Anzio beachhead until 23 May. Evacuating Rome on 4 June and retreating rather faster northwards, the Wehrmacht gave up Florence on 4 August and halted on the 'Gothic Line' on 19 August. Meanwhile on 17 March 1944 the Von Zangen Reinforced Corps (Armeeabteilung von Zangen) was formed in northern Italy, expanding on 31 July 1944 to form *Liguria Army* with two RSI divisions and six German (34 Infantry; 148, 157 Reserve; 42 Rifle; 5 Mountain).

On 25 August 1944 the Allies broke through the Gothic Line, taking Rimini on 21 September, but further advances were slow against determined opposition by Army Group C, which had halted south of Bologna on 29 December 1944. On 10 March 1945 GenObst Heinrich von Vietinghoff, the distinguished 10th Army commander, took over Army Group C on Kesselring's promotion. The final Allied offensive was launched on 1 April 1945; the Germans were soon in headlong retreat towards Austria, abandoning Bologna on 21 April and Genoa on 27 April. German forces in Italy surrendered on 2 May 1945, allowing the Allies to advance into southern Austria by VE-Day.

ARMY UNIFORM

Officers' service uniform

This consisted of the M1935 officer's 'saddle-shaped' peaked cap, M1935 officer's field tunic with ribbons, M1935/M1940 officer's field greatcoat, M1934 officer's brown leather belt, officer's breeches and officer's black leather high-boots, grey suede gloves, pistol and holster. The cloth was a superior quality greenish-grey traditionally called *feldgrau*

Troops of a Volksgrenadier division defending Aachen, October 1944. The soldier being congratulated on just having been awarded the Iron Cross 2nd Class wears a M1935 helmet still bearing the Wehrmacht eagle decal, ordered discontinued from 28 August 1943. He has an entrenching tool – perhaps intended as a hand-to-hand weapon? – thrust into the front of his M1940 field greatcoat, which has no shoulder straps. Contrast the M1924 concussion stick grenade in his belt with that carried by the soldier at right, who wears the M1934 motorcyclist's rubberised coat – the latter's grenade has the M1942 serrated fagmentation sleeve. (Friedrich Herrmann)

(field-grey). These items are described in detail in MAA 330, *The German Army 1939-45 (4).*

Other ranks' service uniform

The service uniform for technical and senior NCOs and many junior NCOs, in lesser-quality field-grey, consisted of the other ranks' M1935 peaked service cap or M1934/M1942 field-cap *Feldmütze)*, M1935 field tunic and M1940 field greatcoat. The M1940 trousers were worn with high black 'dice-cup' marching-boots, or M1943 belted trousers with M1941 field-grey canvas anklets and black lace-up ankle boots. A black leather belt with a M1936 aluminium buckle,

Three platoon leaders of a Panzergrenadier regiment on the Dutch-Belgian border in January 1945 confer over the map while the troops wait in their half-tracks. All three wear the M1934 motorcyclist's rubberised coat with dark green or M1940 *feldgrau* collars. The officer (centre) wears the M1934 'old style' peaked field cap. (Friedrich Herrmann)

from 1941 painted field-grey, a holstered pistol and grey suede gloves were also worn. More junior NCOs and men wore the field cap instead, and a scabbarded bayonet on the belt. The peaked M1943 universal field cap *(Einheitsfeldmütze)*, which officially replaced the M1934/1942 from June 1934 and was by 1944 the most common Army headgear, was essentially the M1942 cap with a deep peak.

The M1942 field tunic omitted the previous pocket pleats, and the M1943 tunic had straight pocket flaps. Some NCOs had the collars sharpened, the skirt shortened in officer style, and the bellows side pockets sewn up for a more elegant appearance. The M1943 belted trousers incorporated a reinforced seat and tapered legs for anklets. The other ranks' field greatcoat had other ranks' quality cloth and insignia, with a wider collar for better protection against the cold on the M1942 model.

These items, and the walking-out uniform for all ranks are described in more detail in MAA 330, *The German Army 1939-45 (4).*

Officers' field uniform

In the field all officers (except platoon leaders – by 1944 only NCOs and the youngest second lieutenants were commanding platoons) wore the M1935 officer's field tunic with officer's belt and holstered pistol; M1935/M1942 steel helmet, officer's M1938 or M1943 field cap and officer's breeches with riding boots.

On 31 October 1939 all officers below general rank in combat units were ordered to wear the other ranks' field tunic, black belt, trousers and marching boots, in order not to be too conspicuous to the enemy; but most officers either totally or partially ignored the order. Many purchased and altered an other ranks' tunic, adding officers' features such as a shortened skirt, roll-back cuffs, pocket pleats, bluish dark green collars, and officer's insignia. The tunic could be worn with the collar unbuttoned when in the field with troops. The other ranks' black belt could no longer be worn by officers after 23 July 1943 and a blackened officer's M1934 belt was prescribed instead, but from 30 October 1943 the M1934 brown belt was reinstated.

On 25 September 1944 the **M1944 field uniform** was introduced for all ranks of the Army, Navy shore units, Luftwaffe and Waffen-SS. The waist-length field jacket or blouse, of inferior quality cloth in a browner green-grey *feldgrau 44* shade, had six front buttons and two plain breast pockets. It was apparently popular for its resemblance to the British battledress blouse and US 'Eisenhower jacket', which were felt to look more modern than the old tunics; some officers imitated these garments further by having fly fronts sewn in. The M1944 trousers, also in *feldgrau 44*, had an integral belt and ankle drawstrings. From 13 December 1944 tailored M1944 jackets could be worn with the collar open over a black tie and a shirt – greenish-grey, green, greenish-brown, beige or white were all seen. Other ranks' M1941 field-grey 'guards braids' were sewn directly onto the collar, as were officer's M1935 collar patches. Officers were prescribed the standard M1944 mouse-grey woven breast-eagle and swastika on a field-grey woven triangle, but most substituted the officer's M1935 pattern in aluminium thread on dark green backing, or the M1944 aluminium woven eagle on a dark green triangle. General officers preferred a dress-quality M1935 gold thread or M1938 celleon eagle.

The M1935 and M1942 steel helmets were painted matt greenish-grey and initially bore a silver-white Wehrmacht eagle decal on the left side, abolished 28 August 1943. The peakless M1938 officer's field cap had aluminium thread pipings, and an aluminium wire embroidered cockade below an aluminium thread eagle on a bluish dark green backing (gold thread or celleon for general officers). Officers also wore the M1943 peaked field cap with aluminium (gold for general officers) cord crown piping, and occasionally the other ranks' eagle and cockade. The obsolete M1934 'old style' officer's peaked field cap with flat machine-woven insignia (called the 'crusher cap' by today's collectors) was worn by many individuals until May 1945. Some officers also unofficially wore the other ranks' M1942 field cap with officers' aluminium or gold piping added.

Subalterns acting as infantry platoon leaders wore the other ranks' black belt supporting the 84/98 bayonet and scabbard, M1939 bayonet frog, M1938 folding shovel, M1941 or M1944 bread bag, M1931 canteen and cup and the M1935 dispatch-case. The M1920 'officers' support

straps' secured two sets of triple M38/40 pouches for the MP38/MP40 sub-machine gun magazines. The anti-gas cape in a pouch was usually tied to a M1930 gas mask canister slung from a shoulder or strapped to the bread bag. Zeiss 6 x 30 binoculars, a signal whistle and a flashlight were also carried.

Other ranks' field uniform

Other ranks wore the service uniform, with M1941 field-grey canvas anklets and black lace-up ankle boots increasingly replacing the traditional marching boots, and a steel helmet. Some senior NCOs preferred the M1934 'old style' peaked field cap to its replacements. The tunic could be worn with the collar unbuttoned by order of the company commander. Technical and senior NCOs carried a pistol in a black holster; NCOs acting as infantry platoon or section leaders wore a subaltern platoon leader's equipment but with other ranks' M1939 infantry support Y-straps. The other ranks' M1944 field uniform had plain round-ended shoulder straps with branch-colour piping, M1940 field-grey 'guards braids' sewn directly onto the collar, no NCO collar edging braid, and the standard M1944 mouse-grey breast eagle on a field-grey woven triangle.

Other NCOs and men wore the standard rifleman's equipment. The waist belt carried the 84/98 bayonet, M1938 folding shovel, M1931 or M1944 bread bag and M1931 canteen and cup. The M1939 infantry support Y-straps and supplementary 'D-ring' straps supported two sets of three M1911 ammunition pouches for the Karabiner 98k rifle on the belt front, and on the back the M1939 canvas A-frame for the M1931 mess kit, M1931 camouflage shelter-quarter, canvas battle pack bag, and the gas cape strapped to the gas mask canister when not worn on the canister shoulder strap. The equipment worn by the section light machine-gun team is described in MAA 311, *The German Army 1939-45 (1)*.

Summer field uniform

Summer field uniforms were worn on the Western and Italian Fronts in hot weather. Tropical uniforms were permitted in southern France and southern Italy, Sicily and Sardinia from summer 1943, after the surrender of North Africa on 12 May 1943 had made them superfluous outside Europe.

The reed-green cotton herringbone twill M1940 fatigue uniform was still occasionally encountered. The tunic, with two skirt pockets only, bore the breast eagle, and collar braid for senior NCOs; they, and officers, added their shoulder straps of rank. The M1941 reed-green pullover-style cotton shirt was worn as an outer garment in warm weather. This had five white plastic buttons and two breast pockets; officers' shoulder-boards, other ranks' piped M1940 field-grey shoulder straps, and arm chevrons or M1942 arm rank insignia were added as appropriate.

Oberleutnant of anti-tank troops captured at Deventer, Holland, in April 1945 by Canadian 1st Army. He wears the M1940 special field grey uniform, with the pink-piped black Panzer collar patches identifying anti-tank battalions in Panzer and Panzergrenadier divisions and those under direct Army or Corps command; he probably commanded a company of self-propelled guns. His shoulder boards have pink underlay and show one gilt 'pip' of rank and the gilt 'P' for Panzerjäger, but no battalion numbers. His other ranks' M1943 field cap has standard insignia and no officer's silver piping, but his breast eagle is the officer's silver model. Note the ribbons of the Eastern Winter 1941/42 Medal and Iron Cross 2nd Class; the Iron Cross 1st Class, General Assault Badge, and silver Wound Badge (three and four wounds) on the left breast; and the Kuban Shield on the left sleeve. (Brian Davis)

The most commonly encountered uniform was the M1942 summer tunic in reed-green or light grey HBT, cut like the M1942 field tunic, with field quality rank insignia and breast eagles. Officers wore M1935 collar patches, NCOs and men M1940 field-grey 'guards braids'. Matching trousers appeared in 1943. A reed-green drill M1944 field blouse and trousers were authorised but almost certainly never produced.

The light olive tropical uniform is described and illustrated in more detail in MAA 316, *The German Army 1939-45 (2)*. It consisted of the distinctive M1940 Afrikakorps peaked field cap; M1940 or M1942 field tunic; M1940 shirt and tie; M1940 breeches or trousers, or M1943 straight-leg trousers; M1940 shorts and knee socks; high lace-up boots or ankle-boots, and brown field greatcoat, worn with the M1940 canvas tropical belt and webbing.

The Luftwaffe tropical uniform, introduced 25 April 1941 in light tan-brown cloth, was worn by Luftwaffe divisions transferred to the Army and by individual soldiers. Individuals also acquired Italian and Waffen-SS tropical items, and often wore them mixed with reed-green Army-issue summer clothing.

Winter clothing

Standard winter uniform items included the woollen balaclava or toque; extra-thick woollen underwear; sweater; woollen mittens, sentry's double-breasted guard coat and felt over-shoes; the vehicle crews' surcoat; fur-lined mittens; and the drivers' and motorcyclists' over-gloves. Other issue winter clothing included sheepskin overcoats, a plain brown quilted jacket and trousers worn over thefield uniform and under the greatcoat, and leather-reinforced felt calf-length boots.

Winter uniforms developed for the Eastern Front were mainly worn on the Western Front during the Ardennes offensive from December 1944 to January 1945 and in the Italian Apennines in winter 1944/45. The M1942 padded reversible white/field-grey winter tunic was issued in lightweight, medium weight and heavyweight versions, with waist and sleeve drawcords, six buttons, two slash waist pockets and an integral hood. Reversible trousers had two thigh pockets, a crutch strap and ankle drawcords. A reversible separate hood was issued with this uniform, but was unpopular. Reversible mittens and leather-reinforced white felt snow boots were also worn. Production of this uniform probably ended in late 1944 due to the chronic raw materials shortage.

Other winter items were the seven-button M1942 one-piece snow overalls, the four-button M1942 snow coverall, the M1942 two-piece snow suit, and the M1942 mountain troops' snow uniform – a reversible anorak and over-trousers, issued to all combat troops. For further details see MAA 330, *The German Army 1939-45 (4)*.

Sturmartillerie-Brigade 12 was raised from Luftwaffe paratrooper volunteers, who wore Luftwaffe headgear and insignia with the M1940 special field-grey uniform. This interesting photograph shows two members of an SP gun crew led by Lt.Heinz Deutsch who distinguished themselves in battle against Allied armour in the Reichswald, February 1945 – the gunner, Oberfeldwebel Berndl (left), and the driver, Feldwebel Stangassinger. Both wear the Army field-grey uniform with yellow Luftwaffe rank collar patches partly enclosed by L-shapes of NCO braid. Both have the Iron Cross 1st Class and the Luftwaffe Ground Combat Badge; Berndl also wears his Parachutist's Badge. (Friedrich Herrmann)

This apprehensive infantry Oberfeldwebel from Army Group B, taken prisoner in the Ruhr Pocket in April 1945, is distinguished from his men as a senior NCO by retaining in the field the M1935 other ranks' service cap, with field-grey crown, dark green band, aluminium insignia, white pipings, and black patent leather chin strap. He still has a M1935 other ranks' field greatcoat with dark green facing cloth collar and shoulder straps, worn here with a coloured civilian scarf at the throat. The looks of the men behind him seem to betray ner- vousness and continued reliance on his leadership. (Brian Davis)

Camouflage uniforms

The M1931 triangular shelter-quarter (Zeltbahn 31), in tightly woven cotton drill, was used as a summer camouflage cape under or over field equipment. It was reversible, between light and dark shades of the first pattern angular 'splinter' camouflage scheme in green, brown and khaki.

The M1942 smock, a collarless cotton drill garment in Zeltbahn 31 camouflage reversible to white, saw limited issue, and was worn over the field uniform. It was closed at the chest by a cord passing through five sets of holes; two breast slits gave access to the tunic beneath; it had a waist drawcord, often two side pockets, and buttoned cuffs. M1942 arm rank insignia was prescribed but usually omitted. Over-trousers in the same material, and helmet covers, were also worn. The first M1942 pattern cover had Zeltbahn 31 reversible to white; the second pattern had added foliage loops; both attached by a drawstring under the helmet rim.

A small number of M1942 padded reversible winter tunics, trousers and mittens were produced in Zeltbahn 31/white from April 1942. A non-reversible winter tunic was also produced in both Zeltbahn 31 and 'marsh pattern' versions – the latter a softer-edged pattern of brown and green on khaki or greyish green background. The M1944 camouflage apron was a sleeveless smock closed by a buttoned chest flap, in Zeltbahn 31 or marsh pattern herringbone twill.

Later production smocks and winter tunics were made in second pattern M1943 splinter camouflage, in marsh pattern, and in a third pattern M1944 rounded 'blotch' version. The M1943 marsh pattern camouflage smock was issued to snipers and Panzergrenadier units.

Personnel of the Luftwaffe field divisions who had transferred to the Army often retained their M1942 thigh-length over-jackets in Luftwaffe splinter camouflage or marsh pattern herringbone twill. M1943 field tunics and M1940 trousers, M1944 field blouses and trousers, and M1940 special tunics and trousers for armoured crews were often privately tailored in Zeltbahn 31 or marsh pattern herringbone twill.

Troops on the Italian Front often wore Italian Army M1929 shelter quarters, or M1942 three-quarter length parachutist smocks, M1942 helmet covers, and Sahariana-style tunics and long trousers made up in standard Italian Army camouflage; this was a rounded 'cloud' pattern in brown, light forest green and ochre. It was also used to manufacture versions of the camouflage items described above, particularly the M1943 field tunic. Waffen-SS camouflage items were also individually acquired; and Luftwaffe troops of the Hermann Göring Division were issued with Waffen-SS camouflage smocks and helmet covers from summer 1942.

Rank insignia

Officers' shoulder boards, NCOs' shoulder straps and mens' arm chevrons are described and illustrated in detail in MAA 311, *The German Army 1939-45 (1)*.

General officers' shoulder boards displayed dress-quality plaited cords on a bright red underlay. The design incorporated two gold bullion or 'celleon' imitation gold cords and one bright aluminium cord. (After 25 April 1944 only generals of combat branches were supposed to wear bright red underlay.) The rank of Generalfeldmarschall was marked by silver crossed marshal's batons (and from 3 April 1941, all-gold cords); the Generaloberst, General, Generalleutnant and Generalmajor wore respectively three, two, one and no silver four-point stars or 'pips'. Generals of specialist branches and élite formations wore appropriate additional shoulder board insignia.

Field officers' shoulder boards had double plaited aluminium cords on a branch-colour underlay; Oberst, Oberstleutnant and Major were differenced by wearing respectively two, one and no gold pips. The company ranks of Hauptmann, Oberleutnant and Leutnant wore doubled flat parallel cords, again differenced by two, one or no gold pips. All officer ranks of specialist branches and élite units wore the appropriate additional insignia in gold. Shoulder boards of field and company ranks were manufactured during wartime in a less conspicuous dull silver-grey cord (sometimes referred to by collectors as 'oxydised silver').

The senior NCO ranks (from Stabsfeldwebel down to Feldwebel) wore dark green or field-grey shoulder straps piped in branch colour and edged with M1935 bright aluminium or M1940 mouse-grey artificial silk or cellulose-fibre braid; to these were applied respectively three, two or one pips, plus appropriate insignia of branch and/or unit, in aluminium. The Hauptfeldwebel (company sergeant major) wore two braid cuff rings. Junior NCOs (Unterfeldwebel and Unteroffizier) wore the same shoulder strap without pips, the latter without braid across the base, with branch and/or unit insignia in branch-colour chain-stitch. If appointed Hauptfeldwebeldiensttuer (acting company sergeant-major – a wartime appointment necessitated by the increasing lack of qualified NCOs) they also wore the two braid cuff rings.

The enlisted men wore plain shoulder straps edged with branch colour piping. Rank was indicated by braid chevrons (or aluminium

On 19 June 1943 Grenadier-Regiment 134 was redesignated Reichsgrenadier-Regiment 'Hoch- und Deutschmeister'. Following regulations Hauptmann Arnult Abele, a battalion commander, wears the M1940 other ranks' field tunic and breast eagle, but has added M1935 officer's collar patches. (Brian Davis)

Belgium, 3 June 1943: a colour-party of Grenadier-Regiment 134 parade their newly awarded regimental flag, in the old Austrian style. That August they transferred to the Italian Front with 44.Reichsgrenadier-Division 'Hoch- und Deutschmeister'. The Oberfeldwebel standard-bearer wears the M1942 other ranks' field tunic but, contrary to German tradition, no carrying sash, gorget or arm badge. He is escorted by two subaltern officers; all three display the Iron Cross 1st Class, Infantry Assault Badge and black Wound Badge in slightly different positions on their left breast pockets. The regiment was awarded the 'Stalingrad Cross' shoulder strap insignia on 31 December 1943. (Brian Davis)

pips) on a bluish dark-green or field-grey triangular (or round) backing patch on the left sleeve. From 25 April 1942 an Obergefreiter of two years' seniority not suitable for junior NCO rank could be promoted to Stabsgefreiter; and many, though not all soldiers ranking as *Obergefreiter mit mehr als 6 Dienstjahren* were promoted to this new pay grade.

The M1942 system of sleeve rank insignia, introduced on 22 August 1942 for wear by officers and NCOs on white winter tunics, anoraks, shirts and drill tunics (i.e. garments on which shoulder straps were not officially worn), is illlustrated in MAA 330, *The German Army 1939-45 (4)*. Consisting of gold or green oakleaf sprays and bars on black rectangular backing, these insignia were not in widespread use until 1944, and even then was relatively unpopular.

Branch insignia

A selective list of branch insignia is shown in the Table on page 40. For security reasons troops of the Army were ordered on 1 September 1939 to conceal or remove their shoulder board/shoulder strap branch letters and unit numerals when outside Germany. Replacement Army personnel, and Army troops on leave or assigned to duties in Germany, could continue to wear these insignia openly. During the war élite units such as the Großdeutschland divisions were permitted their prized GD monogram shoulder strap insignia in the field. By 1944 the OKH recognised that the improved morale – and quick identification of deserters by military police – which the open wearing of unit insignia permitted now outweighed the risk of compromised field security. From 16 February 1944 all Army and Replacement Army officers were ordered to fix gold-coloured galvanised metal branch and unit insignia to their shoulder boards, and senior NCOs bright or matt aluminium insignia to their shoulder straps.

Junior NCOs and men were issued field-grey (or Panzer black) slip-on shoulder loops with insignia in branch-colour artificial silk chain-stitch. Although intended for wearing in the middle of the straps they were often worn at the base. An order of 16 May 1944 prescribed shoulder loop insignia in light grey chain-stitch if the correct branch colour was unavailable. The deteriorating supply situation meant that shoulder loops were not manufactured for, or supplied to, all units, especially for newly formed ones with high 'house-numbers', so in practice the reintroduction of shoulder branch and unit insignia was mainly limited to officers and senior NCOs (many of whom had in fact been wearing them before February 1944).

A Panzer field officer in Italy, summer 1944, wearing the standard field-grey M1935 officer's service cap and the M1940 olive tropical tunic with non-regulation embellishments – he has added the entire M1934 pink-piped black skull patches from his black Panzer Feldjacke. His decorations include Iron Crosses awarded in both World Wars and the German Cross in Gold; on his left sleeve we can just make out what seems to be the '*AFRIKA*' cuff title; yet he has not replaced the factory-applied all-ranks' breast eagle with an officer's pattern. (ECPA)

Special black uniform and insignia for tank crews

Most personnel in Panzer battalions, regiments and brigades, Panzer

NORMANDY & NORTHERN FRANCE, 1944
1: Grenadier, Grenadier-Regiment 914; Omaha Beach, Normandy, 6 June 1944
2: Gefreiter, Panzergrenadier-Lehr-Regiment 901; Barenton, August 1944
3: Oberwachtmeister, Armoured Rocket-Launcher Battery; Normandy, June 1944

A

NORMANDY & NORTHERN FRANCE, 1944
1: Hauptmann, Festungs-Grenadier-Regiment 857; Caen, July 1944
2: Leutnant, Heeres-Flakartillerie-Abteilung 281; Falaise Pocket, August 1944
3: Panzergrenadier, Panzergrenadier-Regiment 192; Lille, September 1944

B

SOUTHERN FRANCE, 1944
1: Legionär, Armenisches Feld-Bataillon I/198; Toulon, August 1944
2: Generalmajor, 11.Panzer-Division; Alsace, September 1944
3: Unterfeldwebel, Panzer-Abteilung 2113; Lorraine, September 1944

BELGIUM AND NETHERLANDS, 1944
1: Grenadier, Grenadier-Regiment 1222; Arnhem corridor, October 1944
2: Feldwebel, Feldgendarmerie-Trupp (Mot.) 189; Dutch-Belgian border, September 1944.
3: Obergefreiter, Grenadier-Regiment 1039; Breskens Pocket, October 1944

D

ARDENNES OFFENSIVE, 1944-1945
1: Unteroffizier, Füsilier-Regiment 39, December 1944
2: Oberstleutnant, Pionier-Bataillon 33, December 1944
3: Panzerobergrenadier, I Panzergrenadier-Bataillon,
Führer-Begleit-Brigade, January 1945

E

WESTERN GERMANY, 1945
1: Oberleutnant, Panzergrenadier-Bataillon 2106; Cologne, March 1945
2: Gefreiter, Grenadier-Regiment 48; Ruhr Pocket, April 1945
3: Panzergrenadier, Panzergrenadier-Regiment 156; Reichswald Forest, February 1945

F

SICILY AND SOUTHERN ITALY, 1943
1: Wehrmachtoberpfarrer, 26.Panzer-Division; Volturno, November 1943
2: Panzergrenadier, Panzergrenadier-Regiment 64; Salerno, September 1943
3: Unterfeldwebel, Panzergrenadier-Regiment 115; Sicily, July 1943

G

CENTRAL AND NORTHERN ITALY, 1944-45
1: Obergefreiter, Jäger-Regiment 25; Gothic Line, September 1944
2: Unteroffizier, Reichsgrenadier-Regiment Hoch- und Deutschmeister; Gustav Line, February 1944
3: Stabsfeldwebel, Panzer-Aufklärungs-Abteilung 26; River Po, April 1945

and Panzergrenadier divisional anti-tank battalions and many on Panzer divisional staffs wore the M1940 black field cap; M1934, M1936 or M1942 field jacket and trousers, with grey shirt, black tie and black lace-up shoes, or marching boots for Armoured Engineer companies. (Against regulations some general officers in Panzer divisions wore the special black uniform with the *Alt-Larisch* collar-patches, sometimes even adding red trouser pipings and stripes.)

A black wool version of the M1942 other ranks' field cap saw limited issue. All sidecaps were superseded from 11 June 1943 by the black wool version of the M1943 peaked field cap, but the peak got in the way when using the optical equipment inside an armoured fighting vehicle; those who had them often preferred to keep the old sidecaps, and this was widely tolerated. Against regulations many officers and senior NCOs also preferred the field-grey officers' M1935 peaked service cap, M1934 'old style' peaked field cap, or the other ranks' M1935 peaked service cap.

Armoured vehicle crews and mechanics and Armoured Artillery and Rocket-Launcher crews were issued cotton one-piece overalls in mouse-grey, field-grey, off-white, light brown or reed-green. Panzer crews sometimes dyed these black, and some crews on the Italian Front had them privately manufactured in Italian camouflage pattern. Crews of armoured car companies wore the M1941 Panzer denim uniform in reed-green herringbone twill or in white or mouse-grey cotton as a fatigue and summer field uniform.

The M1942 Panzer denim uniform in reed-green or light grey HBT was issued for all armoured vehicle crews, including Assault Artillery crews and mechanics. It comprised a loose-fitting jacket with a large left breast pocket with buttoned scalloped flap, with two parallel rows of five concealed buttons on the right side; these allowed adjustment so that it could be worn over the black or field-grey uniform in cold weather, or alone in hot weather. The trousers had a large left thigh pocket. This uniform was also privately acquired in splinter, marsh and Italian M1929 forest-pattern camouflage material.

See MAA 330, *The German Army 1939-45 (4)*, for more detailed descriptions of these uniforms and their insignia worn on them.

Special field-grey uniform and insignia

Eleven categories of troops serving on the Western and Italian Fronts in armoured vehicles but not wearing the black Panzer uniform were issued the special field-grey uniform. These were Assault Artillery; Armoured Artillery with Wespe and Hummel self-propelled guns; army motorised Anti-Aircraft battalions; Armoured Engineers; Armoured Trains; Anti-Tank and Infantry Gun companies on half-tracks in infantry and Panzergrenadier units; Panzergrenadier battalions on half-tracks; Armoured Rocket-Launcher batteries; towed and self-propelled Anti-Tank units in infantry, rifle or mountain divisions or Army or Corps

This Oberst commanding a Panzer regiment in Italy, 1944, wears the olive M1940 tropical field cap; the eagle insignia is woven in light bluish-grey on rust-brown, and a chevron of pink Waffenfarbe (officially discontinued from 8 September 1942) encloses the national cockade, also on a rust-brown patch. The olive M1940 tropical tunic bears the all-ranks collar patches and breast eagle, in light bluish-grey on rust-brown. On the lower lapel he has added the aluminium skulls from the collar patches of his special black uniform – a practice first seen in North Africa. The M1940 light olive tie is worn with a non-regulation dark shirt. His decorations include the Iron Cross 1st Class and German Cross in Gold, a Wound Badge and an unidentified foreign cross. (Brian Davis)

This cheerful Obergefreiter taken prisoner at Lugo near Ravenna, Italy, in January 1945 also wears field-made camouflage trousers, this time in German Zeltbahn 31 splinter-pattern, and cut loose in apparent imitation of M1942 Panzer trousers. His field cap and tunic are of M1943 pattern, with M1936 rank chevrons, and radioman's lightning-flash arm badge in infantry white, on dark green backings.

HQ units; Anti-Tank units under Army or Corps HQ command equipped with the Elefant self-propelled gun; and Signals (not Armoured Signals) personnel in armoured vehicles. General officers sometimes wore this uniform with *Alt-Larisch* collar patches and breeches.

This uniform consisted of the field-grey M1940 version of the black Panzer field uniform – field jacket, trousers, grey shirt, black tie and black leather lace-up boots. Officers wore the M1938 peakless or M1943 peaked field cap, other ranks the M1934 or M1942 peakless or M1943 peaked field cap.

On the jacket officers wore standard M1935 collar patches, NCOs and men M1940 mouse-grey standard 'guards braids' on a field-grey backing sewn onto the rectangular collar patches, piped in branch-colour: bright red for Assault and Armoured Artillery and army Anti-Aircraft battalions; black for Armoured Engineers; pink for Armoured Trains; white for Anti-Tank and Infantry Gun companies in infantry units; grass-green for Panzergrenadier battalions on half-tracks and Anti-Tank and Infantry Gun companies in Panzergrenadier units; and bordeaux red (piping sometimes omitted) for Armoured Rocket-Launcher batteries.

All ranks of Anti-Tank units in infantry, rifle or mountain divisions or Army or HQ units wore the pink-piped field-grey rectangular collar patches with skulls; Signals, lemon yellow-piped field-grey patches with skulls; and self-propelled Anti-Tank units in Panzer and Panzergrenadier divisions or Elefant-equipped Army or Corps HQ units, pink-piped black patches with skulls as for Panzer regiments. Photos from mid-1941 onwards also show many examples of these patches worn with the skulls removed, and an order to this effect was published (or repeated) in January 1943. It was equally often disregarded.

Troops also wore the reed-green fatigue and summer field uniform with appropriate branch insignia.

Special insignia for other branches

The **élite divisions** continued to develop distinctive insignia. From 31 December 1943 personnel (including general officers) of the divisional staff and Reichsgrenadier-Regiment Hoch- und Deutschmeister of the 44th Infantry Division wore on their shoulder boards/straps a grey aluminium 'Stalingrad Cross' – the badge of the medieval Teutonic Order with the campaign title commemorating the original division's destruction at Stalingrad in January 1943. The cross was also worn as an unofficial unit cap badge. A cuff title, probably for the right cuff, was awarded the division on 26 February 1945 when it had transferred to Hungary. Since 3 June 1943 the Grenadier Regiment had already been allowed the unique distinction of carrying the regimental flag of the 4th Infantry Regiment Hoch- und Deutschmeister of the former Austrian Army, with a black imperial Habsburg eagle on a golden yellow ground.

The 106th Feldherrnhalle Panzer Brigade (2106 Panzer and Panzergrenadier Bns) wore the woven brown *Feldherrnhalle* title on the left cuff and the bronze SA 'victory runes' (Siegrunen) shoulder board/strap monogram. During the Ardennes offensive the Führer-Begleit-Brigade wore the GD shoulder-board/strap monogram and *Großdeutschland* right cuff title; personnel assigned to guarding Hitler's various headquarters added the *'Führer-Hauptquartier'* title in hand-embroidered gold wire or machine-embroidered yellow thread Gothic script and edging on a black cloth band, or hand-embroidered aluminium wire 'Sütterlin' script and edging on a black doeskin band. During that operation the Führer-Grenadier-Brigade wore the *'Großdeutschland'* cuff title and GD monogram.

Hitler hoped that strong National Socialist political leadership would transform the understrength, under-equipped and poorly trained **Volksgrenadier** divisions raised after July 1944 into élite units; on 8 October 1944 a distinctive badge, probably a monogram incorporating the letters VGD, was planned, but this was never manufactured.

From 1941 personnel of a number of units, usually in Panzer and Panzergrenadier divisions, wore **unofficial cap badges** on field headgear; these were usually aluminium reproductions of the divisional vehicle sign, worn on the left side just above the ear. The only division on the Western Front with such a badge was the 116th Panzer, who wore the 'Windhund' greyhound in an oval filled in with black. There were three on the Italian Front: 34th Infantry – white and blue shield; 5th Mountain – chamois; and 90th Panzergrenadier – sword over Sardinia map.

On the Italian Front many members of the 5th Mountain Division, which had helped capture Crete in May-June 1941, wore the *'cuff title KRETA'*, and members of the 90th Panzergrenadier Division wore the *'AFRIKA'* title awarded on 15 January 1943 to Afrikakorps veterans. Individual soldiers reassigned to other units retained these titles until May 1945 and, if awarded another title, could wear one above the other on the same cuff.

On 20 August 1944 the staff and cadets of the VI Infantry Officer Candidate (Fahnenjunker) School at Metz in German-annexed Lorraine, under GenMaj Joachim von Siegroth, joined the Krause Battle-Group of Stössel Regiment, 462 Volksgrenadier Division, and held out from 27 August to 20 November 1944 against attacks by US forces. On 24 October 1944 a cuff title was awarded to members of the school who had fought in the battle, and cadets of the school, which was subsequently relocated to Meseritz, central Germany, could wear it whilst training at the school. The black cloth band bore the title *'Metz 1944'* in machine-embroidered silver-grey cotton Roman script and matching edging.

Until 1 September 1943 **reconnaissance battalions** in infantry and mountain divisions wore the cavalry's golden-yellow branch colour, but on that date they were remustered to the infantry as Fusilier Battalions wearing infantry white branch colour. In order to preserve the traditional cavalry association 57 battalions throughout the army were on 23 February 1944 named 'Divisional Fusilier Battalions (AA)', wearing golden-yellow and using cavalry ranks and unit designations. Only the 34th Fusilier Battalion, originally part of 6th Cavalry Regiment, wore its traditional 'dragoon eagle' cap badge. On 25 March 1943 all Armoured Reconnaissance battalions were required to wear the Panzer pink branch colour, but many retained golden-yellow, and on 29 November 1944 this colour was once more prescribed for all such battalions.

The personnel of **military internal security units** apparently feared victimisation if captured by Allied troops, and from early 1944 tended only to wear duty gorgets, armbands and aiguillettes which could be

An Unteroffizier from a Panzergrenadier regiment captured at Castiglione di Lago near Perugia, Italy, July 1944. He wears the M1940 reed-green summer field tunic with M1938 shoulder straps and M1940 collar patches and breast eagle. The cap is the light olive M1940 tropical model; the loose trousers are made up in Italian M1929 forest-pattern camouflage. Note details of other ranks' belt and M1939 leather infantry Y-straps; he carries his bread bag slung. (Brian Davis)

Northern Italy, January 1945: Hauptmann Leopold Berger, of 296th Mountain Regiment, 157th Mountain Division, openly displays his gilt regimental numerals on his shoulder boards in accordance with the regulation of 16 February 1944. His M1935 tunic, collar patches and breast eagle are clear; just cut off by the left edge of the photo is his M1939 Mountain Troops arm badge. Note that he wears an M1943 field cap identified by its single flap button as Waffen-SS issue, with aluminium crown piping and Army insignia. (Friedrich Herrmann)

easily discarded before capture. Thus from 19 March 1944 Military Police (Feldgendarmerie) no longer wore their M1939 arm badge and cuff title, retaining only their distinctive M1939 duty gorget. Field Police (Feldjäger) wore the uniform of their original branch of service and a duty gorget with the inscription *'Feldjägerkorps'*; they were prescribed, but rarely wore, Fj shoulder strap monograms; and a red armband on the left upper or lower sleeve with an official stamp and *'Oberkommando der Wehrmacht/Feldjäger,* in black Roman letters. Wehrmacht Patrol Service (Wehrmacht-Streifendienst) personnel wore their original uniforms with M1935 officers' aiguillettes, and on the left upper sleeve the black-on-white *'Wehrmacht/Streifendienst'* armband. Troops guarding District Command HQs wore the *'Kommandantur'* gorget; railway guards, the *'Zugwachabteilung'* gorget, and railway-station guards the *'Bahnhofswache'* gorget.

Uniforms and insignia of Army Chaplains

Divisional chaplains were classified as senior career Army Officials (Beamten) with equivalent officers' rank, the Chaplain-General (Feldbischof der Wehrmacht) being equivalent to a general officer. From 8 March 1937 chaplains wore the M1935 officer's service dress cap with matt aluminium chin cords and buttons, violet branch-colour pipings and a small aluminium or hand-embroidered Gothic cross between the eagle and the wreathed cockade. A chaplain-general had a gold wire crown and lower cap band piping and violet upper cap band piping (later changed to gold wire); a gold wire or celleon chin cord with gold buttons, and from 1 January 1943 a gold metal eagle, Gothic cross, wreath and cockade. The M1934 'old style' field cap with aluminium or gold thread insignia was also worn, as were the following caps, with aluminium or gold wire crown and front flap pipings, normal army insignia and the Gothic cross badge: M1938 peakless field cap; M1936 mountain cap, introduced 21 July 1942 as the M1942 peaked field cap; and the M1943 peaked field cap. The steel helmet could also be worn in the front line.

The M1935 officer's field tunic had a breast eagle but no shoulder boards, rank being indicated by M1935 violet facing cloth collar patches with two bright wire embroidered 'guards braids' with violet centre cords, gold for the chaplain-general, silver for chaplains ranked as field-officers *(Wehrmachtdekan-Wehrmachtpfarrer).* No collar patches were worn by a war-substantive chaplain ranked as captain *(Wehrmachtkriegspfarrer),* this rank being phased out from October 1942. As non-combatants chaplains wore a white armband, with a violet centre stripe broken by a red cross, on the left upper sleeve; but against regulations some chaplains carried a holstered pistol on their M1934 officers' brown belt for self-protection in the front line.

The full-length pocketless field-grey cassock had a violet standing collar, front and cuff pipings and breast eagle. On their chests Protestant chaplains wore an aluminium cross and chain, and Catholic chaplains a crucifix with a black wooden insert, worn by chaplains-general in gold. For chaplains the M1935 field greatcoat had no shoulder boards, chaplains-general showing violet lapel linings.

The uniform and insignia of other Officials are described in MAA 326 *The German Army 1939-45 (3).*

Uniforms and insignia of European Volunteers

Italian troops in RSI support units with German divisions on the Italian Front wore normal Italian Republican Army uniforms and insignia. From 30 July 1944 individual Italians serving as 'Volunteers' (on the same basis as Hilfswillige on the Eastern Front) in divisional service units were ordered to wear Italian M1940 or German uniforms with German rank insignia and a national badge on the left upper sleeve. The design of the badge is unconfirmed, but was either a black printed armshield with *ITALIA* in white over an inner shield with green-white-red horizontal bars, or a white embroidered eagle and lictor's fasces badge as worn by the Italian 29th SS Infantry Division.

Uniforms and insignia of Osttruppen

From January 1943 ROA personnel in the Eastern Battalions wore standard German uniforms with a Tsarist-style red and blue cap cockade and modified Tsarist rank and collar insignia – illustrated in MAA 330, *The German Army 1939-45 (4)* – and on the left upper sleeve an armshield featuring a blue St Andrew's Cross. In 1944 some troops were issued a distinctive light blue-grey field uniform – possibly using surplus French Army stocks of M1915 'horizon blue' material – with M1943 collar and shoulder insignia and armshield. The pullover field tunic resembled a Soviet M1935 *gymnastiorka*, open at the chest and secured by three field-grey pebbled buttons; it had two breast pockets and two side pockets with V-shaped buttoned flaps, and single-button cuffs. The trousers were worn with M1941 anklets.

From 18 March 1944 personnel who appeared to be 'worthy in character, general performance and political reliability' were permitted German rank insignia and collar patches, a distinction more likely to be gained by battalions integrated into German infantry regiments than independent battalions. In practice ROA officers wore M1943 ROA or M1935 German officers' collar patches, and German shoulder boards with white infantry underlay, while NCOs and men wore M1943 ROA or M1940 German collar patches and M1943 ROA rank-bars on German shoulder straps piped in white. On 2 March 1945 personnel were ordered to remove their German breast eagles, a command often ignored, and German cadres to remove their ROA armshields, to perpetuate the fiction that the ROA/KONR were independent armed forces allied to Germany.

Cossack troops in France wore standard German Army uniforms with breast eagles, M1942 'lance' collar patches and M1943 ROA rank insignia. From 18 March 1944 some troops adopted German collar patches, and many officers added German shoulder boards with white underlay for infantry battalions and golden-yellow for cavalry battalions. Other ranks

On 20 April 1945 Generalleutnant Max Pemsel, commanding 6th Mountain Division in Norway, was appointed Chief of Staff to the German-Italian Liguria Army, only to see it surrender 12 days later on 2 May. His M1935 service cap and tunic bear conventional general officer's distinctions in gold and bright red. At his throat are the Knight's Crosses of the Iron Cross and the War Merit Cross with Swords; in his button hole and on his left breast pocket are the 1914 Iron Cross 2nd Class ribbon and 1st Class decoration, both with 1939 clasps for subsequent World War II awards; and note the very long ribbon bar above. General Pemsel went on to serve in the West German Bundeswehr, and could thus claim the rare distinction of having served in three German Armies. (Brian Davis)

wore M1943 ROA or Cossack shoulder straps or M1940 German shoulder straps with white or golden-yellow piping, all with M1943 ROA/Cossack rank insignia. The M1943 peaked field cap was worn with German or Cossack badges. A red cloth armshield, with additional 1-4 white diagonal stripes probably indicating different battalions, was worn on the left upper sleeve, sometimes with a ROA armshield above.

Eastern Legion battalions continued to wear Legion armshields and German breast eagles as well as the M1942 cap badges, collar patches and shoulder board/strap rank insignia (described and illustrated in MAA 330) until May 1945. Relatively few personnel appear to have adopted German collar patches and shoulder boards/straps with infantry white underlays/pipings after 18 March 1944 – probably because they were considered less reliable than the ROA and Cossacks. German officer and NCO cadres wore German uniforms and insignia with the Legion armshield on the right upper arm.

The disparity in uniforms and insignia and the dejected appearance of these troops captured by the French Expeditionary Corps in Italy, 1944, make a striking contrast with the smartness and confidence of the early war years. The private (left foreground) wears the M1943 tunic with regulation M1940 collar patches, shoulder straps and breast eagle. The young Unteroffizier (centre foreground) has the M1942 tunic with M1940 breast eagle, to which he has attached M1935 dark green collar facing and bright aluminium NCO braid, M1938 collar patches, and long-obsolete M1935 pointed dark green shoulder straps without piping. (Brian Davis)

Medals and awards

By 1944 the German soldier was entitled to wear a substantial number of medals, ribbons, campaign and qualification badges on the field uniform. This may have bolstered morale, but also made much-decorated soldiers obvious targets for snipers.

The principal **medal for bravery and leadership** in the front line remained the Iron Cross, displayed in its 2nd Class by a button hole ribbon and in the 1st Class by a black and silver pin-on cross on the left breast pocket. The German Cross in Gold might be awarded to personnel who already had the Iron Cross 1st Class, and was worn as a swastika within a gilt sunburst on the right breast pocket. For further acts of conspicuous gallantry or leadership four classes of the Knight's Cross of the Iron Cross might be awarded progressively, and were worn at the throat: the basic Knight's Cross, with Oakleaves, with Oakleaves and Swords, and with Oakleaves, Swords and Diamonds – the latter supreme award being granted to only a handful of very distinguished officers.

The War Merit Cross with or without Swords for acts of bravery or leadership away from the front line was in four classes: 2nd Class button hole ribbon, 1st Class cross pinned to the left breast pocket, and silver and gold classes of Knight's Cross worn at the throat. Soldiers admitted to the 'Roll of Honour of the German Army', equivalent to the British Army's 'mentioned in dispatches', were from 30 January 1944 awarded a gilt metal wreathed swastika clasp to be worn in the button hole on the Iron Cross ribbon.

Four combat qualification badges were worn on the left breast pocket: the silver Infantry Assault Badge for infantry, rifle and mountain troops (bronze for motorised infantry); the silver Tank Battle Badge for tank crews (bronze for Panzergrenadiers and armoured car crews); the dull grey Army Anti-Aircraft Badge; and the silver General Assault Badge for other branches, including artillery, anti-tank, engineer and medical personnel. Apart from the Flak badge these were initially awarded for participation in three separate actions, but higher classes were later added.

The Close Combat Clasp, Sniper's Badge. Tank Destruction Badge, and the similar award for shooting down an aircraft with light weapons are described in MAA 330, *The German Army 1939-45 (4)*. Awards such as the Narvik, Cholm, Crimea, Demyansk and Kuban Shields and the Anti-Partisan War Badge, awarded for service on the Eastern Front, could be seen worn by troops transferred from that theatre to the Western and Italian Fronts – see MAA 330. However, only one campaign shield was awarded for service on the latter fronts, and that was unofficial. The submarine base of Lorient in southern Brittany held out as an isolated 'fortress' from 6 August 1944 until 8 May 1945. In December 1944 the base commander, Admiral Henneke, approved a locally-made shield for wear on the left arm, in white metal, copper, aluminium or brass; this featured a defiant warrior naked except for helmet, shield and sword bestriding the base, with the date above and name below. How many were made is unknown.

Cotentin Peninsula, France, summer 1944: a *Fel'dfebel'* of the Russian Liberation Army (ROA) reports to an officer while a German soldier looks on. The Russian NCO is probably from Ostbataillon 439, assigned as 4th Bn to Grenadier-Regiment 726, 716. Infanterie-Division. He wears a M1935 field tunic with the applied ROA rank insignia of 1942, superceded by January 1943 regulations; and the M1943 ROA arm shield - blue saltire on white shield edged red, on dark green backing shield with white or yellow lettering. (Friedrich Herrmann)

Normandy, June 1944: mail for soldiers of 116. Panzer-Division, which would be badly mauled in the fighting against the Allied bridgehead. The Obergefreiter handing it out wears the M1942 reed-green summer tunic with unusual buttoned cuffs; M1938 dark green shoulder straps, M1936 arm chevrons, and on his M1943 field cap the division's unofficial *Windhund* badge. The Oberfeldwebel (centre) – probably a platoon leader in Panzergrenadier-Regiment 60 or 156 – wears the M1940 special field-grey uniform, now no longer the sole preserve of SP gun units but beginning to be issued to the half-track mechanised infantry. On his collar M1940 field-grey patches with standard 'guards braids' are outlined in grass-green Waffenfarbe piping. Note this NCO's MP40 magazine pouches, non-standard 10x50 Voigtländer binoculars, and on his left breast the Close Combat Clasp above the Iron Cross 1st Class. (Brian Davis)

Table: SELECTIVE LIST OF BRANCH AND UNIT INSIGNIA OF UNITS ON THE WESTERN AND ITALIAN FRONTS 10 JULY 1943-8 MAY 1945

Units	Branch colour	Shoulder-strap insignia		Other distinctions
		Western Front 6.6.1944 – 8.5.1945	Italian Front 10.7.1943 – 29.5.1945	
Combat Troops – Staff (Kommandobehörde)				
7 Army Group (Heeresgruppe) Staffs	White	G　　　　　(B,D,G,H,Oberrhein)	G　　　　　　(B,C)	-
10 Army (Armee) Staffs	White	A / 1,7,11,15,19,25 (Blumentritt)	A / 10,14 (Ligurien)	-
2 Reinf. Corps (Armeeabteilung) Staffs	White	None　　　(Von Lüttwitz)	None　　　(Von Zangen)	-
1 Armoured Army (Panzerarmee) Staff	Pink	A /　West/5	-	
30 Corps (Korps) Staffs (* Corps had Latin numbers)	White	Vosegen/13,25,30,37,47,53, 58, 62-4,66-7,74,80-2,84, Kniess/85,86,88-91,Feldt	14,51,Venetisches Küstenland/73,75, 87/Lombardia, Adriatisches Küstenland/97	-
2 Armoured Corps (Panzerkorps) Staff *	Pink	-	14,76	-
Combat Troops – Infantry (Infanterie)				
47 Infantry (Infanterie) Division Staffs	White	D / 16,49,77,84-5,89,106, 176,180,189-90,198,219,249, 269,271-2,275-7,319,331, 338,352-3,361,363,416,703, 716,719, Deichmann,Hamburg,Rässler	D / 34,65,71,92,94,98,148, 162, 278,334, 356,362,715	-
1 Airlanding (Luftlande) Div. Staff	White	D / 91	-	-
1 Infantry (Reichsgrenadig) Div.Staff	White	-	Stalingrad cross	-
23 Static (bodenständig) Inf. Div Staffs	White	D / 59,64,70,226,242-5,265-6, 326,343-4, 346-8,708-9,711-2	D / 232,237,305	-
3 Line Infantry (Grenadier) Div.Staffs	White	D / 36,553,559	-	-
28 Infantry (Volksgrenadier) Div. Staffs	White	D / 9,12,16,18-9,26,36,47, 62,79,167,183, 212,246,256-7, 272,277,326,340,352,361, 363,462,553,559-60,708	-	-
2 Line Infantry (Grenadier) Brigades	White	1005,Baur	-	-
231 Line Infantry (Grenadier) Regts	White	36-1303　　　(179 Regts)	80,107,117,131-2,145-7,191, 194,211,253,267,274,276,281, 285-6,289-90,303,314,329, 576-8,725, 735,754-6,869-71, 956,992-4,954-6,1043-8, 1059-60	
3 Line Infantry (Füsilier) Regts	White	26-7,39	-	-
7 Fortress Inf. (Festungsgrenadier) Regts	White	F / 729,739,851-2,854-5,858	-	-
3 Rifle (Jäger) Div. Staffs	Light green	None　　　(Alpen)	D / 42,114	Jäger badges
6 Rifle (Jäger) Regts	Light green	None　(1 Alpen,2 Alpen)	25,40,721,741	Jäger badges
3 Rifle Field (Feld(L)) Div. Staffs	White	D / 16-8	-	-
1 Assault (Luftwaffe-Sturm) Div. Staff	Gold-yellow	-	D/19	-
9 Rifle (Feld(L)) Regts	White	31-6, 46-8	-	-
3 Rifle (Feld(L)) Regts	Gold-yellow	-	37-8, 45	-
5 Mountain (Gebirgs) Division Staffs	Light green	D / 2,157	D / 5,175/8,188	Edelweiss badges
10 Mountain (Gebirgs) Regts.	Light green	136-7,296-7	85,100,296-7,901-4	Edelweiss badges
7 Reserve (Reserve) Division Staffs	White	D / 158-9,165,172,182,189	D / 157	-
14 Reserve Inf (Reserve-Grenadier) Regts.	White	9,15,18,28,34,36,79,112, 213,221,251,342	7,157	-
1 Res. Mtn (Reserve-Gebirgs) Div.Staff	Light green	-	D / 188	Edelweiss badges
3 Reserve Mtn (Reserve-Gebirgs) Regts.	Light green	-	1,136-9	Edelweiss badges
71　Replacement (Feldersatz) Bns.		3-1560　　　(50 Bns in divisional series)	3-1057　　　(23 Bns in divisional series)	-
1 Training (Feldausbildungs) Div. Staff	White	D / 149	-	-
2 Training (Feldausbildungs) Inf Regts	White	1301-3	-	-
5 Special Div. Staff (Divisionsstab z.b.V)	White	D / 136,406,606,616-7,	-	-
10 Depot (Division Nr.) Div. Staffs	White	D / 176,180,190,405,462,471, 476,526,805, 905	-	-
7 Depot (Grenadier-Ersatz) Inf Regts	White	22,30,269,520,211,253,536	-	-

Units	Branch colour	Shoulder-strap insignia		Other distinctions
		Western Front 6.6.1944 – 8.5.1945	Italian Front 10.7.1943 – 29.5.1945	
Combat Troops – Mobile Troops (Schnelle Truppen)				
7 Armoured (Panzer) Division Staffs	Pink	D / 2,9,11,21,116	D / 16,26	Black Panzer uniform
1 Armoured (Panzer-Lehr) Div. Staff	Pink	D / L	-	Black Panzer uniform
3 Armoured (Panzer) Brigs.	Pink	106-7,108	-	Black Panzer uniform
8 Armoured (Panzer) Regts.	Pink	3,15-6,33,100,130	2,26	Black Panzer uniform
7 Armoured (Panzer) Bns.	Pink	5,103,115,2106-7	103,115,129,190	Black Panzer uniform
12 Armd Recce.(Panzeraufklärung) Bns.	Pink	A / 2,21	-	Black Panzer uniform
12 Armd Recce.(Panzeraufklärung) Bns.	Gold yellow	A / 9,11,103,115-6,125,130	A / 16,26,103,115,129	Black Panzer uniform
5 Armd.Inf.(Panzergrenadier) Div.Staffs	Grass green	D / 3,15,25	D / 3,15,29,90	Grey Panzer uniform
25 Armd.Infantry . (Panzergrenadier) Regts	Grass green	2,8,10,11,29,35,60,104,110-1, 115,119,125, 156,192,304	9,64,76,79,104,115, 155,200,361	Grey Panzer uniform
2 Armd.Infantry (Panzergrenadier) Regts.	Pink	901-2	-	Grey Panzer uniform
2 Armd.Infantry (Panzergrenadier) Bns.	Grass green	2106-7	-	Grey Panzer uniform
5 Motorized (Grenadier(mot.) Regts	White	8,29,1000	8,15,29,71	-
5 Reconnaissance (Aufklärung) Bns.	Gold yellow	-	A / 44,114,142,194,236	
39 Reconnaissance (Füsilier) Bns.	White	59,64,70,84-5,149,176,180, 185,189-90,212,226,272, 275-7,331,344,346-7,361, 363, 405,560,708,712,716,719, 1089,1316, 1553	34,148,192,198, 232,237,278,715	-
14 Div.Recce (Divisions-Füsilier(A.A.)) Bns	Gold yellow	12,26,62,256,269,271,352-3	65,171,305,334,356,362	-
1 Div.Recce(Divisions-Füsilier(A.A.)) Bn	Gold yellow	-	34	Dragoon eagle badge
17 Div. Recce. (Füsilier) Coys.	White	9,47,167,246,257,271, 276-7, 340,352,361,363,553,559, 716,1462,1575	-	-
91 Anti-tank (Panzerjäger) Bns.	Pink	P / 3-1818 (69 Bns in divisional series)	P / 3,16,26,29,33-4,46,95,114, 142,165,171,190,192,194,198,232, 236,278,305,334,356,362, 715,1048,1057	-
Combat Troops – Artillery (Artillerie)				
92 Artillery (Artillerie) Regts.	Bright red	3-1818 (72 Regts in divisional series)	3,29,33-4,96,142,165,171,190, 192,194, 198,232,236-7,278, 305,334,356,362,661, 1048	-
6 Artillery (Artillerie) Bns.	Bright red	28,656,663,GD (Alpen)	671	-
5 Mtn.Artillery (Gebirgsartillerie) Regts	Bright red	111,191,1057	95,1057,1088	Edelweiss badges
8 Armd Artillery (Panzerartillerie) Regts	Bright red	103,119,130,146,155,1818	16,93	Black Panzer uniform
11 Assault Artillery (Sturmartillerie) Brigs.	Bright red	243-4,290,341,394,667, 902,905,911	907,914	Grey Panzer uniform
2 Assault Artillery (Sturmartillerie) Bns.	Bright red	200	242	Grey Panzer uniform
16 Army AA Art. (Heeresflak) Bns	Bright red	273,277,281,287,292,305, 311-2,315,1026, 1036	274,304,312-3,315	Grey Panzer uniform
3 AA Art. (Flak) Coys	Bright red	36,191	1048	Grey Panzer uniform
11 Rocket Launcher (Volks-Werfer) Brigs	Bord. red	4,7-9,15-20	5	-
22 Rocket Launcher (Werfer) Regts.	Bord. red	1,2,14,21-6,51,53-5,83-9	56,71	-
Combat Troops – Engineers (Pioniere)				
92 Engineer (Pionier) Bns	Black	3-1818 (72 Regts in divisional series)	3,33-4,80,114,142,165,171, 190,232,237,278,192,194, 198,305,334,356,362,715, 936,1048	-
4 Mtn. Engineer (Gebirgspionier) Bns	Black	82,1057,	95,1057,1088	Edelweiss badges
9 Armd Engineer (Panzerpionier) Regts	Black	38,86,130,209,220,675,	16,29,93	Black Panzer uniform
Combat Troops – Signals (Nachrichtentruppe)				
91 Signals (Nachrichten) Bns	Lem. yellow	9-1818 (71 Bns in divisional series)	29,33-4,64,114,142,165,171, 192,194,198, 232,236-7,278, 305,334,356,362,715,1048, 1057	-

249

continued on page 42

Units	Branch colour	Shoulder-strap insignia		Other distinctions
		Western Front 6.6.1944 – 8.5.1945	**Italian Front** 10.7.1943 – 29.5.1945	
3 Mot.Signals (Nachrichten) Bns	Lem. yellow	3,33	3	-
3 Mtn Signals (Gebirgsnachrichten) Bns	Lem. yellow	67,1057	95	Edelweiss badges
9 Armd.Sigs (Panzernachrichten) Regts	Lem. yellow	38,85,89,130,200,228	16,93,190	Black Panzer uniform
8 War Correspondent . (Propaganda) Coys	Lem. yellow	605,619,624-5,649,696,698	614	PK cuff-title

Supply Troops (Versorgungstruppen)

Units	Branch colour	Western Front	Italian Front	Other distinctions
98 Div.Supply (Nachschubtruppen) Cdrs	Light blue	D / 3-1818 (73 Cdrs in divisional series)	N / 3-1088 (28 Cdrs in divisional series)	-
50 Supply (Versorgungs) Regts	Light blue	D / 9-1818 (39 Regts in divisional series)	D / 34,165,171,194,198,278, 305,334,356, 715,1048	-
65? Motor Transport (Nachschub) Cols.	Light blue	N / 3-1560 (40 Cols in divisional series)	N / 3-1088 (27 Cols. in divisional series)	-
88? Horse Transport (Nachschub) Cols.	Light blue	N / 9-1818 (69 Cols in divisional series)	N / 3,34,44,114,142,165,171, 192,194,198, 232,237,278, 232,237,278,305,334,356, 362,715,936,1048	Cavalry breeches, boots
4 Mtn Horse Transport (Nachschub) . Cols	Light blue	N / 67,1057	N / 95,1057,1088	Cavalry legwear, Edelweiss badges
86 Horse Medical. (Sanitäts) Coys – men	Dark blue	N / 9-1818 (67 Cols in divisional series)	34,44,114,142,165,171,192, 194,198,232,237,278,305, 334,356,362,715,936,1048	Red Cross armband
4 Mtn.Med. (Gebirgssanitäts) Coys-men	Dark blue	67,1057	95,1057,1088	Red Cross armband
13 Mot.Medical (Sanitäts) Coys – men	Dark blue	3,25,33,60-1,66,82,130,200	3,16,29,33,93,190	Red Cross armband
91 Veterinary (Veterinär) Coys – men	Crimson	9-1818 (70 Coys in divisional series)	34-1088 (22 Coys in divisional series)	Cavalry breeches, boots

Security Troops (Sicherungstruppen)

Units	Branch colour	Western Front	Italian Front	Other distinctions
9 Army Rear-Area Commders (Korück)	White	K / 517,533-5,570,588,591-2	K / 594	-
10 Dist.Comds (Oberfeldkommandantur)	White	K / 520,570,589-91,671-2, 680,894	K / 379	-
64 Sub-Dist.Comds (Feldkommandantur)	White	K / 493-994 (63 Comds)	K / 1017	-
3 MP (Feldgendarmerie) Bns	Orange	690,693	692	Sleeve badge, cuff-title
77 MP (Feldgendarmerie) Troops	Orange	None (3-1560 in divisional series)	None (3-715 in divisional series)	Sleeve badge, cuff-title

Foreign Troops

Units	Branch colour	Western Front	Italian Front	Other distinctions
43 ROA Eastern (Ost) Bns	White	None (285,406,439,441,517, 550,561,600-2,605, 608,615, 618,621,628-30,633-6,642-3, 649, 654,661,663,665-6,669, 680-1,750)	None (263,339,406,412, 556,560,616-7,620)	ROA arm-badge
6 Armenian Ostlegion Bns	Gold yellow	None (II/9,I/198,810,812-3)	None (815)	Armenian arm-badge
6 Azeri Ostlegion Bns	Green	None (807)	None (I/4(Geb),I/97(Jäg), I/101(Jäg),804,806)	Azeri arm-badge
11 Georgian Ostlegion Bns	Red	None (I/9,I/298/II/4(Geb.), 795,797-9,822-3)	None (III/9,II/125,II/198)	Georgian arm-badge
5 North Caucasian Ostlegion Bns	Brown	None (800,803,835-7)	-	North Caucasian badge
9 Turkestani Ostlegion Bns	Light blue	None (781-2,787)	None (I/29,I/44,I/101(Jäg), I/297,I/305,I/384)	Turkestan arm-badge
3 Volga-Tartar Ostlegion Bns	Blue/Green	None (627,826-7)	-	Volga-Tartar badge
5 Cossack (Kosaken) Infantry Bns	White	None I-II/360,570, III/854,III/855	-	Cossack arm-badge
3 Cossack (Kosaken/Ostreiter) Cav. Bns	Gold yellow	None (281,285,403)	-	Cossack arm-badge

Army Officials (Heeresbeamten)

Units	Branch colour	Western Front	Italian Front	Other distinctions
26 Field Security Police (GFP) Groups	Light blue	GFP (2-3,7-9,30,131,161,530, 540,560,590, 625,644,648, 707,710,712,716-7,737-8,743)	GFP (610,637,741)	-

THE PLATES

A: NORMANDY & NORTHERN FRANCE, 1944

A1: Grenadier, Grenadier-Regiment 914; Omaha Beach, Normandy, 6 June 1944

This rifleman of the 352.Infanterie-Division opposing US landings on 'Bloody Omaha' is wearing the Zeltbahn 31 camouflage shelter-quarter with its darker side exposed, over his M1943 field tunic and trousers with M1941 field-grey canvas anklets and lace-up boots. His M1942 helmet has a regulation net and foliage. He wears the other ranks' black belt with tropical M1940 canvas infantry support Y-straps, leather rifle ammunition pouches, and slung M1930 gas mask canister. He carries the rare Walther 7.92mm Gewehr 41(W) semi-automatic rifle, a M1924 stick grenade and two M1939 'egg' grenades.

A2: Gefreiter, Panzergrenadier-Lehr-Regiment 901; Barenton, August 1944

This section first gunner is participating in the unsuccessful Operation Lüttich counterattack, 7-8 August 1944, when his regiment was destroyed. He wears the M1940 special field-grey uniform issued to all Panzer-Lehr-Division troops not entitled to the black Panzer uniform. The dark green M1935 shoulder straps have grass-green branch-colour piping and stitched Gothic L for Lehr, and an NCO candidate's aluminium shoulder loops. The M1940 collar patches are also piped grass-green; rank is indicated by the M1940 left sleeve chevron. His M1942 helmet has the second pattern cover in M1931 splinter-pattern camouflage. He wears M1939 black leather infantry Y-straps, supporting on his belt an MG42 first gunner's spares pouch and P38 Walther pistol in a soft-shell holster.

A3: Oberwachtmeister, Armoured Rocket-Launcher Battery; Normandy, June 1944

The personnel of independent armoured rocket-launcher batteries, equipped with 15cm Nebelwerfer 42 launchers mounted on half-tracks, were issued the M1940 special field-grey uniform. However, this senior NCO wears the M1942 Panzer working uniform in light grey herringbone twill with large left breast and thigh pockets. This was issued with the breast eagle attached; instead of the regulation M1942 sleeve rank insignia he has added M1935 shoulder straps and M1940 collar patches piped with artillery red (patches piped in regulation bordeaux-red were rare); note also his General Assault Badge. He wears a M1943 peaked field cap, a P38 Walther pistol in a soft-shell holster, and lace-up ankle boots; and carries 'liberated' war booty in his M1942 helmet - American cigarettes were particularly prized.

B: NORMANDY & NORTHERN FRANCE, 1944

B1: Hauptmann, Festungs-Grenadier-Regiment 857; Caen, July 1944

This battalion commander from 346.Infanterie-Division wears a privately-made field tunic in Zeltbahn 31 splinter-pattern camouflage, resembling the M1935 other ranks' tunic in cut, with added M1935 officer's collar patches, shoulder boards and breast eagle. It was not uncommon to see such jackets fairly liberally decorated; he displays the ribbons of the Iron Cross 2nd Class and Eastern Winter 1941-42 Medal, his Iron Cross 1st Class and an Infantry Assault Badge. The M1934

Members of a ROA Ostbataillon and their German cadre happy to be taken prisoner by US forces in Normandy, June 1944. All wear German uniforms and insignia; with the exception of the man wearing the fleece cap and the ROA arm shield, the non-Germans are only recognisable by their features. (Friedrich Herrmann)

'old style' soft-peaked field cap has BeVo machine-woven insignia; the M1943 field-grey belted trousers are tucked into M1939 other ranks' short-shaft marching boots. He carries a holstered P08 Luger pistol on his blackened M1934 officer's belt, and Voigtländer short 10x50 binoculars.

B2: Leutnant, Heeres-Flakartillerie-Abteilung 281; Falaise Pocket, August 1944

This young, anti-aircraft battery commander in 116.Panzer-Division wears a version of the M1940 reed-green HBT summer field tunic cut like the M1935 other ranks' field tunic with pocket pleats, with M1935 officers' collar patches, shoulder boards, and other ranks' breast eagle; note matching M1943 issue reed-green trousers. He wears a M1942 helmet, M1941 canvas anklets and lace-up ankle boots; his blackened M1934 officer's belt supports a P38 Walther pistol in a soft-shell holster, and he has tucked under it his M1938 officer's field cap with aluminium front flap and crown pipings. He displays the Army Anti-Aircraft breast badge and Iron Cross 2nd Class button hole ribbon; and carries a M1934 range finder.

B3: Panzergrenadier, Panzergrenadier-Regiment 192; Lille, September 1944

This 21.Panzer-Division soldier wears the M1943 marsh-pattern hooded smock in Zeltbahn 31 splinter-pattern camouflage over his M1940 field tunic, with M1943 field-grey belted trousers, M1941 field-grey canvas anklets and ankle boots. His M1942 helmet has a field-made net of twine and hooks for foliage. He has the black other ranks' belt with field-grey painted buckle, M1939 leather infantry support Y-straps, slung M1930 gas mask canister, a P38 Walther pistol in a soft-shell holster. He carries the 8.8cm M43 Panzerschreck ('tank frightener') anti-tank rocket-launcher, a copy of the US Army 2.36in bazooka introduced late in 1943.

C: SOUTHERN FRANCE, 1944

C1: Legionär, Armenisches Feld-Bataillon I/198; Toulon, August 1944

This Armenian Legion unit formed the 4th Bn of Grenadier-

Regiment 918, 242.Infanterie-Division, and was one of few Eastern Legion units to be awarded German insignia after 18 March 1944; the battalion was destroyed in the defence of Toulon. This rifleman wears the M1943 field tunic with M1940 field-grey shoulder straps piped infantry white, M1940 other ranks' collar patches and breast eagle, and a M1942 national armshield. He wears the M1942 helmet, M1943 field-grey belted trousers, M1941 canvas anklets and ankle boots. The other ranks' black belt with leather M1939 infantry Y-straps supports rifle ammunition pouches, a bayonet and entrenching tool on his left hip, and bread bag and canteen on his right; the M1930 gas mask canister is slung round his body. He is armed with the standard Karabiner 98k rifle and a M1939 grenade.

C2: Generalmajor, 11.Panzer-Division; Alsace, September 1944

Rejecting a general officer's normal affectations such as a privately-tailored field-grey or black Panzer uniform, this divisional commander wears the regulation other ranks' M1943 field tunic with general officers' *Alt-Larisch* collar patches, shoulder boards, gold breast eagle and gilded pebbled buttons. He has a M1943 peaked field cap with gold wire crown piping; officer's breeches with general officer's bright red piping and broad stripes, and officer's riding-boots without spurs. He carries a 7.65mm Walther PPK pistol (his only personal indulgence) holstered on his M1934 officer's brown belt, and 10x50 long Zeiß binoculars. He displays the Knight's Cross, the ribbon of the Eastern Winter 1941-42 Medal and the Tank Battle Badge.

C3: Unterfeldwebel, Panzer-Abteilung 2113; Lorraine, September 1944

This 113.Panzer-Brigade tank commander wears the black M1942 Panzer jacket with M1934 shoulder straps and NCO braid, collar patches and breast eagle. He wears black lace-up ankle-boots, and an M1936 round neck field-grey sweater in preference to the regulation grey shirt and black tie. The M1943 field-grey peaked field cap suggests supply shortages of the black Panzer version. He has a P38 Walther in a soft-shell holster on his belt; and displays the Iron Cross 2nd Class ribbon in his button hole, the Tank Battle Badge, a black Wound Badge (for one and two wounds), and on his left sleeve the Crimea Shield, indicating previous Eastern Front service. He carries the standard field flashlight.

D: BELGIUM AND NETHERLANDS, 1944
D1: Grenadier, Grenadier-Regiment 1222; Arnhem corridor, October 1944

This section third LMG gunner from 180.Infanterie-Division wears the M1943 field tunic and belted trousers with M1941 canvas anklets and ankle boots; his M1942 helmet has a hooked chicken-wire 'basket' cover. His belt and M1939 leather infantry Y-straps support standard rifleman's equipment: M1938 folding shovel in second pattern carrier and 84/98 bayonet on his left hip; M1931 mess kit, bread bag and camouflage shelter-quarter on his lower back; and M1931 canteen and cup behind his right hip. He has tied his gas cape pouch to the M1930 gas mask canister hanging

Part of an infantry section training in France, May 1944. They wear M1940 and M1943 field tunics; M1942 greatcoats; M1940 trousers with M1939 short-shaft marching boots, or M1943 belted trousers with M1941 canvas anklets and ankle boots. The first gunner of the LMG team is at far right; he has a holstered P35 Radom pistol and the MG42 spares pouch on his belt. Left of him we see the second gunner, with holstered pistol, ammunition box, and stick grenades. The third gunner, with standard rifle equipment, holds the late model MG42. All three carry spare ammunition belts. (Friedrich Herrmann)

ABOVE **Very different from the appearance of a German officer of 1939/40 – a Leutnant of infantry wearing the M1943 other ranks' field tunic, to which (like many) he has added non-regulation M1935 collar patches and breast eagle. Note the aluminium officer's crown piping on his M1943 field cap. (Brian Davis)**

from his shoulder. He carries a Karabiner 98k rifle and a spare ammunition belt for the light machine gun.

D2: Feldwebel, Feldgendarmerie-Trupp (Mot.) 189; Dutch-Belgian border, September 1944

This military policeman from 89.Infanterie-Division is on traffic control duty as passenger on a motorcycle combination. He wears a M1942 field-tunic, with scalloped pocket flaps but no pleats, with M1940 shoulder straps, collar patches, breast eagle and NCO collar braid. M1935 helmet with motorcycle goggles, M1943 belted trousers and M1939 short-shaft marching boots complete the uniform. On his belt he wears a second pattern triple magazine pouch for the MP40 sub-machine gun slung around his neck for easy access. He wears his 'chained dog' duty gorget and displays the Infantry Assault Badge; however, following the 19 March 1944 regulations, he has removed his military police left arm badge and cuff title. He carries a baton to direct traffic.

D3: Obergefreiter, Grenadier-Regiment 1039; Breskens Pocket, October 1944

This infantryman of 64.Infanterie-Division trapped in the Breskens Pocket in northern Belgium wears the M1943 field tunic, peaked field cap and belted trousers, M1941 canvas anklets and lace-up boots. As a radioman at company HQ he wears the signaller's qualification badge in infantry white above his M1940 rank chevrons. He carries the Feldfu.B short-range (one mile) radio with 32in antenna and attached headphones suspended from his M1939 leather infantry Y-straps, and the minimum of belt equipment - a P38 Walther in a soft-shell holster and M1931 bread bag, canteen and cup.

Dieppe, August 1944: German POWs have tied and buttoned their Zeltbahn 31 shelter-quarters together to make four-man tents. That in the foreground clearly shows the contrast between the light (outside) and dark (centre) sides of the Zeltbahn. (Brian Davis)

This Panzergrenadier in Italy in 1944 wears the M1938 Mountain Troops' reversible *feldgrau*/white anorak, which its three distinctive chest pockets. He still wears the M1934 field cap rather than the peaked M1943 model. (Brian Davis)

E: ARDENNES OFFENSIVE, 1944-45

E1: Unteroffizier, Füsilier-Regiment 39; Ardennes, December 1944

On 12 November 1942 this infantry regiment in 26.Volksgrenadier-Division was designated *Füsilier* in honour of the Great War commander, GenObst Erich von Ludendorff. This NCO section commander wears the M1942 field greatcoat with extra wide collar for warmth, M1942 helmet with chicken-wire cover, M1942 tubular woollen balaclava pulled down around his neck, woollen gloves, M1943 field-grey belted trousers, M1941 canvas anklets and ankle boots. His other ranks' black leather belt and M1939 infantry Y-straps support two sets of triple canvas magazine pouches for his MP44 (later designated StG44) assault rifle; an 84/98 bayonet and entrenching tool on his left hip; and two M24 stick grenades.

E2: Oberstleutnant, Pionier-Bataillon 33; Ardennes, December 1944

This commander of the 15.Panzergrenadier-Division's combat engineers is wearing a late version of the M1934 rubberised greatcoat with field-grey cloth collar; initially issued to motorcyclists and military police, from 1944 it was privately acquired by many officers and senior NCOs in the front line. He has added his shoulder boards with engineer black underlay. His M1943 officer's peaked field cap has aluminium wire crown piping and a M1943 eagle and cockade on a T-shaped field-grey backing; he wears officers' suede gloves and riding boots. He carries a P38 Walther in a

The M1944 field blouse was popular, but officers often had them privately made or retailored to personal taste. General der Panzertruppen Gerhard Graf von Schwerin, commanding 76 Panzer Corps, was photographed at Bologna, March 1945, wearing one with his shoulder boards, *Alt-Larisch* collar patches, dress-quality gold thread breast eagle (against regulations), gold buttons, and decorations. The open throat displays his Knight's Cross with Oakleaves, Swords and Diamonds. The headgear is the M1934 'old style' field cap with gold machine-woven insignia and gold pipings. (Brian Davis)

M1938 hard-shell holster on his blackened M1934 officer's belt, a standard field flashlight and Voigtländer short 10x50 binoculars.

E3: Panzerobergrenadier, I Panzergrenadier-Bataillon, Führer-Begleit-Brigade; Ardennes, January 1945

The Führer-Begleit-Brigade, a detachment of which formed Hitler's personal bodyguard, was effectively a Großdeutschland unit. This senior private wears M1942 one-piece snow overalls over a M1942 padded non-reversible winter tunic in M1944 marsh-pattern camouflage; a field-grey tubula balaclava around his neck; a M1942 helmet with minimal chicken-wire cover and streaked with whitewash; three-finger reversible mittens, and lace-up ankle boots. He carries leather rifle ammunition pouches and

a M1939 grenade on the right front of his belt, and on the left canvas magazine pouches for the Gew.43 semi-automatic rifle and a 84/98 bayonet. A fighting knife is clipped to the chest of his overalls.

F: WESTERN GERMANY, 1945

F1: Oberleutnant, Panzergrenadier-Bataillon 2106; Cologne, March 1945

This veteran company commander in 106.Panzer-Brigade 'Feldherrnhalle' fighting on the Rhine front wears the M1940 special field-grey jacket displaying M1935 officer's collar-patches and breast eagle, the *'Feldherrnhalle'* shoulder board monogram and cuff title, two silver Tank Destruction Badges, the bronze Tank Battle Badge, the SA Military Sports Badge and Iron Cross 2nd Class ribbon. He also wears the M1942 helmet and field-grey sweater, the trousers of the M1940 special field-grey uniform, and black ankle boots. He carries standard 6x30 binoculars; a M1935 officer's dispatch (map) case and a P38 Walther pistol in a M1938 soft-shell holster on his black other ranks' belt; and a M1943 Panzerfaust 30 ('tank puncher') anti-tank grenade-launcher.

F2: Gefreiter, Grenadier-Regiment 48; Ruhr pocket, April 1945

This section commander from 12.Volksgrenadier-Division wears the M1944 field blouse with M1944 shoulder straps piped infantry white, all-ranks' breast eagle and collar patches; his M1940 rank chevron is just visible on the left sleeve. His M1942 helmet is painted in imitation of the Zeltbahn 31 tan, brown and green camouflage colours. M1944 trousers are tucked into M1941 canvas anklets; note the plain leather lace-up ankle boots. He has M1940 web supporting-straps, canvas magazine pouches for his MP44/StG44 assault rifle, an M1939 grenade, and 84/98 bayonet and folding shovel behind his left hip.

F3: Panzergrenadier, Panzergrenadier-Regiment 156; Reichswald Forest, February 1945

This soldier from 116.Panzer-Division wears a M1942 non-reversible padded winter tunic in M1943 marsh-pattern camouflage, without insignia, over his M1943 field-grey tunic and belted trousers. His M1943 field cap bears the unofficial silver and black (or dark grey) divisional greyhound badge on the left side. Again, note the plain leather of the unblackened ankle boots. He has M1939 leather infantry Y-straps and M1911 ammunition pouches with a grenade attached; behind his left hip are an 84/98 bayonet and his entrenching tool. He also carries a M1924 stick-grenade, his slung Karabiner 98K, and a M1943 Panzerfaust 60 anti-tank grenade-launcher.

G: SICILY AND SOUTHERN ITALY, 1943

G1: Wehrmachtoberpfarrer, 26.Panzer-Division; Volturno, November 1943

This Roman Catholic divisional chaplain wears the M1935 officer's field tunic without shoulder boards but with an M1935 officer's breast eagle. His rank is approximately indicated by the M1935 violet collar patches with aluminium 'guards braids'. His M1937 officer's peaked service cap has violet pipings, and an aluminium Gothic cross between the national insignia. His M1934 officer's belt, M1940 officer's breeches and riding boots are conventional; he wears a

Catholic crucifix around his neck, and the chaplain's armband. On his left breast pocket are pinned the War Merit Cross 1st Class with Swords and a black Wound Badge; he wears the ribbon of the War Merit Cross 2nd Class in his button hole.

G2: Panzergrenadier, Panzergrenadier-Regiment 64; Salerno, September 1943

This member of a rifle section in 16. Panzer-Division, attacking the Allied bridgehead, wears the M1940 light olive tropical shirt with applied M1940 field-grey shoulder straps piped grass-green; M1943 field-grey trousers are confined by M1941 field-grey canvas anklets over black ankle boots. He has dust-goggles on his sand-painted M1935 helmet; a M1940 canvas tropical belt and Y-straps support M1911 black leather rifle ammunition pouches and the rest of the conventional rifleman's belt order, obscured here. Also obscured but slung by a canvas strap over the left shoulder is an olive-green canvas rifle-grenade pouch for the launcher screwed to his Karabiner 98k. The pouch was also manufactured in both reed-green canvas and black leather; and note at his fee a pair of second pattern rifle-grenade carrying bags, designed to be carried by hand.

G3: Unterfeldwebel, Panzergrenadier-Regiment 115; Sicily, July 1943

This section commander from 15.Panzergrenadier-Division, opposing the Allied landings, wears the M1942 light olive tropical field tunic with M1940 machine-woven blue-grey thread breast eagle and collar patches on rust-brown backing, and copper-tan aluminium NCO braid on the collar and olive M1940 tropical shoulder straps. His M1940 light olive tropical peaked field cap has a blue-grey eagle and tricolour national cockade on rust-brown backing. The M1940 light olive tropical trousers are gathered at the ankle over laced leather boots. He wears second pattern tan canvas MP40 magazine pouches on his M1940 tropical canvas belt, with a 84/98 bayonet and entrenching tool; the M1935 sand-painted helmet still bears the Wehrmacht eagle decal on the left side. Note on his left breast the Close Combat Clasp in bronze and the bronze Tank Battle Badge; he also displays the Iron Cross 2nd Class ribbon, and the M1943 'AFRIKA' cuff title for North Africa veterans.

H: CENTRAL AND NORTHERN ITALY, 1944-1945

H1: Obergefreiter, Jäger-Regiment 25; Gothic Line, September 1944

This section third gunner in 42.Jäger-Division wears the M1942 reed-green herringbone twill tunic and trousers. His M1940 field-grey shoulder straps are piped in light green; note also the M1942 machine-embroidered Jäger right arm badge, and M1940 rank chevrons. His M1942 helmet has a second model cover in 1943 marsh-pattern camouflage. He has the M1943 field-grey woollen shirt, M1941 field-grey canvas anklets, and cleated mountain boots. His combat equipment is conventional; note tucked into his belt the

April 1945, Ruhr Pocket: two subaltern officers – appearing rather old for their rank – prepare to leave for a US POW camp, retaining the equipment necessary for an uncertain future. (Left) M1934 motorcyclist's rubberised coat with *feldgrau* cloth collar; wartime-manufactured *feldgrau* canvas rucksack with leather straps, and blanket; M1943 field cap with aluminium crown piping. (Right) M1935 officer's field greatcoat, piped M1943 field cap, M1931 bread bag and mess kit. (Friedrich Herrmann)

M1943 field cap with M1942 aluminium three-leaf Jäger badge on the left side. He carries a Karabiner 98k, M1939 grenades, and a machine gun ammunition box.

H2: Unteroffizier, Reichsgrenadier-Regiment Hoch- und Deutschmeister; Gustav Line, February 1944

This NCO from the Hoch- und Deutschmeister (44.Infanterie-Division) wears the M1942 collarless smock, in Zeltbahn 31 camouflage reversing to white, over his M1943 field tunic and M1942 wide-collar field greatcoat; M1943 field-grey belted trousers, M1941 field-grey canvas anklets and black ankle boots. His M1942 helmet has a rubber foliage retainer ring; and tropical canvas Y-straps support his black leather belt. This section commander has one set of pouches for his MP40 sub-machine gun, a M1935 brown leather map case, and 6x30 binoculars.

H3: Stabsfeldwebel, Panzer-Aufklärungs-Abteilung 26; River Po, April 1945

This senior NCO in 26.Panzer-Division wears the M1942 reed-green HBT Panzer working jacket with a machine-woven M1944 breast eagle and the unpopular M1942 regulation arm rank insignia; he has added – against regulations – Panzer collar patches, piped golden-yellow for Armoured Reconnaissance troops. His M1943 Panzer field cap has machine-woven insignia on a T-shaped backing. His trousers are field-made in Italian M1929 forest-pattern camouflage cloth, to resemble M1942 Panzer denims but with an added second thigh pocket; they are drawstringed at the ankle over lace-up boots. As an AFV crew member he carries a P38 Walther in a hard-shell holster on his other ranks' belt.

INDEX

References to illustrations are shown in **bold**.
Plates are shown with page and caption locators in brackets.

258